OXFORD MONOGRAPHS IN INTERNATIONAL HUMANITARIAN AND CRIMINAL LAW

To Serve the Enemy

OXFORD MONOGRAPHS IN INTERNATIONAL HUMANITARIAN AND CRIMINAL LAW

The aim of this series is to publish original and innovative books on fundamental, topical, or cutting-edge issues in international humanitarian law and international criminal justice. The primary purpose of the series is to publish books which, in addition to surveying existing law critically, also suggest new avenues for improving the law.

Special attention will be given to works by young scholars.

ALSO PUBLISHED IN THIS SERIES

Internationalized Armed Conflicts in International Law
Kubo Mačák

Organizing Rebellion
Non-State Armed Groups under International Humanitarian Law, Human Rights Law, and International Criminal Law
Tilman Rodenhäuser

The Right to Life in Armed Conflict
Ian Park

The Law of Maritime Blockade
Past, Present, and Future
Phillip Drew

To Serve the Enemy

Informers, Collaborators, and the Laws of Armed Conflict

SHANE DARCY

This publication was grant-aided by the Publications Fund of the National University of Ireland Galway

OXFORD
UNIVERSITY PRESS

OXFORD
UNIVERSITY PRESS

Great Clarendon Street, Oxford, OX2 6DP,
United Kingdom

Oxford University Press is a department of the University of Oxford. It furthers the University's objective of excellence in research, scholarship, and education by publishing worldwide. Oxford is a registered trade mark of Oxford University Press in the UK and in certain other countries

First Edition published in 2019

Impression: 2

Published in the United States of America by Oxford University Press
198 Madison Avenue, New York, NY 10016, United States of America

British Library Cataloguing in Publication Data
Data available

Library of Congress Control Number: 2019946162

ISBN 978–0–19–878889–8

Printed and bound by
CPI Group (UK) Ltd, Croydon, CR0 4YY

For Cillian and Oisín

Series Editor's Preface

Collaboration is an area in which there is little scholarship. Nonetheless, it raises very significant legal and moral issues. It involves questions of contested loyalties, multiple, overlapping, and disputed legal authorities, as well as often personal, and political, tumult. In many, if not all cases, the decisions made by collaborators occur against the background threat, or existence, of violence.

Dr Darcy's study is truly pioneering. It is a detailed legal analysis of the issues that arise as a result of choices made under difficult circumstances. The work engages in a thoughtful analysis of collaboration from the point of view of international humanitarian law and human rights law. It shows sensitivity to the law and politics of the matters that collaboration raises. The monograph shows the author's keen eye for the difficulties that legal (or illegal) responses to collaboration involve. The analysis is both a close reading of the law on point and a sophisticated rumination on the choices that collaborators make or have made. The law on the subject, which is explained in detail, is tempered with a sound understanding of the situation of those who are subject to its strictures.

The book deals with issues of great contemporary relevance. The case study it uses humanises the decisions that have been made by the protagonists and their repercussions. Whilst Northern Ireland, like all conflictual situations, could be treated as being *sui generis*, Dr Darcy's study is of far more general application. The issues raised in the work are universal.

The book sheds light on an area which has not yet been the subject of such a comprehensive analysis. Its topic is one which there is little to cast an academic backwards look. The study of the area is subtle, and carefully contextual. We are delighted to have it in the series.

The editors.

Acknowledgements

I am most grateful for the advice and support of a number of people who have made an invaluable contribution to the writing of this book. Thanks are due to friends and colleagues who have read and commented on draft work, including Anthony Cullen, Sandesh Sivakumaran, Michelle Farrell, Yutaka Arai-Takahashi, Brian Farrell, Michael Kearney, Noëlle Quénivet, John Reynolds, Ray Murphy, and Daragh Murray. The manuscript also benefitted greatly from the expert guidance of Rob Cryer, one of the series editors, while Merel Alstein, Natasha Fleming, and Jack McNichol at Oxford University Press have been both encouraging and tolerant and provided professional support throughout the publication process.

As the book was taking shape, it benefitted greatly from papers presented at various conferences and research seminar series, including at the National University of Ireland Galway, Lancaster University, University of Washington, University College Dublin, University of Ulster, the Amsterdam Centre for International Law, and University of Edinburgh. Particular thanks are due to many colleagues and students at the Irish Centre for Human Rights, the School of Law and the National University of Ireland Galway with whom I have engaged on the subject matter of the book. A special thanks to the Director of the Centre, Siobhán Mullally, and to my colleagues Ray Murphy, Anita Ferrara, and Kathleen Cavanaugh. Valuable research assistance has been provided by Marilena Stegbauer, Lisa Buckner, Kathryn Grundy, Katherine Lempres, Courtney Connor, Lauren Martin, Joshua Morency, and Noemi Magugliani. I am also grateful for the financial support provided by the National University of Ireland Galway Publications Fund.

The most heartfelt thanks go to my wife Anna-Marie for her unwavering support and encouragement, both over the years and throughout the writing of the book. Thanks are also very much due to my parents and extended family. My sons, Cillian (7) and Oisín (2) have greatly helped in their special own way, mostly by showing absolutely no interest in the book.

Shane Darcy

Galway, February 2019

Table of Contents

Table of Cases

EUROPEAN COURT OF HUMAN RIGHTS

INTERNATIONAL COURT OF JUSTICE

INTERNATIONAL CRIMINAL COURT

INTERNATIONAL CRIMINAL TRIBUNALS FOR THE FORMER YUGOSLAVIA AND RWANDA

SPECIAL COURT FOR SIERRA LEONE

POST-SECOND WORLD WAR TRIBUNALS

OTHER INTERNATIONAL COURTS

NATIONAL COURTS

Israel

The Netherlands

United Kingdom

United States of America

Table of Treaties

Introduction

A constant yet oftentimes concealed practice in war has been the use of informers and other collaborators by parties to an armed conflict. It has been said that '[c]ollaboration with the enemy is as old as war and the occupation of foreign territory'.[1] Informers may provide valuable intelligence which assists with military and security operations, while various forms of cooperation with an adversary, whether military, administrative, or economic, can further a number of aims of parties to an armed conflict. Collaborators, in some respects, are indispensable for the pursuit of certain wartime objectives, both lawful and otherwise. Surprisingly, despite the prevalence of such activity during wartime, and the serious and at times fatal consequences that befall those who collaborate with an opposing side, international law applicable in times of armed conflict does not squarely address the phenomenon.

The recruitment, use, and treatment of informers and other collaborators is addressed only partially and indirectly by international humanitarian law. No reference to such individuals is found in the various Hague and Geneva treaties aimed at regulating conduct in war and at mitigating the suffering which inevitably occurs during armed conflicts. Informers or collaborators do not feature amongst the categories of persons which the law formally recognises during armed conflict, principally combatants, civilians, prisoners of war, the wounded, sick, and shipwrecked, medical personnel, spies, and mercenaries. But just as the maxim *inter armes leges silent* is no longer accurate, neither is it the case that the laws applicable in armed conflict ignore wartime collaboration, including the use of informers. How the laws of armed conflict address the practice of informing and other forms of collaboration during conflict is the subject of this book.

International law recognises the widespread and enduring phenomenon of individuals cooperating with an opposing side during an armed conflict but treats it with some ambivalence. The lawfulness of resort to the practice is generally accepted in principle, yet international law seeks to place certain limits, including restrictions on the methods employed in the recruitment, use, and treatment of informers and other collaborators during armed conflict. Much as international humanitarian law eschews consideration of the lawfulness of the use of force giving rise to conflict, focusing instead on how parties to an armed conduct themselves, this body of law

[1] Gerhard Hirschfeld, 'Collaboration in Nazi-Occupied France: Some Introductory Remarks' in Gerhard Hirschfeld and Patrick Marsh (eds), *Collaboration in France: Politics and Culture during the Nazi Occupation, 1940–1944* (Berg 1989) 1, 1.

To Serve the Enemy: Informers, Collaborators, and the Laws of Armed Conflict. Shane Darcy, Oxford University Press (2019).
DOI: 10.1093/oso/ 9780198788898.001.0001

does not generally pass comment on the legality of recruiting and using informers or other collaborators, or the lawfulness of individuals engaging in certain forms of cooperation with an adversary, but rather concentrates instead on the treatment of individuals considered as actual or potential collaborators. The limitations imposed are in recognition of the harms frequently associated with the practice, which is itself considered as acceptable under prevailing international law.

International law has broadly adopted a permissive stance when it comes to wartime collaboration. When the Swiss jurist Emer de Vattel considered the question in the mid-eighteenth century, he concluded that measures encouraging an enemy's subjects to collaborate 'are not contrary to the external law of nations, nor can the enemy complain of them as odious proceedings. Accordingly they are practised in all wars.'[2] In the specific realm of wartime intelligence gathering, the 1907 Hague Regulations permit the employment of 'measures necessary for obtaining information about the enemy and the country'.[3] The United Kingdom *Joint Service Manual* states that the gathering of such information about the enemy is not only permissible, but essential, and it specifically envisages the use of collaborators and informers for this purposes. Intelligence can be gathered through 'the employment of informers or agents in enemy-held territory', while it is lawful 'to employ spies; to induce enemy civilians or soldiers to give information [...] or to give false information to the enemy'.[4] International law has not completely forbidden the use of the enemy's population and personnel against it.

On the other hand, international humanitarian law can be seen to place some limitations on the use of informers and other collaborators, including restrictions on the methods of recruitment and the treatment of persons that may have served an opposing side. The Fourth Geneva Convention of 1949, for example, sets out that '[n]o physical or moral coercion shall be exercised against protected persons, in particular to obtain information from them or from third parties'.[5] As will be discussed in this book, the recruitment of informers and collaborators has frequently, although not always, involved the employment of coercive measures. It is the treatment of suspected informers and other collaborators by the aggrieved party, however, that has almost invariably involved the most cruel and vengeful actions. Parties to an armed conflict show little mercy to those who cooperate with an adversary, often subjecting them to ill-treatment and extrajudicial execution. Informers and other collaborators tend to fare far worse than captured members of opposition forces, both during and after a conflict. As the influential Lieber Code of 1863 stated, '[t]he war-traitor is always severely punished. If his offense consists in betraying to the enemy anything

[2] Emer de Vattel, *The Law of Nations*, Book III, *Of War*, Chapter X, §180 (first published 1758, Bela Kapossy and Richard Whatmore (eds), Liberty Fund, 2008) 582–3.

[3] Regulations annexed to Hague Convention IV Respecting the Laws and Customs of War on Land (1907), art 24.

[4] United Kingdom Ministry of Defence, *The Joint Service Manual of the Law of Armed Conflict* (OUP 2004) 63 (footnotes omitted).

[5] Geneva Convention IV Relative to the Protection of Civilian Persons in Time of War (1949), entered into force 21 October 1950, 75 U.N.T.S. 287, art 31.

concerning the condition, safety, operations, or plans of the troops holding or occupying the place or district, his punishment is death.'[6]

The severe punishments inflicted on informers and collaborators in contemporary armed conflicts would tend to run afoul of the prohibitions of Common Article 3 of the 1949 Geneva Conventions. These fundamental guarantees reflect 'elementary considerations of humanity',[7] yet a common and deliberate strategy for dealing with the threat posed by those who might divulge information or cooperate in other ways with an adversary has been to resort publicly to inhumane treatment and brutal execution of those claimed to be traitors. Common Article 3 restricts but does not outlaw capital punishment, prohibiting 'the passing of sentences and the carrying out of executions without previous judgment pronounced by a regularly constituted court, affording all the judicial guarantees which are recognized as indispensable by civilized peoples'. This provision is particularly challenging for non-state armed groups, who have a more limited capacity for counteracting the threat of informers by judicial means.[8]

Unlike the Lieber Code, modern treaties of international humanitarian law have not included provisions specifically addressing the treatment of so-called war traitors, despite this foundational document having significantly influenced the development of the international law of armed conflict in various other ways.[9] This divergent approach underscores the differing treatment by international law and national law of collaboration with an enemy. The Lieber Code was not an international treaty, and comprised a set of 'Instructions for the Government of United States Armies in the Field', issued in the context of a civil war, rather than a conflict taking place between states.[10] Although drawing on existing customary law applicable in wartime, the Code can be seen as a domestic military manual which reflects national laws and standards. While international law has been generally permissive towards cooperation with an opposing side, at least where undertaken voluntarily, national law takes the opposite approach, with collaboration with an enemy invariably treated as a criminal offence such as treason under domestic legal systems. As well as potentially jeopardising military objectives, informers and other collaborators are reviled for having betrayed a country, a people, or a cause. National laws, including military law, invariably criminalise such behaviour given that 'violation of

[6] Instructions for the Government of Armies of the United States in the Field, Prepared by Francis Lieber, promulgated as General Orders No. 100 by President Lincoln, 24 April 1863, art 91 *reprinted in* Dietrich Schindler and Jiří Toman (eds), *The Laws of Armed Conflict: A Collection of Conventions, Resolutions and Other Documents* (Martinus Nijhoff 1988) 3.

[7] *Case Concerning Military and Paramilitary Activities In and Against Nicaragua, (Nicaragua* v *United States of America)*, Merits, 27 June 1986, General List No. 70, para 218.

[8] See generally Jonathan Somer, 'Jungle Justice: Passing Sentence on the Equality of Belligerents in Non-International Armed Conflict' (2007) 89 No. 867 International Review of the Red Cross 655; Sandesh Sivakumaran, 'Courts of Armed Opposition Groups; Fair Trials or Summary Justice?' (2009) 7 Journal of International Criminal Justice 489.

[9] See for example Theodor Meron, 'Francis Lieber's Code and the Principles of Humanity' (1997) 36(1–2) *Columbia Journal of Transnational Law* 269.

[10] Dapo Akande and Laurence Hill-Cawthorne, 'The Lieber Code and the Regulation of Civil War in International Law' (2015) 53(3) Columbia Journal of Transnational Law 638, 639.

an allegiance to one's country is regarded, almost universally, as the most heinous of crimes'.[11] A number of states retain the death penalty for the crime of treason, despite having formally abolished capital punishment for ordinary crimes.[12]

The limited attention given by international humanitarian law to the practice of using informers and collaborators has meant that much of the literature on the law applicable in armed conflict has also been neglectful of the subject. Collaborators or informers are not addressed in any significant detail in key publications in this field,[13] including those which examine civilian participation in armed conflict.[14] The phenomenon is addressed in some detail in disciplines such as history, politics, sociology, and war studies.[15] Even so, the subject of collaboration with an enemy was overlooked in the past; Werner Rings has noted that historical research of the Second World War, for example, paid far greater attention to resistance than to collaboration, with few references to those who 'aided and abetted the occupying power'.[16] As he put it, collaboration was 'regarded as shameful and obnoxious on principle. It is unappealing, and bears the stigma of treason. [...] Unlike collaboration, Resistance testifies to the lionhearted courage and adamantine faith of free men and women.'[17] For David Littlejohn:

> It is understandable that those who endured enemy occupation should today prefer to recall only the heroic aspects of their ordeal. It is equally understandable that those fortunate enough to avoid conquest should not wish to embarrass former friends and allies by reviving unhappy memories. But ... there is a serious risk that its history may become distorted as a result of this delicacy and reticence.[18]

[11] Nigel West (ed), *The Faber Book of Treachery* (Faber and Faber, 1995) 1.

[12] See for example Report of the Secretary General, 'Capital punishment and implementation of the safeguards guaranteeing protection of the rights of those facing the death penalty', 18 December 2009, E/2010/10, paras 3, 12, 16.

[13] For example Frits Kalshoven and Liesbeth Zegveld, *Constraints on the Waging of War* (4th edn, CUP 2011); Dieter Fleck (ed), *The Handbook of International Humanitarian Law* (3th edn, OUP 2013); A.P.V. Rogers, *Law on the Battlefield* (3rd edn, Manchester University Press 2012); Gary Solis, *The Law of Armed Conflict: International Humanitarian Law in War* (CUP 2010).

[14] For example Anicée van Engeland, *Civilian or Combatant? A Challenge for the 21st Century* (OUP 2011); Alexander Gillespie, *A History of the Laws of War: Volume 2; The Customs and Laws of War with Regard to Civilians in Times of Conflict* (Hart 2011); Emily Crawford, *Identifying the Enemy: Civilian Participation in Armed Conflict* (OUP 2015).

[15] See for example István Deák, *Europe on Trial: The Story of Collaboration, Resistance, and Retribution During World War II* (Westview Press 2015); Timothy Brook, *Collaboration: Japanese Agents and Local Elites in Wartime China* (Harvard University Press 2005); Hillel Cohen, *Army of Shadows: Palestinian Collaboration with Zionism, 1917–1948* (translated by Haim Watzman, University of California Press 2008); Werner Rings, *Life with the Enemy: Collaboration and Resistance in Hitler's Europe 1939–1945* (translated by J. Maxwell Brownjohn, Doubleday & Co. 1982).

[16] Rings, *Life with the Enemy* (n 15) 84.

[17] Ibid. For a critique of the tendency in the scholarly literature to view the behaviour of populations under occupation in 'dichotomous terms', such as collaboration or resistance, see Lynne Taylor, *Between Resistance and Collaboration: Popular Protest in Northern France, 1940–1946* (Palgrave McMillan 2000) 2; Tanja Penter, 'Local Collaborators on Trial: Soviet War Crimes Trials Under Stalin (1943–1953)' (2008) 49(2/3) Cahiers du Monde Russe 341, 363–4.

[18] David Littlejohn, *Patriotic Traitors: A History of Collaboration in German-Occupied Europe, 1940–1945* (Heineman 1972) xiii.

International humanitarian law and legal scholarship has thoroughly addressed the subject of armed resistance during time of war, including the status of members of organised resistance movements.[19] In contrast, scant consideration has been given by this body of law and associated scholarship to wartime informers and collaborators as participants in armed conflict.[20] This book seeks to provide a comprehensive consideration of wartime collaboration through the lens of the laws of armed conflict. Before elaborating on the structure of the book, it is necessary first to address the meaning of wartime collaboration by offering understandings of what is meant by informing and other forms of cooperation with an adversary, as well as setting out the various interrelated legal regimes which comprise the laws of armed conflict for the purpose of this study.

Wartime Collaboration: Informers and Collaborators

To collaborate in war is understood as meaning to 'co-operate traitorously with an enemy'.[21] Although the phenomenon of wartime collaboration has a lengthy history, the use of this otherwise benign term in this way can be traced to the widespread occupation of territory during the Second World War. Nazi Germany's seizure of large parts of the European continent prompted a range of responses in those territories:

> German soldiers and policemen were numerous enough to rule the land but not enough to control every town, village, and forest. As a consequence, national governments, local authorities, native populations, and diverse social classes and interest groups, as well as many individuals, were eager, for myriad reasons, to tolerate the inevitable presence of, actively collaborate with, or oppose the ruling Germans.[22]

The first use of the term 'collaboration' in this sense is attributed to Philippe Pétain, the French general and politician who signed an armistice agreement with Germany upon the occupation of French territory during the Second World War, becoming the Chief of State of the French government at Vichy.[23] Following a meeting with Hitler in October 1940, Pétain stated that the defeat of France by Germany meant

[19] See for example Geneva Convention III Relative to the Treatment of Prisoners of War (1949), entered into force 21 October 1950, 75 U.N.T.S. 135, art 4(3); Richard R. Baxter, 'So-called "Unprivileged Belligerency": Spies, Guerillas, and Saboteurs' (1951) 28 British Yearbook of International Law 323; Pertti Joenniemi and Adam Roberts, 'Civil Resistance and the Law of Military Occupation' (1974) 4(1) Instant Research on Peace and Violence 38; W.J. Ford, 'Resistance Movements and International Law' (1967) 7, No. 79 International Review of the Red Cross 515; W.J. Ford, 'Members of Resistance Movements' (1977) 24 (1–2) Netherlands International Law Review 92; W. Thomas Mallison and Sally V. Mallison, 'The Juridical Status of Irregular Combatants under the International Humanitarian Law of Armed Conflict' (1977) 9 Case Western Reserve Journal of International Law 39.

[20] For a recent work addressing certain legal issues relating to collaboration in the context of the Second World War in Asia, see Kerstin von Lingen (ed), *Debating Collaboration and Complicity in War Crimes Trials in Asia, 1945–1956* (Palgrave MacMillan 2017).

[21] *The Oxford English Dictionary* (2nd edn), Volume III (Clarendon Press 1989) 469.

[22] Deák, *Europe on Trial* (n 15) 1.

[23] See generally Charles Williams, *Pétain: How the Hero of France Became a Convicted Traitor and Changed the Course of History* (Palgrave McMillan 2005).

a choice between a 'traditional peace of oppression' or an 'entirely novel peace of collaboration'.[24] The latter was chosen, with Pétain proclaiming that 'I enter, today, into the way of collaboration'.[25] The usage of the term has expanded beyond this first meaning to include a variety of forms of cooperation with an adversary during conflict.

The concept of collaboration in wartime evades precise definition and is seen to be 'simultaneously contested and multifaceted'.[26] No general definition of collaboration or of the individuals who might 'cooperate traitorously' with an opposing party is found in the treaties of international humanitarian law or in the customary international law applicable in armed conflicts. This body of law has not been concerned with prohibiting collaboration with the enemy but rather has sought to ensure humane treatment and respect for other basic protections during conflict by outlawing certain harmful behaviour by all participants in armed conflict, irrespective for the most part of where one's allegiances may lie. In contrast, national laws, including criminal statutes and constitutions, and the military codes of both states and non-state armed groups, frequently address cooperation with an adversary during armed conflict, usually through the establishment of treason or aiding the enemy offences.[27] No attempt is made here to provide a definitive meaning of collaboration during time of war, and instead a practical understanding of the concept and its various forms is set out in order to underpin the legal analysis undertaken.

Wartime collaboration can encompass a spectrum of activity. Taking the Second World War as an illustrative example, clear instances of cooperation with an opposing side would include the bureaucratic collaboration undertaken by the Vichy and Quisling regimes in France and Norway respectively, as well as serving or fighting alongside the armed forces of an adversary, as many thousands did.[28] With betrayal being in the eye of the beholder, however, the concept of collaboration was also frequently interpreted more broadly, and taken to include otherwise seemingly innocuous acts. It could mean 'anything from volunteering for the *Waffen S.S.* to buying a picture postcard of Marshal Pétain', from 'offering a glass of water to a thirsty German soldier all the way to assisting the Gestapo [...] by denouncing, hunting down, torturing and killing potential and real resisters'.[29] French women who fraternised with German soldiers during the War were accused of *collaboration horizontale*.[30] As described in the next chapter, more recent armed conflicts have also seen a range of activities described as collaboration, and the tendency towards broad interpretation has not abated; the International Criminal Tribunal

[24] Rings, *Life with the Enemy* (n 15) 110. [25] Deák, *Europe on Trial* (n 15) 55.

[26] Stathis N. Kalyvas, 'Collaboration in Comparative Perspective' (2008) 15(2) European Review of History—Revue européenne d'histoire 109, 109. See also Henrik Dethlefsen, 'Denmark and the German Occupation: Cooperation, Negotiation or Collaboration?' (1990) 15(1–2) Scandinavian Journal of History 193.

[27] See for example Jabez W. Loane, IV, 'Treason and Aiding the Enemy' (1965) 30 Military Law Review 43.

[28] See generally Deák, *Europe on Trial* (n 15); David Littlejohn, *Patriotic Traitors* (n 18); Peter Davies, *Dangerous Liaisons: Collaboration and World War Two* (Pearson Longman 2004).

[29] David Littlejohn, *Patriotic Traitors* (n 18) 336; Deák, *Europe on Trial* (n 15) 5.

[30] Anthony Beever, 'An Ugly Carnival', *The Guardian*, 5 June 2009.

for Rwanda noted that a Kinyarwanda phrase for collaborators included 'not only collaborators but all Tutsi'.[31]

This book focuses primarily on forms of active cooperation with an adversary that can be considered as offering a military advantage or other substantial benefit to a party to an armed conflict that works to the detriment of the interests of the betrayed party. Key amongst such types of collaboration in armed conflict is the practice of informing. Informers, or informants as they are also known, can comprise both civilians and combatants who provide information of value to enemy forces or intelligence services.[32] With intelligence holding a 'cardinal influence' in military affairs,[33] parties to an armed conflict will invariably seek to gather information from civilians or captured enemy personnel and to recruit such persons as informers. The use of so-called covert human intelligence sources is a common practice both during armed conflict and in domestic policing, criminal justice, and intelligence.[34] Repressive regimes have relied heavily upon informers for the purpose of gathering intelligence on perceived threats. Considerable infamy attaches to the practice of the 'Stasi', the German Democratic Republic's Ministry for State Security, which recruited informers on a considerable scale.[35] According to a United Nations Commission of Inquiry, the security service of the Democratic People's Republic of Korea at one point 'employed an informant network of 400,000 people, an estimated 5 per cent of the population'.[36]

In addition to being a source of information of military value, such as the whereabouts of weapons or particular individuals, the use of informers can significantly weaken the organisational effectiveness of a party to the armed conflict. According to a United States counterinsurgency manual, '[n]othing is more demoralizing to insurgents than realizing that people inside their movement or trusted supporters among the public are deserting or providing information to government authorities'.[37] Military doctrine recognises the value of informers, with military manuals often setting out various methods that might be employed to bring about such cooperation by civilians or captured enemy persons.[38] The recruitment of informers, as will be further discussed later in this book, frequently involves prohibited forms of coercion, while authorities might also be tempted to turn a blind eye to unlawful

[31] *Prosecutor v Akayesu*, Case No. ICTR-96-4-T, Trial Chamber I, Judgment, 2 September 1998, para 150.

[32] For a distinction between informers and collaborators see Michael L. Gross, *The Ethics of Insurgency* (CUP 2015) 109.

[33] Ralph Bennett, *Behind the Battle: Intelligence in the War with Germany 1939–1945* (Pimlico 1999) xvii.

[34] See for example Roger Billingsley (ed), *Covert Human Intelligence Sources: The Unlovely Face of Police Work* (Waterside Press 2009).

[35] See generally Jens Gieseke, *The History of the Stasi: East Germany's Secret Police, 1945–1990* (translated by David Burnett, Berghahn 2014).

[36] United Nations Human Rights Council, *Report of the detailed findings of the commission of inquiry human rights in the Democratic People's Republic of Korea*, A/HRC/25/CRP.1, 7 February 2014, para 111.

[37] United States Army, *Field Manual 3-24, Counterinsurgency*, (Headquarters, Department of the Army December 2006) 1–19.

[38] See for example United States, *Law of War Manual* (Department of Defense, Office of General Counsel 2015) 1040.

or criminal activities by informers in light of their intelligence value. Such practices have prompted intelligence experts to observe that 'events since 9/11 have returned the relatively neglected area of human sources or informers to the centre of controversy'.[39] Informers are often referred to as spies, although the designation is not entirely apt. Humanitarian law refers to spies as 'members of the armed forces of a Party to the conflict . . . engaging in espionage'.[40] While the question of informers as spies is discussed in Chapter 3, it is evident that international humanitarian law does not treat informers as a distinct category, despite their ubiquitous use in armed conflict.

Several other different forms of collaboration that bring a tangible benefit to a party to an armed conflict are examined in detail in this book. Amongst these is bureaucratic or administrative collaboration, typically arising where a governmental authority or its officials agree to cooperate with an invading force or occupying power. Such collaboration is typified by the conduct of a number of European powers or their officials (or fellow nationals who replaced them) that cooperated with Germany during the Second World War. This type of collaboration is less common in contemporary armed conflicts, partly because modern conflicts tend not to be international in nature, with consequently fewer instances of occupation of foreign territory. International humanitarian law is attuned to the existence of this form of collaboration, with the Fourth Geneva Convention seeking to protect public officials and judges from being sanctioned for refusing to serve under a regime of occupation.[41]

The 1949 Conventions also seek to prohibit coerced collaboration of another type that was similarly common during the Second World War: compelling individuals to join the armed forces of the opposing side. It is a grave breach of the Conventions to compel a prisoner of war or a protected person to 'serve in the forces of the hostile Power'.[42] Voluntarily joining the opposing side in a conflict is another matter, as international law does not exclude the practice, unlike national military law. There is no rule against compulsory recruitment in non-international armed conflicts, except with regard to child soldiers, given that many states continue to require conscription into their armed forces. The phenomenon of so-called foreign fighters, whereby nationals of states who have joined a party to a conflict, such as those in Iraq and Syria, constitutes a contemporary manifestation of voluntarily serving in the forces of an adversary where such persons may become involved in hostilities against armed forces of their home state.[43]

In addition to these most prominent forms of cooperation with the other side, the book also touches upon other examples of wartime collaboration involving a contribution to the activities of an opposing party to an armed conflict. In an international armed conflict, for example, a range of persons might 'accompany

[39] Peter Gill and Mark Phythian, *Intelligence in an Insecure World* (2nd edn, Polity Press 2012) 172.

[40] Protocol Additional to the Geneva Conventions of 12 August 1949, and Relating to the Protection of Victims of International Armed Conflicts (Protocol I), (1977), entered into force 7 December 1978, 1125 U.N.T.S. 3, art 46(1).

[41] Fourth Geneva Convention, art 54(1).

[42] Third Geneva Convention, art 130; Fourth Geneva Convention, art 147.

[43] Andrea de Guttry, Francesca Capone, and Christophe Paulussson, *Foreign Fighters under International Law and Beyond* (TMC Asser Press 2016).

the armed forces without actually being members thereof' and where such individuals are drawn from the civilian population of occupied territory, accusations of collaboration inevitably follow.[44] The use of local interpreters is a key example, with many such interpreters in Iraq and Afghanistan having been killed for having provided assistance to the US or UK armed forces.[45] The concept of trading with the enemy or industrial collaboration is more removed from hostilities, yet the economic contribution of such collaboration can offer a significant advantage to a party to an armed conflict. During the Second World War, 'businessmen, industrialists, and financiers placed their factories and financial assets – indeed, whole sectors of the national economy—at the Third Reich's disposal'.[46] While the context, practice, and motivations behind these different types of collaboration may differ, there are often similarities regarding the treatment of individual collaborators, as well as some common applicable legal norms.

The Laws of Armed Conflict

In a situation of armed conflict, a number of legal regimes drawn from both international law and national law will be applicable concurrently. Chief amongst these is international humanitarian law, which comprises the international treaty and customary rules which seek to regulate conduct during armed conflict and to mitigate the suffering that war inevitably brings.[47] Traditionally known as the law of war, this branch of international law is also referred to as the law of armed conflict and is codified primarily in the 1949 Geneva Conventions and their Additional Protocols of 1977.[48] In addition to international humanitarian law, there are various other bodies of laws that are relevant during armed conflict, particularly with regard to the issue of wartime collaboration. Other branches of international law of particular relevance include international criminal law, which provides a sophisticated legal regime for the prosecution of individuals accused of war crimes or other serious international crimes,[49] and international human rights law, a branch of international

[44] Article 4 of the Third Geneva Convention provides that such persons, which may include 'civilian members of military aircraft crews, war correspondents, supply contractors, members of labour units or of services responsible for the welfare of the armed forces', may be entitled to prisoner of war status.

[45] Sean Rayment, '60 Iraqi interpreters murdered working for UK', *Daily Telegraph*, 12 August 2007; Dane Bowker, 'Forget the Syrian refugees. America needs to bring its Afghan and Iraqi interpreters here first', *Washington Post*, 17 September 2015.

[46] Rings, *Life with the Enemy* (n 15) 278.

[47] See generally Kalshoven and Zegveld, *Constraints on the Waging of War* (n 13); Fleck, *The Handbook of International Humanitarian Law* (n 13); Rogers, *Law on the Battlefield* (n 13); Solis, *The Law of Armed Conflict* (n 13).

[48] See however Page Wilson, 'The Myth of International Humanitarian Law' (2017) 93(3) International Affairs 563.

[49] See generally Antonio Cassese, Paula Gaeta, Laurel Baig, Mary Fan, Christopher Gosnell, and Alex Whiting, *Cassese's International Criminal Law* (OUP 2013); Robert Cryer, Håkan Friman, Darryl Robinson and Elizabeth Wilmshurst, *An Introduction to International Criminal Law and Procedure* (3rd edn., CUP 2014).

law that is finding increased application to situations of armed conflict.[50] The laws of armed conflict, in the sense used in this book, focus primarily on these branches of international law, but will also occasionally touch on national legal regimes as may be applicable to wartime collaboration, including both domestic criminal law, human rights and military law.

The analysis of cooperation with an adversary during armed conflict will primarily be undertaken through the lens of international humanitarian law. This branch of international law is characterised by its legitimation of certain acts of violence, the identification of various categories of participants in armed conflict, and the granting of varying legal entitlements or protections to individuals, including whether their status protects them for being the object of attack.[51] As already noted, collaborators, including informers, do not feature as a specific category of persons within this legal regime. In fact, the drafting history of relevant treaties of international humanitarian law reveals some hesitance on the part of states to extending the law's protection to those individuals considered to have collaborated traitorously with an enemy.[52] International law is generally permissive when it comes to the employment of collaborators, yet certain rules and principles of international humanitarian law can be considered as directly relevant to the recruitment, use, and treatment of wartime collaborators. For example, the opprobrium and harsh treatment meted out to suspected informers and collaborators would fall to be assessed under the fundamental guarantees of humanitarian law, including those enshrined in Common Article 3 of the 1949 Geneva Conventions. This has been aptly described as a '[c]onvention in miniature',[53] and its rules can be considered applicable to all armed conflicts.[54] Notwithstanding, international humanitarian law provides a notably more limited legal regime applicable in situations of non-international armed conflict.[55] This may be offset by the growing application of international human rights law during armed conflict, a body of law which has yet to be brought to bear on the practice of wartime collaboration. International criminal law will also come into consideration, particularly where the actions of collaborators or the methods used to recruit or sanction them amount to serious violations of international law constituting international crimes.

While the activities of those who cooperate with an opposing side during armed conflict are not completely ignored by international law, international humanitarian law has some blind sports in this context, and states and non-state parties to an armed conflict have tended to deal with such individuals by way of internal laws

[50] See for example Orna Ben-Naftali (ed), *International Humanitarian Law and International Human Rights Law* (OUP 2011); Chandra Lekha Sriram, Olga Martin-Ortega, and Johanna Herman, *War, Conflict and Human Rights* (2nd edn, Routledge 2014).

[51] See Chris af Jochnick and Roger Normand, 'The Legitimation of Violence: A Critical History of the Laws of War' (1994) 35 Harvard International Law Journal 49.

[52] See discussion in Chapter 2.

[53] Jean Pictet (ed), *Commentary: IV Geneva Convention, Relative to the Protection of Civilian Person in Times of War* (ICRC 1958) 34.

[54] *Nicaragua v United States of America* (n 7), para 218; *Prosecutor* v *Delalić et al.*, Case No. IT-96-21-A, Appeals Chamber, Judgment, 20 February 2001, paras 140–150.

[55] See generally Sandesh Sivakumaran, *The Law of Non-International Armed Conflict* (OUP 2012).

and processes. During the Second World War, for example, the view was expressed at the United Nations War Crimes Commission that '[t]he trial of quislings would be left exclusively to the National Governments'.[56] Many thousands of collaborators were tried and punished after the Second World War for their collaboration on the basis of national treason laws, and a significant number were also executed extrajudicially or punished in other ways without due process.[57] After the Korean conflict, several returning United States' prisoners of war were tried by courts martial for having collaborated with the enemy in violation of the Uniform Code of Military Justice.[58] Contemporary armed conflicts have seen resort to judicial-type bodies or disciplinary measures by non-state armed groups as a means of punishing collaboration and deterring would-be collaborators. For example, the code of conduct of the Bangsamoro Islamic Armed Forces, an armed opposition group active in the Philippines, sets down that:

> Any person who in time of war shall be found lurking or acting as spy in or about any of the fortifications, ports, quarters, or encampments of the Bangsamoro Islamic Armed Forces or elsewhere shall, upon conviction thereof, suffer the penalty of death or as the investigating officer may direct.[59]

Such promulgations by non-state groups prompt consideration of questions regarding legal authority and the compatibility of such laws and their implementation with the rules and precepts of international humanitarian law.

In addition to serving as a vehicle for prosecuting collaborators, national law is also relevant in relation to their recruitment and employment. This is especially the case with regard to informers used for the purpose of gathering information. Military and civilian intelligence work is almost by definition covert and secretive, and the legal regime applicable to such conduct is not always readily apparent. States may grant considerable autonomy to intelligence services to carry out their tasks and at times there may be a 'tenuous relationship between intelligence practices and the law'.[60] Despite the clandestine nature of intelligence activities:

[56] The United Nations War Crimes Commission, *History of the United Nations War Crimes Commission and the Development of the Laws of War* (H.M. Stationery Office 1948) 112.

[57] See generally Deák, *Europe on Trial* (n 15); Jon Elster, *Retribution and Reparation in the Transition to Democracy* (CUP 2006); István Deák, Jan T. Gross, and Tony Judt (eds), *The Politics of Retribution in Europe: World War II and its Aftermath* (Princeton University Press 2000); Benajmin Frommer, *National Cleansing; Retribution Against Nazi Collaborators in Postwar Czechoslovakia* (CUP 2005); Peter Novick, *The Resistance versus Vichy: The Purge of Collaborators in Liberated France* (Columbia University Press 1968); Henry L. Mason, *The Purge of Dutch Quislings: Emergency Justice in the Netherlands* (Springer 1952).

[58] See Elizabeth Lutes Hillman, 'Disloyalty among Men in Arms: Korean War POWs at Court-Martial' (2004) 82(5) North Carolina Law Review 1629; Charles S. Young, *Name, Rank, and Serial Number: Exploiting Korean War POWs at Home and Abroad* (OUP 2014).

[59] Article 59, General Order No. 1: An Order Promulgating a Code of Conduct Regulating the Affairs of the Bangsamoro Islamic Armed Forces, Prescribing its Powers, Duties and Functions, and Other Related Purposes, 2nd edn, June 2006 <http://theirwords.org/media/transfer/doc/sc_ph_milf_biaf_2006_09-9dbc781bd3fc677c268ce003582f4f58.pdf> accessed 29 May 2019.

[60] Gill and Phythian, *Intelligence in an Insecure World* (n 39) 187. See also Benjamin R. Civiletti, 'Intelligence Gathering and the Law: Conflict or Compatability' (1980) 48(6) Fordham Law Review 883.

this does not mean they operate in a legal vacuum. It is vital that their activities are subject to some form of scrutiny whether by an oversight committee or a similar body, such as a commissioner or ombudsperson to ensure the methods used are necessary, proportional, human rights compliant and ethical.[61]

International human rights law and national legislation of relevance are also considered, particularly as they relate to the use of informers, and given the potential for complementing and supplementing international humanitarian law. Consideration is given to issues of legal regulation in relation to the use of informers during the conflict in Northern Ireland. The Chief Constable of the Police Service of Northern Ireland has stated that '[t]here were no rules. There was no regulatory framework for handling of informants at that time',[62] although since the end of the conflict the United Kingdom has enacted legislation which regulates the use of covert human intelligence sources by public authorities and seeks to ensure compliance with applicable human rights standards.[63]

International law's deferential approach to the intelligence practices of states is exemplified in its treatment of spies, with whom informers are frequently compared. Espionage itself by states is not expressly forbidden in instruments of humanitarian law. The relevant articles in the Hague Regulations and Additional Protocol I merely limit the legal protection to which spies are entitled and reinforce the right of states to punish persons engaging in espionage.[64] International law tolerates intelligence activities as 'a necessary evil, something to be mitigated rather than prohibited', as Simon Chesterman has observed.[65] Informers who provide information to an opposing side, whether as civilians or members of the armed forces of a party to a conflict, can be considered as engaging in espionage and may be punished according to national law. International humanitarian law's approach to spies is emblematic of its overall approach to intelligence activities, and has clear resonance with how it addresses the phenomenon of wartime collaboration. Parties to an armed conflict are not prohibited by humanitarian law from encouraging civilians or military personnel to collaborate, yet other laws applicable in armed conflict, namely national criminal and military law, unquestionably forbid and sanction such behaviour in the strongest terms. Humanitarian law restricts how such parties may treat such individuals, but does not exclude the activities they may have engaged in or their prosecution therefore.

[61] Arivinder Sambei, 'Intelligence Cooperation Versus Evidence Collection and Dissemination' in Larissa van den Herik and Nico Schrijver (eds), *Counter-Terrorism Strategies in a Fragmented International Legal Order: Meeting the Challenges* (CUP 2015) 212, 215.

[62] Eamon McCann, 'State role in killings by IRA changes everything', *Irish Times*, 28 January 2016.

[63] Regulation of Investigatory Powers Act 2000.

[64] See for example Hague Regulations 1907, arts 29–31; Additional Protocol I, art 46.

[65] Simon Chesterman, *One Nation under Surveillance* (OUP 2011) 36.

Structure of the Book

The book comprises five main chapters. Chapter 1 describes the historical and contemporary practice of collaboration during times of armed conflict. Key illustrative examples are provided of the principal forms of cooperation with an adversary, namely informing, fighting with enemy forces, and bureaucratic collaboration, as well as other forms of aiding the enemy. With regard to informing, consideration is given to the significance placed on intelligence in warfare and to military doctrine addressed to the recruitment and use of informers. The practice of non-state armed groups is also addressed in this chapter. For other instances of aiding the enemy, the practice of the Second World War looms large, both because of the prevalence of wartime collaboration at that time, and the considerable documentation and scholarly analysis that has followed. The various rationales behind the use of informers and collaborators are explored, as are the diverse motivations of those who engage in wartime collaboration. This chapter aims to provide the conceptual and factual foundation for the detailed legal analysis that follows in the subsequent chapters.

The law of armed conflict as applicable to the recruitment and use of collaborators is examined in Chapter 2. Although international humanitarian law is somewhat permissive regarding such use in principle, key rules within this body of law set certain limits by imposing restrictions on methods of recruitment and by outlawing coerced collaboration of certain kinds. The chapter explores the drafting, application, and interpretation of the humanitarian law rules of relevance. It traces in detail the debates which occurred during the preparation of prominent treaties, including the 1899 and 1907 Hague Regulations, where considerable attention was given to the question of how such laws might be addressed to those persons motivated or compelled 'to serve the enemy'.[66] The legality of certain practices employed by those seeking to recruit collaborators are considered in light of prohibitions under international humanitarian law, such as that of 'physical or moral coercion' against protected persons and prisoners of war for purposes of gathering information.[67] The potential application of human rights law to such practices during armed conflict is touched upon, to be followed by a more detailed treatment of the regulation of the use of informers in domestic policing, criminal justice, and intelligence in Chapter 5.

International humanitarian law is preoccupied with the status of individuals and groups.[68] The activities engaged in by wartime informers and other collaborators

66 This phrase was used during the discussion on the drafting of the 1874 Brussels Declaration on the Laws and Customs of War. See 'Correspondence Respecting the Proposed Conference at Brussels on the Rules of Military Warfare', *United Kingdom Parliamentary Papers,* Miscellaneous No. 1 (1875) [c.-1128], 18, 202.

67 Fourth Geneva Convention, art 31; Third Geneva Convention, art 17.

68 See for example Allan Rosas, *The Legal Status of Prisoners of War*, Institute for Human Rights (Åbo Akademi University 2005); Mallison and Mallison, 'The Juridical Status of Irregular Combatants' (n 19); Lindsey Cameron, 'Private Military Companies: Their Status under International Humanitarian Law and its Impact on Their Regulation' (2006) 88, No. 863 International Review of the Red Cross 573.

may have a bearing on their status under international humanitarian law and the attendant protections which attach to their categorisation. Chapter 3 examines issues regarding status, beginning with civilian informers as spies, before turning to those who might join or fight alongside an enemy's armed forces or provide other forms of assistance, such as interpreting. Recent jurisprudence from the international criminal tribunals on the subject of civilian collaborators and the question of participation in hostilities is analysed.[69] With regard to informers, the International Committee of the Red Cross has taken the view that 'an unarmed civilian sitting in a restaurant using a radio or mobile phone to transmit tactical targeting intelligence to an attacking air force would probably have to be regarded as directly participating in hostilities'.[70] The chapter also considers the concept of protected persons under the Fourth Geneva Convention, the nationality requirement of which may preclude the treaty's full application to local civilian informers working for an occupying power in occupied territory. The chapter will explore developments in international case law which have emphasised allegiance over nationality,[71] as well as the derogations regime under the Fourth Geneva Convention allowing restrictions on the rights and privileges of those who may have engaged in activities hostile to the security of the state or occupying power. The chapter examines finally the question of prisoner of war status for members of the armed forces that may have cooperated with an adversary, including by joining the forces of the other side.

In Chapter 4, the book turns to consider the treatment of individuals suspected or found to have collaborated with an opposing party to an armed conflict and the scope of international humanitarian law's protections. The phenomenon of wartime collaboration with an enemy manifests itself most visibly in the ill-treatment that befalls such persons. Parties to an armed conflict will often subject suspected collaborators to execution, oftentimes extrajudicially, as well as various types of ill-treatment, including torture, as punishment and to deter further betrayal. The severe punishment envisaged by the Lieber Code for traitors has frequently been meted out in armed conflicts; Common Article 3 of the 1949 Geneva Conventions can in some respects be read as a catalogue of the variety of cruelties which have been inflicted on collaborators in wartime. The practice, applicable legal rules, and rationales underlying such actions are examined in this chapter, which also considers potential blind spots on the part of humanitarian law and efforts to expand the scope of the law of war crimes. There is a particular focus on collaborator trials and executions during armed conflict, and an examination of the rules concerning fair trial

[69] See for example *Prosecutor v Limaj et al.*, Case No. IT-03-66-T, Trial Chamber, Judgment, 30 November 2005; *Prosecutor v Haradinaj et al.*, Case No. IT-04-84-T, Trial Chamber, Retrial Judgment, 29 November 2012; *Prosecutor v Fofana and Kondewa*, Case No. SCSL-04-14-A, Appeals Chamber, Judgment, 28 May 2008; *Prosecutor v Sesay, Kallon and Gbao*, Case No. SCSL-04-15-T, Trial Chamber I, Judgment, 2 March 2009.

[70] International Committee of the Red Cross, *Interpretive Guidance on the Notion of Direct Participation in Hostilities under International Humanitarian Law* (ICRC 2009) 48.

[71] See for example *Prosecutor v Tadić*, Case No. IT-94-1-A, Appeals Chamber, Judgment, 15 July 1999, para 166.

guarantees, the permissibility of capital punishment in wartime, and the obligations of non-state actors.

The role of international human rights law and national regulatory regimes regarding the use of informers is considered in Chapter 5. As with international humanitarian law, human rights law accepts the use of informers by national authorities, but seeks to place limits on aspects of the practice to ensure it accords with human rights standards. The European Court of Human Rights has acknowledged a legitimate role for using informers in policing:

> The Court observes at the outset that it is aware of the difficulties inherent in the police's task of searching for and gathering evidence for the purpose of detecting and investigating offences. To perform this task, they are increasingly required to make use of undercover agents, informers and covert practices, particularly in tackling organised crime and corruption.[72]

The chapter begins by outlining human rights standards of relevance to the use of covert human intelligence sources in national policing, criminal justice, and intelligence activities, as interpreted by various international courts and human rights bodies. It then considers national approaches to the regulation of the use of informers, including a case study of Northern Ireland, where human rights law played an ostensibly greater role in regulating conduct than humanitarian law.[73] Informers were both victims and perpetrators of serious crimes during the conflict.[74] The chapter then examines the application of human rights law in times of armed conflict through the lens of the right to life, and considers how national regulation and oversight of the use of informers may be of relevance in situations of armed conflict.

The concluding chapter of the book draws together the analysis from the various chapters and provides an overall reflection and assessment of the treatment by the laws of armed conflict of the phenomenon of wartime collaboration. It considers whether the law's ambivalence towards this perennial yet somewhat neglected aspect of armed conflict may contribute to rather than restrict the harms that invariably accompany the practice.

[72] *Ramanauskas v Lithuania* App no 74420/01 (ECtHR, 5 February 2008), para 49.

[73] See Steven Haines, 'Northern Ireland: 1968–1998' in Elizabeth Wilmshurst (ed), *International Law and the Classification of Conflicts* (OUP 2012) 117; Brice Dickson, *The European Convention of Human Rights and the Conflict in Northern Ireland* (OUP 2010).

[74] *Statement by the Police Ombudsman for Northern Ireland on her Investigation into the circumstances surrounding the death of Raymond McCord Junior and related matters* (Belfast: Police Ombudsman for Northern Ireland, 22 January 2007) 7–8.

1

History and Practice of Collaboration in Armed Conflict

Parties to an armed conflict inevitably place a heavy emphasis on loyalty and encourage a heightened vigilance amongst their members and the population at large against any perceived threats. Suspicion of the presence of internal enemies, particularly of spies or collaborators who might be working with the opposing side, is inevitably generated in such a climate.[1] Individuals or groups that provide assistance to an adversary during wartime are treated at times with as much if not more contempt than the enemy itself.[2] The Second World War Vichy government in France has become synonymous with collaboration, while Vidkun Quisling, described in the Nuremberg judgment as 'the notorious Norwegian traitor',[3] earned the dubious distinction of having his surname adopted as a noun to describe 'a traitor collaborating with an occupying enemy force'.[4]

In understanding the term collaboration, the relative elasticity of the concept, combined with the often-deliberate stoking of wartime anxieties, have led to interpretations of collaboration that go beyond active cooperation with an adversary. The Truth and Reconciliation Commission in Sierra Leone, for example, found that '[t]he notion of 'collaboration' was often applied subjectively and arbitrarily by those who used it. It spread fear and suspicion. "Collaboration" often became a premise upon which violations and abuses were carried out.'[5] Allusions to the omnipresence of traitors, fears of a so-called fifth column, and opportunism have seen the term 'collaborator' deployed against political opponents, minority groups,

[1] Donald R. Hickey, 'The Praeger Affair: A Study in Wartime Hysteria' (1969) 62(2) Journal of the Illinois State Historical Society 117.

[2] See for example Lori J. Ducharme and Gary Alan Fine, 'The Construction of Nonpersonhood and Demonization: Commemorating the Traitorous Reputation of Benedict Arnold' (1995) 73(4) Social Forces 1309; Hans Fredrik Dahl, *Quisling: A Study in Treachery* (translated by Anne-Marie Stanton-Ife, CUP 1999); Colin Holmes, *Searching for Lord Haw-Haw: The Political Lives of William Joyce* (Routledge 2016); Robert O. Paxton, *Vichy France: Old Guard and New Order 1940–1944* (Columbia University Press 2001).

[3] International Military Tribunal (Nuremberg), *Judgment and Sentences* (1947) 41(1) American Journal of International Law 172, 204.

[4] Catherine Soanes (ed), *The Compact Oxford English Dictionary* (2nd edn, OUP 2003) 931.

[5] *Report of the Sierra Leone Truth and Reconciliation Commission*, Vol 3A, 2004, 303, 315; Vol 3B, 286. See also *Chega! The Final Report of the Timor-Leste Commission for Reception, Truth and Reconciliation*, November 2013, Vol II, 1120.

To Serve the Enemy: Informers, Collaborators, and the Laws of Armed Conflict. Shane Darcy, Oxford University Press (2019). © Shane Darcy.
DOI: 10.1093/oso/9780198788898.001.0001

pacifists, conscientious objectors, and human rights defenders.[6] An extreme interpretation of the concept of aiding the enemy saw individuals executed in Nazi Germany for merely criticising the regime or expressing doubt regarding a German victory.[7] During the World Wars, the labelling of Jews and Armenians as 'hostile and traitorous' ultimately served genocidal ends.[8]

This chapter focuses primarily on several forms of cooperation with an adversary which can be said to offer a tangible benefit to an opposing side, while being cognisant of the ready tendency of warring parties to stretch the meaning of the concept of collaboration. The discussion of the history and practice of key forms of collaboration during armed conflict begins with informing by civilians. It then turns to collaboration by combatants and detainees, which has primarily taken the form of serving in the armed forces of the enemy and divulging information when captured. Bureaucratic or administrative collaboration is then explored, while the final section considers a number of residual forms of wartime collaboration, such as trading with the enemy or offering services such as labour or interpreting. The chapter provides illustrative examples of these key types of collaboration and serves to demonstrate the ubiquity of cooperation with an enemy during times of conflict. The various motivations that may underlie such conduct, be they ideological, financial, and even existential, are also discussed.[9] This chapter describes practices which are almost invariably contrary to national law, but which, as later chapters analyse, international law itself has treated with some ambivalence.

1.1 Informers

Intelligence gathering has been a significant and key component of the waging of war for millennia.[10] Successful intelligence enhances the prospects for gaining a military advantage over one's opponent, and can contribute to ensuring compliance with the fundamental principles of distinction, proportionality, and military

[6] See for example *Investigation by the Office of the High Commissioner for Human Rights on Libya: detailed findings*, A/HRC/31/CRP.3, 15 February 2016, paras 228–229; Tom Peck, 'Government Minister Accuses Corbyn of "Collaborating with Russia"', *The Independent*, 12 January 2017; Gavin Weedon, 'Military Resisters, War Resistance, and the Ethics of Disclosure and Exposure' (2014) 14(5) Cultural Studies Critical Methodologies 438.

[7] Ingo Müller, *Hitler's Justice: The Courts of the Third Reich* (translated by Deborah Lucas Schneider, Harvard University Press 1991) 147–8.

[8] István Deák, *Europe on Trial: The Story of Collaboration, Resistance, and Retribution During World War II* (Westview Press 2015) 22–3.

[9] See generally Stanley Hoffmann, 'Collaborationism in France during World War II' (1968) 40(3) The Journal of Modern History 375; Stathis N. Kalyvas, 'Ethnic Defection in Civil War' (2008) 41 Comparative Political Studies 1043; Jon Elster, 'Redemption for Wrongdoing: The Fate of Collaborators after 1945' (2006) 50 Journal of Conflict Resolution 324.

[10] Sun Tzu, *The Art of War*, Chapter XIII, para 3, original translation by Samuel B. Griffith, *reprinted in* Mark McNeilly, *Sun Tzu and the Art of Modern Warfare* (OUP 2001) 211, 290. See generally John Keegan, *Intelligence in War: Knowledge of the Enemy from Napoleon to Al-Qaeda* (Alfred A. Knopf 2003); Ralph Bennett, *Behind the Battle: Intelligence in the War with Germany 1939–1945* (Pimlico 1999).

necessity.[11] The acquisition of human intelligence or HUMINT is prized during armed conflicts and is primarily undertaken by using spies, informers, and agents, and by interrogating detained persons, such as prisoners of war.[12] According to a US army field manual:

HUMINT is vital in all combat operations, regardless of echelon or intensity of conflict. By nature, HUMINT lends itself to the collection of information about the enemy's thought processes and intentions. HUMINT can provide information on almost any topic of intelligence interest, including order of battle (OB) factors, as well as scientific and technical (S&T) intelligence subjects.[13]

Individuals who 'know the enemy situation' have long been considered as particularly valuable.[14] In the wars of Ancient Greece and Rome, human intelligence was obtained from locals, deserters, and collaborators: '[d]isaffected individuals frequently would come forward with vital information'.[15] This section focuses on the use of informers during armed conflict. Human intelligence that might be derived from interrogating prisoners of war or other detainees is examined in section 1.2.

Sun Tzu identified several individuals whose intelligence-gathering activities would unquestionably be considered as collaboration by the opposing party.[16] He described 'native agents' as 'the enemy's country people whom we employ', and 'inside agents' as those 'enemy officials' who provided information.[17] Sun Tzu also advocated turning enemy agents through bribery.[18] Such double agents could then be directed to the recruitment and running of both native and inside agents.[19] Tu Mu, writing in the ninth century, suggested those amongst an enemy's officials who might be recruited:

Among the official class there are worthy men who been deprived of office; others who have committed errors and have been punished. There are sycophants and minions who are covetous of wealth. There are those who remain long in lowly office; those who have not obtained responsible positions, and those whose sole desire is to take advantage of times of trouble to extend the scope of their own abilities. There are those who are two-faced, changeable, and deceitful, and who are always sitting on the fence. As far as all such are concerned you can secretly inquire after their welfare, rewards them liberally with gold and silk, and so tie them to you. Then you may rely on them to seek out the real facts of the situation in their country, and to ascertain its plans directed against you. They can as well create cleavages between the sovereign and his ministers so that these are not in harmonious accord.[20]

[11] Yutaka Arai-Takahashi, *The Law of Occupation: Continuity and Change of International Humanitarian Law, and its Interaction with International Human Rights Law* (Martinus Nijhoff 2009) 277.

[12] On the stages of intelligence see Keegan, *Intelligence in War* (n 10) 5–6. See also Peter Gill and Mark Phythian, *Intelligence in an Insecure World* (2nd edn, Polity Press 2012) 77–102.

[13] Field Manual 34-53, *Intelligence Interrogation* (Headquarters, Department of the Army 28 September 1992) 1–3.

[14] Sun Tzu, *The Art of War* (n 10) Chapter XIII, para 4.

[15] Jonathan P. Roth, 'War' in Philip Sabin, Hans van Wees, and Michael Withby (eds), *The Cambridge History of Greek and Roman Warfare*, Vol. I (CUP 2007) 368, 391.

[16] Sun Tzu, *The Art of War* (n 10) Chapter XIII, para 5.

[17] Ibid para 6.

[18] Ibid para 17.

[19] Ibid para 18.

[20] See McNeilly, *Sun Tzu and the Art of Modern Warfare* (n 10) 290–1.

As regards the handling of informers, Sun Tzu recommended fairness and restraint in dealing with secret agents: 'He who is not sage and wise, humane and just, cannot use secret agents. And he who is not delicate and subtle cannot get the truth out of them.'[21] Severe punishment was required where information was compromised: 'If plans relating to secret operations are prematurely divulged the agent and all those to whom he spoke of them shall be put to death.'[22] Machiavelli proposed a less brutal way of dealing with those persons who are considering to have provided intelligence to an adversary:

> If you suspect anyone in your army of giving the enemy intelligence of your designs you cannot do better than to avail yourself of this treachery by seeming to trust him with some secret resolution which you intend to execute, while you carefully conceal your real design; hence you may perhaps discover the traitor and lead the enemy into an error that may possibly end in its destruction.[23]

He was not hesitant, however, about cultivating the suspicion of collaboration and betrayal in an opponent in order 'to divide the enemy's strength by making him suspicious of his counsellors and confidants'.[24] He proposed tactics such as sparing the property of particular individuals during times of 'general plunder and devastation' and returning detained relatives without requiring that any ransom be paid.[25] He was keenly aware that in addition to being a potentially valuable intelligence source, informers, or even their suspected presence, could serve to undermine the effective functioning of a party to an armed conflict.

The term 'informer' is often understood as referring to individuals who have been recruited by a party to an armed conflict and instructed on how to gather and relay relevant information, but it might also be applied to persons who provide information more informally, including on a once-off basis. Carl von Clausewitz wrote how the general population could constitute a valuable source of information during war:

> We refer not so much to the single outstandingly significant report, but to the countless minor contacts brought about by the daily activities of our army. Here the defender's close relations with the population give him a general superiority. The smallest patrol, every picket, every sentry, every officer on a mission, all have to turn to the local inhabitants for news of friend or foe.[26]

Anyone providing information to an adversary during an armed conflict as a recruited informer or guide during military operations, or on a more casual basis, runs the risk of being considered a collaborator and of facing serious if not lethal consequences for engaging in such activities. While technological developments have significantly changed the warfare described in these historical texts, intelligence

[21] Sun Tzu, *The Art of War* (n 10) Chapter XIII, para 13. [22] Ibid para 15.

[23] Niccolò Machiavelli, *The Art of War*, 1521 (revised edn of the Ellis Farneworth Translation by Neal Wood, 2nd edn, Da Capo Press 2001) 170, 197.

[24] Ibid 173. [25] Ibid.

[26] Carl von Clausewitz, *On War*, Book Six, Chapter Six, 'Scope of the Means of Defence' (first published 1832, edited and translated by Michael Howard and Peter Paret, Princeton University Press 1976) 373.

gathering and the use of enemy civilians and personnel as informers remains relevant in more recent armed conflicts. Throughout the twentieth and twenty-first centuries, warring parties have sought to gather information from the enemy's population, to recruit covertly or plant agents in the opposing party's ranks, and to turn its own spies against it.

1.1.1 Second World War

By the beginning of the Second World War, all the major powers had developed dedicated intelligence services and had become more adept at gathering intelligence on their adversaries.[27] Signals intelligence (SIGINT) played a prominent role during the War,[28] but the protagonists also made use of human intelligence, and counteracted its threat by taking harsh measures against informers, as they had both during and after the First World War.[29] During the first years of the Second World War, British intelligence relied heavily on 'reports from informants abroad'.[30] The Western Allies had limited success in gathering human intelligence at higher levels: 'Neither the British nor the Americans acquired a single highly placed source around the German, Japanese or Italian governments or high commands.'[31] Germany's *Abwehr* gathered intelligence in the territories it occupied through local informers and by interrogating captured prisoners of war,[32] while the Secret Field Police within the *Wehrmacht* established networks of local agents in those territories.[33] Such collaboration was at times voluntary; in the Netherlands, thousands of Dutch nationals 'volunteered to work against their fellow countrymen as agents provocateurs and informers in the service of the Gestapo an Security Police'.[34] For their part, the Allies also acquired information by interrogating captured prisoners of war,[35] as discussed in section 1.2, as well as through the use of civilian informers.

In occupied territories, the use of informers was a means of gathering information, weakening resistance activities, and maintaining control by occupying powers. Such informers were at times forcibly recruited. In the Dutch East Indies, Allied intelligence personnel were alleged to have enlisted locals at gunpoint,[36] whereas in the Japanese-occupied Philippines, informers were also recruited by offers of amnesties or financial rewards to combat guerrillas that were operating under the

[27] Max Hastings, *The Secret War: Spies, Codes and Guerrillas 1939–1945* (William Collins 2015) 2. See also Allen Dulles, *The Craft of Intelligence* (Weidenfeld and Nicolson 1963) 25–7.

[28] Ibid 70.

[29] See for example Markus Pöhlmann, 'German Intelligence at War, 1914–1918' (2005) 5 Journal of Intelligence History 33, 55; Müller, *Hitler's Justice* (n 7) 22.

[30] Hastings, *The Secret War* (n 27) 13.

[31] Ibid xxiv. See also Dulles, *The Craft of Intelligence* (n 27) 66.

[32] Vadim J. Birstein, *SMERSH, Stalin's Secret Weapon: Soviet Military Intelligence in World War II* (Biteback Publishing 2011) 150.

[33] Ibid 150, 165.

[34] Werner Rings, *Life with the Enemy: Collaboration and Resistance in Hitler's Europe 1939–1945* (translated by J. Maxwell Brownjohn, Doubleday & Co. 1982) 96–7.

[35] Kevin Jones, 'From the Horse's Mouth: *Luftwaffe* POWs as Sources for Air Ministry Intelligence During the Battle of Britain' (2000) 15(4) Intelligence and National Security 60.

[36] Hastings, *The Secret War* (n 27) 515.

command of the United States.[37] Civilians were also used as so-called short-range spies or line-crossers during the Second World War by both Allied and Axis powers. According to Max Hastings:

The most ruthless and cynical operations run by all intelligence services were those involving short-range spies – locally recruited civilians dispatched to report what they could see behind the enemy's front line. Their prospects of success or even survival were slight, but this did not deter the Axis or the Allies from thrusting a small army of them into the fray.[38]

For example, Germany recruited 300 French 'stay-behind' agents to be deployed when the Allies gained control over French territory. While most were unemployed men who accepted the work for financial reasons, some were ideologically motivated.[39] As the German army retreated during the final months of the War, 'hundreds of line-crossers recruited by the Allies were thrust forward into Germany'.[40] Their fate was often unknown; a British Special Operations Executive officer 'herded a batch of Poles up a road towards the German lines, with orders to push forward as far as they could in pursuit of information. He wrote, after watching one man go: 'I cannot say I was altogether hopeful about his chances'.[41] Line-crossers deployed by the Soviets, including Russian nationals, German deserters, and exposed double agents, are said to have suffered 'equally devastating attrition'.[42] The phenomenon of line-crossing was not confined to the Second World War; it also occurred during the Korean War.[43]

Informers often suffered at the hands of both those for whom they were gathering information and those whom they were seen to have betrayed. During the First World War, British intelligence officers sat their agents on an 'electric carpet' when questioning them, subjecting them to electric shocks if they were considering to be lying.[44] The Austro-Hungarians, allies of Germany during the First World War, are said to have 'hanged thousands of Serbian and Russian-Ukrainian civilians, among them Orthodox priests, suspected of spying for the enemy'.[45] In the context of the fighting in the Philippines during the Second World War, US Brigadier General Donald Blackburn contended that complying with the laws of war in counteracting the threat posed by informers to US and guerrilla forces, would have meant that they 'could not physically survive':

To avoid extinction and to survive, the American-led guerrilla forces decided to take stringent measures. Through official orders it was announced that spies and informers, considered to be the main problem, would be controlled or eliminated ... Giving these individuals legal or procedural rights that they might have been entitled to was conditioned primarily by reality

[37] Donald Blackburn, 'Irregular Warfare: Legal Implications of the Facts, Policies and Law from World War II to Vietnam: Remarks by Brigadier General Donald Blackburn (USA, Retired)' 70 *Proceedings of the American Society of International Law* (1976) 154, 155.

[38] Ibid 491. [39] Ibid 491–3. [40] Ibid. [41] Ibid. [42] Ibid 494.

[43] John P. Finnegan, 'The Evolution of US Army HUMINT: Intelligence Operations in the Korean War' (2011) 55(2) Studies in Intelligence 57, 58–9.

[44] See Richard Popplewell, 'British Intelligence in Mesopotamia 1914–16' (1990) 5(2) Intelligence and National Security 139, 151–2.

[45] Deák, *Europe on Trial* (n 8) 21.

and was deemed secondary to the primary goal of simply staying alive. The action of the guerrilla forces was consistently conditioned by the fact that compliance with certain legal rules that might have been considered applicable would have resulted, from their point of view, in imminent death. The price of success for guerrilla operations was, simply stated, to destroy spies and informers.[46]

A number of US personnel had been captured and executed by the Japanese on account of this 'relentless, subduing spy system of the enemy'.[47] During the occupation of Malaya in 1942, the Japanese 'rounded up and executed several thousand real or supposed British stay-behind agents and sympathisers'.[48] Informers were also executed by guerrilla forces fighting alongside the United States in Burma, albeit after a rudimentary trial.[49]

Both before and during the Second World War, the Soviet Union under Stalin executed or sent to the gulag many thousands of intelligence officers, soldiers, and civilians suspected of being informers and collaborators.[50] Likewise, Germany sent individuals discovered to be informers 'to the gallows or concentration camps'.[51] The collaborationist Vichy regime ran counter-intelligence operations, including against its principal ally, and is said to have executed or deported dozens of 'secret agents employed by Germany'.[52] The Cold War that followed the end of the Second World War saw an even greater emphasis on espionage by the major powers, including the use of spies and informers for intelligence gathering activities, the encouragement of defection, especially by intelligence officials, and stern and at times excessive measures against real or perceived internal enemies.[53] The next section considers some prominent examples of how informers have continued to be used for the purposes of gathering intelligence and weakening the opposition during times of armed conflict.

1.1.2 Contemporary Conflicts

The legal framework set down in the 1949 Geneva Conventions, adopted in the aftermath of the Second World War and elaborated upon in the 1977 Additional Protocols, firmly distinguishes between international and non-international armed conflicts. The rules of Common Article 3 of the 1949 Geneva Conventions, for example, are said to apply during an 'armed conflict not of an international character occurring in the territory of one of the High Contracting Parties'. International humanitarian law as embodied in these treaties also distinguishes between differing

[46] Blackburn, 'Irregular Warfare: Legal Implications of the Facts' (n 37) 155. [47] Ibid.

[48] Hastings, *The Secret War* (n 27) 515.

[49] James Ward, 'Irregular Warfare: Legal Implications of the Facts, Policies and Law from World War II to Vietnam: Remarks by James Ward', 70 Proceedings of the American Society of International Law (1976) 154, 155.

[50] Hastings, *The Secret War* (n 27) 19–20. See also Birstein, *SMERSH, Stalin's Secret Weapon* (n 32) 174.

[51] Ibid 473. See also Keegan, *Intelligence in War* (n 10) 259.

[52] Rings, *Life with the Enemy* (n 34) 114.

[53] Sanche de Gramont, *The Secret War: The Story of International Espionage since World War II* (A. Deutsch 1962); Dulles, *The Craft of Intelligence* (n 27) 134–43; Milton Bearden and James Risen, *The Main Enemy: The Inside Story of the CIA's Final Showdown with the KGB* (Century 2003) 394, 439–532.

parties to an armed conflict, with Additional Protocol II recognising that an armed conflict might arise between the armed forces of a state and an 'organized armed group'.[54] While questions regarding the consequences of such distinctions on the application of rules of international humanitarian law are addressed in subsequent chapters, these different categories offer a convenient lens through which to view more recent practice regarding the use of informers during armed conflict. Non-international armed conflicts have become more prevalent than their international counterparts,[55] and non-state armed groups more prominent in modern armed conflicts.[56] Informers have been used by states engaged in armed conflict against other states and non-state actors, while organised armed groups themselves have also made use of informers as an intelligence source.

The reliance and emphasis on using informers in British intelligence and counter-insurgency practices provides an appropriate starting point, given their replication in other armed conflicts. The use of informers and agents has been 'a constant feature of the history of British counter-insurgency strategy',[57] and the practice in Ireland over several centuries gave rise to 'a special abhorrence of informers'.[58] During the Irish War of Independence, 'covert intelligence and counter-intelligence operations—involving undercover officers, secret agents and informers—would play a major role in deciding the outcome'.[59] The Irish Republican Army (IRA) recruited and used informers, both casually and from within the military, intelligence, and police services.[60] As to those who may have provided assistance to the British authorities, the IRA engaged in the 'ruthless killing of any members of the public suspected of giving information'.[61] The practices of this particular period in Irish history were repeated in Northern Ireland during the more recent Troubles, with the military and security services vigorously recruiting informers, who in turn were often dealt with severely by paramilitary organisations.[62] This stage of the conflict is discussed in more detail as a case study in Chapter 5.

British General Frank Kitson placed a significant emphasis on the use of informers and other collaborators during counter-insurgency operations:

> An example of a simple Special Operation would be the cordoning of a village and the examination of the occupants by a row of informers concealed in hoods, who are thus able to

[54] Protocol Additional to the Geneva Conventions of 12 August 1949, and relating to the Protection of Victims of Non-International Armed Conflicts (Protocol II) 1977, 1125 U.N.T.S. 609, art 1(1).

[55] M. Cherif Bassiouni, *The Pursuit of International Criminal Justice: A World Study on Conflicts, Victimization and Post-Conflict Justice*, Vol II (Intersentia 2010).

[56] David E. Cunningham, Kristian Skrede Gleditsch, and Idean Salehyan, 'Non-state Actors in Civil Wars' (2013) 30(5) Conflict Management and Peace Science 516; M. Cherif Bassiouni, 'The New Wars and the Crisis of Compliance with the Law of Armed Conflict by Non-State Actors' (2008) 98(3) Journal of Criminal Law and Criminology 711.

[57] Thomas Leahy, 'The Influence of Informers and Agents on Provisional Irish Republican Army Military Strategy and British Counter-Insurgency Strategy, 1976–1994' (2014) 26(1) Twentieth Century British History 122, 123. See also Jon Moran, *From Northern Ireland to Afghanistan: British Military Intelligence Operations, Ethics and Human Rights* (Ashgate 2013).

[58] Paul McMahon, *British Spies and Irish Rebels: British Intelligence and Ireland 1916–1945* (Boydell Press 2008) 4–8.

[59] Ibid 26. [60] Ibid 27–8. [61] Ibid 43.

[62] See John Bowyer Bell, *The Secret Army: The IRA* (Poolbeg 1998) 485.

denounce any enemy without the risk of detection. [...] A more elaborate operation might involve the building up of a pseudo-gang from captured insurgents and the cultivation by them of a local supporters' committee in a particular area designed ultimately to put the pseudo-gang into touch with a genuine armed group.[63]

Such operations were conducted by Germany in occupied territories, by the armed forces of the Philippines in the conflict with the Huk guerrillas, and by the British themselves in the context of colonial conflicts in Kenya and Cyprus.[64] David French has described the use of informers in British-controlled Cyprus against EOKA, the Greek Cypriot nationalist guerrilla force:

cordon and search operations were mounted almost as a matter of routine, to demonstrate to the population that the security forces could exercise a measure of control over their lives. Once the cordon was in place, troops and police erected a barbed wire enclosure nearby, and all of the male inhabitants were required to pass through it for 'screening'. Each man was questioned by the police and, in some instances, made to pass before a hooded informer. If there was anything suspicious about them, or if the informer identified them as an EOKA member, they would be arrested for further questioning.[65]

EOKA had its own network of informers and targeted those suspected of collaborating with the British, including civilians and local police officials.[66]

Such practices have been replicated in contemporary armed conflicts, including those of an international character. While international armed conflicts involving the occupation of enemy territory are less frequent since 1945, the examples of Iraq and Israel/Palestine are illustrative of the use of informers by parties to those conflicts. In Iraq, it became common for US and UK armed forces to deploy specialised human intelligence personnel. Such 'Tactical Humint Teams' accompanied regular patrols and troops conducting military operations and sought to recruit informers from amongst the Iraqi population.[67] A secretive British Army unit, referred to as the Joint Support Group, was trained to 'turn hardened terrorists into coalition spies' and ran dozens of Iraqi double agents during the conflict.[68] According to a military source, their role was 'to recruit and run covert human intelligence sources

[63] Frank Kitson, *Low Intensity Operations: Subversion, Insurgency, Peace-keeping* (Faber and Faber, 1971) 100.

[64] Ibid.

[65] David French, *Fighting EOKA: The British Counter-Insurgency on Cyprus, 1955–1959* (OUP 2015) 132 (footnote omitted). See also ibid 136; David French, *The British Way in Counter-Insurgency, 1945–1967* (OUP 2011) 107, 116.

[66] French, *The British Way in Counter-Insurgency* (n 65) 23.

[67] Mark Urban, *Task Force Black: the Explosive True Story of the SAS and the Secret War in Iraq* (Little, Brown 2010) 50. Field HUMINT teams were also deployed in Afghanistan, see Joop van Reijn, 'Intelligence and the International Security Assistance Force in Afghanistan (ISAF)' in Christopher Andrew, Richard J. Aldrich, and Wesley K. Wark (eds), *Secret Intelligence: A Reader* (Routledge 2008) 510, 516; Nicky Hager and Jon Stephenson, *Hit & Run: The New Zealand SAS in Afghanistan and the Meaning of Honour* (Potton & Burton 2017) 18–21.

[68] Sean Raymant, 'Top Secret Army Cell Breaks Terrorists', *Daily Telegraph*, 4 February 2007.

or agents—we never use the term informer'.[69] Such individuals might have to inform on friends or relatives, and were thus at considerable risk:

> All potential agents are warned that anyone suspected of being a coalition spy will be tortured before being murdered. If he is married, his wife will be gang-raped in front of their children, who will in all probability also be murdered, they are told. Despite the risks, JSG operators deal with dozens of Iraqis every week who are prepared, for a variety of reasons, to become informers.[70]

As well as the prospect of financial reward, some were said to have acted for 'altruistic reasons'.[71] A dedicated phone line was set up to receive confidential information from informers during the war in Iraq.[72]

Iraqi informers accompanied UK and US armed forces on military operations, usually disguised, in order to identify suspected insurgents.[73] The United States relied on a group known as the 'Desert Protectors' for such purposes. In the course of one operation, hundreds of Iraqi individuals were rounded up: 'With the help of a group of locally recruited informants, most with their faces concealed by balaclavas and scarves, the troops pulled 12 suspected insurgents from the lineup, bound them in handcuffs and blindfolds, and took them away.'[74] A US marine commander justified the practice on the basis that '[t]his is the land of 'the enemy of my enemy is my friend'.[75] Given the awareness that such informers could implicate innocent individuals based on 'tribal grievances', the role of informers was confined to initial screenings only, with other evidence and subsequent screenings conducted by intelligence experts and lawyers, leading most to be released.[76]

Questions arise regarding the reliability of human intelligence, including that provided by informers.[77] In the course of the armed conflict in Iraq, intelligence personnel had to sift through a mass of information, some of which may have been false,[78] and account for the detention of innocent persons who were held on the basis of incorrect information received from informers.[79] Despite risks of deliberate misinformation and the presence of double agents, 'there was precious little time for screening once the Iraq War began and the sheer numbers of informants

[69] Ibid. [70] Ibid. [71] Urban, *Task Force Black* (n 67) 198. [72] Ibid 78.

[73] Ibid 239–40. See also 'Report of the Independent International Commission of Inquiry on the Syrian Arab Republic', UN Doc A/HRC/21/50, 16 August 2012, Annex V, para 27.

[74] Kirk Semple, 'U.S. Forces Rely on Local Informants in Ferreting Rebels in West Iraq', *New York Times*, 10 December 2005.

[75] Ibid.

[76] Ibid. See also Andru E. Wall, 'Civilian Detentions in Iraq' in Michael Schmitt and Jelena Pejic (eds), *International Law and Armed Conflict: Exploring the Faultlines: Essays in Honour of Yoram Dinstein* (Martinus Nijhoff 2007) 413, 413.

[77] Keegan, *Intelligence in War* (n 10) 22–3; Hastings, *The Secret War* (n 27) 4; B. Bamford, 'Intelligence in Northern Ireland' in Andrew, Aldrich, and Wark, *Secret Intelligence* (n 67) 259, 266; Gill and Phythian, *Intelligence in an Insecure World* (n 12) 93–4; Matthew Aid, 'All Glory is Fleeting: SIGINT and the Fight Against International Terrorism' in Andrew, Aldrich, and Wark, *Secret Intelligence* (n 67) 40, 56–7; John R. Schindler, 'Intelligence and Strategy in the War on Islamist Terrorism' in Andrew, Aldrich, and Wark, *Secret Intelligence* (n 67) 245, 246.

[78] Urban, *Task Force Black* (n 67) 51–2. [79] Ibid 239–40.

overwhelmed any effort to track them all. Unreliable or difficult operatives were simply dismissed or replaced'.[80] Former CIA Director, James Woolsey, emphasised the value of human intelligence, despite the challenges it presents, including cost and the recruitment of 'unsavoury individuals'.[81] This latter challenge was borne out in Iraq, where local agents run by the US Central Intelligence Agency (CIA) were said to be involved in 'the kidnap business'.[82]

The recruitment, use, and ill-treatment of collaborators has been a recurrent feature of the conflict in Israel/Palestine.[83] According to the Israeli human rights organisation B'tselem:

> Since 1967, the security forces have recruited tens of thousands of Palestinians from the territories to serve as collaborators. This was made possible in part by the great dependence of the Palestinians on the services provided by the Israeli administration. In recruiting collaborators, the security forces used methods that contravened international law, such as providing certain services only on condition that the recipient cooperate with the authorities. They also resorted to extortion and pressure, and offered various inducements.[84]

In addition to networks of informers run by the Israeli intelligence service within prisons, Palestinian institutions, and organised armed groups, the Israeli military has also used Palestinians as informers during military operations. The UN Independent Commission of Inquiry on the 2014 Gaza Conflict documented reports of Palestinians accompanying Israeli soldiers for the purpose of identifying particular individuals.[85] Information from collaborators has also been used in targeted assassinations of alleged members of armed opposition groups.[86] The question of whether such activities amount to direct participation in hostilities is considered in Chapter 3.

The case of Israel/Palestine also highlights how armed forces and intelligence services rely on coercive and other methods to recruit informers. The Israeli authorities have used 'a combination of pressure and sweeteners to entice Palestinians to divulge intelligence'.[87] The UN Fact-Finding Mission in Gaza noted reports of young political

[80] Joby Warrick, *The Triple Agent: The Al-Qaeda Mole who Infiltrated the CIA* (Vintage Books 2012) 144.

[81] United States Senate Committee on the Judiciary Subcommittee on Technology, Terrorism, and Government Information, *Crime, Terror & War: National Security and Public Safety in the Information Age*, Report Submitted by Majority Staff, November 1998, 7.

[82] Urban, *Task Force Black* (n 67) 77.

[83] See generally Palestinian Academic Society for the Study of International Affairs, *The Phenomenon of Collaborators in Palestine* (2001); Hillel Cohen, *Army of Shadows: Palestinian Collaboration with Zionism, 1917–1948* (translated by Haim Watzman, University of California Press 2008); Ron Dudai and Hillel Cohen, 'Triangle of Betrayal: Collaborators and Transitional Justice in the Israeli–Palestinian Conflict' (2007) 6(1) Journal of Human Rights 37.

[84] B'tselem, *Collaborators in the Occupied Territories: Human Rights Abuses and Violations*, 1994, 1. See also Hillel Cohen and Ron Dudai, 'Human Rights Dilemmas in Using Informers to Combat Terrorism: The Israeli–Palestinian Case' (2005) 17 Terrorism and Political Violence 229, 233; Lisa Hajjar, *Courting Conflict: The Israeli Military Court System* (University of California Press, 2005) 211.

[85] *Report of the detailed findings of the independent commission of inquiry established pursuant to Human Rights Council resolution S-21/1*, A/HRC/29/CRP.4, 22 June 2015, para 327.

[86] Mossab Hassan Yousef, *Son of Hamas* (Authentic Media 2014) 156.

[87] 'Israel PM: Hamas will Pay "Heavy Price" after Boy (4) Killed', *Irish Times*, 22 August 2014.

activists being asked under 'threat of arrest or of future difficulties in continuing their studies'.[88] Persons with a criminal past have been particularly vulnerable to recruitment, while the granting of travel permits and access to medical care have been used to achieve cooperation.[89] According to a group of Israeli intelligence officials:

> Personnel were instructed to keep any damaging details of Palestinians' lives they came across, including information on sexual preferences, infidelities, financial problems or family illnesses that could be 'used to extort/blackmail the person and turn them into a collaborator'.[90]

One especially high-profile collaborator, Mosab Hassan Yousef, who was the son of a founder of Hamas, described his torture and ill-treatment at the hands of Israeli soldiers while in detention, and his subsequent recruitment by Shin Bet, the Israeli internal security service. He claims that information he provided was used in arrest operations, targeted assassinations, and the prevention of attacks by Palestinian armed groups.[91]

The ill-treatment and killing of suspected Palestinian informers recruited by the Israeli authorities has been a frequent occurrence during the conflict.[92] In 2012, six alleged collaborators were shot dead in public in Gaza and the body of one dragged through the streets of Gaza City behind a motorbike.[93] When Hamas held a number of collaborator trials and public executions in 2014 under 'Operation Strangling Necks', it was unapologetic about the claimed need 'to send a strong message'.[94] Hamas stated that:

> The resistance will continue to repel collaborators and cut their numbers in Gaza. The resistance will not grant mercy to anyone who provides information about the resistance and its men to the enemy. Field executions will be the number one solution for them.[95]

The UN Independent Commission of Inquiry on the 2014 Gaza Conflict condemned such killings, as well as instances of torture and ill-treatment of collaborators, describing them as war crimes.[96] It also noted the rationale underlying such conduct, 'that they were executed in order to increase pressure on Gaza's population, with a view to preventing others from spying'.[97] Amnesty International also denounced the ill-treatment and execution of collaborators by Hamas,[98] yet neither

[88] Human Rights Council, *Report of the United Nations Fact-Finding Mission on the Gaza Conflict*, A/HRC/12/48, 25 September 2009, para 1722.

[89] Lara Marlowe, 'Collaborating the Only Way to Survive for Some Gaza Families', *Irish Times*, 3 September 2014.

[90] Peter Beaumont, 'Israeli Intelligence Veterans Refuse to Serve in Palestinian Territories', *The Guardian*, 12 September 2014.

[91] Hassan Yousef, *Son of Hamas* (n 86) 70–5, 80, 159, 258.

[92] Yezid Sayigh, *Armed Struggle and the Search for a State: The Palestinian National Movement, 1949–1993* (OUP 1997) 287,

[93] 'Hamas Executes Six Suspected Informants for Israel on Gaza Street', *The Guardian*, 20 November 2012.

[94] Marlowe, 'Collaborating the only way to survive' (n 89).

[95] Amnesty International, *Strangling Necks: Abductions, Torture and Summary Killings of Palestinians by Hamas Forces during the 2014 Gaza/Israel Conflict*, MDE 21/1643/2015, 2015, 14.

[96] *Report of Gaza commission of inquiry* (n 85) para 502.

[97] Ibid para 492.

[98] Amnesty International, *Strangling Necks* (n 95) 13–27.

the Commission of Inquiry nor Amnesty International raised any questions regarding the lawfulness of the use of informers or collaborators per se, or of the authority of relevant non-state armed groups to punish collaboration, so long as such measures accord with the applicable rules of international law.[99] As discussed in subsequent chapters, international humanitarian law permits the practice of using and recruiting informers and other collaborators, but condemns any resort to coercion or ill-treatment of such persons.

1.1.3 Non-State Armed Groups

Contemporary armed conflicts have seen the concerted use of informers by states against armed opposition groups as a means of gathering information on such groups and undermining their activities. According to Michael Herman, 'informers provide almost the only means of penetrating non-state terrorism; and security intelligence has always needed informers on subversive movements and other internal threats'.[100] Intelligence services have encountered difficulties in recruiting informers or running agents within certain groups, such as Al Qaeda, such that after 11 September 2001, the absence of such human intelligence lead to a greater reliance upon interrogating detained individuals, often by the use of unlawful means, including torture.[101] Such techniques are seen both as ineffectual and liable to jeopardise the potential recruitment of voluntary informers.[102] Since that time, however, informers have been recruited within non-state groups and have provided information which has led to the killing by drone of alleged Al Qaeda leaders, including Abu Musad al-Zarqawi.[103] Coalition forces had agents operating inside insurgent groups in Iraq within a number of years,[104] while in Syria, intelligence services successfully infiltrated jihadist groups and turned 'suspects into government collaborators'.[105] Western intelligence agencies are reported to have placed informers within Islamic State, with one former member describing a significant fear of 'the foreign spies who are among them'.[106] Non-state

[99] See discussion in Chapters 2 and 3.

[100] Michael Herman, *Intelligence Power in Peace and War* (CUP 1996) 65.

[101] Aid, 'All Glory is Fleeting' (n 77) 47; Anthony Lewis, 'Introduction' *in* Karen J. Greenberg and Joshua L. Dratel (eds), *The Torture Papers: The Road to Abu Ghraib* (CUP 2005) xiii. See also 'The Mikolashek Report', Department of the Army, The Inspector General Detainee Operations Inspection, 21 July 2004, in Greenberg and Dratel, *The Torture Papers* (n 101) 632, 635, 639.

[102] Andrew, Aldrich, and Wark, *Secret Intelligence* (n 67) 316. See also Mark A. Costanzo and Ellen Gerrity, 'The Effects and Effectiveness of Using Torture as an Interrogation Device: Using Research to Inform the Policy Debate' (2009) 3(1) Social Issues and Policy Review 179; Christopher Michael Sullivan, 'The (in)effectiveness of Torture for Combating Insurgency' (2014) 51(3) Journal of Peace Research 388.

[103] Warrick, *The Triple Agent* (n 80) 39–40. See also Aimee Dean, Paul Cruickshank, and Tim Lister, *Nine Lives: My Time as MI6's Top Spy Inside Al-Qaeda* (Oneworld 2018). On drone warfare see generally see Michael J. Boyle (ed), *Legal and Ethical Implications of Drone Warfare* (Routledge 2017); Peter L. Bergen and Daniel Rothenberg (eds), *Drone Warfare: Transforming Conflict, Law and Policy* (CUP 2014).

[104] Urban, *Task Force Black* (n 67) 243. See also Warrick, *The Triple Agent* (n 80) 119.

[105] Peter Neumann, 'Suspects into Collaborators', 36 London Review of Books 7, 3 April 2014, 19.

[106] Kim Sengupta, 'Inside Isis: How UK Spies Infiltrated Terrorist Leadership', *The Independent*, 19 October 2016.

armed groups themselves have also made use of informers as a means of gathering intelligence on the security services or armed forces of states, as well to accrue information on the civilian population and any perceived enemies.

In the context of guerrilla warfare, Che Guevara's emphasis on the necessity of 'the support of the people' for insurgents was partly based on the population being a valuable source of intelligence.[107] He wrote that:

> Nothing gives more help to combatant forces than correct information. This arrives spontaneously from the local inhabitants, who will come to tell its friendly army, its allies, what is happening in various places; but in addition it should be completely systematized. [...] An intelligence service also should be in direct contact with enemy fronts. Men and women, especially women, should infiltrate; they should be in permanent contact with soldiers and gradually discover what there is to be discovered.[108]

Guevara considered that in the areas where guerrilla forces operate, 'all inhabitants are intelligence agents', although a specific duty concerning intelligence gathering should be designated to certain individuals. In addition to obtaining information, they could 'sow fear and instability by spreading discouraging information'.[109] His writings emphasised the importance of secrecy and loyalty, of the indoctrination of inhabitants, and of the need for 'measures of quarantine [...] against the irreconcilable enemies of the revolution'.[110] Guevara is said to have personally executed a Cuban peasant accused of being a collaborator.[111] He suggested that guerrillas forces be in a state of 'constant distrust', given that 'terrorized peasants in some cases will give them away to the repressive troops in order to save themselves'.[112]

In addition to exploiting the civilian population, non-state armed groups have sought to place agents in or recruit informers from the enemy's military, security, and police apparatus. In the conflict in British-controlled Cyprus, for example, the Greek Cypriot guerrilla group EOKA 'recruited agents from inside the government bureaucracy and police':

> EOKA agents penetrated almost all government departments. Police informers provided EOKA with information about forthcoming security forces operations and the identities of key personnel. EOKA agents working in the post office opened mail addressed to the authorities and thus discovered Greek Cypriot informers, with sometimes fatal consequences for them.[113]

EOKA was able to recruit willing individuals who were politically supportive to act as agents and informers, whereas other persons were threatened or intimidated by the organisation into engaging in such activities.[114] In Colombia, the rules of

[107] Che Guevara, *Guerrilla Warfare* (first published in 1960, translated by J.P. Murry, reprinted in Brian Loveman and Thomas M. Davies Jr. (eds), *Che Guevara: Guerrilla Warfare* (3rd edn, SR Books 1997) 52.

[108] Ibid. [109] Ibid. [110] Ibid. See also ibid 70.

[111] Paul J. Dosal, *Commandante Che: Guerrilla Soldier, Commander, and Strategist, 1956–1967* (Pennsylvania State University Press 2003) 83.

[112] Che Guevara, 'Guerrilla Warfare: A Method', 25 *Cuba Socialista* (first published 1963, reprinted in Loveman and Davies, *Che Guevara* (n 107)) 158–9.

[113] French, *Fighting EOKA* (n 65) 58 (footnotes omitted). [114] Ibid.

conduct used by two armed opposition groups, the FARC and ELN, obliged members of these armed groups to 'respect the various measures taken by collaborators to keep their links to us secret'.[115] Armed groups can thus be seen to have replicated the approaches taken by states to the recruitment and use of informers, while also resorting to harsh measures against those suspected of informing against them. Organised armed groups in Colombia targeted individuals, including children, suspected to have been recruited as informers by police and army units; UN Special Rapporteurs reported accounts of 'assassinations of persons accused by the guerrillas as being informers of the security forces'.[116]

Islamic State operated a sophisticated intelligence operation in both Syria and Iraq which relied heavily on informers and the public and brutal punishment of those suspected of betrayal. A cache of Islamic State documents obtained in Aleppo revealed:

> a highly complex system involving the infiltration and surveillance of all groups, including IS' own people. The jihad archivists maintained long lists noting which informants they had installed in which rebel brigades and government militias. It was even noted who among the rebels was a spy for Assad's intelligence service.[117]

Islamic State had placed a considerable emphasis on human intelligence in its planned takeover of Syria and sought to create an 'Islamic Intelligence State'.[118] Within Syrian villages, individuals were to be 'selected and instructed to spy on their village and obtain a wide range of information', including names, details, political orientation, and potential illegal activities of members of powerful families and rebel groups. The organisation's goal was to have 'everyone keeping an eye on everyone else', and to obtain information that could serve to 'divide and subjugate the local population'.[119] Those recruited as informers by Islamic State included former Syrian intelligence spies and individuals who had opposed the Syrian government but had fallen out of favour with rebel groups.[120]

Islamic State's approach to intelligence gathering is considered to have been influenced by the 2004 document, *The Management of Savagery*, attributed to an Al Qaeda strategist Abu Bakr Naji.[121] The document recognised the likely presence of collaborators, and set out guidance on how to deal with 'the problem of infiltration and spies':

115 'A Collection of Codes of Conduct Issued by Armed Groups', (2011) 93 No. 882 International Review of the Red Cross 483, 493.

116 'Joint report of the Special Rapporteur on the question of torture, Mr. Nigel S. Rodley, and the Special Rapporteur on extrajudicial, summary or arbitrary executions, Mr. Bacre Waly Ndiaye', Commission on Human Rights. 51st session, UN Doc. E/CN.4/1995/111, 4 August 1994, para 57. See also Human Rights Watch, ' "You'll Learn not to Cry": Child Combatants in Colombia', September 2003, 7–11.

117 Christoph Reuter, 'The Terror Strategist: Secret Files Reveal the Structure of Islamic State', *Der Spiegel*, 18 April 2015.

118 Ibid. 119 Ibid. 120 Ibid.

121 See Abu Bakr Naji, *The Management of Savagery: The Most Critical Stage Through Which the Umma Will Pass*, translated by William McCants, 23 May 2006 <https://archive.org/stream/TheManagementOfBarbarismAbuBakrNaji/The+Management+of+Barbarism+-+Abu+Bakr+Naji_djvu.txt> accessed 3 June 2019.

> the people will be good eyes and armor for us and protect us from spies, to say nothing of what we mentioned previously regarding the mastery of surveillance and infiltrating the enemies, a fact which makes it possible for us to discover spies and watch each one of them, especially if our informants infiltrate the security institutions of the enemy.[122]

A strong emphasis was placed on the importance of deterrence when punishing informers, in order that 'the weak souls hesitate in doing likewise'.[123] Especially harsh measures were envisaged for informers and low-ranking 'stool pigeons':

> Working to destroy them completely cripples the movement of the officers of the enemy. Working to destroy them with the utmost coarseness and ugliness even deters those who merely contemplate undertaking something like that. Media coverage is also important for spreading the cause and justifying it to the people.[124]

Islamic State developed an advanced legal system, with courts issuing punishment for offences such as espionage, treason, and collaborating with foreign interests.[125] The presence of informers within Islamic State gave rise to 'paranoia and violent retribution', including extrajudicial killings and beheadings of alleged UK MI6 agents.[126] Such deliberate brutality was not arbitrary but part of a concerted and at times common strategy by non-state parties to an armed conflict aimed at deterring would-be informers.

1.2 Combatants and Detainees

Those engaging in hostilities during an armed conflict, including members of a state's armed forces or fighters belonging to an armed opposition group, are most susceptible to being coerced or persuaded to serve the opposing side when they have been captured and are detained. Throughout the history of war, prisoners of war and other detainees have collaborated with the enemy in various ways, including by joining its ranks and fighting alongside its forces, or by divulging valuable information while held in detention. These are the two principal forms of cooperation with an adversary by combatants and detainees that are considered in this section, although a few others will also be mentioned. A number of historical and contemporary examples of such practices will be elaborated, notably the frequent defection and collaboration by members of armed forces during the Second World War, as well as the activities of a number of US prisoners of war during the Korean war. The legal questions concerning the status of individuals participating in armed hostilities, including their eligibility to be treated as prisoners of war, are addressed in Chapter 3.

During armed conflict, it is not unknown for soldiers or fighters to switch sides and to fight alongside those previously regarded as their enemy, and thus run the risk of being labelled as traitors or collaborators. After an attempted siege of

[122] Ibid 152. [123] Ibid 153. [124] Ibid 154.
[125] Andrew F. March and Mara Revkin, 'Caliphate of Law', *Foreign Affairs*, 15 April 2015.
[126] Sengupta, 'Inside Isis' (n 106).

Medina in 627 by the Meccans, several hundred Jewish soldiers who had fought for Mohammad were 'charged with collaboration with the enemy [...] and beheaded one by one'.[127] During the Thirty Years' War, the execution of defectors was a 'customary practice' on the continent in Europe.[128] The English civil wars saw switching of sides by many soldiers, a practice 'which attracted widespread condemnation, and yet was encouraged and connived at'.[129] Turkey claimed during the First World War that Armenians were siding with Russia as many 'served in the Russian forces either as subjects of the czar or as irregulars from the Ottoman Empire'.[130] While the concept of betrayal might be deployed misleadingly to justify the targeting of certain groups, there is little doubt that shifting alliances and individual circumstances may lead soldiers or even civilians to take up arms on the side of an adversary.

The Second World War provides many examples of soldiers from all sides switching and fighting for the opposing side, with thousands of non-Germans having served in the German armed forces.[131] Around 1 million members of the Soviet army are estimated to have defected to Germany's forces during the Second World War.[132] It has been claimed that around 10 per cent of the Russian population supported the German occupying forces, that 'about 700,000 former Soviet servicemen became "hiwis" (noncombatant volunteers) and 1.4 million participated in the Nazi-controlled military units'.[133] By mid-1944, 'the Wehrmacht had 200 battalions of troops formed of Russians, Ukrainians, Belorussians and other nationalities'.[134] Russian prisoners of war recruited by Germany conducted intelligence operations behind Russian lines and participated in the murder of Jews in Poland.[135]

Numerous Austrian army officers collaborated with the German armed forces by serving as generals, fighting partisans, and staffing Nazi concentration and death camps.[136] Towards the end of the War, there were thousands of Scandinavian, Belgian, and French volunteers in the Waffen SS fighting to defend Berlin.[137] A small group known as the British Free Corps sought to fight on the side of Germany; John Amery, who had proposed the idea, was executed for high treason by the British authorities after the War.[138] Several thousand Indian soldiers who had fought as

[127] Alexander Gillespie, *A History of the Laws of War: Vol 1: The Customs and Laws of War with Regards to Combatants and Captives* (Hart 2011) 128.

[128] Andrew Hopper, *Turncoats and Renegades: Changing Sides during the English Civil Wars* (OUP 2012) 179.

[129] Ibid 2. [130] Deák, *Europe on Trial* (n 8) 23.

[131] Ebrahim Afsah, 'Deserters' in Frauke Lachenmann and Rüdiger Wolfrum (eds), *The Law of Conflict and the Use of Force: The Max Planck Encylopaedia of Public International Law Thematic Series Vol 2* (OUP 2017) 331, 331.

[132] Mark R. Elliott, 'Soviet Military Collaborators during World War II' in Yury Boshyk, *Ukraine during World War II: History and its Aftermath* (Canadian Institute of Ukrainian Studies 1986) 89, 98. See also Deák, *Europe on Trial* (n 8) 2; Mark Edele, *Stalin's Defectors: How Red Army Soldiers became Hitler's Collaborators, 1941–1945* (OUP 2017).

[133] Birstein, *SMERSH, Stalin's Secret Weapon* (n 32) 173. [134] Ibid.

[135] Ibid 168–9; Peter Black, 'Foot Soldiers of the Final Solution: The Trawniki Training Camp and Operation Reinhard' (2011) 25(1) Holocaust and Genocide Studies 1; Lawrence Douglas, *The Right Wrong Man: John Demjanjuk and the Last Great Nazi War Crimes Trial* (Princeton University Press 2016).

[136] Deák, *Europe on Trial* (n 8) 29. [137] Ibid 6.

[138] See Adrian Weale, *Renegades. Hitler's Englishmen* (Weidenfeld & Nicolson 1994) 54–69, 124–43; Robert Loeffel, 'Treasonous Conduct: Assessing the Wartime Activities, Post-War Trials and

colonial subjects alongside the British forces switched allegiance and joined opposing forces on the Axis side in order to fight for independence from Britain following Japan's occupation of Singapore in 1942.[139] While a number of Germans soldiers and civilians resisted the Nazi regime in various ways, there are only a few examples of Axis troops defecting and fighting with the Allies during the Second World War.[140]

In more recent conflicts, examples can also be found of individuals or groups changing their allegiance and fighting alongside parties once considered their enemy. During the war in Iraq, for example, a militia known as the 'Sons of Iraq' switched from waging an insurgency against the United States and other coalition forces to working alongside them and the Iraqi government.[141] Although tasked with carrying out 'defensive missions' only, such as manning checkpoints and gathering intelligence on insurgents, the recruits engaged in fighting against Al Qaeda and, at times, the 'ruthless slaughter' of its suspected members.[142] The 'Sons of Iraq' received salaries and financial rewards from the United States and political recognition from the Iraqi government.[143] In Afghanistan, US soldiers detained a US citizen, John Walker Lindh, who had been fighting with the Taliban, before being captured by the Northern Alliance, a US ally.[144] He had joined the Afghan army prior to 11 September 2001 and the ensuing US-led offensive in Afghanistan. He did so, according to his father, because of his 'youthful idealism':

> [H]e felt it was his religious duty to help defend civilians against Russian-backed warlords, the so-called Northern Alliance, which was seeking to displace the Taliban government. He was deeply moved by stories of horrific human rights abuses by the Northern Alliance.[145]

Labelled a traitor by public figures in the United States, even though he hadn't engaged in any fighting against US forces, he was given a twenty-year prison sentence for two charges, having supplied services to the Taliban and carrying an explosive.[146] Several other US citizens have also been killed or detained by the United States for

Tribulations of Australian Collaborators in the Second World War' (2009) 55(1) Australian Journal of Politics and History 17.

139 See W.L. Cheah, 'Dealing with Desertion and Gaps in International Humanitarian Law: Changes of Allegiance in the Singapore War Crimes Trials' (2018) 8(2) Asian Journal of International Law 350, 350–6.

140 See Randall Hansen, *Disobeying Hitler: German Resistance in the Last Year of WWII* (Faber and Faber 2014); Stephen Harding, *The Last Battle* (Da Capo Press 2014).

141 Mark Wilkbanks and Efraim Karsh, 'How the "Sons of Iraq" Stabilized Iraq' (2010) 17(4) Middle East Quarterly 57, 57. See also Govinda Clayton and Andrew Thomson, 'The Enemy of My Enemy is My Friend ... The Dynamics of Self-Defence Forces in Irregular War: The Case of the Sons of Iraq' (2014) 37(11) Studies in Conflict and Terrorism 920.

142 Wilkbanks and Karsh, 'How the "Sons of Iraq" Stabilized Iraq' (n 141) 61–2.

143 Ibid 66–9.

144 See Jane Mayer, 'Lost in the Jihad', *New Yorker*, 10 March 2003.

145 Frank Lindh, 'How John Walker Lindh Became "Detainee 001"', *The Nation*, 29 August 2014.

146 Paul Theroux, 'Pardon the American Taliban', *New York Times*, 22 October 2016, SR5. With regard to the similar case of Australian national David Hicks, see Leigh Sales, *Detainee 002: The Case of David Hicks* (Melbourne University Press 2007); David Hicks, *Guantanamo: My Story* (Random House Australia 2010).

their alleged involvement with its enemies, including Yaser Esam Hamdi and Anwar al-Awlaki.[147]

Such individuals might be referred to as 'foreign fighters' in some cases.[148] While their actions might not always amount to collaboration with an opposing side during an armed conflict, the phenomenon certainly gives rise to commensurate practices and responses and is similarly not addressed squarely by international humanitarian law. The UN Security Council has expressed its grave concern

> over the acute and growing threat posed by foreign terrorist fighters, namely individuals who travel to a State other than their States of residence or nationality for the purpose of the perpetration, planning, or preparation of, or participation in, terrorist acts or the providing or receiving of terrorist training, including in connection with armed conflict.[149]

Such fighters might 'increase the intensity, duration and intractability of conflicts' and could pose 'a serious threat to their States of origin, the States they transit and the States to which they travel, as well as States neighbouring zones of armed conflict'. The activities of Islamic State, the Al-Nusrah Front, and Al Qaeda were specifically mentioned in Resolution 2178, which called upon Member States to cooperate to address this threat by preventing recruitment and financial support, and to deal with returning fights by way of prosecution, rehabilitation, and reintegration consistent with their existing obligations under international law.[150] Political figures in the United Kingdom have suggested that British citizens who travel and fight with Islamic State should be denied re-entry to the United Kingdom or else tried for treason; according to one Member of Parliament, '[t]heir actions are treachery against Her Majesty, and aiding and abetting enemies of Her Majesty is one of the greatest offences a British citizen can commit'.[151] A number of states have prosecuted a relatively low number of so-called foreign fighters when they have returned to their state of origin.[152]

Members of armed forces or other fighters that choose to join the opposition have done so for various reasons, including a shared ideology, for financial remuneration, or for revenge.[153] For prisoners of war during the Second World War,

[147] See *Hamdi v Rumsfeld*, 542 US 507 (2004); Jeremy Scahill, *Dirty Wars: The World is a Battlefield* (Nation Books 2013).

[148] See for example David Malet, 'Why Foreign Fighters?: Historical Perspectives and Solutions' (2010) 54(1) Orbis 97; Thomas Hegghammer, 'The Rise of Muslim Foreign Fighters: Islam and the Globalisation of Jihad' (2011) 35(3) International Security 53; Andrea de Guttry, Francesca Capone, and Christophe Paulussson, *Foreign Fighters under International Law and Beyond* (TMC Asser Press 2016).

[149] UN Security Council Resolution 2178, 14 September 2014, S/RES/2178 (2014). See also UN Security Council Resolution 2396, 21 December 2017, S/RES/2396 (2017).

[150] UN Security Council Resolution 2178, para 4.

[151] 'Britons Fighting in Iraq and Syria May Face Treason Charges if They Return', *The Guardian*, 17 October 2014.

[152] See Bibi van Ginkel, *Prosecuting Foreign Terrorist Fighters: What Role for the Military?* (International Centre for Counter-Terrorism 2016) 9. See also United Nations Counter-Terrorism Implementation Task Force, *Guidance to States on Human Rights-compliant Responses to the Threat Posed by Foreign Fighters* (United Nations 2018).

[153] See Stathis N. Kalyvas, *The Logic of Violence in Civil War* (CUP 2006) 95–105, 343–51; Ben Oppenheim, Abbey Steele, Juan F. Vargas, and Michael Weintraub, 'True Believers, Deserters, and Traitors: Who Leaves Insurgent Groups and Why' (2015) 59(5) Journal of Conflict Resolution 794.

the motivations for fighting with the enemy often more a question of survival than ideology:

Without question, the collaborator phenomenon included those who were anti-Semitic and who treated Jews and others condemned to death by the Germans despicably. Some did not share their captors' racial perversions, preferred life to death in POW camps, and fought against Stalin rather than Hitler. Simply put, a Soviet soldier in German ranks did not necessarily constitute a Soviet soldier sympathetic to the German cause. [...] so many, caught between the likes of Hitler and Stalin, had scarcely a prayer or a choice.[154]

The majority of Soviet prisoners of war who joined the German forces did so in order to avoid starvation or typhus in the camps, and 'often tried to avoid fighting against fellow Russians and changed back to the Soviet side when it became clear that Germany was losing the war'.[155]

A number of high-ranking Soviet officers willingly volunteered their services to Germany. General Kaminsky, described as 'perhaps the Germans' doughtiest collaborator', voluntarily organised forces to fight against Russian partisans.[156] General Andrei Vlasov chose to collaborate with the Germans because of his opposition to Stalin.[157] Together with other senior officers, Vlasov proposed raising a 'Russian Army of Liberation' to join the Wehrmacht and fight against Stalin, with recruits to be drawn from the prisoner of war population and the inhabitants of occupied territories. Vlasov sought conditions on such collaboration: 'that Russia should not be colonized or enslaved by the Third Reich, and that this should be guaranteed and laid down at the highest level. There must be no recurrence of the "grave abuses" committed by the occupying power'.[158] Germany allowed Vlasov to organise these forces, but they engaged in limited military activities, and eventually surrendered to the United States. Vlasov and other officers were transferred to the Soviets, condemned to death, and hanged in 1946.[159]

Parties to an armed conflict might understandably display some hesitancy towards the voluntary or coerced recruitment of combatants from the opposing side to join their forces, given the mistrust and animosity that frequently exists between opposing sides. Far less caution attaches to using such persons as sources of information when they are detained after capture or surrender. For the 'intentions of an enemy', as Machiavelli wrote, might be 'discovered by the examination of the prisoners you take'.[160] Thus '[e]very army in the world, upon capturing an enemy soldier, attempts to glean military data'.[161] Revealing information when captured, however, usually constitutes an offence under the detainees' national military law. The severest sentence, that of capital punishment, was provided for in the Lieber

[154] Elliott, 'Soviet Military Collaborators during World War II' (n 132) 99. See also Birstein, *SMERSH, Stalin's Secret Weapon* (n 32) 173.

[155] Deák, *Europe on Trial* (n 8) 72–3.

[156] Rings, *Life with the Enemy* (n 34) 104.

[157] Ibid 125. See also Mark Elliott, 'Andrei Vlasov: Red Army General in Hitler's Service' (1982) 46(2) Military Affairs 84.

[158] Ibid.

[159] Ibid 125–7. See also Deák, *Europe on Trial* (n 8) 72.

[160] Machiavelli, *The Art of War* (n 23) 171.

[161] Raymond Lech, *Broken Soldiers* (University of Illinois Press 2000) 103. On the nature of that intelligence see Bennett, *Behind the Battle* (n 10) xix.

Code: 'If a citizen of the United States obtains information in a legitimate manner, and betrays it to the enemy, be he a military or civil officer, or a private citizen, he shall suffer death.'[162] Parties to an armed conflict will, on the one hand, punish those from within their ranks who divulge information of value to the opposing side when captured, while on the other hand, they will actively encourage or even coerce enemy personnel to share information regarding the enemy.

Historical examples attest to the value attached to prisoner intelligence during armed conflict. During the Irish War of Independence, for example, the British authorities considered that the best information was that given by deserters from the IRA and 'prisoners under interrogation'.[163] Information was obtained from prisoners by various means:

> Some prisoners gave information to escape punishment; others gave information unwittingly to skilled interrogators; torture, though officially deemed counter-productive, was used in many cases. Prisoners also yielded intelligence through 'Moutons' or stool pigeons placed in cells; through censorship of the secret mail that the IRA operated from the internment camps; and through listening sets placed in cells.[164]

In Northern Ireland more recently, the recruitment and gathering of information from members of paramilitary organisations was facilitated by extended detention powers and the employment of a various coercive means.[165] According to a former British army officer, questioning a member of a paramilitary group was successful where it led both to the acquisition of information directly, as well as the defection of the individual as an informer who is then capable of providing future intelligence.[166]

During the Second World War, all participating armies sought to gather intelligence from the millions of prisoners of war that were detained throughout the years of the conflict. The 1929 Prisoner of War Convention had set out that a prisoner of war being interrogated was only required to declare 'his true names and rank, or his regimental number', while also forbidding the exertion of pressure to obtain information.[167] These rules were not always observed:

> certain categories of prisoners were placed in special camps, known as 'interrogation camps' before being sent to a normal prisoner-of-war camp. In order to try to secure information, great hardship was inflicted on them. Such camps were outside the control of the protecting powers and the delegates of the International Committee of the Red Cross, which in most cases had no knowledge of their existence. [168]

[162] Instructions for the Government of Armies of the United States in the Field, Prepared by Francis Lieber, promulgated as General Orders No. 100 by President Lincoln, 24 April 1863, art 89 *reprinted in* Dietrich Schindler and Jiří Toman (eds), *The Laws of Armed Conflict: A Collection of Conventions, Resolutions and Other Documents* (Martinus Nijhoff 1988) 3.

[163] McMahon, *British Spies and Irish Rebels* (n 58) 46.

[164] Ibid (footnote omitted).

[165] Fionnuala Ní Aoláin, *The Politics of Force: Conflict Management and State Violence in Northern Ireland* (Blackstaff 2000) 48, 58; Bowyer Bell, *The Secret Army* (n 62) 485.

[166] Robin Evelagh, *Peace Keeping in a Democratic Society: The Lessons of Northern Ireland* (McGill-Queen's University Press 1978) 133.

[167] Convention relative to the Treatment of Prisoners of War, Geneva, 27 July 1929, art 5.

[168] Jean Pictet (ed), *Commentary: III Geneva Convention, Relative to the Treatment of Prisoners of War* (ICRC 1960) 163.

While coercion was used, including torture by local German-recruited collaborators, prisoners of war often divulged information unknowingly because of the 'shock of capture' or during seemingly innocuous conversations with intelligence officers.[169]

Detaining powers also offered inducements to captured soldiers. Some German officers received 'lavish hospitality' from the Soviets in exchange for information.[170] German military intelligence also treated certain senior Russian officers especially well, providing single rooms and full Wehrmacht rations in one particular camp, where the most valuable prisoners stayed and provided 'instant responses' to the information requests of their hosts.[171] A greater willingness on the part of Russian prisoners of war to provide information to their captors was evident when their own country was faring poorly in the War, but '[w]hen the tide of war turned, cooperation declined, because prisoners who aided the Nazis feared their fate—with good reason—if Stalin prevailed'.[172] The Kremlin had considered all captured Red army soldiers as traitors 'simply for having been taken alive',[173] while on the German side, there was a belief amongst captured U-boat crewmen that 'those who divulge information will be punished after the war'.[174] With prisoners of war considered as a valuable source of information, as well as potential propaganda tools, detaining powers frequently disregarded the rules applicable to the treatment of prisoners.

Following the Korean War, a number of US prisoners of war who had been held in North Korean war camps were tried for having collaborated in various ways with their captors.[175] A number of prisoners divulged information, professed support for communism, and denounced the United States, albeit in a context of violence, starvation, torture, death marches, solitary confinement, and appalling camp conditions.[176] Raymond Lech considers that the fear of death explains why the 'majority of the captive Americans did practically everything their North Korean and Chinese captors told them to do'.[177] According to former prisoner of war Captain Robert Wise:

> the Chinese had unquestionably set out to starve us into submission, to force us to come to their terms or to believe in their ways and to accept the ideology. Death had become a commonplace thing rather than something unusual and having an officer due in our room, almost daily, certainly had some effect on a man's reasoning power.[178]

The possibility of certain privileges regarding accommodation, medical care, work assignments, food, money, and early release also contributed to the decision of some

[169] Hastings, *The Secret War* (n 27) 50–1, 270.

[170] Ibid 215. See also Birstein, *SMERSH, Stalin's Secret Weapon* (n 32) 188.

[171] Ibid 225. [172] Ibid.

[173] Elliott, 'Soviet Military Collaborators during World War II' (n 132) 91–2.

[174] Hastings, *The Secret War* (n 27) 215.

[175] See generally Lech, *Broken Soldiers* (n 124); Charles S. Young, *Name, Rank, and Serial Number: Exploiting Korean War POWs at Home and Abroad* (OUP 2014); Elizabeth Lutes Hillman, 'Disloyalty among Men in Arms: Korean War POWs at Court-Martial' (2004) 82(5) North Carolina Law Review 1629.

[176] Lutes Hillman, 'Disloyalty among Men' (n 175) 1639; Lech, *Broken Soldiers* (n 124) 15–17, 23–5, 57–61, 68–80, 121, 170–7.

[177] Lech, *Broken Soldiers* (n 124) 4. [178] Ibid 103.

prisoners to serve the enemy.[179] Some prisoners also cooperated for ideological reason—over twenty prisoners chose to live in China after the war—while others resisted and refused to collaborate.[180]

Chinese camp officials used informers from amongst the prisoner of war population to gather information and to monitor and control the prisoners. For the US prisoners of war, the presence of informers sowed fear and distrust and was 'the chief weapon of the Communists in dividing the prisoners'.[181] United States prisoners of war also undertook 'political indoctrination' at dedicated camps and engaged in propaganda for their captors, through writings, speeches, and hundreds of radio broadcasts.[182] Some were encouraged by their captors to act as secret agents when they returned to the United States, where many were treated with suspicion and accused of cowardice.[183] Several returning prisoners were court-martialled and convicted for having aided the enemy, with the claim of duress having only limited success on account of the defence's requirement of immediate harm.[184] The proceedings were also criticised for their selectivity, given the limited number of prosecutions despite claims of widespread cooperation with the enemy during both the Korean and Vietnam wars.[185]

Detaining powers have often ignored the rule that captured personnel are required to provide only minimal information, while detainees are often placed in the invidious position by the corresponding national duty not to reveal anything more than name, rank, and serial number when questioned.[186] Non-state armed groups have also instructed their members to avoid revealing any information if captured at the risk of serious consequences. The IRA's Green Book warned members to 'say nothing' under interrogation, even when faced with interrogators seeking to 'bleed you of all the information you may have'.[187] The 2006 Taliban Code of Conduct carried a warning that any *mujahedin* that 'becomes a traitor' in this way would forfeit protection of the Taliban.[188] *The Management*

179 Ibid 84; Young, *Name, Rank, and Serial Number* (n 175) 56.

180 Young, *Name, Rank, and Serial Number* (n 175) 56–7; Raymond Lech, *Broken Soldiers* (n 124) 95–96, 128, 150.

181 Young, *Name, Rank, and Serial Number* (n 175) 27, citing Larry Zellers, *In Enemy Hands: A Prisoner in North Korea* (University Press of Kentucky 1999) 160–2.

182 Lech, *Broken Soldiers* (n 124) 81, 122–3, 140–1, 159.

183 Ibid 186–9; Young, *Name, Rank, and Serial Number* (n 175) 116.

184 See 'Misconduct in the Prison Camp: A Survey of the Law and Analysis of the Korean Cases', 56(5) Columbia Law Review (1956) 709, 769–70; *United States v Fleming*, 7 USCMA 543, 23 CMR 7, 57–8. On the defence of duress raised by prisoners of war following the Second World War see *R. v Purdy* (1946) 10 Journal of Criminal Law 182; 'Coercion: A Defense to Misconduct while a Prisoner of War' (1954) 29(4) Indiana Law Journal 603.

185 Lutes Hillman, 'Disloyalty among Men' (n 175) 1632; Young, *Name, Rank, and Serial Number* (n 175) 3.

186 Lech, *Broken Soldiers* (n 124) 105.

187 IRA, *The Green Book*, Vol. II, n.d., Section I(1) <http://cain.ulst.ac.uk/othelem/organ/ira/ira_green_book.htm> accessed 21 May 2019.

188 Article 4, *The Islamic Emirate of Afghanistan: A Jihadi Code of Conduct*, 2006, *reprinted in* Kate Clark, *The Layha: Calling the Taleban to Account*, Afghanistan Analysts Network, July 2011, <http://theirwords.org/media/transfer/doc/ut_af_taliban_2010_2009_2006_03-d8952e65095cf27bd9c8dbc5a328f8eb.pdf> accessed 21 May 2019.

of Savagery goes further regarding the divulging of information, stating that 'a mujahid should not submit to capture in the first place', that he should fight to the death and disregard the notion of acting as a double agent or giving misinformation under interrogation.[189]

The considerable emphasis on gathering information from prisoners of war and detained fighters remains evident in modern conflicts, as does the tendency towards mistreatment for such purposes. Information, and other forms of cooperation, are gained by persuasion, coercion, or a mixture of both. The 2015 US *Law of War Manual* states that 'a combination of threats of criminal punishment and inducements (e.g. amnesty, monetary rewards) may be used to seek to gain the cooperation of captured enemy persons'.[190] The limited number of covert human intelligence sources within certain after 11 September 2001 and during the early phases of the war in Iraq 'left the questioning of prisoners as one of the only viable means of intelligence-gathering'.[191] Both inducements and unlawful coercive measures were used to secure information.[192]

1.3 Bureaucratic Collaboration

Bureaucratic collaboration occurs where a national or local authority or individual officials provide governmental or other administrative cooperation to an invading force or an occupying power.[193] In contrast to informing and the activities of combatants and detainees described earlier, this form of cooperation with an adversary tends to be removed from actual hostilities, yet offers assistance that can be valuable to the opposing power. That government departments or public officials, including civil servants, the judiciary, and the police, might continue in their functions while under the authority of an opposing party to an armed conflict invariably leads to accusations of collaboration. The laws of occupation might be said to provide justifiable grounds for both providing and demanding such cooperation, requiring as they do that an occupying power 'take all the measures in his power to restore, and ensure, as far as possible, public order and safety, while respecting, unless absolutely prevented, the laws in force in the country'.[194]

[189] Abu Bakr Naji, *The Management of Savagery* (n 121) 156.

[190] United States, *Law of War Manual* (Department of Defense, Office of General Counsel 2015) 1040. See generally William H. Boothby and Wolff Heintschel von Heinegg, *The Law of War: A Detailed Assessment of the US Department of Defense Law of War Manual* (CUP 2018); Michael A. Newton, *The United States Department of Defense: Commentary and Critique* (CUP 2019).

[191] Urban, *Task Force Black* (n 67) 36.

[192] Ibid 54–5; Spencer Ackerman, 'Guantánamo Detainee who Wrote Book About his Torture to be Released', *The Guardian*, 20 July 2015.

[193] The phrase 'bureaucratic collaboration' has been used in historical accounts of the Second World War. See for example Jürgen Matthäus, 'What About the "Ordinary Men"?: The German Order Police and the Holocaust in the Occupied Soviet Union' (1996) 10(2) Holocaust and Genocide Studies 134, 150; Megan Koreman, 'The Red Tape Option: Bureaucratic Collaboration and Resistance in Vichy France' (2000) 9(2) Contemporary European History 261.

[194] Hague Regulations 1907, art 43.

Public officials that cooperate with the enemy, especially those at the higher levels of government, have been labelled as collaborators and have suffered harsh consequences for their actions. Bureaucratic collaboration is less common in contemporary armed conflicts and was exemplified by the activities of several European powers and prominent individuals that put themselves in the service of Germany during the Second World War.

In the face of military defeat, European governments, presidents, and monarchs faced two alternatives, according to Werner Rings, 'remain at their posts, or quit and resume the fight against Hitler elsewhere'.[195] While most chose exile in London, others remained and sought assurances from Germany.[196] Henrik Dethlefsen considers that once these politicians had foregone the option of exile, '*collaboration d'état* with all its dangers was not a choice they made: it was an absolute necessity'.[197] Some, such as Philippe Pétain who headed the Vichy regime, and Vidkun Quisling, the Norwegian Nazi collaborator, were more willing to cooperate than others, and acted as 'puppets' for Nazi Germany in occupied territories.[198] This section offers an overview of key examples of bureaucratic collaboration that occurred during the Second World War, as well as a contemporary example.

The phenomenon of bureaucratic collaboration occurred but was not especially prominent during the First World War, in large part because of the limited seizure of territory and the relatively fixed nature of the European front lines during the war.[199] Bureaucratic collaboration was far more common during the Second World War, given the extent of the occupation of enemy territory by the belligerents. The motivations underpinning such cooperation were varied and complex; Stanley Hoffman has described the subject of French collaboration during the War as 'infernally complicated', given that there were 'as many collaborationisms as there were proponents or practitioners of collaboration'.[200] Millions of Europeans adopted an attitude of collaboration with Germany during the War when 'condemned to live with the enemy',[201] although those that engaged in 'active collaboration' comprised only a 'very small percentage of any nation'.[202] In Germany itself at the end of the War, the population generally cooperated peacefully with the Allies during the occupation: 'the Germans proved to be ideal collaborators: submissive, peaceful, hardworking, and well educated'.[203]

195 Rings, *Life with the Enemy* (n 34) 46. 196 Ibid.

197 Henrik Dethlefsen, 'Denmark and the German Occupation: Cooperation, Negotiation or Collaboration?' (1990) 15(1–2) Scandinavian Journal of History 193, 204.

198 Raphaël Lemkin, *Axis Rule in Occupied Europe* (Carnegie Endowment for International Peace 1944) 11.

199 Deák, *Europe on Trial* (n 8) 22.

200 Hoffmann, 'Collaborationism in France during World War II' (n 9) 375.

201 Rings, *Life with the Enemy* (n 34) 278.

202 David Littlejohn, *Patriotic Traitors: A History of Collaboration in German-Occupied Europe, 1940–1945* (Heineman 1972) 336.

203 Déak, *Europe on Trial* (n 8) 183.

Werner Rings offers a typology of collaboration in Europe under Hitler, and explains the motivations and rationales of those that choose to serve the enemy, particularly in the context of bureaucratic collaboration:

Neutral Collaboration or I Conform

The neutral collaborators say: I accept that life must go on. Knowingly and from self-interest, I directly or indirectly work for the occupying power without professing the political and ideological principles of National Socialism. My attitude is dictated by circumstances beyond my control. The sole alternative appears to be bankruptcy, unemployment, starvation, chaos, and destruction. I am determined to survive the war and my country's defeat as best I can.[204]

Unconditional Collaboration or Our Enemy is My Friend

The unconditional collaborator says: I join forces with the occupying power because I endorse its principles and ideal. My attitude is dictated, not by circumstances, but by allegiance to National Socialism. I am prepared to do anything and make any sacrifice for the occupying power as long as I can thereby serve our common cause.[205]

Conditional Collaboration or I Collaborate Up to a Point

The conditional collaborator says: I cooperate with the occupying power although I endorse only some, not all, of the National Socialist doctrines. Subject to that proviso, I am ready and eager to collaborate faithfully because I wish to change the circumstances that dictate my attitude.[206]

Tactical Collaboration or I Do but I Don't

The tactical collaborator says: I agree to collaborate despite my hostility to National Socialism and the Third Reich. I may do so for a variety of reasons: to throw off the foreign yoke and regain my freedom; to prevent the mass murder of innocent people whenever possible; or to consummate a political idea whose fulfilment is obstructed by National Socialism. In every case, collaboration disguises resistance and is part of the fight.[207]

This is a useful encapsulation of the principal reasons underlying the phenomenon of collaboration during the War, notwithstanding some generalisation.[208]

Beginning with the example of bureaucratic collaboration in France during the Second World War, Max Hastings writes that between 1940 and 1944 'many Frenchmen, including hundreds of thousands of servants of the Vichy puppet regime, collaborated with their occupiers'.[209] Following the French surrender and

[204] Rings, *Life with the Enemy* (n 34) 73. [205] Ibid 86. [206] Ibid 106.
[207] Ibid 128.
[208] Ibid 148–9. See also Hoffmann, 'Collaborationism in France during World War II' (n 9) 375.
[209] Hastings, *The Secret War* (n 27) 56. See also Bertram M. Gordon, *Collaborationism in France during the Second World War* (Cornell University Press 1980). For details of other examples see Dethlefsen, 'Denmark and the German Occupation' (n 242); Littlejohn, *Patriotic Traitors* (n 202) 54–82; Timothy Brook, *Collaboration: Japanese Agents and Local Elites in Wartime China* (Harvard University Press 2005).

the armistice agreement between Germany and France in June 1940, Germany remained as the occupying power in the northern half of the country, while the *Zone Libre* in the south was under the authority of the French government at Vichy. The head of the Vichy government, Philippe Pétain, publicly declared the decision to collaborate with Germany.[210] Cooperation by the public with German forces, or at least toleration of their presence, was said to have been facilitated by their 'initial exemplary behaviour' in France, in stark contrast to their conduct in Eastern Europe.[211] A number of French military personnel were even killed by fellow soldiers or by French civilians for failing to submit and continuing to fight the advancing German forces.[212] The new French government at Vichy 'went beyond just trying to live with surrender and foreign occupation', by actively collaborating with the Nazis in the denial of property rights and deportations of French Jews, often in advance of German requests.[213] The Vichy regime shared aspects of the ideology of National Socialism, but its collaboration was also motivated by the desire to preserve French interests in the face of a superior military power.[214] After the War, Pétain and other officials were prosecuted and thousands of alleged collaborators were sentenced to death or killed extrajudicially.[215]

Vidkun Quisling, the Norwegian fascist and leader of the Nasjonal Samling political party, can be considered the archetypal wartime collaborator given that he largely shared and supported the ideology of Nazi Germany and its activities in his own country.[216] Before the outbreak of the Second World War, Quisling met with senior German officials, as described in the Nuremberg judgment:

> Quisling had pointed out the importance of the Norwegian coast in the event of a conflict between Germany and Great Britain, and stated his fears that Great Britain might be able to obtain Norwegian assistance. As a result of this conference Rosenberg arranged for Quisling to collaborate closely with the National Socialists and to receive political assistance by the Nazis.[217]

210 Deák, *Europe on Trial* (n 8) 55. 211 Ibid 44.

212 Rings, *Life with the Enemy* (n 34) 59.

213 Deák, *Europe on Trial* (n 8) 52, 56–7. See further Michael R. Marrus and Robert O. Paxman, *Vichy France and the Jews* (Stanford University Press 1981); Donna F. Ryan, *The Holocaust and the Jews of Marseille: The Enforcement of Anti-Semitic Policies in Vichy France* (University of Illinois Press 1996).

214 See Hoffmann, 'Collaborationism in France during World War II' (n 12) 376–8; Rings, *Life with the Enemy* (n 34) 112–13, 124.

215 Ian Kershaw, *To Hell and Back: Europe 1914–1949* (Penguin Books 2016) 473. See Peter Novick, *The Resistance versus Vichy: The Purge of Collaborators in Liberated France* (Columbia University Press 1968); J. Kenneth Brody, *The Trial of Pierre Laval: Defining Treason, Collaboration and Patriotism in World War II France* (Routledge 2010); Nancy Wood, 'Memory on Trial in Contemporary France: The Case of Maurice Papon' (1999) 11(1) History and Memory 41; Leila Sadat Wexler, 'Reflections on the Trial of Vichy Collaborator Paul Touvier for Crimes Against Humanity in France' (1995) 20(1) Law and Social Inquiry 191.

216 International Military Tribunal (Nuremberg), *Judgment and Sentences* (n 3) 204. See generally Dahl, *Quisling: A Study in Treachery* (n 2).

217 Ibid 286. See also Paul M. Hayes, *Quisling: The Career and Political Ideals of Vidkun Quisling 1887–1945* (David and Charles 1971) 130.

He visited Berlin in December 1939 to propose his plan for a *coup d'état* in Norway, met with Hitler to discuss Germany's views towards Norway and received a promise of financial support.[218] The German invasion of Norway in April 1940 allowed Quisling to exploit the 'political vacuum' left when the Norwegian government and members of the Royal family fled Oslo.[219] He called for a cessation of resistance and declared a new national government, appointing himself as Prime Minister and Minister for Foreign Affairs.[220] He considered himself to be acting in the interests of Norway, that in the circumstances, 'it is the duty of the Nasjonal Samling to take over the business of government in order to defend the vital interests of the Norwegian people and preserve Norway's independence'.[221]

Quisling's attempted peaceful handover with the Norwegian resistance in May 1945 did not prevent his arrest, trial, and execution.[222] His trial was one of many thousands of treason trials held in Norway after the Second World War, but only one of a few where the death penalty was imposed. Norway had previously abolished capital punishment in peacetime, but Quisling was among thirty Norwegians convicted of treason and executed.[223] He had appealed to the Supreme Court of Norway, which upheld the verdict and sentence, dismissing his arguments concerning retroactivity.[224] While the application of the sentence was not in conformity with the principle of legality, it was in keeping with a strong public demand for the death penalty; several of the guards responsible for Quisling's safety during his trial had even gone so far as to agree secretly to kill him if the Court did not hand down a sentence of death.[225] Quisling had argued patriotic motivations for aligning with Nazi Germany,[226] but was without doubt a supporter of fascism.[227] After the War, Norwegian psychiatrists conducted research on collaborators in an attempt to determine the root causes of 'quislingism'.[228]

Other European powers and public officials collaborated with Germany during the Second World War, and even if not subscribing to Nazi ideology, they

[218] Ibid 204. See also Hayes, *Quisling* (n 217) 165–209.

[219] Hayes, *Quisling* (n 217) 211. See also Sigrid Redse Johansen, 'The Occupied and the Occupier: The Case of Norway' in Kjetil Mujenović Larsen, Camilla Guldahl Cooper, and Gro Nystuen (eds), *Searching for a 'Principle of Humanity' in International Humanitarian Law* (CUP 2013) 206, 207–9; Littlejohn, *Patriotic Traitors* (n 202) 1–52.

[220] Hayes, *Quisling* (n 217) 215–17.

[221] Rings, *Life with the Enemy* (n 34) 89.

[222] Hayes, *Quisling* (n 217) 297.

[223] Deák, *Europe on Trial* (n 8) 204. For an account of his arrest, trial, and execution see Dahl, *Quisling: A Study in Treachery* (n 2) 366–415.

[224] Hayes, *Quisling* (n 217) 302–3. See also Dahl, *Quisling* (n 2) 398–400; *Public Prosecutor v Reidar Haaland*, Norway, Supreme Court (Appellate Division), 9 August 1945, 12 *Annual Digest and Reports of Public International Law Cases* (1943–45) 444

[225] Dahl, *Quisling* (n 2) 393.

[226] Littlejohn, *Patriotic Traitors* (n 202) 2. See also Hayes, *Quisling* (n 217) 160.

[227] Rings, *Life with the Enemy* (n 34) 92.

[228] Øyvand Giæver, 'The Psychiatry of Quislingism: Norwegian Psychiatric Research on the Collaborators of World War II' (2004) 17(3) Science in Context 267.

'rendered invaluable service to the German war effort'.[229] In several Western European countries, the view was taken that the need to maintain public services necessitated some cooperation with the occupying power.[230] In Belgium, for example, officials with responsibility for rail and power stations had received an instruction before the War emphasising their duty to continue in their roles even if the country were to be occupied. With references to the Hague Regulations, and a 1935 law on the wartime duties of civil servants, they were instructed not to put up any resistance in the event of an invasion and to refrain from harming the occupying power, although they could resign if an occupying power 'requested them to do something that conflicted with their duty of national allegiance'.[231] The Belgian Prime Minister has apologised for the deportation of thousands of Jews during the occupation, expressing 'the regret and shame that collaboration brought upon us'.[232]

When occupied by Germany during the War, the Channel Islands were said to have practised 'extreme passivity',[233] having been instructed by the British government in 1940 to engage in 'passive cooperation' with the occupiers.[234] The Attorney General of Guernsey called for compliance with German orders and hoped the occupation would be 'a model to the world'.[235] The Islanders practised passive cooperation 'assiduously' during the five-year occupation, failing to oppose the establishment of a concentration camp, and identifying Jewish families for the Gestapo. British officials also arrested 'real and potential resisters',[236] yet after the war, 'not a single islander was tried or punished for collaboration, war crimes or treason'.[237]

The Netherlands had sought to remain neutral during the Second World War, but when it was attacked and invaded by Germany in May 1940, the Dutch government went into exile, and the remaining authorities engaged in bureaucratic collaboration with the occupying power:

> nonideological collaboration was practiced by the so-called secretaries of state who, in the absence of the royal government, ran the everyday affairs and by the national administration at large, which fulfilled the German's political and economic demands. Among other things, governmental offices collected and kept accurate statistics on the country's Jews.[238]

The German Reich Commissioner, Arthur Seyss-Inquart, was said to have informed Dutch under-secretaries who had assumed the responsibilities of the Ministers in exile that they could resign if they felt 'unable to endorse any measure taken by

[229] Rings, *Life with the Enemy* (n 34) 278. [230] Ibid 73. [231] Ibid.

[232] 'Belgian premier apologises for WWII deportation of 25,000 Jews', 9 September 2012, *TheJournal.ie* <http://www.thejournal.ie/belgian-premier-apologises-for-wwii-deportation-of-25000-jews-589903-Sep2012/> accessed 21 May 2019.

[233] David Clark, 'Channel Islanders Committed "Treason" in Second World War', *The Guardian*, 9 October 1974. See also Madeleine Bunting, *The Model Occupation: The Channel Islands Under German Rule, 1940–1945* (Harper Collins 1995).

[234] Deák, *Europe on Trial* (n 8) 59.

[235] Terence O'Neill, *Hitler's Irishmen* (Mercier Press 2008) 55.

[236] Deák, *Europe on Trial* (n 8) 59. [237] Ibid 61.

[238] Deák, *Europe on Trial* (n 8) 49. See generally Gerhard Hirshfeld, *Nazi Rule and Dutch Collaboration: The Netherlands Under German Occupation, 1940–1945* (OUP 1988).

the occupying power'.[239] The Nuremberg Tribunal found that he had been 'ruthless in applying terrorism to suppress all opposition to the German occupation, a program which he described as "annihilating" his opponents'.[240] The Tribunal noted how Seyss-Inquart had used the Dutch police and the courts to pursue opponents of the occupation, which involved the shooting of hostages and deportation to concentration camps:

> Many of the Dutch police were forced to participate in these programs by threats of reprisal against their families. Dutch courts were also forced to participate in this program, but when they indicated their reluctance to give sentences of imprisonment because so many prisoners were in fact killed, a greater emphasis was placed on the use of summary police courts.[241]

During the German occupation of the Netherlands, the Supreme Court judges remained in office 'ostensibly to prevent the Nazification of the Dutch legal system', although none protested, according to Werner Rings, when Jewish judges and staff were removed from office in 1940.[242]

The use by the German authorities of Jews to administer the genocide of the Jewish population of Europe constituted a particularly macabre form of forced collaboration, albeit not one involving two parties to an armed conflict. Administrative structures used to carry out Nazi policies included the Jewish Councils in occupied territories and ghettoes and the *Kapos* system in concentration and death camps.[243] The Councils represented the Jewish leadership in occupied territories in Europe and served ostensibly as a means for communicating between the occupying power and the Jewish population and providing certain services, although they were also authorised to establish a Jewish police force who 'wore special armbands, participated in raids, and rounded up their co-religionists'.[244] While the decision to send individuals to concentration camps was made by the German authorities, the use of the Jewish Councils served to give an air of legitimacy to these actions: 'Human trust was the bait with which unsuspecting victims were lured to their doom by the German authorities and their well-meaning Jewish collaborators'.[245] Most were forced to carry out these activities under duress, although there was also a sense that they might offer some protection to the Jewish population.[246] According to German Rabbi and survivor Leo Baeck:

> When the question arose whether Jewish orderlies should select Jews for deportation, I took the view that it would be better for them to do it because they would at least treat them more gently and be likely to assist them and make their lot easier than the Gestapo. Effective resistance to the task was beyond our power.[247]

239 Rings, *Life with the Enemy* (n 34) 74.

240 International Military Tribunal, *Judgment and Sentences* (n 3) 319.

241 Ibid 320.

242 Rings, *Life with the Enemy* (n 34) 109.

243 See Lemkin, *Axis Rule in Occupied Europe* (n 198) 75; Isaiah Trunk, *Judenrät: The Jewish Councils in Eastern Europe under Nazi Occupation* (University of Nebraska Press 1972); Raul Hilberg, *The Destruction of the European Jews*, Vol III (Holmes & Meier 1985) 1037–40.

244 Rings, *Life with the Enemy* (n 34) 139.

245 Ibid 139–40.

246 Ibid 140.

247 *Cited in* Rings, *Life with the Enemy* (n 34) 140–1.

Those that served in the Jewish Councils or police were not 'committed collaborators', as many had merely sought to prolong their own lives and those of their families.[248]

In the Nazi concentration and death camps, Jewish *Kapos* were inmates who worked with the camps authorities and often received some minor benefits in return. Mark Drumbl explains their function and activities:

Kapos were inmate functionaries whose day-to-day supervision enabled the camps, even sprawling ones, to run with comparatively few SS overseers. They were key cogs in the Nazi policy of 'prisoner self-administration'. *Kapos* exercised their limited agency at times in empathetic ways, at other times to resist, but also to hurt and savage others under their charge. *Kapos* themselves were hierarchically organised—from a chief *Kapo* down to the barrack commander (*Blockältester*) and even lower, ending with the *Sonderkommando*, those inmates engaged to extract teeth and shear hair—mutilations undertaken for the purposes of supplying the Reich—from the dead after the SS gassings and then to burn the bodies in the crematoria.[249]

He notes that many *Kapos* were compelled to undertake these roles, but that some did so voluntarily, albeit under the extreme conditions in the camps. Jacob Tannenbaum, the chief *Kapo* at the camp at Görlitz, was subjected to denaturalization proceedings in the United States decades after the War, [250] while the Israeli authorities prosecuted several *Kapos* under the 1950 Nazi and Nazi Collaborators (Punishment) Law.[251]

A more contemporary example of bureaucratic collaboration consists of the Movement of Palestinian Leagues, or 'Village Leagues', established by the Israeli military in the occupied West Bank in 1978.[252] These administrative and political entities were headed by Palestinian *mukhtars* and served a range of public functions, including the provision of certain services, the issuance of travel or building permits, and policing.[253] Israel funded their activities with a view to providing 'alternative local leadership' to the Palestine Liberation Organisation, exerting control and influence over the local population, and to claim local support for particular actions and policies.[254] The occupying power also provided military training and light arms

[248] Deák, *Europe on Trial* (n 8) 40.

[249] Mark Drumbl, 'Victims who Victimise' (2016) 4(2) London Review of International Law 217, 219.

[250] Eric Lichtblau, *The Nazis Next Door: How America became a Safe Have for Hitler's Men* (Mariner Books 2014) 195–8; Judy Feigin, *The Office of Special Investigations: Striving for Accountability in the Aftermath of the Holocaust* (United States Department of Justice, 2009) 106–16.

[251] See Orna Ben-Naftali and Yogev Tuval, 'Punishing International Crimes Committed by the Persecuted: The *Kapo* Trials in Israel (1950s–1960s)' (2006) 4 Journal of International Criminal Justice 128; Laura Jockusch and Gabriel N. Finder (eds), *Jewish Honor Courts: Revenge, Retribution, and Reconciliation in Europe and Israel after the Holocaust* (Wayne State University Press 2015).

[252] See Salim Tamari, 'In League with Zion: Israel's Search for a Native Pillar' (1983) 12(4) Journal of Palestine Studies 41; Vincent Bernard, Michael Siegrist, and Anton Camen, 'Interview with Raja Shehadeh' (2012) 94 No. 885 International Review of the Red Cross 13, 17. For a similar example in Turkey, see Metin Gurcan, 'Arming Civilians as a Counterterror Strategy: The Case of the Village Guard System in Turkey' (2015) 8(1) Dynamics of Asymmetric Conflict 1.

[253] Tamari, 'In League with Zion' (n 252) 45–7.

[254] Sayigh, *Armed Struggle and the Search for a State* (n 92) 483–4, 508; Raja Shehadeh, *Occupier's Law: Israel and the West Bank* (Institute for Palestine Studies 1985) 174–82.

to members of the Village Leagues.[255] Raja Shehadeh considers that the members were 'recruited from the lowest ranks of society and from among society's outcasts', acting at times like an army militia which mistreated and terrorised the local population.[256] The Leagues and their members were largely unpopular with the Palestinian population and were described as quislings, including by General Benjamin Ben Eliezer, the Israeli Defence Minister's coordinator for the occupied territories.[257] In March 1982, the Jordanian Prime Minister, Mudar Badaran, announced that his government considered those who supported the Leagues as collaborators with Israel, and membership thereof was declared punishable by 'confiscation of property or death'.[258] The Village Leagues were eventually disbanded and disarmed by Israel after a few years, with members facing the risk of retribution for having collaborated with the occupying power.[259]

1.4 Aiding the Enemy

Assistance to the opposing party during an armed conflict can arise in various other ways distinguishable from those already described. Occupying powers have often sought and secured assistance and the cooperation of 'local ... networks of power and large segments of the population' in various ways.[260] This final section will touch briefly on collaboration of an economic nature, including trading with the enemy and industrial collaboration, as well as other forms of assistance, such as providing interpretation, labour, or participating in propaganda efforts. It is difficult to draw clear lines between the various forms of wartime collaboration at times, as different types of cooperation are often intertwined and might be provided simultaneously, such as a locally recruited interpreter who gathers and shares information for intelligence purposes.

During times of armed conflict, economic dealings with parties to the conflict may be restricted by national law forbidding trading with an opposing side or under a sanctions regime imposed by a state unilaterally or by an international body, such as the UN Security Council. With regard to the former, the United Kingdom passed a series of Trading with the Enemy Acts during the First and Second World Wars which established criminal offences for doing business with the enemy state, an individual residing in enemy territory, or companies incorporated under the law of

[255] Sayigh, *Armed Struggle and the Search for a State* (n 92) 484.

[256] Shehadeh, *Occupier's Law* (n 254) 175–8. See also Tamari, 'In League with Zion' (n 252) 48.

[257] Mark A. Tessler, *A History of the Israeli–Palestinian Conflict* (Indiana University Press 1994) 553; George W. Ball, 'The Unbalanced Triangle: The United States, Israel and Palestine' (1988) 10(4) Arab Studies 375, 379.

[258] Tessler, *A History of the Israeli–Palestinian Conflict* (n 257) 553; Sayigh, *Armed Struggle and the Search for a State* (n 92) 610.

[259] Yigal Carmon, 'The Story of the Palestinian Village Leagues' The Middle East Media Research Institute, Daily Brief No. 103, 13 September 2016; John Kifner, 'Palestinians Turn Ire on Collaborators' *New York Times*, 27 March 1988.

[260] Lynne Taylor, *Between Resistance and Collaboration: Popular Protest in Northern France, 1940–1946* (Palgrave McMillan 2000) 3.

an enemy state.[261] The US Trading with the Enemy Act of 1917 remains in force and authorises the President to restrict certain trading activities in time of war.[262] Although individuals or companies that sell goods or conduct business with an enemy or its subjects may find themselves open to the charge of having aided the enemy, the risk of censure or even legal sanction has not prevented the practice from prevailing. According to Levy and Barbieri, '[t]he long-standing and seemingly paradoxical practice of trading with the enemy during wartime continues to the present day'.[263]

The First World War saw hundreds of British companies sanctioned for having voluntarily engaged in trade with Germany.[264] The activities of businesses during the Second World War, including Swiss banks and major US corporations, have also given rise to accusations of collaboration or even complicity in international crimes.[265] Switzerland's private sector contributed to and benefitted from Germany's wartime activates: 'Bankers and industrialists made large profits by exporting commodities to Germany, providing financial services for the Nazi leadership collectively and severally, and exploiting the murder of rich Jews.'[266] Given the emphasis on economic dominance by the Axis powers,[267] companies and industrialists in occupied territories were often compelled to cooperate with the occupying powers. According to the Nuremberg Tribunal, 'industries thought to be of value to the German war effort were compelled to continue and most of the rest were closed down altogether'.[268] Nonetheless, the accusation of economic or industrial collaboration arose as certain businesses or individuals cooperated voluntarily or even enthusiastically with Germany during the War.

With the German occupation of Northern France and the collaborationist Vichy government in the south, France made the largest industrial contribution to Germany's war economy.[269] 'Great industrialists in France', according to Istvan Deák, 'were generally eager to serve and profit from the German war effort'.[270] French automobile companies made a major contribution,[271] while executives of

[261] For example, Trading with the Enemy Act, 1914; Trading with the Enemy Act, 1939, section 2. See also Martin Domke, *Trading with the Enemy in World War II* (Central Book Company 1943).

[262] Trading with the Enemy Act of 1917, 6 October 1917, CH. 106, 40 STAT. 411.

[263] Jack S. Levy and Catherine Barbieri, 'Trading with the Enemy during Wartime' (2004) 13(3) Security Studies 1, 1.

[264] John McDermott, 'Trading with the Enemy: British Business and the Law during the First World War' (1997) 32(2) Canadian Journal of History 201.

[265] See for example Michael Dobbs, 'Ford and GM Scrutinized for Alleged Nazi Collaboration', *Washington Post*, 30 November 1998, A01; Edwin Black, *IBM and the Holocaust: The Strategic Alliance between Nazi Germany and America's Most Powerful Corporation* (2nd edn, Crown Books 2012); Anita Ramasastry, 'Secrets and Lies? Swiss Banks and International Human Rights', 31(2) Vanderbilt Journal of Transnational Law (1998) 325.

[266] Hastings, *The Secret War* (n 27) 347–8.

[267] See Marcel Bordoff and Tetsuji Okazaki (eds), *Economies under Occupation: The Hegemony of Nazi Germany and Imperial Japan in World War II* (Routledge 2015).

[268] See International Military Tribunal (Nuremberg), Judgment and Sentences (n 3) 235–6.

[269] Rings, *Life with the Enemy* (n 34) 279.

[270] Deák, *Europe on Trial* (n 8) 1. See also Taylor, *Between Resistance and Collaboration* (n 260) 18.

[271] Talbot Imlay and Martin Horn, *The Politics of Industrial Collaboration during World War II: Ford France, Vichy and Nazi Germany* (CUP 2014) 1.

France's aircraft industry placed themselves 'wholeheartedly at the service of the German war economy'.[272] Werner Rings notes that 'long before they were compelled to do so, businessmen, industrialists, and financiers placed their factories and financial assets—indeed, whole sectors of the national economy—at the Third Reich's disposal'.[273] In Vichy France, French companies went further in their collaboration than even Pétain's government considered appropriate, circumventing French officials in their eagerness to conduct business with Germany.[274]

Dutch factories, unimpeded by the local administration in the Netherlands, exported billions of guilders-worth of goods to Germany during the War.[275] The Dutch national rail company remained under Dutch management during the German occupation, and its employees cooperated with the occupying power throughout the period of occupation:

They repaired German rolling stock from the very outset. They manned Dutch trains in German frontier areas. They handled the transportation of German loot and German strategic supplies. They did not balk at consigning political prisoners to concentration camps or, later on, Dutch labour conscripts to Germany—410,000 of them, according to official Dutch figures. With disciplined alacrity, they also dispatched ninety-eight freight trains laden with 112,000 Dutch Jews destined for German extermination camps. Their loyalty to the occupying power was almost unbounded.[276]

The Dutch national railway company has since apologised and agreed to make reparations for the role it played in deporting Jews to concentration camps.[277]

At the individual level, the exploitation for slave labour of the local population in occupied territories was 'an integral part of the war economy' of Germany.[278] Compulsory labour, including work of a military nature, was instituted in German-occupied territories and 5 million workers were deported 'to serve Germany industry and agriculture'.[279] While many individuals resisted the compulsory labour,[280] it is estimated that over 2 million workers travelled voluntarily to Germany during the War for the purpose of employment, while some willingly worked for German companies operating in occupied territories.[281] Many of the thousands of Soviet agricultural labourers who worked for the German army were not politically or ideologically motivated:

They did so because they were hungry or afraid, or both. It was hardship, coupled with fear that they might one day be numbered among the countless victims of the manhunt and firing squad, that drove these men into the arms of the Germans. Others, who felt less immediately threatened, collaborated for material reasons.[282]

272 Rings, *Life with the Enemy* (n 34) 77. 273 Ibid 278. 274 Ibid 76–7.

275 Deák, *Europe on Trial* (n 8) 50; Rings, *Life with the Enemy* (n 34) 69.

276 Rings, *Life with the Enemy* (n 34) 80.

277 'Dutch Railway Firm Apologizes for Deporting Jews During WWII, *Reuters*, 29 September 2005; Mike Corder, 'Dutch Railway Firm Plans to Compensate Holocaust Survivors for Role in Second World War Deportations', *The Independent*, 28 November 2018.

278 International Military Tribunal (Nuremberg), Judgment and Sentences (n 3) 224.

279 Ibid. 280 Deák, *Europe on Trial* (n 8) 1.

281 Rings, *Life with the Enemy* (n 34) 80; Tanja Penter, 'Local Collaborators on Trial: Soviet War Crimes Trials under Stalin (1943–1953)' (2008) 49(2/3) Cahiers du Monde Russe 341, 352–353.

282 Rings, *Life with the Enemy* (n 34) 83.

Being compelled to work for the enemy's industries or to support its armed forces of course renders such collaboration involuntary.[283] The Nuremberg Tribunal noted the largely unsuccessful German attempts at voluntary recruitment of workers and thus widespread use of coercive methods, as well as the poor conditions for foreign labourers in Germany.[284]

In addition to economic collaboration, occupying powers have sought cooperation from influential individuals or groups within society. Coco Chanel, the famous fashion designer, is alleged to have spied for the Nazis in occupied Paris.[285] The recruitment of journalists in occupied territory during the Second World War was frequently for the purpose of assisting the propaganda efforts of Nazi Germany. The French journalist Robert Brassilach, for example, was the editor of a pro-Nazi newspaper called *Je Suis Partout* in France and 'collaborated fully with Nazi propaganda efforts'. He also denounced certain individuals in his writings, which 'served as a source of information and an encouragement for many arrests', and was tried and executed for collaboration after the War.[286] William Joyce, who was known as 'Lord Haw Haw', was also put on trial after the Second World War, pursuant to the charge that he 'did traitorously to and aid and comfort' the King's enemies by broadcasting propaganda for Germany.[287] He had acquired a British passport under false pretences, and had seemingly obtained German citizenship at the time of his collaboration, but the sentence of death was upheld.[288]

Finally, the recruitment of locals as interpreters or translators is a common practice for parties to an armed conflict that may be present on enemy territory.[289] The United States recruited around 50,000 local interpreters in Iraq and Afghanistan.[290] While no reference is made to such persons in the Third Geneva Convention amongst those who 'accompany the armed forces', their role is implicitly recognised elsewhere, given that detainees and prisoners of war may have 'the right to the services of an interpreter' if on trial.[291] Interpreters are often viewed as collaborators with the enemy and are targeted by armed opposition groups for that reason.[292] According to one US official, '[i]nterpreters are routinely killed by insurgents because they're aiding the United States'.[293] An Afghan interpreter who provided translation and

[283] Elliott, 'Soviet Military Collaborators during World War II' (n 132) 99.

[284] International Military Tribunal (Nuremberg), Judgment and Sentences (n 3) 240.

[285] Hal Vaughan, *Sleeping with the Enemy: Coco Chanel's Secret War* (Alfred A. Knopf 2011).

[286] Alice Kaplan, *The Collaborator: The Trial & Execution of Robert Brassilach* (University of Chicago Press 2000) ix–x.

[287] *Joyce v Director of Public Prosecutions*, House of Lords [1946] AC 347, 348.

[288] Ibid 348–9; *R. v Joyce* [1945] 2 All ER 673. See further Rebecca West, *The New Meaning of Treason* (The Viking Press 1964); Peter Martland, *Lord Haw Haw: The English Voice of Nazi Germany* (Scarecrow Press 2003); Colin Holmes, *Searching for Lord Haw-Haw: The Political Lives of William Joyce* (Routledge 2016); S.C. Biggs, 'Treason and the Trial of William Joyce' (1947) 7(1) University of Toronto Law Journal 162.

[289] Urban, *Task Force Black* (n 67) 19–20.

[290] Dane Bowker, 'Forget the Syrian Refugees. America Needs to Bring its Afghan and Iraqi Interpreters Here First', *The Washington Post*, 17 September 2015.

[291] See Third Geneva Convention, art 105 and Fourth Geneva Convention, art 72.

[292] Mona Baker, 'Interpreters and Translators in the War Zone; Narrated and Narrators' (2010) 16(2) The Translator 197, 207.

[293] Bowker, 'Forget the Syrian refugees' (n 290).

'intelligence work' by listening to Taliban radio communications described how 'his close work with locals in Helmand led to his identification as a collaborator with the International Security Assistance Force'.[294] A US visa programme was specifically developed to give residence rights to interpreters or translators that had assisted US forces in Iraq and Afghanistan.[295] There have been calls to 'provide better protection for interpreters during and following conflicts'.[296] Ensuring such protection during the context of armed conflict proves challenging, when interpreters, like the other persons described in this chapter, are viewed as collaborators who serve the enemy, and accordingly, are often deliberately subjected to sanctions, cruel treatment and violence.

* * *

This chapter has sought to provide an account of the history and practice of wartime collaboration by providing illustrative examples of the principal forms of collaboration occurring during situations of armed conflict. While there are myriad ways in which individuals might be perceived as providing assistance to an opposing belligerent, the chapter focused on forms of collaboration which entail a substantial benefit or advantage for a party to an armed conflict, principally informing, fighting with the enemy, bureaucratic collaboration, and aiding the enemy through engaging in propaganda, interpreting, trading, or providing labour. The Second World War offers numerous examples of each of these forms of collaboration, although almost all have been practised to some extent in contemporary armed conflicts. Both states and non-state armed groups have sought to use collaborators, particularly informers, on account of the pre-eminent value placed on intelligence during conflict. Both have also punished those considered to have worked in the enemy's favour. The chapter alluded briefly to certain questions of law that arise in relation to the use, recruitment, and treatment of collaborators, and the book now turns to address in detail this broad spectrum of legal issues. The next chapter shows how international humanitarian law displays some ambivalence on this subject, in that it generally permits the recruitment and use of informers and other persons that might collaborate with an opposing power during times of armed conflict, but subjects such actions to certain restrictions, particularly an overarching prohibition on any use of coercion.

[294] Damien Gayle, 'Afghan Interpreter Who Worked with British Army Refused UK Asylum', *The Guardian*, 7 April 2015.

[295] Special Immigrant Visas (SIVs) for Iraqi and Afghan Translators/Interpreters <https://travel.state.gov/content/visas/en/immigrate/iraqi-afghan-translator.html> accessed 21 May 2019. See further Ben Juvinall, 'Heaven or Hell? The Plight of Wartime Interpreters of the Iraq and Afghanistan Conflicts living in the U.S.' (2013) 21(1) Michigan State International Law Review 205.

[296] Parliamentary Assembly of the Council of Europe, 'We should protect interpreters in conflict zones!', Written Declaration No. 442, Document 12239, 29 April 2010.

2

International Humanitarian Law on the Recruitment and Use of Informers and Collaborators

The use of informers and other collaborators is a perennial feature of armed conflict, yet the principal treaties which regulate wartime conduct, the Hague Regulations, the 1949 Geneva Conventions, and the 1977 Additional Protocols, make no explicit reference to such persons. How is the silence of these key instruments to be interpreted? It is not as though the states engaged in their drafting and adoption were unaware of the practice of cooperation with an adversary in times of war. During the drafting of the 1949 Geneva Conventions, for example, the Soviet delegate at the Geneva Diplomatic Conference noted the presence of 'traitors to their country' in occupied territories during the Second World War, and commented that occupying powers 'made use of their services'.[1] Although the main international humanitarian law treaties refer to various categories of persons that participate in or are affected by armed conflicts, neither informers nor other collaborators have been considered as groups of persons that merit specific protections or whose activities require explicit regulation under this body of law.

In considering whether parties to an armed conflict can engage individuals in any of the various forms of cooperation outlined in Chapter 1, the absence of a clear rule against the use of informers or collaborators during armed conflict suggests the applicability of the much-criticised *Lotus* principle, that conduct may be considered permitted under international law absent a specific prohibition.[2] The existence of state practice and *opinio juris* reinforces the position that using informers and collaborators in times of armed conflict is allowed under prevailing international law.[3] Whether the inherent harms and risks associated with such activities require an alternative reading of international law on this question will be returned to at the end

[1] Committee III (Civilians), Forty-Ninth Meeting, 18 July 1949, *Final Record of the Diplomatic Conference of Geneva of 1949*, Vol. II, Section A (Federal Political Department, Berne) 797.

[2] S.S. 'Lotus', *France v Turkey*, Judgment No. 9, 1927, P.C.I.J., Series A, No. 10, 18–21. See for example *Accordance with International Law of the Unilateral Declaration of Independence in Respect of Kosovo*, Advisory Opinion, 22 July 2010, ICJ Reports 2010, 403, Declaration of Judge Simma, para 8. See also An Hertogen, 'Let *Lotus* Bloom' (2016) 26(4) European Journal of International Law 901.

[3] See for example United Kingdom Ministry of Defence, *The Joint Service Manual of the Law of Armed Conflict* (OUP 2004) 63.

To Serve the Enemy: Informers, Collaborators, and the Laws of Armed Conflict. Shane Darcy, Oxford University Press (2019). © Shane Darcy.
DOI: 10.1093/oso/ 9780198788898.001.0001

of the book. International humanitarian law permits, or at least does not expressly prohibit, the use of informers and other collaborators during an armed conflict. But international law also places caveats on this general statement in that specific restrictions under this body of law are relevant to the use of informers and collaborators and to the means of recruiting such persons, even if not explicitly addressed to them. International humanitarian law implicitly recognises both the harms and the utility associated with the practice, and seeks to reconcile the two.

The prohibition of coercion constitutes a key rule that applies to the recruitment and use of informers and other collaborators. While parties to an armed conflict might accept voluntary offers of cooperation, or even seek to persuade individuals to serve an opposing side in various ways, coercing persons to do so is contrary to the rules of international humanitarian law. Most prominently, the Fourth Geneva Convention sets out in Article 31 that '[n]o physical or moral coercion shall be exercised against protected persons, in particular to obtain information from them or from third parties'.[4] While the 1907 Hague Regulations permit the employment of 'measures necessary for obtaining information about the enemy and the country',[5] measures of a coercive nature for such purposes have been prohibited. For prisoners of war, '[n]o physical or mental torture, nor any other form of coercion, may be inflicted . . . to secure from them information of any kind whatever'.[6] As a general rule, neither prisoners of war nor other protected persons can be compelled to serve in the forces of the enemy or to engage in military operations.[7] Regarding bureaucratic collaboration, however, it has been suggested that a certain degree of official cooperation may be required by occupying powers in order for them to fulfil their obligations under the laws of belligerent occupation.[8]

While the international law of armed conflict prohibits coercing protected persons into collaboration, albeit without explicitly using the term, it does not outlaw voluntary cooperation with an adversary by such persons. This is despite the obvious and serious risks arising for those who engage in collaboration during armed conflict. Moreover, as will be discussed, it may be questioned whether an armed conflict allows such conduct to be truly voluntary. Emer de Vattel demonstrated some unease with willing collaboration when he considered the question of 'whether it be

[4] Geneva Convention IV Relative to the Protection of Civilian Persons in Time of War (1949), entered into force 21 October 1950, 75 U.N.T.S. 287, art 31.

[5] Regulations annexed to Hague Convention IV Respecting the Laws and Customs of War on Land (1907), art 24.

[6] Geneva Convention III Relative to the Treatment of Prisoners of War (1949), entered into force 21 October 1950, 75 U.N.T.S. 135, art 17.

[7] See Third Geneva Convention, art 130; Fourth Geneva Convention, art 51; Hague Regulations 1907, art 45.

[8] See Sigrid Redse Johansen, 'The Occupied and the Occupier: The Case of Norway' in Kjetil Mujenović Larsen, Camilla Guldahl Cooper, and Gro Nystuen (eds), *Searching for a 'Principle of Humanity' in International Humanitarian Law* (CUP 2013) 206, 206–7; István Deák, *Europe on Trial: The Story of Collaboration, Resistance, and Retribution During World War II* (Westview Press 2015) 21.

lawful to seduce the enemy's men, for the purpose of engaging them to transgress their duty by an infamous treachery?'[9] Although not 'contrary to the external law of nations', it was dishonourable even if justifiable at times:

> Seducing a subject to betray his country, engaging a traitor to set fire to a magazine, tampering with the fidelity of a governor, enticing him, persuading him to deliver up the town intrusted to his charge, is prompting such persons to commit detestable crimes. Is it honourable to corrupt our most inveterate enemy, and tempt him to the commission of a crime? If such practices are at all excusable, it can be only in a very just war, and when the immediate object is to save our country, when threatened with ruin by a lawless conqueror.[10]

As to voluntary offers of cooperation, 'we may take advantage of his crime, while at the same time we detest it'.[11] While voluntary collaboration might not run afoul of the applicable Hague and Geneva rules, the concept of voluntariness itself is not straightforward in the violent and often inherently coercive circumstances of armed conflict. A decision to cooperate with an adversary may not be directly coerced, but neither might it be said to have been freely made.

This chapter explores the rules of international humanitarian law relevant to the use and recruitment of informers and other collaborators during armed conflict. It considers the prohibition of coercion in the context of the acquisition of information from civilians or detained persons, the rules against forcible recruitment into the enemy's armed forces, as well as those laws applicable in situations of occupation of relevance to bureaucratic collaboration, as well as to other forms of aiding the enemy. While states engaged in the negotiation of the 1949 Geneva Conventions knew of the practice of collaboration during the Second World War, not to mention the often severe treatment of alleged collaborators, the records of the Geneva Diplomatic Conference reveal little discussion of the phenomenon or how the law might address it. In contrast, considerable attention was devoted to these issues during the preparation of prominent predecessor treaties, including the 1899 and 1907 Hague Regulations, and the earlier foundational instrument, the 1874 Brussels Declaration. The debates of the time reveal a notable divergence of views on how the emerging laws of war should address those who either volunteer or are compelled 'to serve the enemy'.[12] This chapter delves into this legal history by examining the drafting, application, and subsequent interpretation of the humanitarian law rules relevant to the use and recruitment of informers and other collaborators.

[9] Emer de Vattel, *The Law of Nations*, Book III, *Of War*, Chapter X, §180 (first published 1758, Bela Kapossy and Richard Whatmore (eds), Liberty Fund 2008) 582–3.

[10] Ibid 583.

[11] Ibid 584. See also H.W. Halleck, *International Law, or Rules Regulation the Intercourse of States in Peace and War* (H.H. Bancroft & Company 1861) 406–9.

[12] This phrase was used during the discussion on the drafting of the 1874 Brussels Declaration on the Laws and Customs of War. See 'Correspondence Respecting the Proposed Conference at Brussels on the Rules of Military Warfare', *United Kingdom Parliamentary Papers,* Miscellaneous No. 1 (1875) [c.-1128] 18, 202.

2.1 Informers

With international humanitarian law seeking to set limits on the conduct of parties to an armed conflict, its treaty and customary rules usually take the form of prohibitions or restrictions on certain types of activities. A key provision relevant to the use of informers during wartime takes the opposite approach: Article 14 of the 1874 Brussels Declaration states that 'measures necessary for obtaining information about the enemy and the country [...] are considered permissible'.[13] Although found in a non-binding declaration devised by a group of European countries well over a century ago, the article is neither anachronistic nor irrelevant for present purposes.[14] The provision was replicated in both the 1899 and 1907 Hague Regulations, which have been found to constitute customary international law, [15] and the principle it embodies, if not the provision itself, continues to be cited by contemporary military manuals.[16] International humanitarian law permits the gathering of intelligence during armed conflict by all 'measures necessary', although, as the 2015 United States *Law of War Manual* states, '[i]nformation gathering measures ... may not violate specific law of war rules'.[17] This section considers those specific rules which are relevant to the recruitment and use of informers who provide information to an opposing side, whether civilians or other persons detained during an armed conflict, such as prisoners of war. Humanitarian law accommodates the intelligence-gathering activities of parties to an armed conflict, but seeks to protect potential sources from certain harms.

The practice of recruiting and using informers is not exclusive to situations of armed conflict, as state authorities employ covert human intelligence sources in the context of crime prevention and prosecution, as well as for international espionage.[18] International law says relatively little about states spying on one another, although certain methods may violate the principle of non-interference or the prohibition on the use of force, the law applicable to diplomatic relations, or human rights standards where coercion is used or privacy violated.[19] In general, international law seems to tolerate much of the spying activities of states, and 'the prevalence of this activity among states suggests that states impliedly have consented to this activity, subject to

[13] Brussels Declaration 1874, art 14.

[14] See generally Tracey Leigh Dowdeswell, 'The Brussels Peace Conference of 1874 and the Modern Laws of Belligerent Qualification' (2017) 54(3) Osgoode Hall Law Journal 805.

[15] See Hague Regulations 1899 and 1907, art 24; International Military Tribunal (Nuremberg), *Judgment and Sentences* 1 October 1946 (1947) 41(1) American Journal of International Law 172, 248–9; *Prosecutor v Mrkšić and Šljivančanin*, Case No. IT-95-13/1-A, Appeals Chamber, Judgment, 5 May 2009, footnote 248.

[16] See for example United Kingdom, *Joint Service Manual* (n 3) 46; United States, *Law of War Manual* (Department of Defense, Office of General Counsel 2015) 309.

[17] United States, *Law of War Manual* (n 16) 309.

[18] See Roger Billingsley, Teresa Nemitz, and Philip Bean (eds), *Informers: Policing, Policy and Practice* (Routledge 2001); Roger Billingsley (ed), *Covert Human Intelligence Sources: The Unlovely Face of Police Work* (Waterside Press 2009).

[19] Simon Chesterman, *One Nation under Surveillance* (OUP 2011) 35–6.

the ability to prosecute those who agree to spy for other governments'.[20] In the context of intelligence gathering, states have tended to avoid legal restraint where possible, and such activities have often involved sanctioning breaches of domestic law.[21] Simon Chesterman has concluded that in the sphere of intelligence, states have been 'reluctant to establish a single regime that would impose undesirable limits on their own freedom of action'.[22] International humanitarian law is somewhat more explicit regarding intelligence gathering during armed conflict, by allowing for 'measures necessary for obtaining information about the enemy and the country', but also laying down specific rules addressed to the use of spies.

Humanitarian law does not prohibit using spies during times of armed conflict or penalise espionage but rather limits the protections available to those considered as spies. According to Hugo Grotius, the sending of spies in wartime is 'beyond doubt permitted by the law of nations'.[23] Spying is 'a deceit in war, allowable by its rules'.[24] However, those members of the armed forces that are caught engaging in espionage can be denied prisoner of war status in certain circumstances and treated as spies.[25] Prior to the development of the present regime of international humanitarian law, spies which were 'usually treated most severely . . . in accordance with that impunity which the law of war accords'.[26] The modern law of armed conflict seeks to limit such treatment to criminal prosecution and punishment:

> The Hague Regulations formally sanctioned the employment of measures necessary for the obtaining of intelligence in enemy-held territory. The collection of such information openly by combatants wearing uniform is a recognized branch of the art of warfare. The obtaining of such information by secret methods is governed by different rules. Thus it is lawful to employ spies and secret agents but the fact that these methods are lawful under international law does not prevent the punishment under domestic or occupation law of individuals who are engaged in procuring intelligence in other than an open manner.[27]

Spying and others means of intelligence gathering are not themselves necessarily unlawful, but certain methods may be: 'It is the disguise, or false pretense, which

[20] Ashley Deeks, 'Confronting and Adapting: Intelligence Agencies and International Law' (2016) 102(3) Virginia Law Review 601, 681; Chesterman, *One Nation under Surveillance* (n 19) 33–4. See further John Kish, *International Law and Espionage* (Martinus Nijhoff 1995); Geoffrey B. Demarest, 'Espionage in International Law' (1996) 24(2) Denver Journal of International Law and Policy 321; Asaf Lubin, 'Espionage as a Sovereign Right under International Law and its Limits' (2016) 24(3) ILSA Quarterly 22; W. Michael Reisman and James E. Baker, *Regulating Covert Action, Practices, Contexts and Policies* (Yale University Press 1992).

[21] Marvin C. Ott., 'Partisanship and the Decline of Intelligence Oversight' in Christopher Andrew, Richard J. Aldrich, and Wesley K. Wark (eds), *Secret Intelligence: A Reader* (Routledge 2009) 318, 320.

[22] Chesterman, *One Nation under Surveillance* (n 19) 36.

[23] Hugo Grotius, *De Jure Belli ac Pacis Libri Tres*, Book III, Chapter IV, Section XVIII, 3 (first published 1646, translated by Francis W. Kelsey, Vol. II, Carnegie Endowment for International Peace, Division of International Law 1925) 655.

[24] Halleck, *International Law* (n 11) 406.

[25] See for example Hague Regulations 1907, arts 29–21; Additional Protocol I, art 46.

[26] Grotius, *De Jure Belli ac Pacis Libri Tres* (n 23) Book III, Chapter IV, Section XVIII, 3, 655–6. Grotius wrote that 'anything is permissible as against an enemy', and that in the case of assassins, 'each decides upon a more severe or more lenient punishment from the point of view of his personal advantage'.

[27] United Kingdom, *Joint Service Manual* (n 3) 46 (footnote omitted).

constitutes the perfidy, and forms the essential elements of the crime, which, by the laws of war, is punishable with an ignominious death', Halleck wrote in 1861.[28] While modern international humanitarian law does not completely outlaw capital punishment, captured spies, like other individuals in the power of a party to an armed conflict, are entitled to the law's basic humanitarian protections, such as those set out in Article 75 of Additional Protocol I.[29] The law applicable to the trial and treatment of those found to have provided information to the enemy is addressed in Chapter 4.

International humanitarian law thus recognises and allows the use of spies as a key means of intelligence gathering while also acknowledging that other means of gathering intelligence might be used during armed conflict. Members of the armed forces who engage in espionage are not collaborators as they are not engaged in intelligence gathering for the enemy's benefit, although humanitarian law treats informers who gather and share information with the opposing side similarly in that such activity is not treated as contrary to international law itself, but those who engage therein can be subjected to punishment under domestic legal regimes. The 1863 Lieber Code envisaged 'death by hanging' for spies and punishment of death for any so-called war traitor who 'gives information of any kind to the enemy, or holds intercourse with him'.[30] Notwithstanding, the Lieber Code also asserted that citizens might be forced to provide information to military forces, given that '[a]ll armies in the field stand in need of guides'.[31] Such persons would not be considered as war traitors and subject to punishment, unless they had served voluntarily as a guide 'against their own country'.[32] As will be discussed, the use of civilians as guides and the extent to which coercion could be employed were highly contested issues during the drafting of the early treaties on the law of armed conflict.

The Lieber Code condemned collaboration with the enemy on the one hand, while taking the view that compelling civilians to provide information was a necessary means of intelligence gathering on the other. This tension was at the heart of several discussions during the drafting of the laws of war. The focus was on the question of compulsion, rather than any questioning of the need for intelligence or its permissibility. While the Lieber Code had accepted that citizens could be forced to act as guides for the enemy, that an army could 'impress them if they cannot obtain them otherwise',[33] and that such individuals would not be liable to punishment, modern international humanitarian law forbids coercion for purposes of obtaining information. The 2015 US *Law of War Manual* states plainly that 'it would be unlawful, of course, to use torture or abuse to interrogate detainees for purposes of gathering information'.[34] It is incorrect to claim that '[n]othing is prohibited for

[28] Halleck, *International Law* (n 11) 407.

[29] United Kingdom, *Joint Service Manual* (n 3) 47. See for example art 75 of Additional Protocol I.

[30] Instructions for the Government of Armies of the United States in the Field, prepared by Francis Lieber, promulgated as General Orders No. 100 by President Lincoln, 24 April 1863, arts 88–91 *reprinted in* Dietrich Schindler and Jiří Toman (eds), *The Laws of Armed Conflict: A Collection of Conventions, Resolutions and Other Documents* (Martinus Nijhoff 1988) 3.

[31] Ibid art 93. [32] Ibid arts 94–96. [33] Ibid art 93.

[34] United States, *Law of War Manual* (n 16) 309.

intelligence by the laws of war, except the torture of prisoners',[35] as the prohibition of torture under Common Article 3 to the 1949 Geneva Conventions extends to all persons 'taking no active part in hostilities'. Civilians are protected from 'physical or moral coercion' where information is being sought from them.[36] Before looking at the substance of these contemporary rules, it is instructive to consider the historical evolution of international humanitarian law as it relates to the use of informers during armed conflict.

2.1.1 Brussels Declaration 1874

The Lieber Code of 1863 reflected but did not create international humanitarian law, which was beginning to emerge in treaty form around this time.[37] The 1899 and 1907 Hague Regulations constitute the first treaties which codified somewhat comprehensively the laws and customs relating to 'war on land'. The content of these instruments was based substantially on the 1874 Brussels Declaration, which arose from a Russian initiative 'to establish by common accord, upon a basis of complete reciprocity, rules which may be binding on all governments and their armies'.[38] The 1874 Brussels Declaration and the document's *travaux préparatoires*, including the Project for an International Convention on the Laws and Customs of War put forward by Russia as a starting point for diplomatic discussion, provide valuable insights as to the views of the participating European states regarding wartime intelligence gathering and the use of civilians for such purposes. The general statement in the 1874 Brussels Declaration that 'measures necessary for obtaining information about the enemy and the country ... are considered permissible' was subject to the caveat that the population of occupied territory 'cannot be forced to take part in military operations against its own country'.[39] The discussions at Brussels regarding civilian participation in intelligence gathering or military operations were closely intertwined and cannot be completely separated, although this section will focus primarily on the discussion of using civilians as informers, while the next section will examine the issue of their participation in military operations.

The Project put forward by Russia sought to permit '[t]he employment of every available means of procuring information about the enemy and the country'.[40] However:

> So long as a province, occupied by the enemy, is not ceded to him by virtue of a Treaty of Peace, the inhabitants thereof cannot be forced either to take part in the operations of war

[35] Michael Herman, 'Ethics and intelligence after September 2001' in Andrew, Aldrich, and Wark, *Secret Intelligence* (n 21) 382, 383.

[36] Fourth Geneva Convention, art 31.

[37] See for example Declaration Respecting Maritime Law, Paris, 1856; Convention for the Amelioration of the Condition of Wounded in Armies in the Field, Geneva, 1864; Declaration Renouncing the Use, in Time of War, of certain Explosive Projectiles, St Petersburg, 1868.

[38] 'Correspondence Respecting the Proposed Conference at Brussels on the Rules of Military Warfare', *United Kingdom Parliamentary Papers,* Miscellaneous No. 1 (1874) [c.-1010], 5–6.

[39] Brussels Declaration 1874, arts 14 and 36.

[40] 'Correspondence Respecting the Proposed Conference at Brussels' (n 38) 13 (§13(e)).

against their legitimate Government, or in acts of such a nature as to further the prosecution of the objects of the war, to the detriment of their own country.[41]

This latter provision was an exception to the more general statement in the former, as forcing civilians to provide information would comprise acts which could advance the war effort to their own country's detriment. These two proposed articles were slightly modified before appearing in the final Brussels Declaration, but were discussed only briefly compared to the lengthy debates at the subsequent Hague Peace Conferences.

During the Brussels Conference, the Russian delegate and President of the Conference, Baron Jomini, proposed a new text concerning compulsion of the inhabitants of occupied territory:

The population of an occupied province cannot be forced to take part either in the operations of war against their legitimate Government or in acts of such a nature as to further the prosecution of the war to the detriment of their own country.[42]

The German delegate, General de Voigts-Rhetz, suggested that 'take part' be replaced with 'take an active part', so as to limit the rule to participation in military operations.[43] Colonel Count Lanza of Italy agreed with the German proposal to delete the last part of the text, as:

[n]o Government would engage ... not to press guides into the service, not to employ the labourers of the country on lines of communication, not to compel carriers to transport the means of subsistence, and to perform other services.[44]

Aside from active participation in military operations, these delegates considered that civilian inhabitants could be compelled to provide information, labour, or various other services to an occupying power.

Baron Lambermont of Belgium expressed concern that limiting the prohibition only to taking an 'active part' in war operations 'might be a source of danger', as belligerents might take advantage 'to justify all the acts which are not included in the qualification proposed'.[45] He thought the second part should be retained 'because its suppression would be contrary to the humane object'.[46] The Committee appointed by the Conference to consider these proposals partly agreed, rejecting the proposal to limit the rule to active participation in military operations, but agreeing to omit the last part of the article. The Committee also supported a suggestion that the words 'against his own country' be added, with the new article reading: 'The population of an occupied territory cannot be compelled to take part in military operations against its own country.'[47]

The provision on intelligence gathering had originally been included in the Project's list of permitted means of warfare, but during the Brussels Conference it was decided that it should be subsumed within a separate article, Article 14, which

[41] Ibid 15 (§48).
[42] 'Correspondence Respecting the Proposed Conference at Brussels' (n 12) 220.
[43] Ibid 267. [44] Ibid. [45] Ibid. [46] Ibid. [47] Ibid.

included a reference to the new Article 36, which prohibited compelling the civilian population to take part in military operations against their own country:

> Strategems ('ruses de guerre'), and the employment of means necessary to procure intelligence respecting the enemy or the country ('terrain') (subject to the provision of Article 36), are considered as lawful means.[48]

Although it was considered impractical to include a list of permitted rather than forbidden measures,[49] the article was retained, with Baron Lambermont of Belgium contending that despite the permissiveness of the provision, '[i]t is, doubtless, not intended to authorize immoral or criminal means'.[50] The Declaration also called for occupying powers to respect '[f]amily honour and rights, and the lives and property of persons, as well as their religious convictions and their practice'.[51] The population of the occupied territory could not be compelled to take an oath of allegiance to the hostile power.[52]

These brief exchanges at the Brussels diplomatic conference are revealing as to the differing views held towards using civilians for gathering information, and they reflect a broader tension between military and humanitarian considerations that was evident at the time. There is some ambiguity in the final document, given that the prohibition in Article 36 is of coerced participation in military operations and not, at least explicitly, of other activities that might contribute to the war effort as initially proposed. A prohibition of the latter might be read in, given that the Conference rejected the proposal that the exclusion be limited only to active participation in military operations by civilians against their country. On the practice of using guides as referred to by the Italian delegate,[53] the Russians had proposed the inclusion of the following provisions:

> An inhabitant of a country, who has 'voluntarily' served as a guide to the enemy, is guilty of high treason; he is not, however, liable to punishment from the moment he has been 'compelled' by the enemy to serve in such capacity.
>
> A guide, even when he has been compelled to serve the enemy, is liable to punishment when he has intentionally pointed out the wrong road.[54]

These proposed articles are likely to have been based on relevant articles of the Lieber Code, which effectively permitted the use of guides, coerced or otherwise, but allowed for the prosecution only of individuals that voluntarily assisted the enemy in this way.[55] The delegates at the Brussels Conference sought instructions from their governments on this proposal as the suggested article had not been included in the original Project, but in the end the proposal was withdrawn without having been submitted to the conference for substantive discussion.[56]

[48] Ibid 165. See also ibid 193–4. [49] Ibid 284 (original emphasis). [50] Ibid.
[51] Brussels Declaration 1874, art 38. [52] Ibid art 37.
[53] 'Correspondence Respecting the Proposed Conference at Brussels' (n 12) 267.
[54] Ibid 18, 202. [55] Lieber Code, arts 93–97.
[56] 'Correspondence Respecting the Proposed Conference at Brussels' (n 12) 181, 201, 281.

2.1.2 Hague Regulations 1899 and 1907

The First Hague Peace Conference of 1899 was initially aimed at addressing the maintenance of international peace and the reduction of excessive armaments, but its focus was subsequently expanded to include revision of the laws and customs of war on land as set out in the 1874 Brussels Declaration.[57] The articles on permissible means of gathering information and prohibiting the compulsion of civilians to take part in military operations were reproduced in the 1899 Hague Regulations with only minor changes. Article 24 of the 1899 Hague Regulations states that 'Ruses of war and the employment of methods necessary to obtain information about the enemy and the country, are considered allowable.' No cross-reference was included to the rule prohibiting forcing the civilian population to take part in hostilities.

Initially, there was no opposition to following the formulation of this article as in the Brussels Declaration,[58] but Edouard Rolin, the *rapporteur* of the Second Subcommission which had been tasked with revising the laws and customs of war, explained that the original wording had been a cause for some concern amongst the delegates. The breadth of Article 24 had been criticised:

> Taken literally this article might indeed be taken to mean that *every ruse of war* and *every method necessary to obtain information about the enemy and the country* should *ipso facto* be considered 'permissible'. It is understood that such is by no means the import of this provision, which aims only to say that ruses of war and methods of obtaining information are not prohibited as such. They would cease to be 'permissible' in case of infraction of a recognized imperative rule to the contrary.[59]

As to the omission of a cross-reference in Article 24 to the rule concerning forced participation in military operations, Rolin explained that this was one of many imperative rules, 'and not being able to recall all these rules with regard to Article 24, the subcommission thought it was better to mention none of them'.[60]

The rule forbidding the compelling of the population of occupied territory to take part in military operations was retained as Article 44 of the 1899 Hague Regulations largely in the form it had appeared in the Brussels Declaration, albeit after a brief reprise of the debate on the scope of the prohibition.[61] Colonel Gross von Schwarzhoff of Germany, for example, reiterated that 'this provision does not deprive the belligerents of the right to force an individual to perform some service,

[57] Circular Note Proposing the First Peace Conference, August 12, 1898, by Count Mouravieff, Russian Minister for Foreign Affairs *reprinted in* James Brown Scott (ed), *The Reports to the Hague Conferences of 1899 and 1907* (Carnegie Endowment for International Peace/Clarendon Press 1917) 1–4.

[58] Twelfth Meeting of the Second Commission: Second Subcommission, 1 July 1899, *The Proceedings of the Hague Peace Conferences, Translation of the Official Texts: The Conference of 1899* (OUP 1920) 557, 567.

[59] *Report to the Conference*, by Edouard Rolin, Annex 1 to the Minutes of the Fifth Plenary Meeting, 5 July 1899, *The Proceedings of the Hague Peace Conferences: The Conference of 1899* (n 58) 50, 59 (original emphasis).

[60] Ibid 59.

[61] Fourth Meeting of the Second Commission: Second Subcommission, 1 June 1899, *The Proceedings of the Hague Peace Conferences: The Conference of 1899* (n 58) 487.

for instance to show the road'.[62] While such a service could assist the invading army or occupying power, that it placed the individual in question at risk of being considered a collaborator with the enemy was raised as a concern by delegates at the Second Hague Peace Conference in 1907.

The 1907 Hague Regulations retained Article 24 on the permissibility of methods necessary for obtaining information from the 1899 Regulations, but added an explicit rule prohibiting occupying powers from forcing civilians to divulge such information: the stand-alone provision prohibiting forced participation in military operations in Article 44 of the 1899 Hague Regulations, was replaced by Article 44 of the 1907 Hague Regulations which provides that it is unlawful for an occupying power 'to force the inhabitants of territory occupied by it to furnish information about the army of the other belligerent, or about its means of defense'. Rules against forcing the population to take part in military operations are now found in both Article 23(h) and Article 52 on requisition and services, as examined further in the next section. A prohibition on compelling the taking of the oath of allegiance to the occupying power was included in Article 45. The result of the lengthy and often convoluted discussions at the Second Hague Conference on these interrelated rules was the introduction for the first time in international law of a rule explicitly prohibiting occupying powers from forcing civilians to act as informers. Having civilians provide information was 'not prohibited as such', to borrow Rolin's phrase, but neither could they be forced to cooperate with an opposing side in this way.

The text which ultimately became Article 44 of the 1907 Hague Regulations was proposed by the Netherlands' Lieutenant General Jonkheer den Beer Poortugael.[63] He demonstrated an intention to depart from previous practice:

> By disclosing to the enemy that which he desires to know, the inhabitant of the country would become a traitor to his native land. In our day it is no longer fitting to make disloyal demands and to permit a man to commit acts which would render him despicable in his own eyes and in those of every man of spirit.[64]

While these comments seem also to suggest that accepting voluntary offers of information was similarly no longer appropriate, Article 44a as proposed focused only on forced collaboration: 'It is forbidden to compel the population of occupied territory to give information concerning their own army or the means of defence of their country.'[65] Germany was responsible for the proposal to replace the original Article 44 on forced participation in military operations with Article 22a:

> It is forbidden to compel *ressortissants* of the hostile party to take part in the operations of war directed against their own country, even if they were enrolled in its service before the commencement of the war.[66]

[62] Ibid.

[63] First Meeting of the Second Commission: First Subcommission, 3 July 1907, *The Proceedings of the Hague Peace Conferences: The Conference of 1907*, Volume III (OUP 1921) 98.

[64] Ibid 98–9.

[65] Second Meeting of the Second Commission: First Subcommission, 10 July 1907, *The Proceedings of the Hague Peace Conferences: The Conference of 1907* (n 63) 108.

[66] Ibid 107.

These two proposed articles gave rise to intertwined, lengthy, and at times fraught debates between the delegates in 1907, revealing diverging views of these military powers as to how civilians might be required to assist the enemy in times of war.

From the *travaux préparatoires* of the Second Hague Peace Conference there is an evident tension between the claimed demands of military necessity in allowing resort to a valuable method of intelligence gathering and the proposed attempts to embed greater humanitarian protections in the laws of war and place limits on an inherently risk-laden practice.[67] At a meeting of the Committee of Examination, President Beernaert of Belgium sought to draw the attention of the delegates to the central dilemma posed by using the civilian population in activities connected to military operations, by referring to:

> the cruelty of compelling the inhabitants of a country under pain of death to become traitors to their fatherland, by leading an enemy army or by erecting its fortifications. On the other hand the necessities of war are invoked, it being at the same time recognized that they must always be mitigated as far as possible conformably to the principles of humanity inspiring all civilized nations; but since these necessities are in certain cases unavoidable it would therefore be more loyal to sanction them.[68]

Tentative votes in the Committee of Examination saw the Dutch article accepted by seven votes to six and a proposed Austro-Hungarian amendment to add 'as combatants' to the rule in article 22A defeated by eleven votes to two.[69]

When the discussion of these articles was taken up by the First Subcommission, the delegate of Austria-Hungary, Major General Baron Giesl von Gieslingen, explained the proposed amendment was grounded in military necessity and that 'offensive action remains ... the basis of success'.[70] Where troops are present on enemy or neutral territory 'a military commander cannot, or at least not always, forego securing temporary assistance in the form of military services which can be rendered him only by the said enemy or neutral population'.[71] Aware that such issues may 'alarm the non-military men', von Gieslingen sought to explain that in the absence of detailed maps '[t]he commander upon whom rests the entire responsibility for so many lives entrusted to him cannot often hesitate to have recourse to information furnished by an enemy or neutral guide'.[72] The civilian population might also be required in the construction of bridges or fortifications, given that troops may be 'weakened from fighting'.[73] The delegate of Austria-Hungary acknowledged the potential impact on the civilian population when he concluded, somewhat ominously, that 'the population will not be mistreated and this work will assuredly be the least

[67] Ibid.

[68] Third Meeting of the Second Commission: First Subcommission, 24 July 1907, *Annex; Report made in the name of the Committee of Examination, The Proceedings of the Hague Peace Conferences: The Conference of 1907* (n 63) 127.

[69] Ibid.

[70] Third Meeting of the Second Commission: First Subcommission, 24 July 1907, *The Proceedings of the Hague Peace Conferences: The Conference of 1907* (n 63) 117.

[71] Ibid. [72] Ibid. [73] Ibid 118.

of the inconveniences to which it might be subjected during the campaign'.[74] If his own country was invaded:

we should consider it perfectly justifiable and natural for the enemy to employ our population to safeguard its superior military interests. [. . .] As, according to us, it can be a question of immorality only if the population is forced to fight with weapons in hand against its own country, we propose to have the words 'as combatants' inserted in the German amendment.[75]

Russia also supported the view that the line should be drawn at forced participation of civilians as combatants in military activities against their own country.

The Russian delegate, Major General Yermolov, felt that it was necessary to distinguish 'between "the service" in which the enemy population cannot be forced to participate and "the services" which this population can in case of imperative and grave necessity be compelled to render'.[76] The latter:

in the form of work on roads, camps, hospitals, trains, etc., are often absolutely indispensable to armies. These services are already authorized by the text of Article 52 which stipulates that they may be required of the inhabitants for the needs of the army. Consequently, if Article 22a were adopted without adding the amendment of the words 'as combatants' it would be in contradiction with the meaning of Article 52 and would contribute to the whole question only ambiguity, obscurity and confusion.[77]

In response, Major General von Gündell of Germany explained that the proposed Article 22a principally sought to extend the scope of application of the 1899 article beyond occupied territory to all the '*ressortissants* of the hostile party'.[78] He also supported the continued use of guides, given 'the necessity of ensuring the march of the armies in mountainous countries'.[79]

The issue of using guides prompted an intervention by den Beer Poortugael of the Netherlands who was keen to stress that the article proposed by his delegation was not solely concerned with guides.[80] He sought to challenge the claim that guides are indispensable from a military perspective:

If the enemy has invaded a certain country, it can send for the inhabitants, men and women, and interrogate them with threats of shooting them instantly if they do not give satisfactory information. [. . .] it is not for peaceful inhabitants to furnish the means of making war upon their fatherland. It is up to the soldiers, the generals, to find out for themselves what they want to know. They have the means to do it. They have maps, scouts; they have only to send in front of their columns their light cavalry, patrols, well-mounted officers to make raids; they have their spies and their intelligence bureaus.[81]

He considered that the need to use guides was no longer as acute as in previous conflicts, and that is was a dangerous method of gathering information, given troops had been led into ambushes by guides on more than one occasion.[82]

The motivations of the delegate of the Netherlands were primarily humanitarian, and he was of the view that the issue should not be dealt with 'from a technical point

[74] Ibid. [75] Ibid. [76] Ibid 118–19. [77] Ibid 119. [78] Ibid.
[79] Ibid 126. [80] Ibid 119–20. [81] Ibid 120. [82] Ibid.

of view but from the point of view of what is moral and right'.[83] den Beer Poortugael highlighted the serious predicament faced by members of the civilian population:

The situation of an inhabitant of an occupied country is not very different from that of a paroled prisoner. He still enjoys relative freedom but he does not dare to cross certain barriers: geographical barriers and moral barriers. He remains in the country, he sees all that happens, but woe to him if he ever opens his mouth. He would be immediately brought before a war council which knows only the penalty of death. And do you think it right that this same man, upon whom the enemy imposes the obligation of silence regarding the movements and situation of the occupying army, should be forced by this same enemy to communicate the movements of his countrymen or any other important information concerning them? In my opinion this would be immoral in the highest degree. That cannot become law. It is not for us to create an incubus.[84]

The delegates were at risk of creating a 'fatal position' for the inhabitants of an occupied territory: 'on the one hand, if he betrays his country he will be guillotined, hung or imprisoned for life; on the other hand, if he refuses he will be shot'.[85] He seemed to take some comfort from the view of Yermolov of Russia that 'forced services' would not be demanded where volunteers could be found and money used to obtain information; this would mean 'only as an exceptional case that recourse will be had to this monstrous threat'.[86]

The delegations of Switzerland and France supported the Dutch proposal. The Swiss delegate Colonel Borel endorsed the position that 'if absolutely necessary one can do without the services of guides when it would not be possible to procure them otherwise than by compulsion'.[87] Forcing assistance from the population in military operations was inhumane and 'of little or no significance' from an operational perspective:

volunteer service only produces good results and the employment of force yields bad results. That is true particularly in the matter of the employment of guides, for a measure of this kind realized by means of compulsion is always aleatory; it may become dangerous for the one who has recourse to it; it will be easily replaced to-day by maps, reconnaissance, etc.[88]

He also took the view that the 1899 Hague Regulations, specifically Articles 44 and 52, 'in a wholly general way forbid already the employment of force to obtain services such as those of a guide against his own country'.[89] In particular, he disagreed that providing information in this way was not considered armed service or was somehow less serious: 'it is an incontestable fact that in guiding the enemy an individual may do infinitely more serious harm to his country and thus commit a greater crime than if he were to fight in a line of riflemen or artillerists'.[90] The Swiss delegation did not want their acceptance of the Dutch article to cast any doubt on the meaning of the original Article 44, which in its view 'forbids the belligerents to require of the population of the enemy State any act whatsoever connected with the military operations'.[91]

[83] Ibid. [84] Ibid. [85] Ibid. [86] Ibid 120–1. [87] Ibid. [88] Ibid.
[89] Ibid. [90] Ibid 122. [91] Ibid.

The delegate of France, General Amourel, took a similar view with regard to both the need for using guides and the relevance of the 1899 Hague Regulations. With regard to the latter, he put it that 'the use of forced guides constitutes a useless violence in contradiction with the very spirit of the Regulations of 1899'.[92] This view was based on the possibility of finding volunteer guides, whether paid or not, the availability of maps, and the communications which armies maintain in the theatre of operations.[93] Forced guides were also potentially harmful, and could lead an army 'to destruction'.[94] General Amourel put it that 'such guides are often more dangerous than useful for those who employ them when they are recruited in a patriotic and fanatic population'.[95] He sought agreement from the other delegates that the use of forced guides be 'henceforth forbidden'.[96]

The discussion of the proposals by the Netherlands, Germany, and Austria-Hungary continued into the fourth meeting of the First Subcommission. President Beernaert proposed a compromise wording in the form of a single article that would replace Article 44, but would merge with the original rule with the Dutch proposal:

> It is forbidden to force the inhabitants of occupied territory to take part personally, either directly or indirectly, collectively or individually, in military operations against their country and to demand of them information in view of such operations.[97]

Having described as 'antipodal' the Dutch proposal and the mooted Austro-Hungarian amendment on adding 'as combatants', the President clearly favoured the former of these opposing provisions.[98] Beernaert explained that military operations were not to be interpreted narrowly:

> They refer not only to the act of carrying arms and fighting, but to all personal cooperation demanded of the inhabitant against his country, works of fortification, strategic routes, and above all the requisitions, under threats, of guides or information, that is to say, acts of felony contrary to honor and endangering life.[99]

He reiterated, though, that belligerents would remain permitted to make requisitions under Article 52.[100]

President Beernaert spoke of the likely fate that would befall those who collaborated with the enemy, whether voluntarily or under compulsion. 'It is certain', he put it, 'that the inhabitant who has betrayed his country, even though compelled to do so, may be executed by his own troops'.[101] How could such a situation, where an inhabitant might be exposed 'equally on both sides through no fault of his own', be reconciled with the provisions of the Hague Regulations which 'solemnly guarantees to him life, liberty and honor?'[102] He warned strongly against permitting forced collaboration in a treaty:

> Permit me to call attention again to the new character which the requisition of a guide by the enemy would take if it were made henceforth by virtue of a world convention. It would

92 Ibid. 93 Ibid. 94 Ibid 123. 95 Ibid 126. 96 Ibid 123.

97 Fourth Meeting of the Second Commission: First Subcommission, 31 July 1907, *The Proceedings of the Hague Peace Conferences: The Conference of 1907* (n 63) 131.

98 Ibid 130. 99 Ibid 131. 100 Ibid. 101 Ibid 132. 102 Ibid.

no longer be a question of an act of force, of an act of violence explicable if not justifiable by a situation which would admit of no deliberation. Each of our countries would admit by a solemn act that its children could be required to inflict upon it perhaps a mortal blow.[103]

The force of his arguments did not persuade all the delegates to support his proposed rewording, although the 1907 Hague Regulations did ultimately reflect the content of Beernaert's proposed compromise article.

The delegate of Austria-Hungary, von Gieslingen, expressed his delegation's opposition to the inclusion of a prohibition of demanding information concerning military operations from the inhabitants of occupied territory.[104] The existing restrictions had gone far enough and 'more restrictive stipulations would compromise in a scarcely justifiable manner the freedom of action of troop commanders without increasing the protection of the inhabitants of occupied territory'.[105] In emphasising military imperatives, von Gieslingen put it that the gathering of information from civilians or prisoners of war 'cannot be relinquished', as one 'cannot refuse to troops the means of accomplishing their duties'.[106] The lives of those troops needed to be taken into account.

The existence and the fate of a body of troops, composed of several thousand men seems to us to merit at least as much consideration as the conscience of a peasant under interrogation, a conscience which will be easily tranquilized by the compulsion under which its possessor acts.[107]

von Gieslingen also suggested that a defence of duress to civilians who divulge information should be available.

When one yields to superior force he cannot be accused of failing in a patriotic duty, and his guilt is not established by any code if his offence has been committed under the domination of an irresistible compulsion.[108]

The Lieber Code similarly considered that civilians could be compelled to act as guides, but that punishment would be excluded for such individuals.[109]

During the debate on Beernaert's proposed combined article, the President confirmed that voluntary collaboration was not prohibited by this provision. When it was remarked by Réchid Bey, the representative of Turkey, that the article concerned only 'forced services', and that 'the prohibition cannot be applied to services offered voluntarily and without compulsion', the President agreed that there can be 'no doubt on this point. To accept and to demand are two entirely different things.'[110] This was and to a large extent remains the crux of how international humanitarian law treats the phenomenon of cooperation with an adversary during armed conflict. In 1907, though, upon the first vote on the Belgian proposal in the First Subcommission, eighteen delegations supported it, with fifteen against.[111] The

103 Ibid. 104 Ibid 133. 105 Ibid. 106 Ibid. 107 Ibid.
108 Ibid. 109 Lieber Code, arts 93–97.
110 Fourth Meeting of the Second Commission: First Subcommission, 31 July 1907, *The Proceedings of the Hague Peace Conferences: The Conference of 1907* (n 63) 133.
111 Ibid 135–6.

text was then abandoned due to 'the smallness of this majority and with a view to reach a more complete accord'.[112] The focus returned to the Dutch and German articles with a continued divergence of views in the Second Commission of the Peace Conference.

In opening the debate at the Second Commission, its President, Beernaert, noted the importance and the 'long discussions' that had been generated by the proposals on restricting the use of civilians either in military operations against their own country or for the purpose of gathering intelligence.[113] The issue of guides had been left unresolved at the First Peace Conference, leaving ambiguity as to whether a belligerent could 'require the inhabitants of occupied territory to serve as guides for his troops or furnish them with information looking toward military operations'.[114] Beernaert reminded the delegates that the Austro-Hungarian amendment sought to limit the scope of the German proposal, whereas the Netherlands' proposed article sought to 'solve the question in a humanitarian sense and to respect the conscience of the inhabitants of occupied territories as is intended by the Convention of 1899'.[115] It was no easy task for the Second Commission to resolve these issues, given that the proposals revealed 'diametrically opposite tendencies'.[116]

The Russian delegate could not accept any amendment or addition to Article 44 of the 1899 Hague Regulations, but was amenable to it being replaced by Germany's proposed Article 22a.[117] Major General Baron von Gieslingen voiced Austria-Hungary's support for this approach, although President Beernaert noted that this sidestepped 'the question of the use of guides and of exacted information, without solving it either affirmatively or negatively'.[118] With other delegates also expressing support for this Russian suggestion, den Beer Poortugael spoke up in order to gain further backing for the Dutch proposal.[119] He reminded the conference of how it was prohibited in a number of countries to 'force inhabitants to betray their country'.[120] He put it that:

> [i]f in the occupying army, the information and spy service is well regulated, it will find many cosmopolitans, individuals without heart and without country, Judases who would betray even the Messiah for a sequin. If this service is not well regulated, whose is the fault? Should the inhabitants who must remain apart from the struggle be forced to supply the lack of instruction and foresight of the invader? If a State has not sufficient means to make war let it keep the peace or make peace. It is not for us to make war easy. The best means the belligerent has to obtain his end in the minimum of time is to prevent the inhabitants of an occupied territory from going to join the armed forces of the adversary. To that end there is no more efficacious means than to pay in cash for everything that one takes and never to force the inhabitants to commit villainies.[121]

He added that '*to force the inhabitants* means nothing but threatening them with death and that the threat in a war is followed very closely by execution'.[122] The

[112] Second Meeting of the Second Commission, 14 August 1907, *The Proceedings of the Hague Peace Conferences: The Conference of 1907* (n 63) 9.
[113] Ibid. [114] Ibid. [115] Ibid.
[116] Ibid. For a summation of developments up to this point see ibid 21–2. [117] Ibid.
[118] Ibid 10. [119] Ibid. [120] Ibid. [121] Ibid.
[122] Ibid 11 (original emphasis).

Dutch delegation accepted the permissibility of persons voluntarily acting as informers, but could not countenance compelling civilians to provide information to an adversary.

The representative of the Netherlands also took the opportunity to remind the delegates of the rules in the proposed 1874 Russian Project which prohibited treachery and cruelty towards the enemy, and stated that '[t]o threaten with death one who does not wish to become a traitor is at the same time violence and cruelty'.[123] It would not be acceptable to make such threats against 'peaceable inhabitants who have done no wrong and forcing them to treason'.[124] He received loud applause from those in attendance with his concluding remarks:

> War is made by State upon State and not upon individuals, private persons, inhabitants of the country. This is the fundamental principle of the law of war that we find repeatedly throughout the minutes of our Conferences. What should we think of all that? Shall they be but phrases, but empty words? [...] If it is true that war is made by State upon State, let us not force inhabitants to mingle in the struggle; above all let us not force them to commit villanies [sic].[125]

With a number of delegates expressing support for the original Netherlands' proposal of Article 44a, it was put to a vote as to whether the German and Dutch articles should be adopted as two separate articles.[126] Twenty-three voted in favour, with nine against and one abstaining.[127] A lack of unanimity continued in the subsequent plenary session of the conference.

While Germany's proposed Article 22a was accepted at plenary without discussion, and became Article 23(h) of the 1907 Hague Regulations,[128] the Netherland's Article 44a encountered some hostility and a number of delegations made known their reservations to this article.[129] The delegate of Austria-Hungary stated that his country could not consent to the article, as they had agreed to Article 22a on the basis that the original Article 44 would be retained, while several other delegates simply stated that their delegation 'makes reservations on the subject of the new wording of the said Article 44a'.[130] The President closed the discussion of Article 44a by noting that '[t]he Conference records the reservations just expressed'.[131] When a vote was taken on the complete set of amendments to the 1899 Hague Regulations, thirty-five delegations voted in favour without reservations, whereas ten delegations voted in favour but with reservations.[132] The overwhelming majority of those reservations

[123] Ibid. [124] Ibid. [125] Ibid. [126] Ibid.

[127] Ibid 12. In favour: Belgium, Brazil, China, Cuba, Denmark, Dominican Republic, France, Greece, Haiti, Italy, Luxemburg, Mexico, Norway, Panama, Paraguay, Netherlands, Persia, Serbia, Siam, Sweden, Switzerland, Spain, Turkey. Against: Austria-Hungary, Bulgaria, Germany, Great Britain, Montenegro, Portugal, Roumania, Russia, United States of America. Abstaining: Japan.

[128] Article 23(h) of the 1907 Hague Regulations states that: 'A belligerent is likewise forbidden to compel the nationals of the adverse party to take part in operations of war directed against their country, even when they have been in the service before the commencement of the war.'

[129] Fourth Meeting of the Plenary Conference, 17 August 1907, *The Proceedings of the Hague Peace Conferences: The Conference of 1907,* Volume I (OUP 1921) 84. For a summary of the developments to date see ibid 97–9.

[130] Ibid. Those States were Montenegro, Russia, Roumania, and Bulgaria. [131] Ibid.

[132] Ibid 85.

were in relation to Article 44a, which became Article 44 in the final 1907 Hague Regulations. The dissatisfaction with the provision was further evidenced by Russia, Montenegro, Japan, Germany, and Austria-Hungary maintaining their reservations to Article 44 on signature or ratification of Hague Convention IV, to which the 1907 Regulations are annexed.[133] Aside from one other reservation by Turkey to Article 3, Article 44 is the only article in the 1907 Hague Regulations to be formally objected to in this manner.

It is not clear how these reservations serve to modify or exclude the legal rule, as they mostly referred back to the statement of reservation noted in the minutes of the plenary session of the Second Peace Conference, which merely stated the existence of the reservation rather than elaborate on its substance.[134] The States parties in question did not state explicitly in their reservations that they did not consider themselves bound by the article, despite the clear opposition that was expressed by a number of them at various times. Article 44 of the 1907 Hague Regulations as eventually adopted constitutes an unprecedented legal restriction on occupying powers seeking to gather information from the civilian population. The simplicity of the provision belies the long, complex, and fraught debates that lead to its eventual adoption.[135]

2.1.3 Geneva Conventions 1949 and Additional Protocols 1977

The rapid development which international humanitarian law underwent with the adoption of the four 1949 Geneva Conventions after the Second World War did not involve any fundamental change in how this body of law approaches the use and recruitment of informers during situations of armed conflict. It has remained permissible for parties to an armed conflict to use civilians or detained persons as sources of information or as informers for the purpose of gathering intelligence. There was no altering of the basic premise that such was both allowable and necessary; with regard to prisoners of war, for example, the United Kingdom delegate at the 1949 Geneva Diplomatic Conference observed that states 'would always try to obtain military information from them'.[136] To think otherwise, would be 'to harbour illusions'.[137]

[133] Table of States Signatories of the Conventions, Declaration and Final Act of the Second Peace Conference, *The Proceedings of the Hague Peace Conferences: The Conference of 1907* (n 129) 701. See also James Brown Scott (ed), *The Hague Conventions and Declarations of 1899 and 1907, accompanied by Tables of Signatures, Ratifications and Adhesions of the Various Powers, and Texts of Reservations* (OUP 1915) 131–2.

[134] Ibid.

[135] There are some slight inconsistencies in the versions of Article 44 of the Hague Regulations included in the documentation published at the time, which is likely due to different translations of the authoritative French text. Compare Annex B, Fourth Meeting of the Plenary Conference, 17 August 1907, *The Proceedings of the Hague Peace Conferences: The Conference of 1907* (n 129) 108; IV Convention Respecting the Law and Customs of War on Land, *The Proceedings of the Hague Peace Conferences: The Conference of 1907* (n 129) 629; A. Pearce Higgins, *The Hague Peace Conferences and Other International Conferences Concerning the Laws and Usages of War: Texts of Conventions with Commentaries* (CUP 1909) 245; Scott, *The Hague Conventions and Declarations of 1899 and 1907* (n 133) 123.

[136] Committee II (Prisoners of War), Fifth Meeting, 29 April 1949, *Final Record* (n 1) 251.

[137] Ibid.

The new treaties did clarify, however, that the means of intelligence gathering, to borrow a phrase concerning the means of warfare, are 'not unlimited'.[138] In addition to elaborating specific prohibitions aimed at ensuring humane treatment, the 1949 Geneva Conventions confirm that civilians and prisoners of war in the context of international armed conflicts cannot be compelled to provide information. The adoption of the 1949 Geneva Conventions was also significant in that the previous hostility to the relevant Hague rules had evaporated by this time. This was most likely on account of the frequent cruelty that had accompanied the compulsion and coercion of the victims of armed conflict that characterised so much conduct in the Second World War.

This section begins with a discussion of the rules applicable to prisoners of war as a source of information. The 1899 and 1907 Hague Regulations contain several rules concerning prisoners of war and their protection, although neither includes a clear prohibition on compelling prisoners to provide information, as they do for civilians in occupied territories. The 1880 Oxford Manual had proposed that prisoners of war should not be compelled 'to give information about their country or their army'.[139] While this rule was not replicated in the 1899 and 1907 Regulations, both these instruments include a general rule that prisoners of war must be treated humanely which would be of obvious relevance to interrogations.[140] The 1929 Prisoner of War Convention provides that a prisoner of war when interrogated need only to declare 'his true names and rank, or his regimental number', and in what might have been then interpreted as an insurmountable obstacle to obtaining intelligence from prisoners, sets down that '[n]o pressure shall be exercised on prisoners to obtain information regarding the situation in their armed forces or their country. Prisoners who refuse to reply may not be threatened, insulted, or exposed to unpleasantness or disadvantages of any kind whatsoever.'[141] This rule did not prohibit voluntary disclosures of information by prisoners, but neither did it prevent in practice the pressuring of prisoners for intelligence as occurred during the Second World War.[142] Intelligence gathering was one of the reasons which lead to prisoners of war being 'ill-treated and tortured and murdered, not only in defiance of the well-established rules of international law, but in complete disregard of the elementary dictates of humanity'.[143]

The Third Geneva Convention of 1949 sets out the modern standard of what is required of prisoners of war when questioned during their captivity. A prisoner is bound to give only 'surname, first names and rank, date of birth, and army, regimental, personal or serial number, or failing this, equivalent information'.[144] This comprises an elaboration of the similar provision in the 1929 Convention,

[138] Hague Regulations 1907, art 22.

[139] Article 70, Oxford Manual on the Laws of War on Land (British Institute of International Law, 1880).

[140] 1899 and 1907 Hague Regulations, art 4.

[141] Convention relative to the Treatment of Prisoners of War, Geneva, 27 July 1929, art 5.

[142] See discussion in Chapter 1.

[143] International Military Tribunal (Nuremberg), *Judgment and Sentences* (n 15) 225.

[144] Third Geneva Convention, art 17.

but still remains in keeping with national articulations of the duty of members of armed forces to give only such minimal information when questioned. The Code of Conduct for Members of the Armed Forces of the United States, for example, imposes the following ethical duties:

> I will give no information or take part in any action which might be harmful to my comrades. [...] When questioned, should I become a prisoner of war, I am required to give name, rank, service number, and date of birth. I will evade answering further questions to the utmost of my ability. I will make no oral or written statements disloyal to my country and its allies or harmful to their cause.[145]

Prisoners may find themselves in the invidious position of having to choose which of the competing demands of opposing parties to an armed conflict to satisfy, which is especially daunting where the detaining power disregards the rules concerning humane treatment of prisoners of war in order to gather information.

Article 17 of the Third Geneva Convention was specifically developed with this context in mind:

> No physical or mental torture, nor any other form of coercion, may be inflicted on prisoners of war to secure from them information of any kind whatever. Prisoners of war who refuse to answer may not be threatened, insulted, or exposed to any unpleasant or disadvantageous treatment of any kind.[146]

The Convention does not prohibit the seeking of information from prisoners—'it would be unrealistic to expect that the Detaining Power would not try to take advantage of its control of prisoners to discover details regarding the military planning of the enemy, as well as any other useful information'[147]—but restricts the ways in which this may be done. It prohibits both physical and mental torture and any other form of coercion of prisoners for the purpose of obtaining any kind of information, and not merely that relating to 'the situation in their armed forces or their country', as per the 1929 Convention.[148] A prisoner of war who provides information in order to avoid mistreatment runs the risk of prosecution upon repatriation, although it would be expected that the defence of duress would be available in such circumstances.[149]

Turning to civilians as potential informers during armed conflict, the Fourth Geneva Convention contains largely similar rules prohibiting the use of torture or coercion against protected persons for purposes of gathering intelligence. While

[145] President of the United States Executive Order 10631, 17 August 1955 (as amended by Executive Order 12017, 3 November 1977), reprinted in Raymond Lech, *Broken Soldiers* (University of Illinois Press 2000) 297–8.

[146] Third Geneva Convention, art 17.

[147] Silvia Sanna, 'Treatment of Prisoners of War' in Andrew Clapham, Paola Gaeta, and Marco Sassòli (eds), *The 1949 Geneva Conventions: A Commentary* (OUP 2015) 977, 992.

[148] Jean Pictet (ed), *Commentary: III Geneva Convention, Relative to the Treatment of Prisoners of War* (ICRC 1960) 163.

[149] For an articulation of this defence to a criminal charge see Rome Statute of the International Criminal Court (1998), UN Doc. A/CONF.183/9, entered into force 1 July 2002, 2187 U.N.T.S. 90, art 31(1)(d).

no equivalent to the 1929 Prisoners of War Convention came into force in the inter-war period, the Draft Civilians Convention proposed by the International Committee of the Red Cross (ICRC) in 1934 had retained the rule in Article 44 of the 1907 Hague Regulations forbidding the compelling of civilians to provide information concerning the army or its defence.[150] The Fourth Geneva Convention includes a broader prohibition than the Hague precedent; according to Article 31, '[n]o physical or moral coercion shall be exercised against protected persons, in particular to obtain information from them or from third parties'.[151] The records of the 1949 Geneva Diplomatic Conference do not reveal any discussion of this provision and the wording remained exactly as had been proposed by the ICRC in its 1948 Draft Civilians Convention.[152] During the preparatory work leading to the Draft Convention, there was some suggestion that such a strong prohibition might not be acceptable to States. The report of the Conference of Government Experts convened in Geneva in 1947 at the invitation of the ICRC includes the following observations on an earlier incarnation of Article 31:

> a distinction should be drawn between information of a general kind and that of a family nature. As regards the first class of information, civilians may be submitted to a certain degree of constraint, in so far as this does not include physical or moral torture. Any form of constraint to obtain information of a family nature from civilians is, however, prohibited.[153]

Such a view did not prevail and by the following year the ICRC had adopted the wording that appears in Article 31, together with a prohibition of torture and corporal punishment. It had been persuaded by the view expressed at a subsequent meeting of Government Experts in 1947 that it was necessary 'to lay down the categorical prohibition of any physical or moral torture, as also of any other form of coercion, whatever its reason or purpose'.[154]

The prohibition in Article 31 of the Fourth Geneva Convention of using physical or moral coercion against protected persons, in particular for the purpose of gathering information, is significant both because of the wording used and where the article is placed in the treaty. The article is broader in its scope than Article 44 of the 1907 Hague Regulations and therefore an 'enormous step forward in the protection of civilians'.[155] The authoritative Pictet *Commentary* explains its scope:

[150] See Projet de Convention Internationale Concernant la Condition et la Protection des Civils de Nationalité Ennemie qui se trouvent sur le Territoire d'un Belligérant ou sur un Territoire Occupé par Lui, Comité International de la Croix-Rouge, *Quinzième Conférence Internationale de la Croix-Rouge Tenue à Tokio Du 20 Au 29 Octobre 1934, Compte Rendu* (International Publishing and Printing Co. 1935), art 18.

[151] Fourth Geneva Convention, art 31.

[152] See Draft Convention for the Protection of Civilian Persons in Time of War, Draft as approved by the XVIIth International Red Cross Conference, *Final Record of the Diplomatic Conference of Geneva of 1949*, Vol. I (Federal Political Department, Berne) 118, art 29.

[153] International Committee of the Red Cross, *Report on the Work of the Conference of Government Experts for the Study of the Conventions for the Protection of War Victims, Geneva, April 14–26, 1947* (ICRC 1947) 276.

[154] International Committee of the Red Cross, *Draft Revised or New Conventions for the Protection of War Victims* (ICRC May 1948) 166.

[155] Iris van der Heijden, 'Other Issues Relating to the Treatment of Civilians in Enemy Hands' in Clapham, Gaeta, and Sassòli, *The 1949 Geneva Conventions: A Commentary* (n 147) 1242, 1255.

The prohibition laid down in this Article is general in character and applies to both physical and moral forms of coercion. It covers all cases, whether the pressure is direct or indirect, obvious or hidden [. . .]. Furthermore, coercion is forbidden for any purpose or motive whatever. The authors of the Convention had mainly in mind coercion aimed at obtaining information, work or support for an ideological or political idea.[156]

The reference to both physical and moral coercion, and Pictet's understanding of this phrase prevents any narrow interpretation of the rule as addressing physical violence only, as might have occurred with Article 44 of the Hague Regulations with its explicit reference to 'force'. Article 31 does not limit its prohibition to information concerning the occupied state's army or its means of defence. While the reservations to Article 44 meant that the lawfulness of using guides was not fully resolved by the Hague treaties, no reservations were entered to Article 31 of the Fourth Geneva Convention. Pictet's *Commentary* states that the use of guides 'is now forbidden' on account of Article 31, having noted 'the custom, hitherto accepted in practice but disputed in theory' of forcing inhabitants in occupied territories to serve in this way.[157] The reach of Article 31 goes beyond protected persons in occupied territories, as it is found in Section I of Part III of the Fourth Geneva Convention which is also addressed to civilian aliens found on the territory of a party to the conflict.

In interpreting the prohibition of physical and moral coercion in Article 31, the most serious forms of such coercion would also be covered by Article 32 of the Fourth Geneva Convention, which includes prohibitions of murder, torture, corporal punishment, and 'any other measures of brutality whether applied by civilian agents'. Common Article 3 of the 1949 Geneva Conventions, applicable to non-international armed conflicts, similarly prohibits such violent acts against those taking no active part in hostilities, although no corresponding rule against 'moral coercion' is found here. The connection between torture and other serious forms of ill-treatment and attempts at gathering information is well-recognised in international law; torture has been defined 'any act by which severe pain or suffering, whether physical or mental, is intentionally inflicted on a person for such purposes as obtaining from him or a third person information or a confession'.[158] While the prohibition of torture is absolute in nature and comprises customary international law,[159] the rule against coercion does not have such standing.

Despite the language of Article 31, the prohibition of physical or moral coercion is not absolute. According to the Pictet *Commentary* 'there is no question of absolute prohibition':

The prohibition only applies in so far as the other provisions of the Convention do not implicitly or explicitly authorize a resort to coercion. Thus, Article 31 is subject to the unspoken

[156] Jean S. Pictet (ed), *Commentary; IV Geneva Convention, Relative to the Protection of Civilian Person in Times of War* (ICRC 1958) 219–20.

[157] Ibid 220.

[158] Convention Against Torture and Other Cruel, Inhuman or Degrading Treatment or Punishment (1984) 1465 U.N.T.S. 85, art 1(1).

[159] See Jean-Marie Henckaerts and Louise Doswald-Beck, *Customary International Humanitarian Law, Volume I: Rules* (CUP 2005) 315.

reservation that force is permitted whenever it is necessary to use it in the application of measures taken under the Convention.[160]

Coercion might thus be used to take permitted measures such as evacuation, internment, assigned residence, or removing public officials from their posts in occupied territories.[161] The use of 'in particular' in Article 31, as opposed to 'in order', gives a misleading impression as to the nature of the prohibition on the use of physical or moral coercion. There is little doubt, however, that protected persons cannot be coerced for the stated reason of providing information to a party to an armed conflict of which they are not nationals.

The precise meaning of moral coercion, where such conduct does not rise to the level of torture or other forms of cruel treatment, is elusive, although some guidance is available. The Pictet *Commentary*, for example, refers to direct and indirect pressure, and to that which is 'obvious or hidden', giving the example of 'a threat to subject other persons to severe measures, deprival of rations or of work'.[162] A more recent elaboration of the meaning of coercion has been developed in relation to the crime of rape in the Rome Statute of the International Criminal Court.[163] According to the Elements of this crime, the act must have been committed 'by force, or by threat of force or coercion, such as that caused by fear of violence, duress, detention, psychological oppression or abuse of power, against such person or another person, or by taking advantage of a coercive environment'.[164] This was influenced by the *Akayesu* Trial Chamber judgment of the International Criminal Tribunal for Rwanda,[165] which had stated that 'coercive circumstances need not be evidenced by a show of physical force. Threats, intimidation, extortion and other forms of duress which prey on fear or desperation may constitute coercion, and coercion may be inherent in certain circumstances, such as armed conflict or [...] military presence.'[166] In applying the concept of a coercive environment, the Appeals Chamber of the International Criminal Tribunal for the Former Yugoslavia (ICTY) found that the conditions of detention for certain victims of rape amounted to 'circumstances that were so coercive as to negate any possibility of consent'.[167] Such interpretations of coercion are instructive for the practices under consideration, even though they relate to a different context which involves patently criminal acts.

160 Pictet, *Commentary IV Geneva Convention* (n 156) 220.

161 Ibid.

162 Ibid 219–20.

163 Rome Statute of the International Criminal Court, art 8(2)(b)(xxii). See further Wolfgang Schomburg and Ines Peterson, 'Genuine Consent to Sexual Violence under International Criminal Law' (2007) 101(1) American Journal of International Law 121.

164 *Elements of Crimes*, International Criminal Court, 2011, 28.

165 Knut Dörmann, *Elements of War Crimes under the Rome Statute of the International Criminal Court* (CUP 2002) 328.

166 *Prosecutor v Akayesu*, Case No. ICTR-96-4-T, Trial Chamber I, Judgment, 2 September 1998, para 688. See also *Prosecutor v Bemba*, Case No. ICC-01/05-01/08, Trial Chamber III, Judgment, 21 March 2016, paras 103–104; *Prosecutor v Bemba Gombo*, Case No. ICC-01/05/-01/08, Decision Pursuant to Article 61(7)(a) and (b) of the Rome Statute on the Charges, Pre-Trial Chamber II, 15 June 2009, para 162.

167 *Prosecutor v Kunarac, Kovac and Vukovic*, Case No. IT-96-23 & IT-96-23/1-A, Appeals Chamber, Judgment, 12 June 2002, para 132.

Moral coercion could encompass threats of physical violence against a person or a third party, as well as intimidation, harassment, the instilling of fear, or the denial or threatened denial of access to basic necessities, services, or employment. With regard to inherently coercive circumstances or a 'coercive environment', a situation of armed conflict might be considered as such, particularly a situation of military occupation, given the power asymmetry that exists between an occupying power and the civilian population. It may be going too far to suggest that the mere request for information by members of an armed force to a protected person in a context of armed conflict or military occupation would amount to moral coercion in and of itself. Such an interpretation, in the absence of other coercive elements or where the official took advantage of the coercive circumstances, would almost negate the rule in Article 31, as it would amount effectively to prohibiting the seeking of information from protected persons during an armed conflict except in the most benign of circumstances. A key element in assessing whether such a request might amount to moral coercion would be whether the protected person could refuse the request without suffering any negative consequences. But, as was shown in Chapter 1, the recruitment of would-be informers often involves the deliberate exploiting of individuals that find themselves in situations of vulnerability.

Military manuals offer examples of what states perceive as lawful means of recruiting informers. According to a US counterinsurgency manual, informants or deserters from insurgent groups might be attracted 'by arousing fear of prosecution or by offering rewards'.[168] The 2015 US *Law of War Manual* notes that bribery and other rewards are permitted, including those 'intended to corrupt enemy combatants or civilians'.[169] With regard to captured enemy personnel in non-international armed conflicts, the *Manual* recommends 'a combination of threats of criminal prosecution and inducements', such as amnesties or monetary rewards.[170] In addition to obviously unlawful practices such as torture and ill-treatment, the practice of recruiting informers has also involved such bribery and blackmail, as well as other threats or offers of various kinds.[171] David French recounts how the British Special Branch in Malaya recruited agents in the Malayan Communist Party (MCP) by using bribery and threats of 'long prison sentences if potential agents did not cooperate, or exposure to the MCP as "traitors" with the resulting likelihood of assassination'.[172]

Contemporary examples can also be found of the coerced use of civilians as 'guides' by armed forces in occupied territory. The United Nations Independent Commission of Inquiry on the 2014 Gaza conflict documented accounts of Palestinian civilians accompanying Israeli soldiers and providing information during the conduct of searches,[173] and according to testimony, coercion has been used in order to achieve such cooperation:

168 Field Manual 3–24, *Counterinsurgency* (Headquarters Department of the Army 2006) 1–19.

169 United States, *Law of War Manual* (n 16) 310.

170 Ibid 1040.

171 Peter Gill and Mark Phythian, *Intelligence in an Insecure World* (2nd edn, Polity Press 2012) 172; Max Hastings, *The Secret War: Spies, Codes and Guerillas 1939–1945* (William Collins 2015) xviii.

172 David French, *The British Way in Counter-Insurgency, 1945–1967* (OUP 2011) 31.

173 *Report of the detailed findings of the independent commission of inquiry established pursuant to Human Rights Council resolution S-21/1*, A/HRC/29/CRP.4, 22 June 2015, para 327.

I definitely remember three cases, at least, where a farmer was taken and literally forced to come with us and show us where there are caves, where there are water cisterns, since we had intelligence information about terrorists supposedly hiding out in them. [...] he didn't want to come with us. He also said: I don't want to be seen with you, I'll be seen as a collaborator. I don't want to go with you. And he was still forced to come.[174]

Assessing whether a request for assistance amounts to coercion will depend on the specific instance and the context in which it is made. In the absence of overt threats, it may be difficult to draw a line between prohibited moral coercion and permitted inducements, such as offers of money or access to medical treatment that might not otherwise be available to a civilian. This ambiguity on the part of international humanitarian law grants considerable leeway to parties to an armed conflict in recruiting informers with the evident risks of abuse and exploitation of civilians.

The relevant Geneva and Hague rules apply mainly to persons who find themselves under the authority of foreign power during an armed conflict, whether as prisoners of war, civilians in occupied territory, or civilian aliens on enemy territory. Despite such persons not owing any allegiance to the detaining or occupying power,[175] they are generally obliged to obey the lawful directions of those powers and can be subject to proceedings and punishment for failure to do so. Traditionally, a civilian in occupied territory who engaged in hostile acts against an occupying power was liable to be prosecuted for 'war treason'.[176] The occupying power was entitled to take such measures against a 'war traitor' on account of the powers and duties accruing to it under the laws of occupation.[177] Violation of those same laws by the occupier by compelling the inhabitants in occupied territory to provide information puts those civilians at risk of prosecution by their own national authorities to whom a duty of allegiance is owed. Bert Röling, who sat on the Tokyo Tribunal, wrote that:

[t]he duties of the civilian population derive from their domestic law, which demands loyalty to their own national government, and which puts penalties on collaboration. International law tolerates such national law.[178]

A similar situation prevails for prisoners of war, and international humanitarian law has sought to reconcile these competing duties of obedience to the detaining power and allegiance to their own state. Civilian aliens in the territory of party to an armed

[174] *Breaking the Silence*, Testimony Catalog Number 186839 <https://www.breakingthesilence.org.il/testimonies/database/186839> accessed 28 May 2019.

[175] See for example Third Geneva Convention, art 87; 1907 Hague Regulations 1907, art 45.

[176] See Richard R. Baxter, 'The Duty of Obedience to the Belligerent Occupant' (1950) 27 British Yearbook of International Law 235; L. Oppenheim, 'On War Treason' (1917) 33 Law Quarterly Review 266; J.H. Morgan, 'War Treason' (1916) 2 Problems of the War 161; Yutaka Arai-Takahashi, *The Law of Occupation: Continuity and Change of International Humanitarian Law, and its Interaction with International Human Rights Law* (Martinus Nijhoff 2009) 43.

[177] Yves Sandoz, Christophe Swinarski, and Bruno Zimmermann (eds), *Commentary on the Additional Protocols of 8 June 1977 to the Geneva Conventions of 12 August 1949* (ICRC/Martinus Nijhoff Publishers 1987) 562–3.

[178] B.V.A. Röling, 'The Law of War and the National Jurisdiction since 1945' (1960) 100(II) Recueil de Cours 323, 404–5.

conflict might lose their rights and privileges under the Fourth Geneva Convention as protected persons if they engage in 'activities hostile to the security of the State'.[179] In the context of non-international armed conflicts and wars of national liberation on the territory of a single state, the tension that may arise between duties of obedience and allegiance based on nationality is not present in the same way. Participants in such conflicts, as well as the civilian population, will by and large share the same nationality, with the attendant duties of obedience and allegiance, although clearly they may not all profess or share the same sense of allegiance to the state.[180] With regard to the use of informers, the law applicable to such conflicts does not mirror that which applies in international armed conflicts.

Neither of the two Additional Protocols of 1977 contain equivalent articles to those of the 1949 Geneva Conventions which prohibit the coercion of prisoners of war or civilians for the purpose of gathering information. As might be expected, neither contain a prohibition on treating such persons as intelligence sources during armed conflict, bearing in mind that the concept of prisoners of war as recognised in Protocol I only extends the application of this category to so-called wars of national liberation, and not to all conflicts taking place within the territory of a state.[181] This instrument can be seen to recognise implicitly the importance of intelligence for both military and humanitarian purposes, by not outlawing the use of spies and by requiring that those planning attacks 'do everything feasible to verify that the objectives to be attacked are neither civilians nor civilian objects'.[182]

Despite the absence of any positive rule similar to Article 31 of the Fourth Geneva Convention, the prohibition of physical and moral coercion of protected persons in order to garner information can be seen as covered by the fundamental guarantees articles of both Protocols. The ICRC had proposed that such a rule be included in Protocol I, but this was considered unnecessary in light of the other prohibitions.[183] Article 75 of Protocol I and Article 4 of Protocol II notably expand the prohibitions first codified in Common Article 3 and forbid 'violence to the life, health, or physical and mental well-being of persons'.[184] In addition to specifying a range of prohibited acts, the Protocols also forbid intimidation by making threats to commit any of those acts.[185] As noted in the ICRC Commentary to the Protocols, threats may 'constitute a formidable means of pressure and undercut the other prohibitions'.[186] These more expansive prohibitions apply in non-international armed conflicts, as well as in wars of national liberation, which are treated as international conflicts under Additional Protocol I.[187]

179 Fourth Geneva Convention, art 5. See discussion in Chapter 3.

180 See *Prosecutor v Tadić*, Case No. IT-94-1-A, Appeals Chamber, Judgment, 15 July 1999, para 166.

181 See Additional Protocol I, art 44.

182 See Additional Protocol I, arts 46 and 57(2)(a)(i).

183 See CDDH/407/Rev.1 *Official Records of the Diplomatic Conference on the Reaffirmation and Development of International Humanitarian Law Applicable in Armed Conflicts, Geneva (1974–1977)*, Volume XV, 461.

184 Additional Protocol I, art 75(2)(a); Additional Protocol II, art 4.

185 Additional Protocol I, art 75(2)(e); Additional Protocol II, art 4(2)(h).

186 Sandoz, Swinarski and Zimmermann, *Commentary on the Additional Protocols* (n 177) 1376.

187 Additional Protocol I, art 1(4); Additional Protocol II, art 1(1).

The limited discussion during the drafting of the Protocols of the ICRC's proposal to include the prohibition of physical and moral coercion for purpose of gathering information prompted some revealing comments by states on the potential application of such a rule to their own nationals. Most prominently, the United States supported the deletion of the ICRC's proposed prohibition:

> Nationals of a State Party to an armed conflict could use that provision to avoid having to give evidence during an inquiry or trial. Under all national legislations, however, courts could insist on persons within their jurisdiction supplying the information necessary for the application of the law. The right to demand such information was accompanied by penal provisions including imprisonment, and that might be equated with physical coercion. Under United States law, there were, however, exceptions to that general rule. An individual was not obliged to incriminate himself in a penal case. Moreover, there were certain established privileges, such as the professional secrecy binding on lawyers and priests.[188]

The relevant provisions of the Third and Fourth Geneva Conventions 'did not of course apply to a Party's own nationals'.[189]

For the delegate of Australia, who had proposed deleting the ICRC's proposed article, the suggested prohibition of physical and moral coercion was 'far too general and quite unrealistic'.[190] In any event, 'the evils' which it sought to avoid were 'already largely covered' by the prohibition of violence to life, health, and the physical or mental well-being of persons.[191] These comments reinforce the attenuated approach of states to the regulation of conflicts on their own territory, which has been characterised by a notable reluctance to apply as extensive a set of rules as those which apply in international armed conflicts. When it comes to gathering information during such conflicts, there is no express exclusion of bribery, blackmail, or other forms of moral coercion, although the rule against violence to the 'mental well-being of persons' would clearly be relevant where non-physical coercion is used.[192] In such contexts, the human rights law obligations of a state and their applicability to the conflict also need to be considered.[193] In considering the law applicable to participation in military activities, the next section demonstrates that it may be permissible in certain circumstances in non-international armed conflicts to compel members of a non-state armed group to fight alongside state forces against their own group. Such coerced collaboration is excluded under the law of international armed conflicts.

2.2 Participation in Military Activities

The survey of various forms of wartime collaboration in Chapter 1 provided examples of instances where members of armed forces or armed opposition groups voluntarily or under compulsion joined or fought alongside forces which were

188 CDDH/III/SR.43, *Official Records of the Diplomatic Conference* (n 183) 36.
189 Ibid. 190 Ibid 40. 191 Ibid. 192 Additional Protocol II, art 4(2).
193 See Chapter 5.

previously regarded as their adversary. While this occurred on a considerable scale during the Second World War, such collaboration is less common, but not unheard of, in contemporary armed conflicts. Participation in military activities is not limited to combatants in practice, as civilians might also collaborate with an opposing side to an armed conflict by joining as fighters or contributing to military activities in other ways. This section considers how international humanitarian law addresses the use of an opposing side's personnel or civilians in military activities. While this issue did not generate as much controversy during the drafting of the early treaties on the law of armed conflict compared to the rules concerning civilians and information gathering, there were nevertheless some points of contention. A lengthier discussion of the precise meaning of the concept of direct participation in hostilities will follow in Chapter 3, in the examination of the status of collaborators, particularly civilians who contribute to military operations.

The 1949 Geneva Conventions prohibit and criminalise the coercing of protected persons into serving in armed forces or taking part in military operations during an international armed conflict. The Fourth Geneva Convention sets out that an occupying power cannot forcibly recruit protected persons into its armed or auxiliary forces, and that it may not compel such persons 'to undertake any work which would involve them in the obligation of taking part in military operations'.[194] The Third Geneva Convention permits the forced labour of prisoners of war, but not in work that has a 'military character or purpose'.[195] Universal criminal jurisdiction is envisaged under the Third Convention for the grave breach of 'compelling a prisoner of war to serve in the forces of the hostile Power', and under the Fourth Convention for 'compelling a protected person to serve in the forces of a hostile Power'.[196]

These treaties do not outlaw voluntary service in the forces of a hostile power. Although the Fourth Geneva Convention prohibits 'pressure or propaganda which is aimed at securing voluntary enlistment', it does not declare that such enlistment is itself unlawful. As those who would serve the enemy by fighting for it would inevitably be put in harm's way, both by taking part in military activities and in facing harsh consequences from their own side as collaborators, international humanitarian law has sought to exclude coerced collaboration of this type, at least in the context of international armed conflicts. There are no equivalent rules against forcible recruitment in non-international armed conflicts however. Additional Protocol II establishes only that children should not be recruited into armed forces or groups, or allowed to participate in hostilities.[197] The absence of similar rules reflects the refusal of states to transpose the law of international armed conflict, including the concept of prisoners of war, into non-international armed conflicts, as well as their continued assertion of a right to conscript citizens into their armed forces.[198]

194 Fourth Geneva Convention, art 51.

195 Third Geneva Convention, art 50.

196 Third Geneva Convention, art 130; Fourth Geneva Convention, art 147. See also Rome Statute of the International Criminal Court, arts 8(2)(a)(v) and 8(2)(b)(xv).

197 Additional Protocol II, art 4(3)(c). See also Additional Protocol I, art 77(2).

198 See for example Rita J. Simon and Mohamed Alaa Abdel-Moneim, *A Handbook of Military Conscription and Composition the World Over* (Lexington 2011); Pertti Joenniemi (ed), *The Changing Face of European Conscription* (Ashgate 2006).

With regard to the legal rules concerning the labour of prisoners of war, the earliest attempts at devising an international law of war sought to exclude any work that was directly connected to 'the operations of the war'.[199] The formulation of Article 6 of both the 1899 and 1907 Hague Regulations, that the labour of prisoners must not be excessive and 'shall have no connection with the operations of war', was seen as overly strict, given that much of the work done by prisoners of war could be interpreted as being connected to the war in some way.[200] Accordingly, the 1929 Prisoner of War Convention sought to bring some clarity by including specific examples:

> Work done by prisoners of war shall have no direct connection with the operations of the war. In particular, it is forbidden to employ prisoners in the manufacture or transport of arms or munitions of any kind, or on the transport of material destined for combatant units.[201]

The precise meaning of this rule was contested during the Second World War, after which the element of compulsion was emphasised in the relevant article of the Third Geneva Convention.[202] With regard to prohibited forms of labour, some delegates at the 1949 Diplomatic Conference had sought to exclude the removal of mines from the proposed list.[203] Others expressed concern that the terms 'military character or purpose', as ultimately used in Article 50 of the Third Convention, were 'so restrictive that violation would be practically inevitable'.[204]

At the 1949 Diplomatic Conference, the delegate of Switzerland emphasised the limited agency of prisoners when addressing whether the Convention should specify forms of labour that prisoners could be compelled to undertake or instead those in which they could be employed:

> If it was desired to make a distinction between 'obliged' and 'employed', and to allow prisoners of war to perform work other than that specified in Article 42, account must be taken not only of the degree of individual liberty enjoyed by the prisoner and of how far he was free to choose, but also of the fact that, although a prisoner, he was still in the service of the Power in whose armed forces he had fought. The Detaining Power must not be given the possibility of bringing pressure to bear on prisoners of war to induce them to carry out work which they could not be compelled to do.[205]

This was a minority view amongst the delegates which did not prevail; the UK delegate responded curtly that 'prisoners should have complete liberty in the matter of choosing voluntary work'.[206] The delegate of the ICRC shared the Swiss perspective and pointed out that such freedom of choice was not always to a prisoner's advantage.[207]

Nevertheless, the Third Geneva Convention lists certain types of labour that prisoners may be compelled to undertake, and prohibited types of work, particularly that of a military character or purpose. This approach effectively allows prisoners

[199] See Brussels Declaration 1874, arts 25–26.
[200] Pictet, *Commentary III Geneva Convention* (n 148) 264.
[201] Prisoners of War Convention 1929, art 31.
[202] Third Geneva Convention, art 50. See Pictet, *Commentary III Geneva Convention* (n 148) 264.
[203] Committee II, *Prisoners of War*, 23rd Meeting, 4 July 1949, *Official Records* (n 1) 342–3.
[204] Ibid 343. [205] Ibid. [206] Ibid. [207] Ibid.

of war to voluntarily take part in work of any kind.[208] Unquestionably, the practice during the Second World War of compelling captured prisoners of war to serve in the armed forces of a hostile power would contravene both the 1929 and 1949 Conventions; as a US Military Tribunal held in 1949, 'it is not illegal to recruit prisoners of war who volunteer to fight against their own country, but pressure or coercion to compel such persons to enter into armed forces obviously violates international law'.[209] It has been suggested that the prohibition on the renunciation of rights in Article 7 of the Third Geneva Convention would prevent prisoners of war, even those forcibly conscripted in the first place, from 'joining the enemy forces by their own free will'.[210] The ICRC has acknowledged but not proffered a firm view of this interpretation, although it has queried whether persons finding themselves in such vulnerable circumstances can truly make such decisions freely.[211]

Civilians in occupied territory cannot be compelled to join the forces of the hostile party or to take part in military operations against their will.[212] Although such rules are long-established in international humanitarian law, it has frequently been debated as to where the line of prohibited conduct should be drawn, given that parties to an armed conflict have often relied on the civilian population for certain services or contributions that assist the war effort but fall short of taking part in the actual fighting. At the 1874 Brussels Conference, the issue was discussed by the delegates at length who agreed on a truncated version of the original article proposed by Russia,[213] which set out that '[t]he population of an occupied territory cannot be compelled to take part in military operations against its own country'.[214] In considering the proposed rules on requisitions and contributions from the population in occupied territory, a proposal was put forward that an explicit reference should be made to the rule forbidding coerced participation in military operations.[215] The delegate of Germany, Colonel de Voigts-Rhetz, explained that the civilian population 'may be called upon to supply food, clothing, conveyances, horses etc., or they may have horses billeted on them; all of which are an aid to the object of the war'.[216]

As private property should be respected, the enemy will demand from parishes (communes) or the inhabitants, only such payments and services as are connected with the necessities of war generally acknowledged, in proportion of the country, and which do not imply, with

[208] Sanna, 'Treatment of Prisoners of War' (n 147) 1003.

[209] *The Ministries case*, Judgment, XIV *Trials of War Criminals Before the Nuernberg Military Tribunals* (1952) 308, 549.

[210] Pierre D'Argent, 'Non-Renunciation of the Rights Provided by the Conventions' *in* Clapham, Gaeta, and Sassòli, *The 1949 Geneva Conventions: A Commentary* (n 147) 145, 148–9. See also Marco Sassòli, 'The Status, Treatment and Repatriation of Deserters under International Humanitarian Law' (1985) Yearbook / International Institute of Humanitarian Law 9, 10, 24–5; W.L. Cheah, 'Dealing with Desertion and Gaps in International Humanitarian Law: Changes of Allegiance in the Singapore War Crimes Trials' (2018) 8(2) Asian Journal of International Law 350, 365.

[211] ICRC, *Commentary on the First Geneva Convention: Convention (I) for the Amelioration of the Condition of the Wounded and Sick in Armed Forces in the Field* (2nd edn, CUP 2016) para 995.

[212] Fourth Geneva Convention, art 51.

[213] 'Correspondence Respecting the Proposed Conference at Brussels' (n 38) 15 (§48).

[214] 1874 Brussels Declaration, art 36. See 'Correspondence Respecting the Proposed Conference at Brussels' (n 12) 267.

[215] Ibid 269. [216] Ibid.

regard to the inhabitants, the obligation of taking part in the operations of war against the enemy.[217]

This article was adopted,[218] with the last words subsequently changed to 'against their own country', as reflected in Article 40 of the Brussels Declaration.[219]

At the First Hague Peace Conference, after some debate, the approach of the Brussels Declaration was replicated by the 1899 Hague Regulations including a stand-alone prohibition against compelling civilians in occupied territory to take part in military operations and a second reference in the articles on requisitions and contributions.[220] The 1907 Hague Regulations also follow this approach, but expanded the prohibition to 'the nationals of the adverse party'.[221] At the 1899 Hague Peace Conference, Edouard Rolin, the *rapporteur* of the Second Subcommission noted how both invaders and occupiers 'will necessarily be forbidden to force the population of a territory to take part in military operations'.[222] A debate amongst the delegates, as touched upon in the previous section, centred on whether the prohibition should apply only to taking a direct part in military operations.[223] With regard to requisitions of services from the population, it was agreed that this could not include their involvement in operations of war and could only be based on 'the needs of the occupying army', rather than 'the rather vague criterion of "necessities of war" '.[224] Article 52 of the 1899 Hague Regulations states:

Requisitions in kind and services shall not be demanded from municipalities, or inhabitants except for the needs of the army of occupation. They shall be in proportion to the resources of the country, and of such a nature as not to involve the population in the obligation of taking part in the operations of the war against their country.[225]

This article was retained at the Second Peace Conference following a slight rewording.[226]

The 1907 Hague Regulations also include a prohibition in Article 23(h) of compelling the nationals of the adverse party to take part in military operations that expands the original rule's application beyond the inhabitants in occupied territory:

A belligerent is likewise forbidden to compel the nationals of the adverse party to take part in operations of war directed against their country, even when they have been in the service before the commencement of the war.

217 Ibid 273–9. 218 Ibid 287. 219 Ibid 323.

220 Hague Regulations 1899, art 44 and 52.

221 Hague Regulations 1907, art 23(h) and 52.

222 *Report to the Conference*, by Edouard Rolin, *The Proceedings of the Hague Peace Conferences: The Conference of 1899* (n 58) 50, 67.

223 Fourth Meeting of the Second Commission: Second Subcommission, 1 June 1899, *The Proceedings of the Hague Peace Conferences: The Conference of 1899* (n 58) 487, 574.

224 *Report to the Conference*, by Edouard Rolin, *The Proceedings of the Hague Peace Conferences: The Conference of 1899* (n 58) 63–4.

225 *The Proceedings of the Hague Peace Conferences: The Conference of 1899* (n 58) 260–1.

226 See for example Second Meeting of the Second Commission, 14 August 1907, *The Proceedings of the Hague Peace Conferences: The Conference of 1907* (n 63) 24.

This article is based on the proposed Article 22a introduced by Germany at the Second Hague Peace Conference, discussed in the previous section, and which Austria-Hungary had unsuccessfully sought to narrow to compelling nationals to serve 'as combatants'. While delegates had divergent approaches to the question of coercing military assistance from the civilian population,[227] there was at least unanimous agreement regarding 'the necessity of respecting the legitimate sentiments of the inhabitants of an occupied region; there should be no question of enrolling them as combatants against their own country'.[228] The prohibition in Article 23(h) of the 1907 Hague Regulations grants 'the benefit of the prohibitions' to all enemy nationals, not just those in occupied territory.[229]

In 1949, the Fourth Geneva Convention provided a revision of the Hague rules by prohibiting an occupying power from forcibly recruiting protected persons into its armed or auxiliary forces.[230] This is an absolute rule, which cannot be derogated from, and which aims to protect the population in occupied territory 'from actions offensive to their patriotic feelings or from attempts to undermine their allegiance to their own country'.[231] The Convention also prohibits the compelling of protected persons 'to undertake any work which would involve them in the obligation of taking part in military operations'.[232] The equivalent Hague rules have retained some currency, as demonstrated by the pertinent war crime in the Rome Statute of the International Criminal Court.[233]

While acknowledging the possibility of voluntary enlistment, the Fourth Geneva Convention prohibits 'pressure or propaganda' for that purpose.[234] The United Kingdom had opposed the prohibiting of such propaganda at the 1949 Diplomatic Conference, but its proposal to have it excluded from the provision in question was rejected by a majority, 'no doubt because of the bad impression left by certain propaganda in the last two wars'.[235] While the prohibition of pressure itself might seem unnecessary, given that enlistment under pressure would not be voluntary, it would seem to be aimed at addressing recruitment activities that are less overt than directly forcing inhabitants into the armed or auxiliary forces. It also reinforces how international humanitarian law prohibits coercion in the context of serving in the forces of the enemy or contributing to the war effort in international armed conflicts, while allowing voluntary service, in keeping with the 'established practice of States to accept the services of defectors'.[236]

[227] See for example Third Meeting of the Second Commission: First Subcommission, 24 July 1907, *Annex; Report made in the name of the Committee of Examination, The Proceedings of the Hague Peace Conferences: The Conference of 1907* (n 63) 117, 127.

[228] Fourth Meeting of the Second Commission: First Subcommission, 31 July 1907, *The Proceedings of the Hague Peace Conferences: The Conference of 1907* (n 63) 134

[229] Third Meeting of the Second Commission: First Subcommission, 24 July 1907, *The Proceedings of the Hague Peace Conferences: The Conference of 1907* (n 63) 119.

[230] Fourth Geneva Convention, art 51.

[231] Pictet, *Commentary IV Geneva Convention* (n 156) 293.

[232] Fourth Geneva Convention, art 40 and 51.

[233] Rome Statute of the International Criminal Court, art 8(2)(b)(xv).

[234] Fourth Geneva Convention, art 51.

[235] Committee III (Civilians), Forty-Fourth Meeting, 8 July 1949, *Final Record* (n 1) 775.

[236] Sassòli, 'The Status, Treatment and Repatriation of Deserters' (n 210), 22–3.

The application of these rules by national courts presents an opportunity for judicial consideration of the existing prohibitions. A more stringent interpretation excluding even voluntary participation in military activities arose in the context of a legal challenge to the Israeli army's 'early warning procedure', a military practice whereby local civilians were asked to enter buildings in which wanted persons were claimed to be present, in order to warn the occupants and avoid unnecessary military or civilian casualties.[237] Various non-governmental organisations have described many cases in which the Israeli Defence Forces 'made use of local residents for military needs', such as using them as hostages or human shields.[238] The Supreme Court of Israel sitting as the High Court of Justice issued a temporary injunction in 2002 against the use of Palestinian civilians as human shields or hostages, including 'for any military acts', such as 'the neighbor procedure'.[239] A military order authorising this 'early warning' procedure stipulated that no compulsion, violence, or threat of violence was permitted in the requesting of such assistance.[240] Subsequent reports, however, raised the concern of the unlawful use of coercion and of civilians in military operations.[241] At a hearing in 2003, the Court restated the injunction against the use of human shields or hostages, but did not prohibit the use of the 'new procedure' per se.[242]

The Supreme Court declared these practices unlawful in a final judgment issued in 2005. President Barak in his opinion, with which the other judges concurred, acknowledged that although humanitarian law prohibited the use of 'human shields', there was no specific rule addressing the consensual granting of assistance by local residents as envisaged under the 'early warning' procedure.[243] The latter involved conflicting considerations between the occupying power's duty to protect the life and dignity of those living close to the wanted person, and those of the civilian asked to deliver the warning. For the latter, the Court found fault with both coerced and voluntary cooperation:

> That is certainly the case when he does not consent to take upon himself the task he has been given, and when its performance is likely to cause him damage. But that is also the case when he gives his consent, and when performance of the role will cause him no damage. That is so not only since he is not permitted to waive his rights pursuant to the humanitarian law [...], but also since, de facto, it is difficult to judge when his consent is given freely, and when it is the result of overt or subtle pressure.[244]

[237] See Roland Otto, 'Neighbours as Human Shields? The Israel Defence Forces' "Early Warning Procedure" and International Humanitarian Law' (2004) 86 No. 856 International Review of the Red Cross 771.

[238] HCJ 3799/02 *Adalah et al. v GOC Central Command, IDF et al.*, Supreme Court sitting as the High Court of Justice, 23 June 2005, para 2.

[239] Ibid para 4.

[240] See Military Order (Israel), 'Advance Warning Procedure', 26 November 2002 <http://www.btselem.org/english/legal_documents/advanced_warning_procedure.doc> accessed 28 May 2019.

[241] Otto, 'Neighbours as Human Shields?' (n 237) 775.

[242] *Adalah et al. v GOC Central Command, IDF et al.* (n 238) para 8.

[243] Ibid paras 21–23.

[244] Ibid para 23.

In finding that the protection of the local civilian used in the early warning procedure should prevail, President Barak referred to 'a common thread running through all of the law of belligerent occupation, [...] the prohibition of use of protected residents as a part of the war effort of the occupying army'.[245] A prohibition on the use of local civilians for relaying warnings from the army to a wanted person was to be derived from this principle, read together with the prohibition on using coercion to obtain intelligence from the civilian population.

The 'early warning' procedure was declared as contrary to international law on several other grounds also. Humanitarian law requires that efforts be made to keep civilians separate from hostilities, with the Court advancing the view that 'a local resident is not to be brought, even with his consent, into a zone in which combat activity is taking place'.[246] Given the asymmetrical relationship between occupier and occupied, a request for cooperation is unlikely to be rejected and thus such consent 'will not be real'. In the Court's view, an occupying army should avoid a situation in which such consent would be requested. Finally, the Court noted that the harm which a cooperating resident might face cannot be determined in advance: 'one must consider not only the physical danger of damage from gunfire originating in the wanted person's location, or from various booby-traps, but also the wider danger which a local resident who "collaborates" with the occupying army can expect'.[247] In alluding to the ill-treatment that has tended to befall collaborators, and restricting the military practices of an occupying army in light of this, the Court provides a rare example of an interpretation of international law that restricts the use of civilians as voluntary collaborators.

In declaring the 'early warning procedure' at odds with international law, Barak acknowledged the law's ambiguity, stated that the practice 'comes too close to the normative "nucleus" of the forbidden, and is found in the relatively grey area (the penumbra) of the improper'.[248] In her concurring opinion, Justice Beinisch added that 'even if the procedure were legal, the danger of sliding into the practice forbidden by a categorical prohibition is inherent in the means permitted by the procedure'.[249] She placed particular emphasis on the question of consent:

> The validity of consent is conditional upon it being given of free will. When a local resident is asked by a military commander, accompanied by armed army forces, to assist in an act performed against the population to which he belongs, even if the request is made for a desirable objective, the resident has no real option of refusing the request, and therefore his consent—is not consent.[250]

Similar sentiments were expressed when the Supreme Court subsequently rejected the State's application for a second hearing, with Justice Rivlin holding that:

> [t]o place this resident, who is caught in the middle of a battlefield, in a position where he has to choose whether or not to acquiesce to the army's request to pass a warning to a wanted

245 Ibid para 24. 246 Ibid. 247 Ibid. 248 Ibid para 25.
249 Ibid para 4. 250 Ibid para 5.

gunman is to place him in an impossible position. The choice itself is immoral and impairs the dignity of man.[251]

This jurisprudence offers a compelling interpretation of the applicable rules of international humanitarian law going beyond a mere consideration of whether coercion was present, by emphasising the impossibility of free choice inherent in the circumstances in question. It has been cited in support of the ICRC's customary international humanitarian law rule that '[u]ncompensated or abusive forced labour is prohibited'.[252]

The law of non-international armed conflict is almost completely silent on the question of forced or voluntary recruitment into armed forces. This more modest body of law neither prohibits pressure nor propaganda aimed at the voluntary enlistment of civilians or detained fighters into armed forces, nor the compulsory conscription of the nationals of a state into its armed forces. The obvious exception is children, with the Rome Statute, for example, including the war crime of '[c]onscripting or enlisting children under the age of fifteen years into armed forces or groups or using them to participate in hostilities'.[253] The evidence cited by the ICRC in support of the existence of a customary international humanitarian law prohibition of uncompensated or abusive forced labour in non-international armed conflicts consists primarily of the rule in Additional Protocol II that persons whose liberty has been restricted 'shall, if made to work, have the benefit of working conditions and safeguards similar to those enjoyed by the local civilian population'.[254]

From the perspective of collaboration in armed conflict, international humanitarian law thus effectively leaves open the door for states to coerce opposition fighters or adult civilians to take part in military activities directed against a non-state armed group, including one of which they may have been a member or have supported. This is starkly demonstrated in the statement on 'pseudoforces' in the US *Law of War Manual*:

Under international law, a State may compel its nationals to serve in its armed forces and to fight against non-State armed groups. For example, in contrast to POWs, captured insurgents who are nationals of that State could be required to serve in that State's armed forces or to take part in operations directed against their former comrades.[255]

While it might be considered 'distressing and dishonourable' to force persons take part in military operations against their own country,[256] such a rationale is also

[251] Cited in Adalah, 'Supreme Court Rejects State's Motion to Rehear Human Shields Case', 6 March 2006 <https://www.adalah.org/en/content/view/8182> accessed 28 May 2019. See further Sharon Weill, *The Role of National Courts in Applying International Humanitarian Law* (OUP 2014) 148–52; Michael N. Schmitt, 'Human Shields in International Humanitarian Law' (2008) 38 Israel Yearbook on Human Rights 17, 35–8.

[252] International Committee of the Red Cross, *Customary International Humanitarian Law Database*, Practice Relating to Rule 95 <https://ihl-databases.icrc.org/customary-ihl/eng/docs/v2_cha_chapter32_rule95_sectionb> accessed 28 May 2019.

[253] Rome Statute of the International Criminal Court, art 8(2)(e)(vii).

[254] Henckaerts and Doswald-Beck, *Customary International Humanitarian Law* (n 159) 332.

[255] United States, *Law of War Manual* (n 16) 1039–40 (footnotes omitted).

[256] Henckaerts and Doswald-Beck, *Customary International Humanitarian Law* (n 159) 334.

applicable in non-international armed conflicts, yet no commensurate rule has been adopted. In such instances, such individuals might seek to object to participation in such military operations for reasons of conscience, although humanitarian law does not address conscientious objection, and international human rights law does not explicitly provide such a right.[257]The International Covenant on Civil and Political Rights recognises the lawfulness of compulsory military service, by excluding from the definition of forced or compulsory labour '[a]ny service of a military character and, in countries where conscientious objection is recognized, any national service required by law of conscientious objectors'.[258]

As it remains for states to legislate for conscientious objection domestically, those countries that are engaged in a non-international armed conflict may be able to compel participation in military activities, although there would be an obvious reluctance to do so where individuals have pledged themselves to an opposing party to the conflict. For such individuals, however, there may be an argument that compelling their participation amounts to a form of 'abusive forced labour'; the ICTY's Appeal Chamber held that:

> the use of persons taking no active part in hostilities to prepare military fortifications for use in operations and against the forces with whom those persons identify or sympathies is a serious attack on human dignity and causes serious mental (and depending on the circumstances physical) suffering or injury. Any order to compel protected persons to dig trenches or to prepare other forms of military installations, in particular when such persons are ordered to do so against their own forces in an armed conflict, constitutes cruel treatment.[259]

The Tribunal's finding that such acts involving 'non-combatant detainees' constituted war crimes occurring in a non-international armed conflict would also be of relevance to fighters coerced into participating in hostilities against their former armed groups. For non-state armed groups, the silence of international humanitarian law with regard to recruiting persons to participate in military activities cannot be interpreted as an authorisation to do so, particularly in light of the prescriptions of national law.

The clear dichotomy in the law of armed conflict between international and non-international armed conflicts, and the far more limited set of rules applicable to the latter is glaringly highlighted in this context. While judges at the ICTY had some success in their efforts to 'jettison this stupid distinction', as Antonio Cassese once described it,[260] support is unlikely to be found amongst states for a transposition of the relevant rules prohibiting compulsory participation in military activities into

[257] See generally Office of the High Commission for Human Rights, *Conscientious Objection to Military Service* (United Nations 2012); Marie-France Major, 'Conscientious Objection and International Law: A Human Right?' (1992) 24 Case Western Reserve Journal of International Law 249.

[258] International Covenant on Civil and Political Rights (1966), entered into force 23 March 1976, 999 U.N.T.S. 171, art 8(3)(c)(ii).

[259] *Prosecutor v Blaškić*, Case No. IT-95-14-A, Appeals Chamber, Judgment, 29 July 2004, para 597.

[260] 'To be an International Criminal Court Judge: Conversation with Antonio Cassese', *Distinguished Fellows Lecture Series*, 4 September 2003, Hauser Global Law School Program, NYU School of Law, reprinted in (2011) 22(4) European Journal of International Law 931, 942. See also *Prosecutor v Tadić*, Case No. IT-94-1-A, Appeals Chamber, Judgment, 15 July 1999, paras 128–135.

non-international armed conflicts. 'Pseudoforces' made up of former insurgents that have been turned against their own side are considered of 'immense importance' and have been used 'in virtually every insurgency since World War II'.[261] International humanitarian law does not include an equivocal prohibition of forced recruitment into armed forces applicable in all armed conflicts, although the practice could run afoul of prohibitions of cruel and inhuman treatment.

2.3 Bureaucratic Collaboration

Bureaucratic collaboration by a national government, local authorities, or individual officials is most often associated with situations of belligerent occupation.[262] International humanitarian law in times of occupation establishes certain rights and benefits for the local population, as well as duties of the occupying power that are of relevance in this context. In particular, an occupying power must 'take all the measures in his power to restore, and ensure, as far as possible, public order and safety, while respecting, unless absolutely prevented, the laws in force in the country'.[263] It has been said that an occupying power 'may to some extent require the collaboration of the occupied population [. . .] but only in relation to respecting the security and the basic needs of the occupier, not to promote its military and political aims'.[264]

Given that an occupying power is considered a temporary authority in occupied territory with an obligation to ensure that daily life continues in those territories to the extent that the circumstances permit, a more legally justifiable ground for demanding local cooperation arguably arises from the obligation to maintain public order and services in occupied territory. According to István Deák, Articles 42 and 43 of the Hague Regulations can be read as having 'legalized a limited degree of collaboration'.[265] In contrast, however, a Belgian Military Tribunal sitting in the aftermath of the Second World War held that 'the German policy of appointing Belgians loyal to Germany to key positions in the state's apparatus, of protecting collaborators and indeed promoting treason, was contrary to [Article 43 of the Hague Regulations]'.[266] The 1949 Geneva Conventions only touch on the issue of bureaucratic collaboration by providing certain protections for local officials in occupied territory who refuse to cooperate with an occupying power 'for reasons of conscience'.[267] While earlier instruments do not provide clear stipulations concerning bureaucratic collaboration, their *travaux préparatoires* reveal acknowledgment of the tensions generated in situations of occupation between obedience to an occupying

[261] Donald A. MacCuish and Spencer C. Tucker, 'Pseudoforces' in Spencer C. Tucker (ed), *Encyclopedia of Insurgency and Counterinsurgency: A New Era of Modern Warfare* (ABC-CLIO, 2013) 452.

[262] See Chapter 1, section 1.3.

[263] Hague Regulations 1907, art 43.

[264] Redse Johansen, 'The occupied and the occupier: the case of Norway' (n 8) 206–7.

[265] Deák, *Europe on Trial* (n 8) 21.

[266] *Von Falkenhausen and others*, Brussels, Belgium, Court Martial, 9 March 1951 (1950–1951) 31 Revue de droit pénal et criminologie 863–3, *summary translation in* Antonio Cassese (ed), *The Oxford Companion to International Criminal Justice* (OUP 2009) 963–4.

[267] Fourth Geneva Convention, art 54(1).

power and allegiance to the displaced sovereign for those who might continue in their existing roles or assume positions under a new administration.

At the 1874 Brussels Conference and the First Hague Peace Conference, the question of the role of local authorities in situations of occupation was the subject of 'detailed study'.[268] There was a view expressed that public officials could be compelled to continue their functions under the occupying power without exception. This reflected the far-reaching powers envisaged for occupying powers proposed in Russia's Project for an International Convention on the Laws and Customs, which included the power to maintain, modify, or suspend 'altogether' existing laws in occupied territory.[269] It was put forward that the commander of the occupying army could compel 'the Departments, as well as the officers of the Civil Administration of Police and Justice to continue in the exercise of their duties under his superintendence and control'.[270] Moreover:

> [t]he military authority may require the local officials to undertake an oath, or on their word, to fulfil the duties required of them during the hostile occupation; it may remove those who refuse to satisfy this requirement, and prosecute judicially those who shall not fulfil the duties undertaken by them.[271]

Coerced bureaucratic collaboration was foreseen by the Russian proposal and a failure to cooperate with an occupying power could lead to criminal prosecution. At the Brussels Conference, the Belgian delegate raised a doubt as to 'whether under the constitution of his country, any other power than the will of the Belgian people itself could acquiesce in a decree submitting the country to the jurisdiction of a foreigner'.[272] Ultimately, the delegates did not support the stern tenor of the Russian text and agreed to a more moderate article.

The report of the British delegate to the 1874 Conference notes that the proposed articles were modified, and the 'harsh treatment to which public officials were liable to be exposed by the provisions of the latter, disappears in the version adopted'.[273] In cases of invasion, 'every official is free to follow the line of conduct his conscience may dictate with regard to continuance in office'.[274] The final version of Article 4 of the Brussels Declaration placed an emphasis on consent:

> The functionaries and officials of every class who at the instance of the occupier consent to continue to perform their duties, shall be under his protection. They shall not be dismissed or be liable to summary punishment ('punis disciplinairement') unless they fail in fulfilling the obligations they have undertaken, and shall be handed over to justice, only if they violate those obligations by unfaithfulness.[275]

Several versions of this article were discussed during the conference,[276] with the delegates broadly having accepted that an occupying power could rely on local administrations but taking issue with the imposition of penalties on non-cooperative

[268] Pictet, *Commentary IV Geneva Convention* (n 156) 303.
[269] 'Correspondence Respecting the Proposed Conference at Brussels' (n 38) 12.
[270] Ibid. [271] Ibid.
[272] 'Correspondence Respecting the Proposed Conference at Brussels' (n 12) 161.
[273] Ibid. [274] Ibid. [275] Ibid 162. [276] Ibid 202, 228, 240, 248.

individuals. For Baron Lambermont of Belgium, resigning from office should not be an offence for 'a functionary who, after consenting to remain in office, influenced perhaps by a feeling of patriotism, subsequently withdraws such consent'.[277] Russia's General de Leer considered that those remaining in office 'will be rendering a service to their country, because they will be in a position to be useful to the population; but they should always have the power to resign their posts'.[278] The French delegate, Baron Baude, highlighted the distinction between 'the fact of not fulfilling obligations and treachery', and sought to have the article exclude summary punishment or dismissal unless officials 'fail in fulfilling the obligations they have undertaken, or be handed over to justice unless they violate those obligations by unfaithfulness'.[279] It was broadly agreed that a functionary 'cannot be deprived of his right to resign his office'.[280]

At a full sitting of the conference on August 26, Baron Blanc of Italy expressed the view that civil servants and other public officials may 'consider themselves morally bound not to abandon their posts in the face of an occupation':

> It would be unjust to place their patriotism in collision with the sentiment of their moral obligation towards society, by establishing that they shall remain in office by a kind of assignment on the part of the occupier, that is to say, in virtue of his invitation which they accept.[281]

He felt that it should be understood that the obligations in question, and relevant penalties, were to be determined 'according to the ordinary laws and jurisdiction'.[282] Baron Jomini of Russia clarified that according to the proposed wording, 'functionaries are always at liberty to decline, but as long as they remain in office their responsibility exists'.[283] These efforts at Brussels to address the relationship between an occupying power and local authorities and officials had little influence on subsequent treaty-making endeavours.

The delegates at the First Hague Peace Conference in 1899 rejected Article 4 of the Brussels Declaration and agreed that any similar article should be omitted from the proposed instrument. There was opposition to any provision that might be interpreted as requiring or allowing public officials to serve an opposing power in this way. For example, van Karnebeek of the Netherlands was opposed to:

> any provision that might seem directly or indirectly to give the public officers of an invaded country any authority to place themselves at the service of the invader. It was not denied, however, that certain officers, particularly municipal officers, might sometimes best perform their duty, in a moral sense at least, towards their people if they remained at their posts in the presence of the invader.[284]

The Belgian delegate Beernaert questioned whether an international treaty should grant what might be seen as expansive rights to an occupying power:

[277] Ibid 240. [278] Ibid. [279] Ibid 240. [280] Ibid 243. [281] Ibid 306.
[282] Ibid. [283] Ibid 307.
[284] *Report to the Conference*, by Edouard Rolin, Annex 1 to the Minutes of the Fifth Meeting, 5 July 1899, *The Proceedings of the Hague Peace Conferences: The Conference of 1899* (n 58) 62.

Is it conceivable that the State that is beaten would grant rights to its conqueror in its own territory, in advance and in case of war, and that it would organize a régime of defeat? Could it be by the anticipated and written consent of the conquered party that the conqueror would levy taxes and impose fines or engage in his service officials whose first duty is to be faithful to their own country? I admit that there might in fact be some advantages to this, that civil order would be better preserved, and that the invaded populations would suffer less; but such a regulation would encounter objections of a moral and patriotic nature, which seem hardly surmountable. It does not seem to me that one can sanction in advance as a right that which necessarily belongs to the domain of fact and force.[285]

Beernaert was of the view that the delegates could not 'transform fact into law' and that the conference could adopt provisions which 'admitting the fact without recognizing the right of the conqueror, would involve a pledge on the part of the latter to exercise his right moderately'.[286] The Swiss delegate Odier felt it would be 'impossible to ask the conquered State to subscribe in advance, by means of a convention, to measures which might be vexing to the populations; it is also impossible to delegate, so to speak, to the occupant the powers which the *de jure* States has been forced to relinquish'.[287] Another delegate, Eyschen of Luxemburg agreed that such an article should be omitted but emphasised that 'the duties of economic, legislative and military guardianship which devolve upon the occupant ought to be construed in the sense of the Brussels Declaration'.[288] After having been put to a vote, Article 4 of the Brussels Declaration was 'tentatively eliminated' by fifteen votes to seven.[289]

When the delegates at the First Hague Peace Conference returned once more to Article 4 of the Brussels Declaration, their hostility towards the provision was still evident, although they also demonstrated some recognition that continued service by local authorities during an occupation might be of benefit to the civilian population. While Beernaert reiterated his view that it was 'impossible for a State to authorize its officials in advance to pass into the service of its adversary', van Karnebeek saw the article as placing limitations on the authority of the occupying power, rather than granting it a right.[290] He felt that '[i]n many cases it would be a patriotic duty of the highest importance to remain to the end the most determined and resolute opponents and enemies of the invader'.[291] Germany's Gross von Schwarzhoff took the view that the article did not concern 'political functionaries alone, but also ... those of all other categories, including those elected by the inhabitants. The inhabitants have a right to have the mayors and municipal employees remain in their places.'[292] This could be of mutual benefit for the occupier and occupied, he argued.[293] The

[285] Sixth Meeting of the Second Commission: Second Subcommission, 6 June 1899, *The Proceedings of the Hague Peace Conferences: The Conference of 1899* (n 58) 503.

[286] Ibid 503–4.

[287] Seventh Meeting of the Second Commission: Second Subcommission, 8 June 1899, *The Proceedings of the Hague Peace Conferences: The Conference of 1899* (n 58) 513–14.

[288] Ibid. [289] Ibid.

[290] Eighth Meeting of the Second Commission: Second Subcommission, 10 June 1899, *The Proceedings of the Hague Peace Conferences: The Conference of 1899* (n 58) 521.

[291] Ibid. [292] Ibid. [293] Ibid.

debates provide evidence of a notable wariness on the part of the smaller countries to the idea of legislating for the putting of their bureaucracies and officials at the disposal of an occupying power.

Edouard Rolin, *rapporteur* of the Second Subcommission, was unable to devise a workable formulation for an article and took the view that it should be omitted. He too considered that such cooperation with an occupying power could be of benefit to the local population and should not be contingent on authorisation from their own government:

> It is necessary to take into account the interest of the populations, which require that the local and municipal functionaries shall be present in order to defend the rights and property of the populations as far as possible against the demands of the invader.
>
> In acting thus the functionaries not only do not fail in their duties, but from a certain standpoint it may even be said that they fulfil an obligation towards their own country. It would therefore be dangerous to adopt a form of wording which might be construed to mean that the functionaries could not remain at their posts without having received permission from their own country.[294]

Martens, the delegate of Russia, agreed to the abolition of the article in light of the difficulties it gave rise to, but advocated for cooperation between an occupying power and local officials:

> If the enemy does not find any functionary at hand, he has no means of being equitable and just, and it is by virtue of the mandate of their own country that the functionaries are the natural defenders and protectors of the inhabitants in their relations with the occupant.[295]

While officials could serve to protect the local population by remaining in their posts, those with responsibility for vital infrastructure, for example, could end up serving the military aims of occupying power: 'if they were to enter his service this might constitute an act of treason at a time when it is a question of the defence of the country'.[296] Veljkovitch of Serbia considered that the inclusion of an article requiring observance of the law in force of the occupied territory 'already decided' the question, in that respect for the law 'implies the retention of the functionaries appointed by virtue of those laws'.[297] Article 4 was thus 'unanimously omitted' in the end.[298] There was no discussion of the issue of bureaucratic collaboration at the Second Hague Peace Conference in 1907 and thus little guidance from international law on the matter prior to the two World Wars.

The inconclusive debates of 1874 and 1899 focused almost exclusively on local officials and judges, the so-called functionaries who find themselves under an alien authority in a situation of occupation, rather than the government or national authorities who may choose to surrender and cooperate. It will be recalled from Chapter 1 that during the Second World War, both national and local authorities cooperated with occupying powers to various degrees. As Pictet notes:

294 Ibid 522. 295 Ibid. 296 Ibid. 297 Ibid. 298 Ibid.

In their dealings with judges and public officials, the occupation authorities aimed at inducing them to support the Occupying Power's policies and to place themselves in opposition to the legal government to which they had sworn allegiance.[299]

Germany did find willing collaborators, including at the highest levels, such as Pétain and the Vichy regime in France, and in some cases effectively placed persons into positions of authority, notably Quisling in Norway. During the War, the territories under occupation experienced 'changes in constitutional forms or in the form of government, the establishment of new military or political organizations, the dissolution of the State, or the formation of new political entities'.[300] But, as Pictet asserts:

[i]nternational law prohibits such actions, which are based solely on the military strength of the Occupying Power and not on a sovereign decision by the occupied State. Of course the Occupying Power usually tried to give some colour of legality and independence to the new organizations, which were formed in the majority of cases with the co-operation of certain elements among the population of the occupied country, but it was obvious that they were in fact always subservient to the will of the Occupying Power. Such practices were incompatible with the traditional concept of occupation (as defined in Article 43 of the Hague Regulations of 1907) according to which the occupying authority was to be considered as merely being a de facto administrator.[301]

Legal challenges to bureaucratic collaboration during the Second World War were largely based on national law, whether the criminal law of treason or constitutional law. In France, for example, Professor René Cassin, who was subsequently one of the drafters of the Universal Declaration of Human Rights, argued that French constitutional law had been breached by the Vichy regime, as 'the circumstances of the occupation did not make a free consultation possible'.[302] In adopting the 1949 Geneva Conventions after the War, and bringing into force an expanded set of international laws that could be brought to bear in future situations of occupation, states introduced only limited rules addressing bureaucratic collaboration.

The Fourth Geneva Convention recognises that an occupation can have an impact on the administration of the territory, foreseeing potential changes in 'the institutions or government of the said territory' as a result of occupation.[303] It also accepts that national and local administrations might continue with their functions under the authority of an occupying power. For example, the Convention specifies the occupier 'shall, with the cooperation of the national and local authorities, facilitate the proper working of all institutions devoted to the care and education of children'.[304] Any changes that do occur cannot deprive protected persons of the benefits they enjoy under the Convention, while public officials and judges are protected where they decline to serve under the occupying power:

[299] Pictet, *Commentary IV Geneva Convention* (n 156) 303. [300] Ibid 273.

[301] Ibid. See however Adam Roberts, 'Transformative Military Occupation: Applying the Laws of War and Human Rights' (2006) 100(3) American Journal of International Law 580, 586.

[302] Peter Novick, *The Resistance versus Vichy: The Purge of Collaborators in Liberated France* (Columbia University Press 1968) 23. See also ibid 191–7.

[303] Fourth Geneva Convention, art 47. [304] Ibid art 50.

The Occupying Power may not alter the status of public officials or judges in the occupied territories or in any way apply sanctions to or take any measures of coercion or discrimination against them, should they abstain from fulfilling their functions for reasons of conscience.[305]

The rule concerning status here reflects the temporary nature of an occupation and the need to ensure the continuation of public order and civil life in occupied territory. Judges and public officials are to retain their 'pre-occupation status' in order that they can 'continue carrying out the duties of their office as in the past, without being the object of intimidation or unwarranted interference'.[306] As Pictet observes, public officials and judges must remain sufficiently independent and be allowed to act according to their conscience, so as not to 'run the risk of being called to account for disloyalty when the national authorities resume their rights after the occupation ceases'.[307] Ties of allegiance to the displaced sovereign remain during a period of occupation.[308]

Pursuant to Article 54(1), public officials or judges refusing to carry out their functions cannot be sanctioned because of their loyalty to the displaced regime.[309] Their 'right to resign is clearly guaranteed'.[310] The Fourth Geneva Convention tries to manage the tension between the obedience owed by public officials and judges under the control of the occupying power and their allegiance and loyalty to the displaced national authorities. Pictet considers that while 'this duty of obedience does not cancel out the duty of allegiance which subsists during the period of occupation', there is a requirement of conformity with Convention rules in order to reconcile the two to the extent possible:

The occupation authorities may not, therefore, compel judges or public officials to swear allegiance to them, nor demand that they should exercise their functions or pronounce their decisions and sentences in the name of the Occupying Power. There is not in general any inconsistency between the two ideas, provided that the Occupying Power, in exercising its authority, keeps strictly to the Convention and to other rules governing occupation and that it demands nothing of public officials and judges which might constitute an act of treason towards their country. The position is still, of course, a very delicate one in practice; for it is very difficult to avoid some conflict between these duties. It is for that reason that persons holding public posts are left free to abstain for reasons of conscience. In such cases the Occupying Power cannot hold it against them, nor apply sanctions or take any measures of coercion or discrimination.[311]

An occupying power which compels the cooperation of public officials or judges against their will renders such persons open to charges of collaboration with the enemy, yet the Convention leaves the door to such compulsion open.

305 Ibid art 54(1).
306 Pictet, *Commentary IV Geneva Convention* (n 156) 304.
307 Ibid.
308 Ibid.
309 Michael Bothe, 'The Administration of Occupied Territory' in Clapham, Gaeta, and Sassòli, *The 1949 Geneva Conventions: A Commentary* (n 147) 1455, 1466.
310 Yutaka Arai-Takahashi, 'Lawmaking and the Judicial Guarantees in Occupied Territories' in Clapham, Gaeta, and Sassòli, *The 1949 Geneva Conventions: A Commentary* (n 147) 1421, 1428.
311 Pictet, *Commentary IV Geneva Convention* (n 156) 305.

The exceptions to these rules are found in Article 54(1), devised by the drafters so as to ensure that they complied with the rules on compulsory labour in Article 51(2), as well as to grant some discretion to the occupier by recognising 'the right of the Occupying Power to remove public officials from their posts'.[312] Protected persons can be compelled to carry out work 'necessary either for the needs of the occupying army, or for the public utility services or for the feeding, clothing, sheltering, transportation or health of the population of the occupied territory'.[313] Accordingly, an occupying power could refuse to allow public officials or judges to abstain from fulfilling their roles; in its final report to the plenary of the 1949 Diplomatic Conference, Committee III expressed the view that 'it might be necessary for certain of these officials or judges to be compulsorily employed'.[314]

Pictet's *Commentary* interprets this rule somewhat benignly, seeing it as justifiable in the context of officials working in the provisions of essential public services.[315] The need for a continuation of the judicial role is also mentioned:

> Judges and other members of the judiciary, for their part, are the natural guardians and protectors of the inhabitants of the country in their relations with the Occupying Power and their resignation might well paralyse the whole administrative and judicial machinery, in which case protected persons would be the first to suffer. It is therefore generally agreed that it is their moral duty to remain at their posts in the interests of their fellow citizens; such a requirement is all the more justified as the non-political nature of their duties is generally such as to remove any conscientious scruples they might have.[316]

The limitation on participation in military operations in Article 51(2) has been interpreted as prohibiting the compelling of local police forces 'to act against lawful combatants, such as resistance movements that fulfil the criteria of distinction'.[317] That local police can be lawfully required by an occupying power to take measures against hostile acts by persons other than those covered by Article 4 of the Third Geneva Convention would surely leave them open to accusations of collaboration. Pictet considers that 'the occupation authorities, being responsible for maintaining law and order, are within their rights in claiming the co-operation of the police' in order to address what may amount to offences at common law.[318]

Situations of belligerent occupation are less common in contemporary armed conflicts, having been supplanted in some instances by the control of territory by states through 'puppet' regimes or non-state armed groups.[319] Yet occupations remain a fertile breeding ground for collaboration with an occupying power, both real and imagined. Previous sections have addressed the limitations placed on occupiers by the laws of occupation with regard to coercion of protected persons for purposes of intelligence gathering or recruitment into armed forces and participation in

312 Fourth Geneva Convention, art 54(2). 313 Ibid art 51(2).

314 Report of Committee III to the Plenary Assembly, *Final Record* (n 1) 829.

315 Pictet, *Commentary IV Geneva Convention* (n 156) 306. 316 Ibid 306.

317 Arai-Takahashi, 'Lawmaking and the Judicial Guarantees in Occupied Territories' (n 310) 1429.

318 Pictet, *Commentary IV Geneva Convention* (n 156) 307.

319 See Bogdan Ivanel, 'Puppet States: A Growing Trend of Covert Occupation' (2015) 18 Yearbook of International Humanitarian Law 43; International Committee of the Red Cross, *Occupation and Other Forms of Administration of Foreign Territory* (ICRC 2012) 23.

military activities. The permissiveness of this body of law towards voluntary cooperation in those contexts is also present in relation to the activities of public authorities in occupied territory. Moreover, there is something of an expectation that certain national and local authorities, including judges, will continue to fulfil their functions even when under the authority of an occupying power. While the Fourth Geneva Convention recognises that public officials should not be sanctioned for refusing to continue in their roles, perhaps due to allegiance to the displaced sovereign, it also effectively permits an occupying power to compel them to do so. In the absence of compulsion, officials will be left to decide whether engaging in their professional activities will serve, or be perceived to serve, the local population or the enemy occupying power. The laws of occupation seek to offer humanitarian protection to those who decline to serve under a regime of occupation, but without providing any easy solution to their pressing dilemma.

2.4 Aiding the Enemy

The remaining activities discussed in Chapter 1—conducting business and trade, providing labour, acting as an interpreter, or contributing to propaganda efforts—have at times been viewed as aiding the enemy and are not squarely addressed by the main treaties of international humanitarian law. While certain general rules are laid down with regard to the labour of civilians, for example, the international law of armed conflict does not seek to regulate trade or business activities between armed forces and individuals or companies. With regard to interpreters, the 1949 Geneva Conventions guarantee that civilian detainees or prisoners of war facing trial have 'the right to the services of an interpreter', but do not elaborate specific rules applicable to their use or recruitment.[320] The reference in Common Article 3 to 'judicial guarantees which are recognized as indispensable by civilized peoples' indicates that interpreters may also need to be available during trial proceedings in non-international armed conflicts.[321] This is buttressed by human rights law, which insists on the 'free assistance of an interpreter' as a minimum guarantee.[322] The provision of interpretation or translation in such instances is less likely to be conceived as collaboration with the enemy, unless the trials are a mere sham, although interpreters that accompany armed forces during military operations or participate in the interrogation of detained persons are more likely to be viewed as collaborators.[323]

[320] Third Geneva Convention, art 105 and Fourth Geneva Convention, art 72. See also Giulio Bartolini, 'General principles of international humanitarian law and their application to interpreters serving in conflict locations', 9 March 2010, <http://aiic.net/p/3396> accessed 28 May 2019.

[321] Additional Protocol II does not specifically refer to the right to an interpreter, it does require that an accused be informed of the charges and have 'all necessary rights and means of defence', Additional Protocol II, art 6(2)(a).

[322] International Covenant on Civil and Political Rights, art 14(3)(f).

[323] See Mona Baker, 'Interpreters and Translators in the War Zone: Narrated and Narrators', 16(2) The Translator (2010) 197, 207.

While an occupier can require protected persons to engage in work that is 'necessary ... for the needs of the army of occupation', they cannot be obliged to take part in military operations.[324] International humanitarian law does not prohibit interpreters taking part in such operations on a voluntary basis, and those working for an occupying power would be entitled to fair wages and conditions of work, including 'compensation for occupational accidents'.[325] The latter provision could be interpreted as implying a duty on the part of an occupying power to protect such persons from retaliation as perceived collaborators.[326] The expansive protections of the right to life under international human rights law, as examined in Chapter 5, require positive obligations on the part of states to take measures where imminent threats exist.

With regard to economic collaboration, international humanitarian law does not prevent a party to an armed conflict from trading with local businesses or accepting voluntary offers of labour.[327] While an occupying force might compel labour that is necessary for its 'needs', or those of the local population, '[u]ncompensated or abusive forced labour is prohibited' as already noted.[328] A US Military Tribunal made the following pertinent observations regarding the economy of an occupied territory in the *Krupp* case:

> The economy of the belligerently occupied territory is to be kept intact, except for the carefully defined permissions given to the occupying authority – permissions which all refer to the army of occupation. Just as the inhabitants of the occupied territory must not be forced to help the enemy in waging war against their own country or their own country's allies, so must the economic assets of the occupied territory not be used in such a manner.[329]

International law neither requires nor prohibits legislative measures proscribing trade with an enemy, although during the late nineteenth and early twentieth centuries, considerable attention was devoted to the question of trading with belligerents, including by neutral countries that were dealing in 'contraband of war'.[330] Shipments of arms and ammunition were liable to be confiscated in wartime.[331]

During an examination of the laws of naval warfare as they related to neutral shipping at the Second Hague Peace Conference in 1907, the delegates considered whether the destruction of neutral prizes might be necessary to prevent arms and ammunition reaching an enemy. The Russian delegate, Captain Behr, argued that being prevented from seizing or destroying a captured neutral prize carrying arms and ammunition, because of an inability to bring it before a prize court, would be tantamount to aiding the enemy on the part of the commanding officer:

324 Fourth Geneva Convention, art 51(2). 325 Ibid. 326 Ibid.

327 On commercial activities during times of war, see generally James Thuo Gathii, *War, Commerce, and International Law* (OUP 2010).

328 ICRC, Practice Relating to Rule 95 (n 252).

329 *Trial of Krupp and eleven others*, United States Military Tribunal, Nuremberg, 17 November 1949–30 June 1948, X *Law Reports of the Trials of War Criminals* (1949) 69, 134.

330 See for example Halleck, *International Law* (n 11) 496–512, 569–90; T.J. Lawrence, *The Principles of International Law* (Sixth Edn., D.C. Heath & Co. 1915) 697–723.

331 Halleck, *International Law* (n 11) 496.

Do you not think that he will feel that he would be a traitor to his country if he obeyed the Convention and sent these cannon and projectiles to the enemy? [. . .]

And then everybody will see that, while the Second Commission forbids the invading enemy to require of the inhabitants of occupied territory any participation in military operations against their country, the Fourth Commission requires a naval officer in certain cases actually to aid the enemy by sending him cannon, arms, etc., which this enemy needs to do more damage to the officer's own fellow countrymen.[332]

Delegates were divided as to whether there should be an absolute prohibition under international law of the destruction of neutral prizes or a general prohibition subject to limited exceptions.[333] The latter approach eventually prevailed, thus naval officers could avoid having to aid the enemy, as Behr put it, against their will.[334] For the most part, international law leaves open the question of trading with the enemy, although national law and sanctions regimes may prohibit such activities.[335] This exemplifies the divergent approaches of national and international to the phenomenon of cooperation with an opposing side during armed conflict.

Finally, while a party to an international armed conflict might accept the propaganda services of enemy nationals, such individuals run the risk of being prosecuted for treason. The trial of William Joyce for his broadcasting activities for Nazi Germany was referred to by delegates at the 1949 Diplomatic Conference. Wershof, the delegate of Canada, commented that 'the famous traitor Lord Haw-Haw committed his treason in Germany', and raised a concern that a proposed amendment to the article concerning offences committed prior to an occupation might preclude such prosecutions.[336] The proposed Article 60, which after some alterations became Article 70 of the Fourth Geneva Convention, included a provision that restricted the arrest, prosecution, conviction, or deportation of nationals of an occupying power who had sought refuge in the territory of the occupied state prior to the outbreak of hostilities as a consequence of an offence committed outside the occupied territory, unless, 'according to the law of the occupied State, the said offence would have justified extradition in time of peace'.[337]

A joint amendment proposed by India and France sought to ensure that the provision covered both refugees that had committed such an offence, and those who had not.[338] The delegate of India, Haksar, responded forcefully to the claim of Canada

[332] Eighth Meeting of the Fourth Commission: Committee of Examination, 24 July 1907, *The Proceedings of the Hague Peace Conferences: The Conference of 1907* (n 63) 979–80.

[333] See for example Fourteenth Meeting of the Fourth Commission: Committee of Examination, 10 September 1907, *The Proceedings of the Hague Peace Conferences: The Conference of 1907* (n 63) 1061–3. See also ibid 1086–8.

[334] Eighth Meeting of the Plenary Conference, 10 October 1907, *The Proceedings of the Hague Peace Conferences: The Conference of 1907* (n 63) 314–15.

[335] See for example the United Kingdom's Trading with the Enemy Act, 1914; Trading with the Enemy Act, 1939.

[336] Twenty-Eighth Plenary Meeting, 4 August 1949, *Final Record of the Diplomatic Conference of Geneva of 1949*, Volume II, Section B (Federal Political Department, Berne) 433.

[337] Draft Convention for the Protection of Civilian Persons in Time of War, Draft as approved by the XVIIth International Red Cross Conference, *Final Records* (n 152) I, 123.

[338] Twenty-Eighth Plenary Meeting, 4 August 1949, *Final Record* (n 336) 433.

that this 'last moment' amendment would have prevented the United Kingdom from bringing Joyce to London for trial:

It has been said that Lord Haw-Haw (William Joyce), for instance, would have been protected by the second paragraph of Article 60. If I may say so respectfully, I do not agree. Common criminals, including those committing treasonable offences during hostilities, are not protected. In fact, Lord Haw-Haw could have been apprehended under the provisions of the second paragraph of Article 60, tried and hanged.[339]

Article 60 and the proposed amendment were submitted to the Drafting Committee,[340] and the new wording of paragraph 2 subsequently devised was agreed upon by all delegates.[341] Article 70 allows for trial or deportation for 'offences committed after the outbreak of hostilities, or for offences under common law committed before the outbreak of hostilities which, according to the law of the occupied state, would have justified extradition in time of peace'.[342] The representative of the Netherlands reiterated that the delegates 'must make it possible for a man who flees from his country and, after the outbreak of hostilities, commits acts against his country—such as giving propaganda talks on the radio—to be arrested, brought to trial and convicted in his own country'.[343] This discussion is a telling demonstration of how states were favourably disposed to the use of collaborators during wartime and did not prohibit their use as a matter of international law, but insisted on the right under national law to punish individuals that engaged in such activities.

* * *

This chapter has analysed the historical development and contemporary understanding of rules of international humanitarian law applicable to the use and recruitment of informers and other collaborators during armed conflict. Despite the absence of any specific reference to such persons in the main treaties, considerable attention has been paid by states to the various questions that arise concerning their use in wartime and how international law might be addressed to the practice. This was especially the case during the preparation of the Brussels Declaration and the Hague Regulations, where competing considerations of military necessity and humanitarian protection featured in the debates regarding whether civilians might be compelled to serve the enemy in various ways. States even disagreed on the substance of relevant articles in the adopted treaties. The contemporary law of armed conflict emphasises the prohibition on the use of coercion to force protected persons to provide information, participate in military activities or collaborate in other ways with opposition forces or authorities. Although *prima facie* it would seem that coerced collaboration is absolutely prohibited, while voluntary collaboration with an enemy power is permitted under international law, there are some exceptions. As discussed, captured members of an armed opposition group might be compelled to serve in

339 Ibid 434. 340 Ibid 435.
341 Thirty-Second Plenary Meeting, 6 August 1949, *Final Record* (n 336) 481.
342 Fourth Geneva Convention, art 70(2).
343 Thirty-Second Plenary Meeting, 6 August 1949, *Final Record* (n 336) 480.

the state forces which they had previously fought against during a non-international armed conflict, while judges and other public officials in occupied territory might be compelled to serve under an occupying power, albeit for the ostensible benefit of the local population. Certain interpretations of international humanitarian law have it that civilians and prisoners of war should not be permitted to contribute to military activities for the enemy even if they wish to do so.

The chapter's greater focus on the law applicable in international armed conflict addressing the use and recruitment of informers and collaborators demonstrates that the law of non-international armed conflict touches even less on these issues. How human rights law may be brought to bear on the phenomenon of informers and collaborators is explored further in Chapter 5. International humanitarian law remains relevant, however, in relation to several other aspects of the phenomenon of wartime collaboration in both international and non-international armed conflicts. The next chapter continues this analysis through the lens of humanitarian law by considering the at times complex issue of the status of those persons that have collaborated with the enemy.

3

Individual Status under International Humanitarian Law

This chapter explores the question of status under the law of armed conflict for persons who actively cooperate with an opposing party to an armed conflict. While it has been noted that informers and other collaborators as participants in armed conflict are not explicitly recognised by this body of law as a distinct category, that is not to say that individuals who collaborate with an opposing force may not fall within the recognised categories of persons addressed by international humanitarian law. For persons already within a particular category, be they prisoners of war or civilians in occupied territory, for example, activities that involve collaborating with an adversary may have a bearing on their status and the protections afforded to them on that basis. Those who assist an opposing side might not only be exposed to public hostility and the rigours of domestic criminal law if their activities become known but they might also lose certain protections to which they may have been entitled under international law. Protected person status under the 1949 Geneva Conventions might not arise for certain civilians, including 'the detaining power's own nationals who may have collaborated with the enemy'.[1] As will be discussed, international humanitarian law's fundamental guarantees concerning humane treatment and fair trial would nevertheless be generally applicable to such persons, given that these protections increasingly apply regardless of status.

The emphasis on status under international humanitarian law is a reflection of the fundamental principle of distinction which obliges parties to an armed conflict to distinguish at all times between civilians and civilian objects on the one hand, and members of armed forces and military objectives on the other. It also reflects how particular groups of persons have been considered as being especially vulnerable during wartime and deserving of legal protection. Owing to the risks they face after having fallen into the hands of the enemy, prisoners of war and civilians in occupied territory have long been treated as two such principal categories; the Appeals Chamber of the International Criminal Court has observed how '[p]rotection is required in particular against harm suffered from the enemy forces since violence—and potential abuses—during armed conflict are typically directed against, or inflicted on, enemy

[1] Nils Melzer, *International Humanitarian Law: A Comprehensive Introduction* (ICRC 2016) 207.

To Serve the Enemy: Informers, Collaborators, and the Laws of Armed Conflict. Shane Darcy, Oxford University Press (2019). © Shane Darcy.
DOI: 10.1093/oso/ 9780198788898.001.0001

combatants or enemy civilians'.[2] Since its earliest treaties, humanitarian law has also offered protection to other specific groups, such as the wounded, sick, and shipwrecked members of armed forces.[3] More recent instruments seek to extend protections more broadly, with Common Article 3 of the 1949 Geneva Conventions applying its fundamental guarantees to all persons 'taking no active part in the hostilities'.[4] This includes 'members of armed forces who have laid down their arms and those placed "hors de combat" by sickness, wounds, detention, or any other cause'. Other participants in armed conflict recognised by humanitarian law, such as spies and mercenaries, receive more limited protection,[5] while certain civilians may be denied particular rights and privileges for 'activities hostile to the security of the State'.[6]

In examining the key issues concerning the status of informers and other collaborators in times of armed conflict, this chapter will begin with civilians who actively cooperate with an adversary, before turning to members of armed forces who do so. As discussed in Chapter 1, it is not uncommon for civilians to provide information to enemy forces as guides or informers, while those who contribute to military operations, serve under an occupying power or engage in propaganda efforts have also been condemned as collaborators for aiding the enemy. The first section examines whether civilian informers might be considered as spies under the law of armed conflict, following which civilian participation in hostilities is discussed, given its relevance for certain forms of collaboration. The section then turns to the category of protected persons under the Fourth Geneva Convention in order to consider the status of nationals of the occupied state that collaborate with an occupying power. This section will consider evolving understandings of the nationality requirement for protected person status,[7] the Fourth Convention's derogations regime under Article 5, and the claim that civilians in occupied territory 'who furnish information to the enemy, fall outside the provisions of Additional Protocol I'.[8] Analysing the status of civilians who collaborate with an adversary reveals certain deliberate blind spots on the part of international humanitarian law.

With regard to members of armed forces, this chapter's second section examines the status implications for those who choose to serve the enemy, whether by providing information or by engaging in military activities. Prisoner of war status might not apply to those individuals who defect to join the enemy's ranks or to fight alongside an enemy's armed forces. For persons already entitled to prisoner of war status, the potential implications of engaging in acts of collaboration are also addressed. The chapter considers the status of members of armed forces in non-international

[2] *Prosecutor* v *Ntaganda*, Appeals Chamber, Judgment on the appeal of Mr Ntaganda against the Second Decision on the Defence's challenge to the jurisdiction of the Court in respect of Counts 6 and 9, Case No. ICC-01/04-02/06 OA5, 15 June 2017, para 57.

[3] See for example Convention for the Amelioration of the Condition of Wounded in Armies in the Field, Geneva, 1864.

[4] Geneva Conventions 1949, art 3.

[5] See Additional Protocol I, arts 46–47.

[6] Fourth Geneva Convention, art 5.

[7] See for example *Prosecutor v Tadić*, Case No. IT-94-1-A, Appeals Chamber, Judgment, 15 July 1999, para 166.

[8] United Kingdom, *The Joint Service Manual of the Law of Armed Conflict* (OUP 2004) 46.

armed conflicts who serve the opposing side in some way. Given the absence of the doctrine of combat immunity for non-state fighters in non-international armed conflicts, it explores whether there are any legal implications under the law of armed conflict, as opposed to national laws, for those members of such forces who collaborate with an adversary. Hersh Lauterpacht's description of the law of war being 'at the vanishing point of international law' is germane in this context,[9] for when it comes to those in the ranks of armed forces or amongst the civilian population who cooperate with an opposing side, international humanitarian law itself appears to be at a vanishing point in certain significant respects.

3.1 Civilians

3.1.1 Civilian Informers as Spies

The gathering and disclosure of information by civilian informers invariably leads to the term spies being used to describe such persons.[10] International humanitarian law, like international law more generally, does not prohibit espionage, but it denies certain rights and privileges to those persons found to have engaged in spying activities.[11] The term 'spies' is generally understood to refer to members of a state's intelligence services, although in the context of armed conflict, the most recent treaty reference in humanitarian law is to 'members of the armed forces of a Party to the conflict ... engaging in espionage'.[12] While Additional Protocol I does not refer to civilians engaging in espionage, it seems to acknowledge that spies are not limited to members of the armed forces, given its pronouncement that a member of armed forces undertaking espionage 'may be treated *as a spy*' and denied prisoner of war status.[13] The Fourth Geneva Convention recognises that civilians can engage in spying activities by allowing the punishment of protected persons found 'guilty of espionage'.[14]

For captured members of armed forces who have engaged in espionage, being treated 'as a spy' means denial of prisoner of war status and being liable prosecution for having engaged in espionage. The Hague Regulations prohibited extrajudicial punishment of spies by establishing that '[a] spy taken in the act shall not

[9] Hersch Lauterpacht, 'The Problem of the Revision of the Law of War' (1952) 29 British Yearbook of International Law 360, 381–2.

[10] See for example Republic of Liberia, Truth and Reconciliation Commission, Volume II, *Consolidated Final Report*, June 30 2009, 169; *From Madness to Hope: The 12-year war in El Salvador: Report of the Commission on the Truth for El Salvador*, UN Doc. S/25500, 1 April 1993, 44, 150; *Chega! The Final Report of the Timor-Leste Commission for Reception, Truth and Reconciliation*, November 2013, Volume II, 1054–5.

[11] See Richard R. Baxter, 'So-called "Unprivileged Belligerency": Spies, Guerillas, and Saboteurs' (1951) 28 British Yearbook of International Law 323; Simon Chesterman, 'The Spy Who Came in from the Cold War: Intelligence and International Law' (2006) 27 Michigan Journal of International Law 1071.

[12] Additional Protocol I, art 46(1). See also Hague Regulations 1907, arts 29–31.

[13] Additional Protocol I, art 46(1) (emphasis added).

[14] Fourth Geneva Convention, art 68.

be punished without previous trial'.[15] The death penalty was often applied to spies, with Vattel writing that spies are 'generally condemned to capital punishment, and with great justice, since we have scarcely any other means of guarding against the mischief they may do to us'.[16] While Additional Protocol I does not specify sanctions for those members of armed forces who have engaged in espionage, the Fourth Geneva Convention permits the death penalty for protected persons found guilty of espionage.[17] International law accepts both espionage and its punishment in armed conflict, and interjects only to ensure humane treatment of those considered as spies, including where this has led to a loss of prisoner of war status.

To designate a civilian as a spy would not trigger the application of Article 46 of Additional Protocol I, given that civilians engaging in espionage are not members of armed forces and thus cannot be denied a status as prisoner of war which they would not have been entitled to in the first place.[18] A civilian engaging in espionage could, however, be 'treated as a spy' and subject to the punitive consequences that flow from such a designation. Additional Protocol I does not provide a definition of a spy,[19] but Article 29 of the 1907 Hague Regulations does not confine its description of a spy only to members of armed forces: 'A person can only be considered a spy when, acting clandestinely or on false pretences, he obtains or endeavours to obtain information in the zone of operations of a belligerent, with the intention of communicating it to the hostile party.'[20] The US *Law of War Manual* states that 'any person—military or civilian' whose actions meet the definition of Article 29 'may be considered a spy under the law of war'.[21] The question then arises as to whether the international rules on spies and espionage address the situation of civilian informers who are spying for the enemy against their own country or party to an armed conflict, as opposed to spies conventionally understood as those engaging in espionage against the opposite side.

The provisions of the Hague Regulations relating to spies are based largely on corresponding articles of the 1874 Brussels Declaration.[22] Spies were 'by no means without protectors and advocates' at the 1874 Brussels Conference,[23] according to the British delegate General Horsford, who claimed that other delegates failed to appreciate fully the threat they posed and the necessity of their punishment:

[15] Hague Regulations 1907, art 30.

[16] Emer de Vattel, *The Law of Nations*, Book III, *Of War*, Chapter X, §179 (first published 1758, Bela Kapossy and Richard Whatmore (eds), Liberty Fund, 2008) 582.

[17] See Yutaka Arai-Takahashi, 'Lawmaking and the Judicial Guarantees in Occupied Territories' in Andrew Clapham, Paola Gaeta, and Marco Sassòli (eds), *The 1949 Geneva Conventions: A Commentary* (OUP 2015) 1421, 1429.

[18] On the categories of persons entitled to prisoners of war status see Third Geneva Convention, art 4.

[19] Yves Sandoz, Christophe Swinarski, and Bruno Zimmermann (eds), *Commentary on the Additional Protocols of 8 June 1977 to the Geneva Conventions of 12 August 1949* (ICRC/Martinus Nijhoff Publishers 1987) 565.

[20] Hague Regulations 1907, art 29.

[21] United States, *Law of War Manual* (Department of Defense, Office of General Counsel 2015) 151. See also United Kingdom, *The Joint Service Manual of the Law of Armed Conflict* (n 8) 45.

[22] Brussels Declaration 1874, arts 18–22.

[23] 'Correspondence Respecting the Proposed Conference at Brussels on the Rules of Military Warfare', *United Kingdom Parliamentary Papers*, Miscellaneous No. 1 (1875) [c.-1128] 167.

The danger to which an army is exposed by the enemy obtaining information through spies was perhaps, not fully realized by some of the Delegates, who failed to see that the punishment inflicted on spies is intended simply to be a deterrent.[24]

The original Russian Project defined a spy as a member of the military who 'secretly collects information in districts occupied by the enemy, with the intention of communicating it to the opposing force'.[25] Such a person, if caught, was to 'be handed over to justice', as was '[a]ny inhabitant of the country occupied by the enemy communicating information to the opposing force'.[26] The delegates agreed that military spies would not be liable to punishment if they re-joined their own forces, and would be entitled to prisoner of war status if captured again, but as they could not agree on whether this 'exemption from punishment' could be applied to civilians, they unanimously agreed to suppress the proposed article on spying by inhabitants of an occupied territory.[27] The opposition to the proposed rule that captured spies could be punished by the authorities of an enemy state was pacified by a modified article allowing trial in accordance with military law of the capturing state.[28] This 'guarantee of humanity' to prevent captured spies being 'placed beyond the pale of the law' had some detractors, however.[29]

New wording was adopted in the 1899 and 1907 Hague Regulations concerning the trial of those accused of espionage, as both prohibited the punishment of apprehended spies 'without previous trial'.[30] For Rolin, this enunciated 'a guaranty that is always indispensable, and the new phrasing was adopted with the purpose of saying this more explicitly'.[31] The Hague Regulations expanded the scope of application from occupied territory to 'the zone of operations of a belligerent'.[32] During the drafting process, it was acknowledged that private citizens might be considered as spies, in light of the adopted definition.[33] However, civilians or soldiers tasked with delivering dispatches to their own army or the enemy, and doing so openly, were not to be considered as spies.[34] *Parlementaires*, those tasked with communicating with the enemy and required to carry a white flag, were forbidden from taking advantage of their mission 'to obtain information', and would lose their 'rights of inviolability' if they 'provoke or commit an act of treason'.[35] A *parlementaire* engaging in espionage, or provoking collaboration, is not committing a violation of international humanitarian law per se, but like a spy, is liable to be denied certain entitlements which he or she may have been owed on account of such activities.[36]

[24] Ibid. [25] Ibid 166–7. [26] Ibid. [27] Ibid. See also ibid 200–1.
[28] Ibid 199–200. [29] Ibid. 199–200, 286.
[30] Hague Regulations 1899 and 1907, art 30.
[31] *Report to the Conference*, by Edouard Rolin, *The Proceedings of the Hague Peace Conferences, Translation of the Official Texts: The Conference of 1899* (OUP 1920) 60.
[32] See brief exchange during the Fourth Meeting of the Second Commission: Second Subcommission, 1 June 1899, *The Proceedings of the Hague Peace Conferences: The Conference of 1899* (n 31) 489.
[33] Ibid 490. [34] Hague Regulations 1899 and 1907, art 30.
[35] Brussels Declaration 1874, arts 44–45; Hague Regulations 1907, arts 33–34. See further *Report to the Conference*, by Edouard Rolin, *The Proceedings of the Hague Peace Conferences: The Conference of 1899* (n 31).
[36] Federal Republic of Germany, *Humanitarian Law in Armed Conflicts—Manual* (Federal Ministry of Defence 1992) para 229.

In the context of civilian informers, international humanitarian law does not exclude civilians from being considered as spies. Article 29 of the Hague Regulations sets out that an individual may be considered as a spy when 'acting clandestinely or on false pretences, he obtains or endeavours to obtain information in the zone of operations of a belligerent, with the intention of communicating it to the hostile party'. A civilian informer would arguably satisfy these requirements. The territorial element, that the clandestine intelligence gathering occurs 'in the zone of operations of the belligerent', has been understood broadly to include 'areas supporting the war effort'.[37] Physical presence is required in such areas; according to the US *Law of War Manual*, 'a person who engages in surveillance or information gathering from outside territory controlled by a hostile party would not meet this element, and would not be considered a spy'.[38] There are a number of implications for finding that a civilian who has shared information of value with the opposing side is a spy, bearing in mind the such persons would not be entitled to prisoner of war status in the first place.

Civilians engaging in spying activities for the enemy are liable to prosecution and punishment. They do not enjoy 'combat immunity', whereas members of armed forces engaging in espionage effectively forfeit such immunity on account of their actions.[39] The legal basis for prosecuting spying offences is national law, rather than international law.[40] An early attempt to devise an international code of crimes and punishment, the unsuccessful French proposal at the 1874 Brussels Conference for a 'uniform code for dealing with all instances of infringement of international law', had sought to include espionage among its offences.[41] However, as the Dutch Special Court of Cassation declared in 1949, espionage 'is a recognised means of warfare and therefore is neither an international delinquency on the part of the State employing the spy nor a war crime proper on the part of the individual concerned'.[42] The Court accepted that a civilian could be a spy within the meaning of Article 29 of the Hague Regulations, and although their activity 'was not forbidden by the laws of war', it was 'very hazardous for the person concerned' and they could be 'subject to sanctions on the part of the opposing belligerent'.[43]

International humanitarian law is not irrelevant to prosecutions for espionage, even if the legal basis for such lies in national law, given its insistence on fair trials and humane treatment (as discussed further in Chapter 4). With regard to prosecuting civilians for espionage, the UK *Joint Service Manual* makes the following claim:

> Civilians in occupied territory, even outside the zone of operations, who furnish information to the enemy, fall outside the provisions of Additional Protocol I and will usually be dealt

[37] United States, *Law of War Manual* (n 21) 152. [38] Ibid.
[39] William H. Boothby, *The Law of Targeting* (OUP 2012) 535.
[40] United Kingdom, *Joint Service Manual* (n 8) 46–7.
[41] 'Correspondence Respecting the Proposed Conference at Brussels' (n 23) 181.
[42] *In re Flesche*, Holland, Special Court of Cassation, 27 June 1949, Case No. 87 Annual Digest and Reports of Public International Law Cases (1949) 266, 272.
[43] Ibid 271.

with under the law of the belligerent or occupying power against whom their activities are directed.[44]

On its face, the *Manual* seems to exclude any role for international humanitarian law in this context. However, the intention seems that such persons 'fall outside' Article 46 of Additional Protocol I as they are not members of the armed forces for whom the issue of prisoner of war status arises, rather than the entirety of the instrument, given that the fundamental guarantees in Article 75 apply broadly to persons in the power of a party to the conflict. The fair trial provisions of Article 75 are critically important for those suspected of having engaged in espionage, especially those persons accused of having betrayed their country in doing so. The Fourth Geneva Convention accepts that offences of espionage can be prosecuted pursuant to penal provisions introduced by the occupying power, but stipulates that sentences may only be imposed only after a 'regular trial'.[45]

An occupying power will not be interested in prosecuting civilian informers who gather information for its benefit. Such persons may face trial before their own national courts after the conflict and the termination of the occupation, or before then if parts of the territory have remained unoccupied and the national justice system has continued to function. Until such time, however, civilian informers engaging in espionage may face other potentially more serious consequences, as mentioned almost in passing in Canada's *Joint Doctrine Manual*:

> Espionage means to gather or attempt to gather information of military value through an act of false pretence or deliberately in a clandestine manner. Generally speaking, persons engaging in espionage *may be attacked* and if captured while doing so shall NOT have the right to the status of prisoner of war.[46]

The reference to being 'attacked' suggests that spying activities, including those engaged in by civilian informers, may amount to a form of participation in hostilities and lead to the forfeiture of immunity from attack. The following section thus turns to consider the contested concept of direct participation in hostilities in the context of certain forms of collaboration by civilians.

3.1.2 Direct Participation in Hostilities

Civilians are not entitled to take part in hostilities during an armed conflict, in contrast to combatants, who have the right to participate in hostilities and who enjoy immunity from prosecution for doing so during an international armed conflict at least.[47] International humanitarian law does not explicitly prohibit civilian participation in armed conflict and even contemplates that certain civilians taking up

[44] United Kingdom, *Joint Service Manual* (n 8) 46.

[45] Fourth Geneva Convention, arts 68 and 71.

[46] Canada, *Joint Doctrine Manual; Law of Armed Conflict at the Operational and Tactical Levels*, (Office of the Judge Advocate General, 2001) 3–6 (emphasis added).

[47] Additional Protocol I, art 44. For non-international armed conflicts see Additional Protocol II, art 6(5).

arms may be entitled to prisoner of war status during a *levée en masse*.[48] However, the protection which is afforded to civilians under the law of armed conflict is very often contingent on such persons not taking part in armed hostilities. The basic rules of Common Article 3 of the 1949 Geneva Conventions apply to those persons 'taking no active part in the hostilities', a condition followed by Additional Protocol II which sets out that fundamental guarantees apply to those 'who do not take a direct part or who have ceased to take part in hostilities, whether or not their liberty has been restricted'.[49] Additional Protocol I is more forthright by stating that civilians will enjoy certain protections—most prominently the prohibition of being 'the object of attack'—'unless and for such time as they take a direct part in hostilities'.[50] These instruments do not provide a definition of direct participation in hostilities, although the concept has received considerable attention.[51] The issue of participation by civilian collaborators in hostilities, including by engaging in intelligence activities, has occasionally been touched upon.

Jurisprudence from the ad hoc international criminal tribunals has treated 'direct' and 'active' participation synonymously,[52] although the International Criminal Court has interpreted the latter term more broadly to include direct and indirect forms of participation by children in hostilities.[53] The Appeals Chamber of the International Criminal Tribunal for the former Yugoslavia (ICTY) has explained how direct participation in hostilities may go beyond combat activities, but rightly warned that it should not be understood as embracing 'all activities in support of one party's military operations or war effort'.[54] It considered the following to constitute examples of direct participation in hostilities:

> bearing, using or taking up arms, taking part in military or hostile acts, activities, conduct or operations, armed fighting or combat, participating in attacks against enemy personnel, property or equipment, transmitting military information for the immediate use of a belligerent, transporting weapons in proximity to combat operations, and serving as guards, intelligence agents, lookouts, or observers on behalf of military forces.[55]

[48] See Third Geneva Convention, art 4(A)(6). See generally Emily Crawford, *Identifying the Enemy: Civilian Participation in Armed Conflict* (OUP 2015).

[49] Additional Protocol II, art 4(1).

[50] Additional Protocol I, art 51(2)-(3).

[51] See for example *Abella* v *Argentina*, Case No. 11.137, Report No. 55/97, 18 November 1997, para 178; *Prosecutor* v *Akayesu*, Case No. ICTR-*96-4-T*, Trial Chamber I, Judgment, 2 September 1998, para 629; *Prosecutor* v *Strugar*, Case No. IT-01-42-A, Appeals Chamber, Judgment, 17 July 2008, paras 173–179; International Committee of the Red Cross, *Interpretive Guidance on the Notion of Direct Participation in Hostilities under International Humanitarian Law* (ICRC 2009); Michael N. Schmitt, 'The Interpretive Guidance on the Notion of Direct Participation in Hostilities: A Critical Analysis' (2010) 1 Harvard National Security Law Journal 5; Nils Melzer, 'Keeping the Balance between Military Necessity and Humanity: A Response to Four Critiques of the ICRC's Interpretive Guidance on the Notion of Direct Participation in Hostilities' (2009) 42 New York University Journal of International Law and Policy 831; Dapo Akande, 'Clearing the Fog of War? The ICRC's Interpretive Guidance on Direct Participation in Hostilities' (2010) 59 International and Comparative Law Quarterly 181.

[52] *Akayesu*, Trial Chamber Judgment (n 51) para 629; *Strugar*, Appeals Chamber Judgment (n 51) para 173.

[53] *Prosecutor v Lubanga Dyilo*, Case No. ICC-01/04-01/06, Trial Chamber 1, Judgment, 14 March 2012, paras 619–631; *Prosecutor* v *Katanga*, Case No. ICC-01/04-01/07, Trial Chamber II, 7 March 2014, Judgment, paras 788–790, 1043–1045.

[54] *Strugar*, Appeals Chamber Judgment (n 51) para 176.

[55] Ibid para 177 (footnotes omitted).

While civilians would lose their immunity from attack while taking part in hostilities in these ways, the Appeals Chamber also described forms of indirect participation where such protection would not be foregone:

participating in activities in support of the war or military effort of one of the parties to the conflict, selling goods to one of the parties to the conflict, expressing sympathy for the cause of one of the parties to the conflict, failing to act to prevent an incursion by one of the parties to the conflict, accompanying and supplying food to one of the parties to the conflict, gathering and transmitting military information, transporting arms and munitions, and providing supplies, and providing specialist advice regarding the selection of military personnel, their training or the correct maintenance of the weapons.[56]

The examples of civilian collaboration with enemy forces as described in Chapter 1 encompass both direct and indirect forms of participation in hostilities, as well as other forms of cooperation with an opposing side which are clearly unrelated to actual hostilities.

Civilians taking up arms and engaging in fighting alongside the enemy would clearly lead to such persons losing their immunity from being the object of attack for such time as they are directly participating in hostilities, but those who trade with the enemy, provide labour, or are engaged in bureaucratic collaboration should not be considered as direct participants in hostilities. The assistance provided by interpreters in some limited instances, such as during raids or searches, may be considered as amounting to direct participation in hostilities.[57] In Afghanistan, armed opposition groups have threatened that local interpreters working with foreign forces would be targeted; 'even if an Afghan or an interpreter was standing next to an International Security Assistance Force soldier, it would be them that would be targeted first rather than the soldier'.[58] For civilian informers, the question of direct participation in hostilities is more complex, given the range of potential intelligence gathering activities which may constitute either direct or indirect participation according to the ICTY's list.

The case law of the international criminal tribunals has touched on the phenomenon of real or perceived collaboration by civilians with an opposing force during armed conflict, including examples of civilians acting as informers. In the *Limaj* case, an ICTY Trial Chamber addressed the treatment of Serbian and Kosovar Albanian civilians suspected of collaboration by the Kosovo Liberation Army (KLA). Businesses and businesspeople 'believed to be collaborating with Serbs' were attacked, and the KLA detained, interrogated, and abused persons 'accused of working as spies for the Serbian regime or accused of having knowledge of perceived collaborators operating in Kosovo'.[59] Suspected spies and other 'traitors to their people' were 'singled

[56] Ibid (footnotes omitted).

[57] Giulio Bartolini, 'General Principles of International Humanitarian Law and Their Application to Interpreters Serving in Conflict Locations', 9 March 2010 <http://aiic.net/p/3396> accessed 29 May 2019.

[58] 'Opposing militants forces threaten local nationals working for International Security Assistance Force', 10 Marine 2007, TFU intelligence summary 222 (NSI), 9 March 2007 <https://wardiaries.wikileaks.org/id/774CFC16-2219-0B3F-9FA240E18C7B122F/> accessed 29 May 2019.

[59] *Prosecutor* v *Limaj et al.*, Case No. IT-03-66-T, Trial Chamber, Judgment, 30 November 2005, para 196, 203.

out for especially severe treatment in detention'.[60] A communiqué from the KLA promised 'death to enemies and traitors'.[61] Defence counsel argued that such persons were targeted for taking an active part in hostilities and as collaborators they were not entitled to civilian status.[62] The Trial Chamber concluded that it did not have sufficient evidence to conclude that the alleged collaborators could be denied civilian status for the purpose of crimes against humanity, but held that 'as a general rule, perceived collaborators abducted by the KLA were entitled to civilian status' in accordance with Article 50(1) of Additional Protocol I.[63] As they were not taking an active part in hostilities at the time they were subject to cruel treatment,[64] the issue of whether informing would amount to direct participation in hostilities was not broached by the Tribunal.

The Appeals Chamber of the Special Court for Sierra Leone adopted a similar position in holding that 'perceived "collaborators" are accorded civilian status under international law'.[65] The parties to the civil war in Sierra Leone had used the term collaborators broadly so as to include those that supported or cooperated with other armed groups, as well as persons who were perceived as not offering their support to a particular party to the conflict.[66] The Special Court focused primarily on this passive variety of perceived collaborator, although it also considered briefly those that might have collaborated more actively:

> The Chamber is of the opinion that persons accused of 'collaborating' with the government or armed forces would only become legitimate military targets if they were taking direct part in the hostilities. Indirectly supporting or failing to resist an attacking force is insufficient to constitute such participation. In addition, even if such civilians could be considered to have taken a direct part in hostilities, they would only qualify as legitimate military targets during the period of their direct participation.[67]

The attacks on unarmed 'rebel collaborators' largely took place outside the context of military operations, according to the Special Court.[68]

In considering whether the activities of civilian informers might amount to direct participation in hostilities, the jurisprudence offers some guidance by distinguishing between certain types of intelligence activities. From the sources drawn upon by the ICTY in *Strugar*, 'transmitting military information for the immediate use of a belligerent' would amount to direct participation in hostilities, as would serving as an 'intelligence agent', although 'gathering and transmitting military information'

[60] Ibid para 208. [61] Ibid para 216. [62] Ibid para 219. [63] Ibid para 224.

[64] Ibid paras 290–507. See also *Prosecutor v Haradinaj et al.*, Case No. IT-04-84-T, Trial Chamber, Judgment, 3 April 2008; *Prosecutor v Haradinaj et al.*, Case No. IT-04-84-A, Appeals Chamber, Judgment, 19 July 2010; *Prosecutor v Haradinaj et al.*, Case No. IT-04-84-T, Trial Chamber, Retrial Judgment, 29 November 2012.

[65] *Prosecutor v Fofana and Kondewa*, Case No. SCSL-04-14-A, Appeals Chamber, Judgment, 28 May 2008, para 260. See also ibid para 264.

[66] See for example *Prosecutor v Brima, Kamara and Kanu*, Case No. SCSL-2004-16-T, Trial Chamber II, Judgment, 20 June 2007, para 1778.

[67] *Prosecutor v Sesay, Kallon and Gbao*, Case No. SCSL-04-15-T, Trial Chamber I, Judgment, 2 March 2009, para 86.

[68] *Prosecutor v Fofana and Kondewa*, Case No. SCSL-04-14-T, Trial Chamber, Sentencing Judgment, 9 October 2007, para 47.

would only amount to indirect participation.[69] The Supreme Court of Israel did not draw such distinctions when asserting that 'a person who collects intelligence on the army, whether on issues regarding the hostilities … or beyond' ought to be considered as taking a direct part in hostilities.[70]

To try to draw a distinction between such forms of intelligence gathering, the ICTY Appeals Chamber noted that an individual's participation might be 'intermittent and discontinuous', as is often the case with informers, and that establishing 'whether a victim was actively participating in the hostilities at the time of the offence depends on the nexus between the victim's activities at the time of the offence and any acts of war which by their nature or purpose are intended to cause actual harm to the personnel or equipment of the adverse party'.[71] This language is echoed in the International Committee of the Red Cross' (ICRC) *Interpretative Guidance on the Notion of Direct Participation*, which provides the following criteria for an act to be considered as direct participation:

1. The act must be likely to adversely affect the military operations or military capacity of a party to an armed conflict or, alternatively, to inflict death, injury, or destruction on persons or objects protected against direct attack (threshold of harm), and
2. there must be a direct causal link between the act and the harm likely to result either from that act, or from a coordinated military operation of which that act constitutes an integral part (direct causation), and
3. the act must be specifically designed to directly cause the required threshold of harm in support of a party to the conflict and to the detriment of another (belligerent nexus).[72]

For a civilian informer, the act of supplying information would need to involve intelligence of significant value to the opposing side, and its transmission to the opposing side would have to lead directly to the causing of adverse military impact or harm of the necessary severity to constitute direct participation. The ICTY's inventory of forms of participation in hostilities set out in *Strugar* presented the 'immediate use' of military information as being a distinguishing factor in determining whether intelligence gathering amounts to direct or indirect participation in hostilities.

The activities of civilian informers may not always meet the high threshold of the ICRC's formulation, particularly if the information is of limited or no direct value for military operations. The general undermining of the effectiveness of an armed group by the recurring acts of informers would seem to have a cumulative effect and not be reducible to single acts that in and of themselves would constitute direct participation in hostilities. However, the activities of hooded informers in identifying wanted persons during military search operations, as described in Chapter 1,

[69] *Strugar*, Appeals Chamber Judgment (n 51) para 177.

[70] *The Public Committee against Torture in Israel et al. v Government of Israel et al.*, HCJ 769/02, 13 December 2006, para 35.

[71] Ibid para 178.

[72] ICRC, *Interpretive Guidance on the Notion of Direct Participation* (n 51) 16–17.

would more readily constitute direct participation. Similarly, a civilian in occupied territory who communicates to the armed forces of the occupying power the whereabouts of a particular individual, who is then subsequently targeted and killed, could be considered to have directly participated in hostilities, as in the following example:

On August 4, 2001, I was sitting in my car outside of Barghouti's office when I saw Halawa walk in. A couple of hours later, he came out, got into his gold VW Golf, and drove off. I called the security forces and assured them that Halawa was alone.

From inside a tank at the top of a nearby hill [Israeli Defence Force] soldiers watched Halawa's car, waiting for a clear shot with no civilians close by. The first armor-piercing missile headed for the windshield, but Halawa must have seen it coming, because he opened his door and tried to jump out. He wasn't fast enough. The missile exploded and threw him out of the car. My car—which was sitting several hundred yards away—shook with the force of the blast. A second missile missed and hit the street. The Golf was in flames, and so was Halawa—but he wasn't dead. As I watched him run through the streets, screaming in pain as the flames engulfed his body, my heart nearly pounded out of my chest.[73]

Halawa was subsequently killed by missiles fired from Israeli helicopters, after an 'Israeli spy spotted him [leaving a restaurant] and verified his identity'.[74] In both instances, the information supplied by the civilian informers was used immediately and played a key role in the attacks.[75]

The ICRC's *Interpretive Guidance* views the gathering of intelligence as a preparatory act amounting to direct participation where 'carried out with a view to the execution of a specific hostile act'.[76] This suggests that the gathering and sharing of military information of a more general nature by a civilian informer does not amount to direct participation in hostilities. The ICRC also refers specifically to 'transmitting tactical targeting information for an attack',[77] which is similar to the 'immediate use' requirement referred to by the ICTY in *Strugar*. The following example of such an action is offered in the *Interpretive Guidance*:

an unarmed civilian sitting in a restaurant using a radio or mobile phone to transmit tactical targeting intelligence to an attacking air force would probably have to be regarded as directly participating in hostilities.[78]

Even though unarmed, such an individual can be considered as directly participating in hostilities and as not enjoying immunity from being the object of attack during that time. Other sources offer support for this position, including the US *Air Force Commander's Handbook* (1980), which states in notably broader terms that:

[c]ivilians who collect intelligence information, or otherwise act as part of the enemy's military intelligence network, are lawful objects of attack. Members of a civilian ground

[73] Mossab Hassan Yousef, *Son of Hamas* (Authentic Media 2014) 167–8. [74] Ibid 169.

[75] On the lawfulness of such attacks themselves see Nils Melzer, *Targeted Killings in International Law* (OUP 2008); Noam Lubell, *Extraterritorial Use of Force against Non-State Actors* (OUP 2010). On the causative link between intelligence and an attack see Michael N. Schmitt, 'Deconstructing Direct Participation in Hostilities: The Constitutive Elements' (2009) 42 New York University Journal of International Law and Politics 697, 728.

[76] ICRC, *Interpretive Guidance on the Notion of Direct Participation* (n 51) 66.

[77] Ibid 83. [78] Ibid 48.

observer corps who report the approach of hostile aircraft would also be taking a direct part in hostilities.[79]

The 2013 *Manual on International Law Applicable to Air and Missile Warfare*, prepared by the Harvard Program on Humanitarian Law and Policy Research, asserts that '[p]articipation in target acquisition' amounts to direct participation in hostilities.[80]

In *Strugar*, the ICTY Appeals Chamber included serving as 'an intelligence agent' as a form of direct participation in hostilities.[81] The sources relied upon by the Tribunal are naval and air force manuals of Ecuador and the United States, the former of which states that 'civilians serving as guards, intelligence agents or lookouts on behalf of military forces may be attacked'.[82] Using similar language, the 2007 US *Naval Handbook* considers that civilians 'serving as lookouts or guards, or intelligence agents for military forces may be considered to be directly participating in hostilities'. While intelligence agents would normally mean those members of a state's intelligence service,[83] civilian informers could arguably fall under this category, or be considered as lookouts. The sources relied upon by the ICTY do not offer any clarification nor do they refer to the agents as having supplied specific information of particular value, such as that to be used immediately for a military attack, only that they serve in that role 'for military forces'.

An interpretation that being in the role of an intelligence agent leaves a civilian open to being the object of attack for such a time as they assume that role seems overly broad given the frequently irregular and piecemeal nature of informing, and would arguably not constitute a 'continuous combat function'.[84] It is submitted that direct participation in hostilities would only arise where such persons are specifically engaged in intelligence-gathering activities, including the transmission of tactical targeting information. The position of a number of non-state armed groups that members of a state's intelligences services constitute legitimate military targets would not accord with international humanitarian law where those persons' activities are unconnected with military activities.[85] Sivakumaran has noted other overly broad interpretations, including the assertion by the National Democratic Front of the Philippines that intelligence personnel would include 'casual Government

[79] United States, *Air Force Commander's Handbook* (1980) cited in Jean-Marie Henckaerts and Louise Doswald-Beck, *Customary International Humanitarian Law, Volume II: Practice* (CUP 2005) 117. On the controversial reference in the United States *Law of War Manual* to journalists 'collecting intelligence or even spying' see United States, *Law of War Manual* (n 21) 175; Yeganeh Torbati, 'Pentagon revises law of war manual after criticism of press treatment', *Reuters*, 22 July 2016; United States, *Law of War Manual*, (Office of General Counsel, Department of Defence, 2015 (updated May 2016)) 171–6.

[80] Harvard Program on Humanitarian Policy and Conflict Research, *Manual on International Law Applicable to Air and Missile Warfare* (Bern 2013) art 29(iv).

[81] *Strugar*, Appeals Chamber Judgment (n 51) para 177.

[82] Ecuador, *Aspectos Importantes del Derecho Internacional Maritimo que Deben Tener Presente los Commandantes de los Buques*, Academia de Guerra Naval, 1989, §11.3, cited in Henckaerts and Doswald-Beck, *Customary International Humanitarian Law* (n 79) 116.

[83] See for example Ian Henderson, 'Civilian Intelligence Agencies and the Use of Armed Drones' (2010) 13 Yearbook of International Humanitarian Law 133.

[84] ICRC, *Interpretive Guidance on the Nation of Direct Participation* (n 51) 33–4.

[85] Sandesh Sivakumaran, *The Law of Non-International Armed Conflict* (OUP 2012) 368–70.

informers' such as peasants who identify members of the Communist party or who call the police when faced with threats of extortion.[86] The Sudan People's Liberation Army included '[p]ersons acting as agents or spies for the Sudan Government' on its list of declared enemies.[87]

Spies, both civilian and military, might be open to lawful attack while engaged in intelligence-gathering activities:

> Espionage [...] and indeed the gathering of militarily useful information from outside territory controlled by the adverse party are both likely to constitute direct participation in the hostilities. Any person so engaged, including a civilian, will be liable to be lawfully attacked by the adverse party to the conflict, in the case of a civilian for such time as he is so engaged.[88]

A significant practical problem arises in this context in that determining whether an individual is a spy, an intelligence agent, or is engaged in the transmission of tactical targeting information for immediate use is inherently difficult on account of the clandestine nature of such activities. These tend to be undertaken in such a way as 'to conceal the identities of the persons concerned ... or to conceal that fact that the activity has occurred at all'.[89] Moreover, a civilian informer who alerts an attacking force to the location of a wanted individual, for example, might be directly participating in hostilities only for however long it takes to make a phone call or send an electronic message. To treat such an individual as an 'intelligence agent' would expand the period of time in which such a person might be considered as participating in hostilities, but seems be an inaccurate designation that would be open to abuse. In the context of irregular armed groups, Nils Melzer has taken a similar line that informers and collaborators 'without fighting function' could hardly be considered as members of such groups, and thus are to be treated as civilians and subject to attack 'only for such time as they directly participate in hostilities'.[90]

Two further dilemmas arise in the context of informers and direct participation in hostilities: first, civilian collaborators supplying information of military value may have been coerced into doing so, and second, it is not the opposing force that might seek to make them the object of attack but rather the party to the armed conflict that they have informed on. The ICRC's *Interpretive Guidance* does not discuss these issues, touching only briefly on the concept of collaboration. The *Guidance* explains that 'the refusal of a civilian to collaborate with a party to the conflict as an informant, scout or lookout would not reach the required threshold of harm regardless of the motivations underlying the refusal'.[91] The corollary, therefore, would seem to be that the actions of a civilian who does collaborate might reach the required threshold of harm, and such an individual could be open to attack if the other requirements are met.

That collaboration may have been coerced might not necessarily prevent the loss of immunity and protect individuals from being the object of attack. Only in 'exceptional circumstances' does this arise, such as civilians physically forced to act as

[86] Ibid 369. [87] Ibid. [88] Boothby, *The Law of Targeting* (n 39) 535.
[89] Ibid. [90] Melzer, *Targeted Killing in International Law* (n 75) 320.
[91] ICRC, *Interpretive Guidance on the Notion of Direct Participation* (n 51) 48.

human shields.[92] Persons forced to engage in hostilities, including child soldiers, may lose the protection from being attacked, even if such participation can be said to have been against their will.[93] For a party to an armed conflict, it may not be possible to determine during the conduct of hostilities whether a civilian informer has voluntarily provided information to the opposing force, or indeed what the nature of that information is. Knowledge of the activities of a particular individual sharing information with the enemy would seem more likely to arise after an attack has occurred, in which case such a person would no longer be directly participating in hostilities, and thus not a lawful object of attack. If such a person were to be captured and held by their own side, the question arises as to the extent to which international humanitarian law offers protection or even applies to them, as is explored in the next section.

3.1.3 Protected Persons

Common Article 3 and Additional Protocols I and II codify a series of fundamental guarantees that are owed to all persons not participating in hostilities. This set of protections constitutes the legal foundation for the protection of civilians during contemporary armed conflict. A considerable swathe of the legal protections of the Fourth Geneva Convention, the so-called Civilians Convention, do not apply to all civilians, but rather only to 'protected persons', as defined in Article 4:

> Persons protected by the Convention are those who at a given moment and in any manner whatsoever, find themselves, in case of a conflict or occupation, in the hands of persons a Party to the conflict or Occupying Power of which they are not nationals.[94]

This emphasis on nationality reflects the original focus of the international law of war which was on inter-state conflicts and the protection of persons falling in to the hands of the enemy, primarily prisoners of war and civilians in occupied territory. The considerable expansion of this body of law during the twentieth century has led to its scope extending to both international and non-international armed conflicts, and its protections to all civilians, not only those of a different nationality. Common Article 3, for example, 'provides for unqualified protection against inhumane treatment irrespective of a person's affiliation, requiring only that the persons were taking no active part in hostilities at the material time'.[95] Situations of belligerent occupation, however, remain somewhat distinct and are governed by a specific set of rules set out in the Fourth Geneva Convention, as well as pertinent provisions of the Hague Regulations, Additional Protocol I, and applicable human rights law.

Civilians who collaborate with an occupying power during an occupation are in a potentially precarious position under the Fourth Geneva Convention. While the

[92] Ibid 59–60.

[93] Ibid. See further Chris Jenks, 'Law as Shield, Law as Sword: the ICC's Lubanga Decision, Child Soldiers and the Perverse Mutualism of Participation' (2013) 3 University of Miami National Security & Armed Conflict Law Review 106.

[94] Fourth Geneva Convention, art 4(2). See also Article 13, which applies Part II to 'the whole of the populations of the countries in conflict'.

[95] *Prosecutor v Ntaganda*, Appeals Chamber Judgment on Jurisdiction (n 2) para 60.

treaty protects civilians from being coerced by the occupying power into joining its armed forces or providing it with information, as discussed in Chapter 2, the potential harm faced by collaborators who engage in these or other similar activities emanates from sources other than the occupying power, principally the local population, armed resistance groups, or agents of the occupied state. Informers or collaborators would not seem to meet the definition of 'protected persons' vis-à-vis these persons or groups, as they would not be considered as being 'in the hands of a party to the conflict of which they are not nationals' under Article 4. For example, following the killing of Muhaned Abu Halawa as discussed in the previous section, a seventeen-year-old Palestinian youth was allegedly interrogated and tortured by the Al-Aqsa Martyrs Brigades and 'confessed to collaborating with the Israelis'.[96] Members of this Palestinian armed group then 'shot him, tied his body to the back of a car, dragged it through the streets of Ramallah, and hung him from the tower in the square'.[97] This treatment is clearly contrary to the fundamental guarantees of international humanitarian law, such as those laid out in Common Article 3, but such conduct could not be addressed under the Fourth Geneva Convention's provisions related to specifically to occupied territories on account of the 'protected persons' definition. It is a reflection of how international humanitarian law has at times paid little heed to how parties to a conflict treats those perceived as internal enemies.

A literal reading of the Fourth Geneva Convention would have it that informers or other collaborators who fall into the hands of armed resistance groups or forces of the ousted sovereign do not enjoy the full range of the treaty's protections on account of their shared nationality. Local interpreters, for example, would not be entitled to protected person status under the Fourth Geneva Convention if detained by forces of the occupied country.[98] At first glance, neither would Common Article 3 of the 1949 Geneva Conventions be applicable to situations of belligerent occupation, given that it applies '[i]in the case of armed conflict not of an international character'. The ICRC originally contended that Common Article 3 'applies to non-international armed conflicts *only*', but the fundamental principle of humane treatment and its elaboration in this 'Convention in miniature' applies *a fortiori* in international armed conflicts.[99] The contemporary view is that Common Article 3 applies in 'all conflicts'.[100] Nevertheless, it comprises a more limited set of rules. The broader protections of the Fourth Geneva Convention addressed to 'protected persons' apply only to individuals who are not nationals of the party or occupying power into whose hands they have fallen, even though such persons have no duty of

[96] Hassan Yousef, *Son of Hamas* (n 73) 169. [97] Ibid.

[98] Bartolini, 'General Principles of International Humanitarian Law and Their Application to Interpreters' (n 57).

[99] Jean S. Pictet (ed), *Commentary: IV Geneva Convention, Relative to the Protection of Civilian Person in Times of War* (ICRC 1958) 34, 38 (emphasis added).

[100] *Prosecutor v Tadić*, Case No. IT-94-1-T, Trial Chamber, Judgment, 7 May 1997, para 607. See also *Case Concerning Military and Paramilitary Activities In and Against Nicaragua, (Nicaragua* v *United States of America)*, Merits, 27 June 1986, General List No. 70, para 219; *Prosecutor* v *Tadić*, Case No. IT-9-14-AR72, Appeals Chamber, Decision on the Defence Motion for Interlocutory Appeal on Jurisdiction, 2 October 1995, para 98.

allegiance to that power.[101] The Convention's protections are consciously delimited in this way, as the treaty, 'remains faithful to a recognized principle of international law: it does not interfere in a State's relations with its own nationals'.[102]

A scholarly and judicial push for a more expansive interpretation of the definition of protected persons in the Fourth Geneva Convention occurred in the 1990s with a view to adapting humanitarian law 'to the principal challenges of contemporary conflicts'.[103] In *Čelebići*, an ICTY Trial Chamber applied the article 'in a more flexible manner' in order to cover 'as broad a category of persons as possible'. [104] The Serb victims in that case, although of the same nationality as those detaining them, 'were clearly regarded by the Bosnian authorities as belonging to the opposing party in an armed conflict and as posing a threat to the Bosnian State'.[105] The Appeals Chamber of the ICTY in *Tadić* claimed that the limited instances where the Fourth Geneva Convention did not apply the general nationality requirement—for certain refugees and persons lacking diplomatic protection—demonstrated that 'the legal bond of nationality was not regarded as crucial'.[106] For the Appeals Chamber, the character of international armed conflicts necessitated an emphasis on 'substantial relations more than on formal bonds':

> While previously wars were primarily between well-established States, in modern inter-ethnic armed conflicts such as that in the former Yugoslavia, new States are often created during the conflict and ethnicity rather than nationality may become the grounds for allegiance. Or, put another way, ethnicity may become determinative of national allegiance. Under these conditions, the requirement of nationality is even less adequate to define protected persons. In such conflicts, not only the text and the drafting history of the Convention but also, and more importantly, the Convention's object and purpose suggest that allegiance to a Party to the conflict and, correspondingly, control by this Party over persons in a given territory, may be regarded as the crucial test.[107]

The Appeals Chamber saw allegiance as being a key element, which might be determined by considering an individual's ethnicity, rather than nationality alone, as well as the exercise of control over that person. The Extraordinary Chambers in the Courts of Cambodia also emphasised the issue of 'allegiance—or lack thereof—that an individual has to a party to the conflict'.[108]

The ICTY's efforts at expanding the category of protected persons under the Fourth Geneva Convention can be considered as a progressive development of international humanitarian law.[109] The International Criminal Court has given an

[101] Fourth Geneva Convention, art 68(3).

[102] Pictet, *Commentary IV Geneva Convention* (n 99) 46.

[103] Theodor Meron, 'Classification of Armed Conflict in the Former Yugoslavia: *Nicaragua's* Fallout' (1998) 92 American Journal of International Law 236, 242.

[104] *Prosecutor* v *Delalić et al.*, Case No. IT-96-21-T, Trial Chamber, Judgment, 18 November 1998, para 262.

[105] Ibid para 264.

[106] *Tadić*, Appeals Chamber Judgment (n 7) para 166.

[107] Ibid.

[108] Extraordinary Chambers in the Courts of Cambodia, Case File/Dossier No. 001/18-07-2007/ECCC/TC, Trial Chamber, Judgment, 26 July 2010, para 419.

[109] See further Shane Darcy, *Judges, Law and War: The Judicial Development of International Humanitarian Law* (CUP 2014) 118–22; Allison Marston Danner, 'When Courts Make Law: How the International Criminal Tribunals Recast the Laws of War' (2006) 59 Vanderbilt Law Review 1.

imprimatur to this approach by not insisting on nationality as an element of protected person status for grave breaches and requiring that the perpetrator 'needs only to know that the victim belonged to an adverse party to the conflict'.[110] In *Katanga and Chui*, Pre-Trial Chamber I followed *Tadić* and held that civilians would be considered as protected persons when in the territory under the control of a party to the conflict 'provided they do not claim allegiance to the party in question'.[111] As a determining factor of protected person status, nationality is perhaps more easily assessed than the potentially elusive concepts of allegiance or belonging to a party to an armed conflict.[112] With regard to civilian collaborators in occupied territory, such persons are used by occupying powers because they share the same nationality or ethnicity as the local population and anti-occupation forces. Could it be argued that such persons no longer belong to the occupied state, that their allegiance is instead with the occupying power?

An individual who has voluntarily cooperated with enemy forces might be said to have switched allegiance, and arguably could be entitled to protected person status under *Tadić* if they fall into the hands of forces fighting against the occupying power. But if the collaboration was coerced, then there has been no genuine change of allegiance and such an individual might not be entitled to protected person status under the Fourth Geneva Convention. This slightly absurd outcome, and somewhat convoluted analysis, demonstrates one challenge arising from a move away from the nationality requirement under Article 4. Moreover, as Sassòli and Olson have argued, 'one should wonder whether states involved in international armed conflicts would be ready to give their own nationals the additional benefit of being treated as protected persons when—and just because—they bear no allegiance to the state (and are therefore surely seen by the state as disloyal to it in the midst of an external threat)'.[113]

In the case of collaborators, it may not be possible to extend all the protections of the Fourth Geneva Convention to a class of individuals which states patently did not want to be so covered by the treaty.[114] The obvious exception to this general exclusion is provided by Common Article 3, while Article 70 of the Fourth Convention also offers protections to certain nationals of an occupying power, namely those who sought refuge in occupied territory prior to the outbreak of hostilities. Such persons 'shall not be arrested, prosecuted, convicted or deported from the occupied territory, except for offences committed after the outbreak of hostilities, or for offences under common law committed before the outbreak of hostilities which, according

[110] See *Elements of Crimes*, International Criminal Court, 2011, 13; Knut Dörmann, *Elements of War Crimes under the Rome Statute of the International Criminal Court* (CUP 2002) 28–33. See also *Prosecutor v Thomas Lubanga Dyilo*, Case No. ICC-01/04-01/06, Pre-Trial Chamber 1, Decision on the Confirmation of Charges, 29 January 2007, paras 277–281; *Lubanga*, Trial Chamber Judgment (n 53) Separate and Dissenting Opinion of Judge Odio Benito, paras 9–14.

[111] *Prosecutor v Katanga and Chui*, Case No. ICC-01/04-01/07-PT, Pre-Trial Chamber I, Decision on the Confirmation of Charges, 30 September 2008, paras 290–293.

[112] Marco Sassòli and Laura M. Olson, '*Prosecutor v Tadić* (Judgement). Case No. IT-94-1-A. 38 ILM 1518 (1999), International Criminal Tribunal for the Former Yugoslavia, Appeals Chamber, July 15, 1999' (2000) 94 American Journal of International Law 571, 576.

[113] Ibid. [114] Pictet, *Commentary IV Geneva Convention* (n 99) 46.

to the law of the occupied State, would have justified extradition in time of peace'.[115] During the drafting of this article, as discussed in Chapter 2, it was accepted that this would cover both 'traitors' and common criminals.[116] Pursuant to this provision, an occupying power can take proceedings against those 'guilty of action prejudicial to their home country', such as propaganda in favour of the enemy after the start of hostilities.[117] Before then, these acts would be seen as 'political agitation', but once the war has begun 'such agitation becomes treason and the higher interests of the state take precedence over the protection of the individual'.[118] Article 70 allows the occupying power to prosecute its own nationals, who are not protected persons according to the wording of this article. The underlying logic of the provision would surely also apply to the occupied state, in that it would retain the right to prosecute civilians who assist an adversary and to deny them protected person status under the Fourth Geneva Convention. Whether armed opposition groups can prosecute alleged collaborators as a matter of international humanitarian law is explored in the next chapter.

The power of certain parties to an armed conflict to take measures against persons considered to present a security threat is confirmed in the article on 'Derogations'.[119] Described as 'an important and regrettable concession to State expediency',[120] Article 5 seeks to limit the rights or privileges for protected persons who may have engaged in activities deemed hostile to the security of the state or an occupying power.[121] The first paragraph of Article 5 applies to the territory of a party to a conflict, and covers situations where the party in question is satisfied that:

> an individual protected person is definitely suspected of or engaged in activities hostile to the security of the State, such individual person shall not be entitled to claim such rights and privileges under the present Convention as would, if exercised in the favour of such individual person, be prejudicial to the security of such State.[122]

In occupied territories, lesser potential restrictions apply, where:

> an individual protected person is detained as a spy or saboteur, or as a person under definite suspicion of activity hostile to the security of the Occupying Power, such person shall, in those cases where absolute military security so requires, be regarded as having forfeited rights of communication under the present Convention.[123]

These provisions are not specifically addressed to collaborators, but their content and the debates leading to their adoption serve to demonstrate the attitude of

115 Fourth Geneva Convention, art 70(2).

116 See Thirty-Second Plenary Meeting, 6 August 1949, *Final Record of the Diplomatic Conference of Geneva of 1949*, Vol. II, Section B (Federal Political Department, Berne) 480.

117 Pictet, *Commentary IV Geneva Convention* (n 99) 351.

118 Ibid.

119 Fourth Geneva Convention, art 5.

120 Pictet, *Commentary IV Geneva Convention* (n 99) 58.

121 See Anne-Laurence Graf-Brugère, 'The Derogation Clause' in Clapham, Gaeta, and Sassòli, *The 1949 Geneva Conventions; A Commentary* (n 17) 1123; Yutaka Arai-Takahashi, *The Law of Occupation: Continuity and Change of International Humanitarian Law, and its Interaction with International Human Rights Law* (Martinus Nijhoff 2009) 275–8.

122 Article 5(1), Fourth Geneva Convention, art 5(1).

123 Ibid art 5(2).

States towards civilians that may present a threat to security during an international armed conflict. Such persons are not entitled to the full range of protections of the Convention.

During the 1949 Diplomatic Conference, the perceived tension between the protections proposed for civilians and the right of States to ensure their security prompted attempts to limit the rights of protected persons considered hostile. Colonel Hodgson of Australia voiced his delegation's concerns at the direction of the legislative efforts underway, claiming that:

> the rights of the State in relation to certain persons such as spies, saboteurs, fifth columnists and traitors, had been insufficiently defined. The only laws which protected a State against its enemies were, it seemed, the Criminal Laws in force before hostilities. It was desirable to provide for the necessary exceptions to the rules for protection contained in the Convention.[124]

Amendments were thus proposed to the article on protected persons 'with the object of excluding spies and traitors from the benefits provided by that Article'.[125] Such persons were not to be without any protection, as even for a spy, 'it would not be right to submit him to inhumane treatment, to torture, and so forth'.[126]

For some delegates at the 1949 Diplomatic Conference, the proposed article on derogations was to allow States to 'get round the Convention'.[127] Colonel Hodgson countered testily that 'you would think this afternoon that our main purpose in coming to this Conference was to draft Conventions or Articles for the protection of Quislings, saboteurs and traitors'.[128] The UK's delegation explained that it should be possible 'to counteract the dangers to which a country could be exposed in wartime by the activities of traitors and saboteurs [...] by the adoption of effective measures against individuals suspected of giving assistance to the enemy'.[129] The derogations article would only apply to a particular class of individuals:

> the people with whom we are generally dealing here are people who have entered the country of the Home Power in time of peace and with their permission, and who have taken all that the country had to give them and have turned out to be conspirators and traitors in war-time against the country which has sheltered them.[130]

The report of Committee III to the conference plenary explained that the proposed article was to prevent enemy agents benefitting from the treaty:

[124] Committee III (Civilians) Second Meeting, 26 April 1949, *Final Record of the Diplomatic Conference of Geneva of 1949*, Vol. II, Section A (Federal Political Department, Berne) 622.

[125] Committee III (Civilians) Tenth Meeting, 6 May 1949, *Final Record* (n 124) 644–5.

[126] Ibid 645.

[127] Twenty-Third Plenary Meeting, 1 August 1949, *Final Record* (n 124) 382. For the proposed article see Annex No. 195, *Final Record of the Diplomatic Conference of Geneva of 1949*, Vol. III (Federal Political Department, Berne) 100–1.

[128] Twenty-Third Plenary Meeting, 1 August 1949, *Final Record* (n 124) 382.

[129] Committee III (Civilians), Forty-Ninth Meeting, 18 July 1949, *Final Record* (n 127) 797.

[130] Twenty-Third Plenary Meeting, 1 August 1949, *Final Record* (n 124) 380. See also Annex No. 196, *Final Record* (n 127) 101.

Many Delegations have therefore felt the fear that, under cover of the protection offered by our Convention, spies, saboteurs or other persons dangerous to the State may be able to abuse the rights which it provides for them.[131]

The existence of this threat was seen as a necessary justification for giving each state 'a free hand in its defence measures without imposing any obligations under the Convention other than the duty to ensure humane and legal treatment'.[132] The final paragraph of Article 5, as adopted, reflects this latter stipulation and requires that such persons 'be treated with humanity', and subject to a 'fair and regular' trial if prosecuted.[133] Full rights and privileges should be restored 'at the earliest date consistent with the security of the State or Occupying Power'.[134]

The inclusion of an article on derogations in the Fourth Geneva Convention served to ensure that international humanitarian law did not prevent states from taking lawful measures against individuals presenting a wartime security threat. In occupied territory, where the domestic laws of the occupier should generally not apply, occupying powers are permitted to subject the local population to those 'provisions' necessary for fulfilling its treaty obligations and ensuring security and public order.[135] Protected persons engaging in subversive activities, including 'actions which are of direct assistance to an enemy Power', might lawfully be subjected to internment or assigned residence, for example.[136] This derogations regime allows for the rights and privileges of such persons to be restricted, but occupying powers are not given a 'free hand'—the forfeiture of rights under Article 5(2) is 'equivalent to placing the accused in solitary confinement'.[137] Nevertheless, this article is open to subjective interpretation by States as to what constitutes hostile activity or a security threat. Committee III of the 1949 Diplomatic Conference acknowledged that the proposed formulation was problematic:

The wording of this Article will perhaps be criticised as being almost too elastic. It must however be pointed out that threats to security can take so many different forms that it is hardly possible to give a more exact definition of the 'rights and privileges' which may be withdrawn. It has in any case been specified that the elasticity of the wording must not be taken as justification of any arbitrary action and that the provision would only apply in the case of serious and definite suspicions.[138]

These recommendations are reflected also in the Pictet *Commentary*, which stresses that Article 5 should only be applied 'in individual cases of an exceptional nature, when the existence of specific charges makes it almost certain than penal proceedings will follow. This Article should never be applied as a result of mere suspicion'.[139] The *Commentary* expresses concern with the breadth of the article's scope, while noting that some degree of protection was necessary for spies, saboteurs and other irregular combatants that 'act outside the laws of warfare'.[140] Terms such as espionage,

[131] Report of Committee III to the Plenary Assembly, *Final Record* (124) 814. [132] Ibid.
[133] Fourth Geneva Convention, art 5(3). [134] Ibid. [135] Ibid art 64(2).
[136] Pictet, *Commentary IV Geneva Convention* (n 99) 258; Fourth Geneva Convention, art 42.
[137] Report of Committee III to the Plenary Assembly, *Final Record* (n 124) 815.
[138] Ibid 814–15. [139] Pictet, *Commentary IV Geneva Convention* (n 99) 58.
[140] Ibid 53.

sabotage, and intelligence with the enemy 'have so often been used lightly, and applied to trivial offences, that it was not advisable to leave the accused to the mercy of those detaining them'.[141]

Protected person status under the Fourth Geneva Convention is restricted by nationality to certain civilians, but even those who are eligible to be included in this category may lose certain rights and privileges if they engage in activities hostile to a party to the armed conflict or an occupying power. The Convention, however, seeks to ensure a baseline of humane treatment and to prevent arbitrary action even in such instances. In times of armed conflict, mere suspicion or even prejudice have led to stern measures in the name of security against enemy nationals, as well as a state's own citizens. The internment of tens of thousands of Japanese-Americans in the United States during the Second World War, motivated by racism and war hysteria, was considered by the US Supreme Court as required by the 'military urgency of the situation'.[142] A presidential apology was issued many decades later.[143] Had it been in force, the provisions of the Fourth Geneva Convention would have offered protection to those Japanese nationals on US territory, but those US citizens of Japanese ancestry who were interned would not have been considered protected persons under the Convention, at a time when international human rights law had yet to emerge.

For civilians who do collaborate with an opposing belligerent, ineligibility for protected person status is based on their nationality, rather than their activities. While they may not satisfy the definition of Article 4, other rules of international humanitarian law, as well as applicable human rights standards, would be relevant. As Nils Melzer has observed:

> Persons detained for reasons related to an armed conflict without being entitled to a status specifically protected under the Geneva Conventions, such as the detaining power's own nationals who may have collaborated with the enemy, likewise benefit from the fundamental guarantees of IHL with regard to humane treatment and fair trial until their final release, repatriation or return.[144]

Common Article 3, as noted, does not make any reference to nationality, while Article 75 of Additional Protocol I elaborates on fundamental guarantees for persons in the power of a party to the conflict who do not benefit from more favourable treatment under the 1949 Conventions or the Protocol.[145] Despite the Protocol not enjoying the near-universal ratification of the Fourth Geneva Convention, the fundamental guarantees provisions may be considered as comprising customary international law.[146] International human rights law, as discussed further in Chapter 5,

[141] Ibid.

[142] *Korematsu v United States*, 323 US 214 (1944) 223. See Richard Reeves, *Infamy: The Shocking Story of the Japanese-American Internment in World War II* (Henry Holt and Company 2015).

[143] Julie Johnson, 'President Signs Law to Redress Wartime Wrong', *New York Times*, 11 August 1988.

[144] Melzer, *International Humanitarian Law* (n 1) 207.

[145] Article 75(1), Additional Protocol I.

[146] Jean-Marie Henckaerts and Louise Doswald-Beck, *Customary International Humanitarian Law, Volume I: Rules* (CUP 2005) 299–383.

would also clearly be of relevance for how a state treats its own citizens, including during times of armed conflict. While there may be other sources of legal protection for civilian collaborators, the issue of protected persons status remains relevant for the prosecution of those alleged to have committed grave breaches by mistreating or killing collaborators.[147]

The law applicable to non-international armed conflicts, the application of which may have obviated the ICTY's expansion of protected person status in *Tadić*,[148] eschews both the category of protected persons and that of prisoners of war as found in the 1949 Geneva Conventions. Civilian protection is not dependant on nationality in a non-international armed conflict; Common Article 3 offers the protection of its rules to those not or no longer taking part in hostilities. The law of non-international armed conflict 'does not contain the notion of a "collaborator" ',[149] as with the law applicable in international armed conflicts, but in contrast, it does not address spies and their treatment, or their activities more generally.[150] Authorities have taken the position that civilians who engage in collaboration during an internal armed conflict remain civilians; in one of the few references to the concept of collaboration in the ICRC *Customary International Law Study*, it cites practice from Rwanda which states that 'unarmed civilians who collaborate with one of the parties to the conflict always remain civilians. [...] this distinction is justified by the fact that in internal armed conflicts civilians are forced to cooperate with the party that holds them in power'.[151] As the judicial sources cited in the previous section clarified, civilians, including those cooperating with an opposing side, only lose their protection from being the object of attack for such time as they directly participate in hostilities. A civilian collaborator who assists the state's enemies during a non-international armed conflict may remain a civilian but is also likely to at least face prosecution under national law for subversive activities.

3.2 Members of Armed Forces

Collaboration with an opposing side by members of armed forces, whether by informing and passing sensitive information, or defecting and fighting alongside their previous opponents, may have an impact on their status under international humanitarian law. The armed forces of a party to a conflict, according to Additional Protocol I, consist of 'all organized armed forces, groups and units which are under a command responsible to that Party for the conduct of its subordinates, even if that Party is represented by a government or an authority not recognized by an adverse Party'.[152] Aside from chaplains and medical personnel, such members are considered as combatants and 'have the right to participate directly in hostilities'.[153]

[147] See Rome Statute of the International Criminal Court, art 8(2)(a). See discussion in Chapter 4.
[148] Sassòli and Olson, '*Prosecutor v Tadić*' (n 112) 576–7.
[149] Sivakumaran, *The Law of Non-International Armed Conflict* (n 85) 359.
[150] Boothby, *The Law of Targeting* (n 39) 276.
[151] Henckaerts and Doswald-Beck, *Customary International Humanitarian Law* (n 146) 23.
[152] Additional Protocol I, art 43.
[153] Additional Protocol I, art 43(2).

If they fall under the power of the adverse party during an international armed conflict, they are entitled to prisoner of war status, as are various other persons that accompany the armed forces.[154] While Common Article 3 refers to 'members of armed forces', and Additional Protocol II to 'armed forces', 'dissident armed forces' and 'organized armed groups', neither combatant status entailing immunity from prosecution for participating in hostilities, nor prisoner of war status are said to apply in non-international armed conflicts. None of the instruments explicitly address the status consequences for those members of the armed forces who choose or are coerced into serving the enemy. Irrespective of the impact of their collaboration on their status, such persons are likely to be subjected to the full weight of relevant internal disciplinary processes, if not worse.

In international armed conflicts, it is not unknown for members of armed forces to defect to the opposing side, and parties to a conflict would not hesitate to encourage such defection.[155] Although the terms 'defection' and 'desertion' are at times used interchangeably, defectors in this context would normally consist of those members of armed forces who voluntarily take up arms with the other side, while deserters are those who leave the armed forces to which they belong without permission to avoid military service and without necessarily seeking to participate in hostilities for an adversary.[156] International law neither prohibits defection nor the prosecution of defectors. The harshest of penalties was envisaged in the Lieber Code for members of armed forces that fought for the opposing side: 'if a deserter from the enemy, having taken service in the Army of the United States, is captured by the enemy, and punished by them with death or otherwise, it is not a breach against the law and usages of war, requiring redress or retaliation'.[157] Members of the US forces who fought on the side of Mexico during the United States–Mexico war of 1846–47 were sentenced to death, flogged, imprisoned, and branded by a hot-iron 'with a two-inch letter "D" for deserter'.[158] Most soldiers 'approved of the executions as just punishment for wartime treason and as a deterrent to future desertions'.[159]

Propaganda encouraging members of the enemy's armed forces to desert or defect, and thus act in violation of the domestic law of their own state, is considered permissible in times of armed conflict,[160] even though this is specifically prohibited

[154] Additional Protocol I, art 44(1); Third Geneva Convention, art 4.

[155] See discussion in Chapter 1.

[156] Heike Niebergall-Lackner, *Status and Treatment of Deserters in International Armed Conflicts* (Brill/Nijhoff 2016) 20–2; Ebrahim Afsah, 'Deserters' in Frauke Lachenmann and Rüdiger Wolfrum (eds), *The Law of Conflict and the Use of Force: The Max Planck Encyclopedia of Public International Law Thematic Series Volume 2* (OUP 2017) 331. See also James D. Clause, 'The Status of Deserters under the 1949 Geneva Prisoner of War Convention' (1961) 11 Military Law Review 15; Marco Sassòli, 'The Status, Treatment and Repatriation of Deserters under International Humanitarian Law' (1985) Yearbook / International Institute of Humanitarian Law 9; W.L. Cheah, 'Dealing with Desertion and Gaps in International Humanitarian Law: Changes of Allegiance in the Singapore War Crimes Trials' (2018) 8(2) Asian Journal of International Law 350.

[157] Lieber Code 1863, art 48.

[158] Robert Ryal Miller, *Shamrock and Sword: The Saint Patrick's Battalion in the US—Mexican War* (University of Oklahoma Press 1989) 92–112.

[159] Ibid 108. [160] United States, *Law of War Manual* (n 79) 307.

in relation to civilians in occupied territory.[161] It might be assumed that defectors which serve in the armed forces of the enemy might be entitled to be treated in the same manner as those whom they fight alongside. However, not only might they be prosecuted for their defection, the prevailing view is that defectors can also be denied the status of prisoner of war if captured by forces of the State party to the armed conflict from which they defected:

> The privileges of members of armed forces cannot be claimed by members of the armed forces of a belligerent who go over to the forces of the enemy and are afterwards captured by the former. They may be, and always are, treated as criminals. The same applies to traitorous subjects of a belligerent who, without having been members of his armed forces, fight in the armed forces of the enemy. Even if they appear under the protection of a flag of truce, deserters and traitors may be seized and punished.[162]

The view that defectors falling into the hands of their home state can be denied prisoner of war status is reflected in national case law and contemporary military manuals, although such status may be retained if acquired prior to defection.[163] The UK *Joint Service Manual* states that:

> [d]eserters in the military law sense become prisoners of war if they are captured. On the other hand, defectors from the enemy are considered not to be entitled to be treated as prisoners of war. However, prisoners of war who defect during captivity retain their status and cannot be deprived of it.[164]

The US *Law of War Manual* also takes the view that defectors are 'generally not regarded as POWs while serving in their new armed force'.[165] The rationale for excluding defectors from prisoner of war status is that they have not 'fallen into the power of the enemy' against their will; the Third Geneva Convention is concerned with 'combatants who pass into enemy hands, not of their own free will but by a force beyond their control because they are under its restraint'.[166] Defectors who voluntarily join the enemy's armed forces will not be treated as prisoners of war by that party, although persons who have already been designated as prisoners of war arguably cannot defect under the Third Geneva Convention.[167]

Defectors who fall into the hands of their original state are not considered entitled to be treated as prisoners of war. According to the US *Law of War Manual*:

161 Fourth Geneva Convention, art 51.

162 Lassa Oppenheim, *International Law: A Treatise*, Volume II (Hersh Lauterpacht (ed), 7th edn, Longmans 1952) 268.

163 See *Public Prosecutor v Oie Hee Koi and Associated Appeals*, [1967] UKPC 21, 4 December 1967. See however Susan Elman, 'Prisoners of War under the Geneva Convention' (1969) 18(1) International and Comparative Law Quarterly 178.

164 United Kingdom, *Joint Service Manual* (n 8) 147.

165 United States, *Law of War Manual* (n 79) 114–15.

166 *Manual of Military Law*, part III, (United Kingdom 1958) para 126. See also Albert J. Esgain and Waldemar A. Solf, 'The Geneva Convention Relative to the Treatment of Prisoners of War 1949: Its Principles, Innovations, and Deficiencies' (1963) 41(3) North Carolina Law Review 537, 555–63.

167 Third Geneva Convention, art 7; Cheah, 'Dealing with Desertion' (n 156) 5.

Defectors serving in the forces of the enemy who are captured by the State to which they originally owed an allegiance generally would not be entitled to POW status because the privileges of combatant status are generally understood not to apply, as a matter of international law, between nationals and their State of nationality.[168]

On this interpretation, international humanitarian law thus again refrains from offering a protected status under the 1949 Geneva Convention to a state's own nationals. This denial of prisoner of war status has been criticised for refusing specific protections of international humanitarian law to persons that are lawfully participating in armed conflict.[169] Heike Niebergall-Lackner argues that the specific judicial guarantees of the Third Geneva Convention could protect a defector from 'vengeful and expedited punishment while the conflict is ongoing',[170] without preventing prosecution for the act of defection. As with civilian collaborators who do not meet the definition of protected person under Article 4 of the Fourth Geneva Convention, defectors from the armed forces are entitled to be treated in accordance with fundamental guarantees under Article 75 of Protocol I, as well as applicable human rights law.[171]

A member of the armed forces who divulges information or acts as an informer for the enemy while remaining within the ranks of his or her armed forces would be liable to criminal prosecution but would not forfeit any particular status under international law. The context of captivity as a prisoner of war, however, is when members of armed forces are more likely to provide information to the enemy. Prisoners of war that serve the enemy in this way, or even those that might seek to defect during captivity, do not lose their status as prisoners of war. Article 7 of the Third Geneva Convention prohibits the renunciation by prisoners of war of the rights guaranteed under the treaty and serves to remove 'a possible additional incentive for the Detaining Power to indoctrinate prisoners of war'.[172] During the drafting of the Geneva Conventions, the delegate of Belgium raised an objection to forced repatriation on account of certain practices of seeking to turn prisoners of war:

> the Germans had brought pressure to bear on certain prisoners of war who might, they thought, be useful to them in the future, and had included them automatically in the lists of sick persons to be repatriated to their respective occupied countries. Once they had returned home, such prisoners were forced to collaborate in economic and in some cases in political or even military connections.[173]

With regard to coerced collaboration, whether in captivity or subsequently, prisoners of war should be entitled to raise a defence of duress, notwithstanding its exacting standards.[174] For members of armed forces who voluntarily collaborate

[168] United States, *Law of War Manual* (n 79) 115.

[169] Niebergall-Lackner, *Status and Treatment of Deserters* (n 156) 145.

[170] Ibid.

[171] Additional Protocol I, art 45(3).

[172] Marco Sassòli, 'The Status, Treatment and Repatriation of Deserters' (n 156) 24.

[173] Committee II, *Prisoners of War*, 14th Meeting, 17 May 1949, *Final Records* (n 124) 291. See Third Geneva Convention, art 109(4).

[174] See for example 'Misconduct in the Prison Camp: A Survey of the Law and Analysis of the Korean Cases', 56(5) Columbia Law Review (1956) 709, 769–70; *United States v Fleming*, 7 USCMA 543, 23 CMR 7, 57–58; *R. v Purdy* (1946) 10 Journal of Criminal Law 182.

while detained by the enemy as prisoners of war, they would not be entitled to such status were they to fall into the hands of their home state.

The status implications of switching sides by members of armed forces in an international armed conflict has been somewhat complicated by the adoption of Additional Protocol I, which has expanded the definition of such conflicts to include 'armed conflicts in which peoples are fighting against colonial domination and alien occupation and against racist régimes in the exercise of their right of self-determination'.[175] In such conflicts, the concept of prisoner of war is deemed applicable by the Protocol, even though the members of the armed forces of the parties to the conflict might be of the same nationality.[176] States have traditionally contended that prisoner of war status is not owed to their own nationals, and Article 44 of the Protocol, which foresees the granting of such status to certain guerrilla fighters, was 'one of the most bitterly disputed articles' during the drafting of the Protocol.[177] While a significant number of states abstained from the vote on this article during its drafting, most have now ratified the Protocol I without reservation on this matter.[178] The long-standing hesitancy to apply prisoner of war status to one's own nationals is likely to be amplified where the individual in question has defected during such conflicts. The relevant treaties are silent on the issue of defectors, while no clear practice to date has emerged to date.

The armed conflict in Afghanistan from 2001 saw the United States detain a number of its own nationals who had fought with the Taliban, albeit without necessarily having engaged in armed hostilities against US forces, including John Walker Lindh and Yaser Esam Hamdi. The United States sought to treat these individuals as 'enemy combatants', and in the case of Hamdi, to detain him 'indefinitely—without formal charges or proceedings—unless and until it makes the determination that access to counsel or further process is warranted'.[179] The Supreme Court found there to be 'no bar to this Nation's holding one of its own citizens as an enemy combatant', but that Hamdi was entitled to due process and to challenge the factual basis of his detention.[180] Justice Souter considered that as 'he was taken bearing arms on the Taliban side of a field of battle in Afghanistan [...] He would therefore seem to qualify for treatment as a prisoner of war under the Third Geneva Convention'.[181] John Walker Lindh was denied 'lawful combatant status' by reliance on the criteria for prisoner of war status under Article 4 of the Third Geneva Convention, which the Taliban had failed to meet, it was contended.[182] The court in *Lindh* noted that it was not asked to consider whether combatant immunity could arise for 'one who takes up arms in combat against his own country'.[183] The approach of the United

[175] Additional Protocol I, art 1(4).

[176] Melzer, *International Humanitarian Law* (n 1) 176.

[177] Sandoz, Swinarski, and Zimmermann, *Commentary on the Additional Protocols* (n 19), 521.

[178] Henckaerts and Doswald-Beck, *Customary International Humanitarian Law* (n 146) 387–9.

[179] *Hamdi v Rumsfeld*, 542 U.S. 507 (2004) 510–11.

[180] Ibid 509, 519.

[181] Ibid 549.

[182] *United States v Lindh*, 212 F. Supp. 2d 541, 557–58 (E.D. Va. 2002), 553–8. See Ray Murphy, 'Prisoner of War Status and the Question of the Guantanamo Detainees' (2003) 3 Human Rights Law Review 257.

[183] Ibid footnote 24.

States to these individuals might have been different had it been a party to Additional Protocol I which provides for a presumption in favour of prisoner of war status.[184] Moreover, a denial of prisoner of war status does not equate to an absence of protection under international humanitarian law: 'there is no room whatsoever for the argument that certain categories of person deprived of their liberty fall outside the protection of the law, regardless of whether they are called "terrorists," "traitors" or "unlawful combatants" '.[185]

The law applicable to non-international armed conflicts does not provide for the category of combatants with the attendant right to participate in hostilities or be treated as prisoners of war, although scholars and judicial bodies have suggested a commensurate status.[186] During the drafting of Common Article 3, there was heated discussion amongst the delegates regarding a proposal to shield from prosecution those taking up arms against the state. Norway suggested that participants in a non-international armed conflict should not be punished for taking part in the conflict, although this privilege would not apply to 'the instigators of such conflicts, nor criminals in common law, war criminals or traitors'.[187] The United Kingdom opposed the proposal as it implied that 'a country must suspend its law of allegiance in the event of a rebellion', entailing 'an abnegation of sovereignty by a government responsible for maintaining order'.[188] Governments were entitled to suppress rebellions and punish participants for treason, including resident aliens who 'owe local allegiance'.[189]

Common Article 3 remains silent on prosecution for taking part in hostilities, as the Norwegian proposal was unsuccessful, and contains a proviso that its application does not 'affect the legal status of Parties to the conflict'.[190] The inclusion of this clause was 'essential' to the adoption of these nascent rules, given that Common Article 3:

> does not limit in any way the Government's right to suppress a rebellion by all the means—including arms—provided by its own laws; nor does it any way affect the Government's right to prosecute, try and sentence its adversaries for their crimes, according to its own laws.[191]

[184] See Melysa H. Sperber, 'John Walker Lindh and Yaser Esam Hamdi: Closing the Loophole in International Humanitarian Law for American Nationals Captured Abroad while Fighting with Enemy Forces' (2004) 40 American Criminal Law Review 159, 164–5; Niebergall-Lackner, *Status and Treatment of Deserters* (n 156) 144–5.

[185] Melzer, *International Humanitarian Law* (n 1) 177.

[186] See for example Antonio Cassese, 'Should Rebels be Treated as Criminals? Some Modest Proposals for Rendering Internal Armed Conflict Less Inhumane' in Antonio Cassese (ed), *Realizing Utopia: The Future of International Law* (OUP 2012) 519; Emily Crawford, *The Treatment of Combatants and Insurgents Under the Law of Armed Conflict* (OUP 2010) 153–69; Tom Ruys, 'The Syrian Civil War and the Achilles Heel of the Law of Non-International Armed Conflict' (2014) 50(2) Stanford Journal of International Law 247; *Prosecutor v Mrkšić and Šljivančanin*, Case No. IT-95-13/1-A, Appeals Chamber, Judgment, 5 May 2009, paras 69–74.

[187] Committee II (Prisoners of War) Nineteenth Meeting, 14 June 1949, *Final Record* (n 124) 322.

[188] Ibid.

[189] Special Committee of the Joint Committee, 6 May 1949, *Final Record* (n 116) 42; Thirty-First Plenary Meeting, 5 August 1949, *Final Record* (n 116) 475.

[190] See also Additional Protocol II, art 3.

[191] Pictet, *Commentary IV Geneva Convention* (n 99) 58.

While laws relating to sedition, treason, and terrorism are frequently deployed to prosecute those taking up arms against the state,[192] Additional Protocol II embraces a reconciliatory approach by encouraging authorities 'to grant the broadest possible amnesty to persons who have participated in the armed conflict'.[193] But given the recommendatory nature of this provision, and the formal absence of the categories of prisoner of war or combatant from the law of non-international armed conflicts, the activities of defectors do not give rise to any change of status in internal conflicts, although the treatment of such individuals should remain governed by applicable international humanitarian and human rights law.

* * *

International humanitarian law's *modus operandi* requires an assessment of the status of particular individuals during situations of armed conflict in order to determine the legal protections to which they are entitled and the treatment which they may lawfully be subjected to. While informers and other collaborators are not amongst the categories of persons recognised by the laws of armed conflict, the question of status must be considered for civilians or members of armed forces who collaborate with an opposite side. Civilians informers who collaborate with enemy forces by providing information may be treated as spies, and prosecuted for their activities. Such activity, and other acts of collaboration, may in some instances even amount to direct participation in hostilities, and lead to the loss of the protection that civilians normally enjoy from being the object of attack.

The status of protected persons under the Fourth Geneva Convention tends not to arise for civilian collaborators in occupied territory, despite the prevalence of their use and the serious harm which may befall them. The firm reluctance of states to afford protected person status under the 1949 Geneva Conventions to their own nationals is also evident in the general denial of prisoner of war status to members of armed forces that defect to the other side. Despite their creation of an extensive set of laws regulating situations of armed conflict, states have at times sought to retain a 'free hand' to deal with internal security threats. National law rather than international law provides the legal basis for prosecuting civilians or members of the armed forces who collaborate with the enemy. Nevertheless, fundamental guarantees of international humanitarian law, including those relating to fair trial, apply to all persons irrespective of any status under the laws of armed conflict. The next chapter explores the application of such fundamental guarantees in the trial and treatment of informers and collaborators during situations of armed conflict, practices that have almost invariably been characterised by brutality, contempt, and revenge.

[192] See for example United Kingdom, *Joint Service Manual* (n 8) 398.
[193] Additional Protocol II, art 6(5).

4

Wartime Trial and Treatment of Collaborators

The most visible manifestation of the phenomenon of wartime collaboration is the frequently violent treatment and killing of those believed to have assisted an opposing side during an armed conflict. In contrast to the often clandestine nature of certain acts of collaboration, particularly informing, the ill-treatment to which collaborators are subjected is often deliberately public with a view to deterring others from serving the enemy. The brutal treatment meted out to suspected informers, collaborators, and other perceived traitors has at times been the outcome of some form of trial process, although doubts invariably arise regarding the fairness of such proceedings. While the question of direct participation in hostilities was considered in the previous chapter, in practice, alleged collaborators are most likely to be attacked outside the conduct of actual hostilities. International law is of most relevance in relation to collaboration during armed conflict in this context on account of its general prohibition of such practices, albeit with an occasional blind spot as to how a party to a conflict may treat those on its own side. The fundamental guarantees in Common Article 3 of the 1949 Geneva Conventions, and subsequently elaborated upon in the 1977 Additional Protocols, are key in considering the treatment meted out to collaborators during armed conflict. International human rights law is also of relevance for states and, increasingly, non-state armed groups.[1]

This chapter begins with a recitation of 'the gruesome repercussions for collaborating', to borrow a phrase from the Special Court for Sierra Leone.[2] The first section provides examples of the litany of brutal treatment to which collaborators have been subjected during armed conflict, from the Second World War to the present. It remains evident that a special contempt has been reserved for collaborators during times of war. The chapter then considers the legal standards applicable to such conduct and the extent to which international humanitarian law addresses or ignores how a party to an armed conflict might treat those that cooperate traitorously with an opposing side. This section analyses whether there are any potential implications for protection arising from the exclusion of a state's own nationals from the categories of protected persons or prisoners of war under the 1949 Geneva

[1] As discussed further in Chapter 5. On the applicability of human rights law to non-state groups see generally Darragh Murray, *The Human Rights Obligations of Non-State Armed Groups* (Hart 2016); Katharine Fortin, *The Accountability of Armed Groups under Human Rights Law* (OUP 2017); Andrew Clapham, *Human Rights Obligations of Non-State Actors* (OUP 2006) 271–316.

[2] *Prosecutor v Sesay, Kallon and Gbao*, Case No. SCSL-04-15-T, Trial Chamber I, Judgment, 2 March 2009, para 1125.

To Serve the Enemy: Informers, Collaborators, and the Laws of Armed Conflict. Shane Darcy, Oxford University Press (2019). © Shane Darcy.
DOI: 10.1093/oso/ 9780198788898.001.0001

Conventions as discussed in Chapter 3. It considers the evolution of the law of war crimes and crimes against humanity, and their application to crimes against collaborators, as well as the potentially expansive approach to Common Article 3 taken in the *Ntaganda* jurisprudence before the International Criminal Court.

The harshness with which informers and other collaborators are often dealt can be distinguished at times from similar treatment meted out to other victims of armed conflict on account of the claims to legality, or at least legitimacy, that regularly accompany such action. The lawfulness of prosecuting collaborators was noted by Hersh Lauterpacht, who wrote that '[a]lthough a belligerent acts lawfully in employing spies and traitors, the other belligerent, who punishes them, likewise acts lawfully'.[3] International law tolerates their activities and their being punished, while national law, public opinion, and the betrayed parties to an armed conflict will usually demand the latter. Thus, informers and other collaborators can be said to exist in a similar 'legal limbo' to that in which spies operate.[4] The final section of the chapter focuses on the rules of international humanitarian law relating to trials in times of armed conflict and the use of capital punishment, looking closely at trials by non-state armed groups.

4.1 'The Gruesome Repercussions of Collaborating'

International humanitarian law conceives of armed conflict as involving two or more opposing enemies, of states waging war against one another, or in a non-international armed conflict, a state and organised armed opposition, or several armed groups fighting against each other.[5] The treaties variously make reference to the armed forces, property, or population of 'the enemy', to 'opposing forces', and to 'the adverse party' of an armed conflict.[6] Yet participants might not consider the enemy as being limited to the armed forces of the opposing side, and might treat collaborators as also being adversaries. The Popular Front for the Liberation of Palestine, for example, stated that 'the enemy's informers are an integral part of the enemy ... we do not distinguish between them'.[7] For parties to an armed conflict, collaborators may present as significant a threat to their ability to wage conflict as the combatants of the opposing side. With this threat effectively emanating from within the ranks of their own armed forces or civilian population, greater ill-treatment

[3] Lassa Oppenheim, *International Law: A Treatise*, Volume II (Hersh Lauterpacht (ed), 7th edn, Longmans 1952) 422. See also *International Military Tribunal for the Far East, Judgment of Justice Pal, in* Neil Boister and Robert Cryer (eds), *Documents on the Tokyo International Military Tribunal* (OUP 2008) 809, 1403.

[4] See Simon Chesterman, *One Nation under Surveillance* (OUP 2011) 26, 35.

[5] See for example Fourth Geneva Convention, art 2; Additional Protocol II, art 1(1); Rome Statute of the International Criminal Court, art 8(2)(f).

[6] See for example Fourth Geneva Convention, arts 18, 19, 22, 23, 36, 40, 44, 83; Additional Protocol I, arts 2, 13, 17, 23–27, 41, 65; Rome Statute of the International Criminal Court, arts 8(2)(b)(xiii) and 8(2)(e)(xii).

[7] Yezid Sayigh, *Armed Struggle and the Search for a State: The Palestinian National Movement, 1949–1993* (OUP 1997) 287.

and abuse is often meted out to those collaborators as traitors than might be to the enemy's forces or civilians as conventionally understood.

Informers and other collaborators, including defectors from the armed forces, have usually fared particularly badly during times of armed conflict. They have been subjected to public executions and various other cruelties, in overt displays of the harsh fate that awaits those considered to have betrayed their own side. Treachery in war, like cowardice, has been 'traditionally answered with attacks on the body: flogging it, incarcerating it, displaying it'.[8] There are countless examples of such practices throughout the history of war.[9] The punishment for high treason in medieval England—men were 'hung, drawn and quartered' and women were burned at the stake[10]—was also applied to those involved in armed insurrection, such as the 1745 Jacobite rebellion in Scotland, which was followed by widespread executions and 'ritual disemboweling of the victims'.[11] Such practices are not historical artefacts, and similar examples can be found in more recent armed conflicts. In the Vietnam War, for example, upon the capture of a village which was considered to have 'defected' to the Government, the Vietcong seized 'the headman and his family, disemboweled his wife in front of him, hacked off his children's arms and legs and then emasculated him'.[12] The Special Court for Sierra Leone has described the brutal treatment to which perceived collaborators, and even their corpses, were subjected to during the civil war; one individual's severed head was impaled on a pole and another's intestines were used as a checkpoint.[13] The purpose of these acts was 'to illustrate the gruesome repercussions of collaborating or being perceived to collaborate with enemies of the [Revolutionary United Front] and so to terrorise and subdue the population'.[14]

The brutal treatment of collaborators may be part of a strategy directed at subjugating a population, with punishment as retribution for the betrayal of one's allegiance to a country or cause, or for failing to offer support, but it is frequently aimed at deterring would-be collaborators from divulging information, defecting to the other side, or offering other forms of assistance. The severity of the treatment to which informers and other collaborators are subjected mirrors the eagerness with which parties to an armed conflict seek to recruit such persons in the first place. Their value to one side is directly related to the risk they present to the other. While the forms of punishment imposed on collaborators may run afoul of contemporary humanitarian law and human rights standards, there is little scope for challenging the underlying authority, of states at least, to prosecute persons for crimes of

[8] Charles S. Young, *Name, Rank, and Serial Number: Exploiting Korean War POWs at Home and Abroad* (OUP 2014) 125.

[9] Alexander Gillespie, *A History of the Laws of War: Volume 1; The Customs and Laws of War with Regards to Combatants and Captives* (Hart 2011) 128.

[10] Matthew Lockwood, 'From Treason to Homicide: Changing Conceptions of the Law of Petty Treason in Early Modern England' (2013) 34(1) Journal of Legal History 31, 34.

[11] John Fabian Witt, *Lincoln's Code: The Laws of War in American History* (Free Press 2012) 21.

[12] Robert Thompson, *Defeating Communist Insurgency* (Chatto and Windus 1966) 25.

[13] *Prosecutor v Sesay, Kallon and Gbao*, Case No. SCSL-04-15-T, Trial Chamber I, Judgment, 2 March 2009, para 1124.

[14] Ibid para 1125.

collaboration such as treason, defection, or aiding the enemy. The frequent recourse to law and claimed justifications is evident in the practice of both states and non-states actors in their treatment of internal enemies.

4.1.1 Second World War

Prior to the Second World War, Nazi authorities showed little mercy to the real or perceived enemies of Germany. Political opponents and those accused of treason or espionage often faced the death penalty.[15] A Luftwaffe major who had shared an order of battle with Czechoslovakian intelligence was 'arrested, tried and beheaded'.[16] In the lead-up to the War, the courts of the Third Reich had significantly increased the penalties for offences of treason, crimes which were applied broadly to perceived enemies of the state.[17] Political opponents were labeled as traitors, and according to the Reich Minister of Justice Franz Gürtner, a traitor 'has always been regarded everywhere as the most heinous of criminals'.[18] The criminal law in Germany was treated as a 'law of war', with its goal being 'not merely to resist the opponent, but to annihilate him'.[19]

During the Second World War, the Third Reich 'executed wholesale spies, traitors and saboteurs who threatened its security'.[20] It is estimated that Nazi military tribunals sentenced 30,000 people to death for treason or desertion, 20,000 of whom were executed, and sentenced 100,000 to prison sentences.[21] The Gestapo is said to have found systematic betrayal of Germany by hundreds of Germans, including 'penetration of some of the highest headquarters of the Third Reich' by its citizens engaging in espionage.[22] For example, members of the Red Orchestra who passed information to the Soviet Union about Germany's war plans were arrested, often along with family members, and executed:

> Amongst those seized were a married couple, Hans and Hilda Coppi. He a radio-operator, was killed almost immediately. She, however, heavily pregnant, was kept alive until her son had been born and attained the age of eight months. She was then decapitated, and her child handed over to his grandparents.[23]

The bodies of Red Orchestra members were 'dispatched for anatomical dissection, in order that the remains should be unidentifiable'.[24] One of the most high-profile

[15] See for example 'Woman and 3 Men Executed in Germany', *New York Times*, 21 June 1938, 9; 'Germany to Execute Wartime Traitors', *The Victoria Advocate*, Vol. 43 (81), 1 September 1939, 1; 'Reich Extends Death Penalty', *New York Times*, 8 October 1939, 37.

[16] Max Hastings, *The Secret War: Spies, Codes and Guerillas 1939–1945* (William Collins 2015) 2.

[17] Ingo Müller, *Hitler's Justice: The Courts of the Third Reich* (translated by Deborah Lucas Schneider, Harvard University Press 1991) 50–8.

[18] Ibid 77. [19] Ibid 76. [20] Hastings, *The Secret War* (n 16) 551.

[21] 'Lawmakers clear names of German "war-time traitors"', *Deustsche Welle*, 8 September 2009, <http://www.dw.de/lawmakers-clear-names-of-german-war-time-traitors/a-4650568> accessed 29 May 2019.

[22] Hastings, *The Secret War* (n 16) 242.

[23] Ibid 243. See also ibid 114–22; Randall Hansen, *Disobeying Hitler: German Resistance in the Last Year of WWII* (Faber and Faber 2014) 18.

[24] Hastings, *The Secret War* (n 16) 246.

prosecutions for treason in Germany during the Second World War was that of Admiral Wilhelm Canaris, the chief of the Abwehr, Germany's military intelligence.[25] While the extent to which he may have contributed to the efforts of Germany's enemies remains contested,[26] Canaris was convicted of treason and sent to Flossenbürg concentration camp, where he suffered 'considerable mistreatment'[27] and was 'hanged slowly with a piano-wire noose'.[28]

Resistance fighters in the territories occupied by Germany also targeted members of the local population seen to be collaborating with the occupying power. Although attacks were directed against Germany's armed forces and supply lines, the armed resistance often had a preference for attacking local collaborators:

> His or her target was seldom a Gestapo agent or a German soldier; more often the target was a compatriot – a policeman, a factory guard, a railroad engineer, or anyone whom one's superiors in the resistance movement suspected of being a traitor, a spy, an obstacle, or a dangerous rival.[29]

This was at times a deliberate strategy owing to the risk of retaliatory hostage killings by German troops; 'rather than ordering the murder of Germans, they ordered the murder of traitors and collaborators'.[30] Killing collaborators would also contribute to creating a climate of terror, according to the French resistance:

> if the traitors continued to get away with their crimes, they would be joined by other cowards and opportunists. Justice and public welfare demand that they be pitilessly punished. Those that strike them down are instituting a reign of terror only in the camp of the traitors.[31]

The editor of *Défence de la France* considered that there was a duty to kill Germans, *miliciens* and traitors: 'kill those who denounce, those who have aided the enemy. Kill the policeman who in any way at all has contributed to the arrest of patriots.'[32]

In addition to summary execution in France, collaborators were blacklisted by certain professions and had their homes targeted, while certain resistance groups threatened to kill family members of informers and to punish those who opposed their way of dealing with this threat.[33] Death was often considered the only penalty available to resistance forces and the fate of condemned individuals was at times decided by a secret 'trial'.[34] In Poland, underground courts operated throughout

[25] See John H. Waller, 'The Double Life of Admiral Canaris' (1996) 9(3) International Journal of Intelligence and Counter Intelligence 271; Michael Mueller, *Canaris: The Life and Death of Hitler's Spymaster* (Naval Institute Press 2007).

[26] Hastings, *The Secret War* (n 16) 63–4, 223.

[27] Waller, 'The Double Life of Admiral Canaris' (n 25) 286.

[28] Vadim J. Birstein, *SMERSH, Stalin's Secret Weapon: Soviet Military Intelligence in World War II* (Biteback Publishing 2011) 316.

[29] István Deák, *Europe on Trial: The Story of Collaboration, Resistance, and Retribution During World War II* (Westview Press 2015) 113.

[30] Ibid 135.

[31] *Combat*, No. 49, 15 October 1943, *cited in* Peter Novick, *The Resistance versus Vichy: The Purge of Collaborators in Liberated France* (Columbia University Press 1968) 31.

[32] *Défence de la France*, No. 44, 15 March 1944, cited in Novick, *The Resistance versus Vichy* (n 31) 31–2.

[33] Novick, *The Resistance versus Vichy* (n 31) 26–31.

[34] Ibid 32, 35.

the Second World War 'trying and sentencing traitors in as legalistic circumstances as possible'.[35] In Burma, a cursory process for dealing with informers was used by Burmese guerrillas conducting operations with the United States: 'When informers were captured, the mountain people would go through the formality of a judicial trial: a three man jury would be selected and given instructions to execute the informers after the trial'.[36]

Of the major Allies, the United States prosecuted a relatively small number of members of the armed forces and citizens during the Second World War for collaboration. A handful of US soldiers were tried for helping German prisoners of war to escape, and several citizens were convicted for treason for assisting enemy agents engaged in sabotage in the United States, or for engaging in propaganda activities.[37] Collaboration with the Japanese authorities by US prisoners of war prompted the addition of a new crime of 'Misconduct as a Prisoner' to the Uniform Code of Military Justice.[38] The internment of Japanese Americans was not on the basis of convictions for collaboration offences, even though it was perceived as punitive in nature.[39] There were a number of British treason trials after the end of the Second World War, including that of William Joyce for his propaganda activities for Nazi Germany and John Amery for his efforts with the British Free Corps.[40] In its colonial territories, the British also punished former subjects for having aided the enemy by fighting alongside Axis forces.[41] The greatest number of post-war trials, as well as retaliatory violence, occurred in countries that had been occupied during the Second World War. For example, around 25,000 alleged collaborators with Japan were tried by the Chinese after the War,[42] and thousands of Vichy collaborators were killed either extrajudicially or following cursory court-martials.[43]

The Soviet Union punished tens of thousands of its soldiers and citizens for allegedly having collaborated with its enemies during the Second World War.[44]

[35] Deák, *Europe on Trial* (n 29) 201.

[36] James Ward, 'Irregular Warfare: Legal Implications of the Facts, Policies and Law from World War II to Vietnam: Remarks by James Ward' (1976) 70 Proceedings of the American Society of International Law 154, 155.

[37] Raymond Lech, *Broken Soldiers* (University of Illinois Press 2000) 231; *Haupt v United States* 330 U.S 631 (1947); *Cramer v United States* 325 U.S. 1 (1945); *Best v United States*, 184 F.2d 131 (1st Cir. 1950).

[38] Young, *Name, Rank, and Serial Number* (n 8) 87.

[39] *Korematsu v United States*, 323 US 214 (1944) 223. See Richard Reeves, *Infamy: The Shocking Story of the Japanese-American Internment in World War II* (Henry Holt and Company 2015).

[40] *Joyce v Director of Public Prosecutions*, House of Lords [1946] A.C. 347; *R. v Joyce* [1945] 2 All ER 673. See further Rebecca West, *The New Meaning of Treason* (The Viking Press 1964); 'Wartime Collaborators: A Comparative Study of the Effect of their Trials on the Treason Law of Great Britain, Switzerland and France' (1946–1947) 56 Yale Law Journal 1210.

[41] See W.L. Cheah, 'Dealing with Desertion and Gaps in International Humanitarian Law: Changes of Allegiance in the Singapore War Crimes Trials' (2018) 8(2) Asian Journal of International Law 350.

[42] Dongyoun Hwang, 'Wartime Collaboration in Question: An Examination of the Postwar Trials of the Chinese Collaborators' (2005) 6(1) Inter-Asia Cultural Studies 75, 75. See also Kerstin von Lingen (ed), *Debating Collaboration and Complicity in War Crimes Trials in Asia, 1945–1956* (Palgrave MacMillan 2017) 1.

[43] Ian Kershaw, *To Hell and Back: Europe 1914–1949* (Penguin Books 2016) 473. See also Novick, *The Resistance versus Vichy* (n 31); István Déak, *Europe on Trial* (n 29).

[44] Cherif M. Bassiouni, *Crimes against Humanity: Historical Evolution and Contemporary Application* (CUP 2011) 157–8.

Following the Axis invasion of the Soviet Union in June 1941, Stalin had publicly appealed that '[c]onditions must be made unbearable for the enemy and his collaborators; they must be pursued and annihilated wherever they are'.[45] Germany had found willing collaborators in the territories it occupied, at times through the promise of greater rations or exemption from forced labour.[46] The Soviet Union ran a military counter-intelligence organisation known as SMERSH, an acronym of the Russian phrase 'Death to Spies', which was charged with 'the detection and liquidation of traitors'.[47] The Soviet Union sentenced 472,000 servicemen as war criminals or traitors, of whom 217,000 were shot, and 600,000 prisoners of war and civilians were sent to the Gulag upon their return from slave labour in Germany.[48] Cases pursued by SMERSH were based primarily on the Russian Criminal Code's 'counter-revolutionary crimes', which included treason and espionage, and which allowed capital punishment and confiscation of property.[49] The Soviets also executed several thousand suspected collaborators with Germany operating within the partisan groups active in territories occupied by German forces.[50] Germany's recruitment of Soviet collaborators was often based on ethnicity, and Stalin responded by deporting entire ethnic groups to Central Asia and Siberia as 'traitors to the Soviet Motherland'.[51] Those that could not be deported, such as hospital patients, were 'burned, buried alive, or drowned in lakes'.[52]

Relatives of those considered as traitors to the Soviet Union were subject to collective punishment, imprisonment, and generally treated with suspicion.[53] Stalin authorised automatic arrest and five years exile for those whose relatives had engaged in 'spying for Germany and its allies; changing sides; aiding the German occupiers; participation in the punitive organs or administration established by the Germans in the occupied territories; attempted or intended treason'.[54] Deserters and surrendering Russian soldiers were liable to be 'shot on the spot' as traitors, and their families arrested and 'deprived of all State allowances and assistance'.[55] Although the Soviet authorities had recourse to domestic criminal law and trial processes at times, the trials have generally been viewed as unfair and arbitrary.[56] A judge from one of the Soviet field courts deployed in recaptured territories gave the following account:

> Frequently, I have to act as the third judge in a military tribunal and I condemn people to death. You can never understand how disgusting the whole business is. The prosecutor reads his charges, then demands capital punishment. Our triumvirate always confirms that sentence and the prisoner is taken out and shot.[57]

[45] Hastings, *The Secret War* (n 16) 316. [46] Ibid 324.
[47] Ibid 236; Birstein, *SMERSH; Stalin's Secret Weapon* (n 28) 1. [48] Ibid 2, 124.
[49] Ibid 52–3. [50] Ibid 218–19, 235; Hastings, *The Secret War* (n 16) 325–7.
[51] Deák, *Europe on Trial* (n 29) 71; Birstein, *SMERSH, Stalin's Secret Weapon* (n 28) 245.
[52] Birstein, *SMERSH, Stalin's Secret Weapon* (n 28) 246 (footnote omitted).
[53] Ibid 54–5, 129.
[54] Ibid 130. See also Tanja Penter, 'Local Collaborators on Trial: Soviet War Crimes Trials under Stalin (1943–1953)' (2008) 49(2/3) Cahiers du Monde Russe 341, 345.
[55] Ibid 105. [56] Ibid 235–7. [57] Ibid 191–2.

A mere pretence of legality accompanied much of the harsh punishment and ill-treatment that was meted out to the many thousands of real or suspected enemy collaborators during the Second World War. However, even the pretence itself was dispensed with at times. This has also been a recurrent feature of more recent armed conflicts.

4.1.2 Contemporary Conflicts

Armed conflicts of the twentieth and twenty-first century have continued to involve the most violent treatment for those considered as collaborating with an opposing party. International armed conflicts, including wars of national liberation, non-international armed conflicts, as well as instances of armed violence not qualifying as an armed conflict have all witnessed the severe and frequently unsparing treatment of informers and other collaborators. As the examples provided here illustrate, those who serve the enemy often fall victim to what can appropriately be described as 'man's inhumanity to man'.[58]

In the context of colonial conflicts, violence has been directed by liberation movements not only against the colonial power itself but also against those locals deemed to be working on their behalf. In British-controlled Cyprus in the 1950s, the majority of Greek Cypriots died at the hands of EOKA as 'traitors'.[59] The armed group had adopted an expansive definition of this term, which included Greek Cypriot policemen, police informers, and officials who collaborated with the British. The definition of 'traitor' used by EOKA 'was widened to include anyone who did not give active assistance to the organization'.[60] In one incident in August 1957, the Mukhtar of Asha was abducted and tied to the iron palings of a church with a sign on his chest which read 'this is what happens to collaborators'.[61] The consequences for betrayal under EOKA's interpretation were at times even more serious, with dozens killed.[62] The British authorities claimed that only around a fifth of those killed were known to them, and even fewer had provided information.[63] EOKA had a 'tendency to act on the merest unsubstantiated suspicion' in their view.[64] The killings of alleged traitors was often carried out publicly, in cafés and in front of family members, with victims shot or even bludgeoned to death in order 'to send a message to people that they must not betray EOKA'.[65] The summary nature of EOKA executions meant that they were open to abuse for the settling of old scores and prone to error, despite it being claimed that they had to be authorized at highest level.[66]

In Malaya, the British authorities relied upon informers in the conflict with the Malayan National Liberation Army. Jack Morton of MI5, and the Director of

[58] Robert Burns, *Man was Made to Mourn: A Dirge* (1784). See also *United States of America v Wilhelm von Leeb et al.*, Judgment, 27 October 1948, Case No. 12, XI *Trials of War Criminals before the Nuernberg Military Tribunals under Control Council Law No. 10* 462, 495; *Prosecutor v Kupreškić et al.*, Case No. IT-95-16-T, Trial Chamber, Judgment, 14 January 2000, para 755.

[59] David French, *Fighting EOKA: The British Counter-Insurgency on Cyprus, 1955–1959* (OUP 2015) 112.

[60] Ibid 159 (footnotes omitted). [61] Ibid 164. [62] Ibid 165. [63] Ibid 162.

[64] Ibid (footnotes omitted). [65] Ibid 162–3. [66] Ibid 163.

Intelligence in Malaya, explained how a series of successful British operations lead to one such agent being 'liquidated' in a Communist party purge: 'He was made to dig his own grave and two strong men then slowly strangled him to death. It was, however, some consolation to know that other comrades who were not agents were also executed. The Communists were taking no chances.' [67]

The replication of these practices in more recent armed conflicts has been documented by various official bodies. The International Commission of Inquiry on Darfur reported that rebels had abducted, tortured, and ill-treated individuals they accused of 'collaborating with Government and Arab tribes'.[68] During the civil war in Sri Lanka, the Liberation Tigers of Tamil Eelam targeted and killed 'suspected informers'.[69] In Eritrea, the state authorities are alleged to have killed both Eritreans and Ethiopians suspected of collaborating with the Government of Ethiopia.[70] Following Eritrean independence in 1993, 150 alleged collaborators were executed and buried in a mass grave, while several years later, the same number of Eritrean civilians 'were rounded up and shot for allegedly being collaborators of the Eritrean Islamic Jihad'.[71] The case law of the Special Court for Sierra Leone has detailed the beating, ill-treatment, and killing of alleged collaborators.[72] A seventeen-year-old boy accused of having collaborated with rebel groups in Sierra Leone was reportedly killed in 'a cannibalistic ritual',[73] while women were frequently targeted and subjected to sexual abuse for their alleged collaboration.[74] In cases concerning the Kosovo conflict, the International Criminal Tribunal for the Former Yugoslavia adjudicated charges relating to those of perceived as collaborators having been abducted, detained in inhumane conditions, assaulted, tortured, and murdered.[75]

The practice of contemporary armed conflicts and situations of internal violence demonstrates that suspected informers and other collaborators continue to be the subjects of public spectacles of overt violence. In South Africa, for example, such individuals were killed by the practice of 'necklacing', which involved 'a tyre

[67] David French, *The British Way in Counter-Insurgency, 1945–1967* (OUP 2011) 31.

[68] *Report of the International Commission of Inquiry on Darfur to the United Nations Secretary-General*, Geneva, 25 January 2005, para 402.

[69] *Report of the Office of the United Nations High Commissioner for Human Rights on Promoting Reconciliation, Accountability and Human Rights in Sri Lanka*, 16 September 2015, UN Doc. A/HRC/30/61, para 26.

[70] *Report of the detailed findings of the Commission of Inquiry on Human Rights in Eritrea*, 5 June 2015, UN Doc. A/HRC/29/CRP.1, para 1103.

[71] Ibid paras 1103, 1110, 1118.

[72] See for example *Sesay, Kallon and Gbao*, Trial Chamber Judgment (n 13) paras 1049, 1124–5. See also Amnesty International, *Sierra Leone: The Extrajudicial Execution of Suspected Rebels and Collaborators,* AFR 51/02/92 (Amnesty International 1992)

[73] Amnesty International, *Sierra Leone: 1998—A year of atrocities against civilians*, AFR 51/022/1998, Amnesty International, 1 November 1998, 37.

[74] *Report of the Sierra Leone Truth and Reconciliation Commission*, 2004, Volume 2, 101; Volume 3, 177, 180.

[75] See for example *Prosecutor v Limaj et al.*, Case No. IT-03-66-PT, Second Amended Indictment, 6 November 2003.

filled with lighted petrol placed around the neck'.[76] The South African Truth and Reconciliation Commission described the rationale behind this technique:

From evidence before the Commission, it appears that the burning of a body was a sign of contempt for the victim and his/her deeds. No act could convey a deeper sense of hatred and disrespect. The practice was also used to make an example of the victim, so that others would be inhibited from behaving like the deceased.[77]

In Northern Ireland, banishment or the killing of suspected informers 'with a bullet to the back of the head' was common, and individuals who were considered by the IRA to have associated with the enemy were tarred and feathered in some instances.[78] During the Anfal campaign against the Kurds, a senior Iraqi official stated that there was 'no objection to cutting off the heads of traitors' other than such persons should be interrogated for intelligence purposes beforehand.[79] Brutal methods of execution have been used by Islamic State against suspected spies and collaborators, most notoriously public beheadings and crucifixions,[80] as well as by other armed groups in Syria.[81] Other methods have also been used; in Colombia, the ELN imposed taxes on those 'who collaborate unconditionally with the armed forces of the government and paramilitary forces',[82] and in East Timor the burning of the homes of suspected collaborators was used to warn 'about the consequences of collaboration'.[83]

International armed conflicts, particularly those involving the occupation of enemy territory, have seen violence and threats against those considered as informers or collaborators. In Afghanistan, the Taliban proclaimed that it would 'kill all individuals suspected of collaboration with Coalition Forces'.[84] According to US intelligence reports, opposing forces in Afghanistan claimed 'they would dig up and violate

[76] Marie Breen Smyth, *Truth Recovery and Justice after Conflict: Managing Violent Pasts* (Routledge 2007) 50. On the question of the status of the conflict in South Africa see Neil Boister and Richard Burchill, 'The International Legal Definition of the South African Armed Conflict in the South African Courts: War of National Liberation, Civil War or No War at All?' (1998) 45 Netherlands International Law Review 348.

[77] *Truth and Reconciliation Commission of South Africa Report*, 1998, Volume 2, 386–8.

[78] Breen Smyth, *Truth Recovery and Justice after Conflict* (n 76) 50.

[79] See *Saddam Hussein: Crimes and Human Rights Abuses* (United Kingdom Foreign and Commonwealth Office, 2002) 13.

[80] See generally Michael Weiss and Hassan Hassan, *ISIS: Inside the Army of Terror* (2nd edn, Regan Arts 2016); Jessica Stern and J.M. Berger, *ISIS: The State of Terror* (Harper Collins 2015).

[81] *Oral Update of the Independent International Commission of Inquiry on the Syrian Arab Republic*, U.N. Doc. A/HRC/20/CRP.1, 26 June 2012, paras 90, 92; *Report of the Independent International Commission of Inquiry on the Syrian Arab Republic*, U.N. Doc. A/HRC/21/50, 16 August 2012, Annex V, para 42. See also Amnesty International, *'Torture was my punishment'; Abductions, torture and summary killings under armed group rule in Aleppo and Idleb, Syria*, MDE 24/4227/2016, July 2016, 29; 'Syria conflict: Boy beheaded by rebels "was fighter" ', BBC News, 21 July 2016 <http://www.bbc.com/news/world-middle-east-36843990> accessed 29 May 2019.

[82] National Liberation Army (ELN) of Colombia, *Code of war*, reprinted in Olivier Bangerter and Nelleke van Amstel, 'A Collection of Codes of Conduct Issued by Armed Groups' (2011) 93 No. 882 International Review of the Red Cross 491.

[83] *Chega! The Final Report of the Timor-Leste Commission for Reception, Truth and Reconciliation*, November 2013, Volume II, 1050. See also *Report of the Independent International Commission of Inquiry on the Syrian Arab Republic* (n 81) Annex V, para 19.

[84] 'TB Planning to use fake checkpoints', Threat Report, 15 March 2006 <https://wardiaries.wikileaks.org/id/772734B3-2219-0B3F-9FDC8D9E5DBBE357/> accessed 29 May 2019.

the mothers of those who worked for International Security Assistance Force'.[85] During the occupation of Iraq by the United States and other countries, alleged informers and other collaborators were frequently targeted and killed by armed opposition groups. The body of an alleged collaborator was found in Baghdad with a broken arm and multiple stab wounds, while another was discovered having been shot over twenty times and with a sign which read: 'This is a traitor with a British occupation. This is what happens to traitors.'[86] In Baghdad, a human head was found in a bag suspended from an electricity pole with an accompanying note claiming that the person had collaborated with coalition forces.[87] An entire Iraqi family of seven was murdered in Mosul with a note found on one of the bodies stating that '[t]his is the end of traitors'.[88]

The consequences for Palestinians collaborating with the Israeli authorities have also been severe, with many hundreds killed since the occupation began in 1967.[89] Public lynching of alleged collaborators were common, as was the mutilation of the bodies of collaborators.[90] The United Nations has documented reports of alleged collaborators with Israel being 'killed or maimed by being shot in the leg or otherwise severely injured'.[91] Palestinian armed groups are alleged to have tortured and murdered a number of Palestinian detainees in Israeli prisons who were considered as collaborators.[92] Six alleged collaborators were publicly executed in Gaza in 2012 and the body of one was dragged through the streets of Gaza City behind a motorbike.[93] In 2014, Hamas held trials and publicly executed a number of collaborators under 'Operation Strangling Necks', having stated that '[t]he resistance will not grant mercy to anyone who provides information about the resistance and its men to the enemy'.[94] At times, those Palestinians labeled and targeted as collaborators with Israel have been political opponents, common criminals, or the 'victims of personal vendettas'.[95] While such practices are obviously contrary to fundamental tenets of

[85] 'Opposing militants forces threaten local nationals working for International Security Assistance Force', 10 Marine 2007, TFU intelligence summary 222 (NSI), 9 March 2007 <https://wardiaries.wikileaks.org/id/774CFC16-2219-0B3F-9FA240E18C7B122F/> accessed 29 May 2019.

[86] '(Criminal Event) Murder Report by Not Provided in vicinity of Basrah (Route Unknown): Civilian killed in action', 6 August 2007 <https://wardiaries.wikileaks.org/id/407F0C75-F6E8-01BD-0EB4C65EEA325641/> accessed 29 May 2019. See also 'Body Found in the vicinity of Baghdad (Zone 60): 1x Civilian killed', 14 January 2005 <https://wardiaries.wikileaks.org/id/56859857-6DD3-4ADB-B255-02BC02C103C8/> accessed 29 May 2019.

[87] 'Dismembered head found by IP in Baghdad: 1 NEU killed', 24 April 2004 <https://wardiaries.wikileaks.org/id/FB375BB5-20FC-4381-A187-2FDDECA5DB22/> accessed 29 May 2019.

[88] 'Attack on IZ family in Mosul', 13 September 2004 <https://wardiaries.wikileaks.org/id/F2874C60-3685-45CC-964A-0FEE5E5D4765/> accessed 29 May 2019.

[89] Sayigh, *Armed Struggle and the Search for a State* (n 7) 287. [90] Ibid 636.

[91] Human Rights Council, *Report of the United Nations Fact-Finding Mission on the Gaza Conflict*, A/HRC/12/48, 25 September 2009, para 1368.

[92] Mossab Hassan Yousef, *Son of Hamas* (Authentic Media 2014) 97–8.

[93] 'Hamas executes six suspected informants for Israel on Gaza street', *The Guardian*, 20 November 2012.

[94] Amnesty International, *Strangling Necks; Abductions, Torture and Summary Killings of Palestinians by Hamas Forces during the 2014 Gaza/Israel Conflict*, MDE 21/1643/2015, 2015, 14.

[95] *Report of the detailed findings of the independent commission of inquiry established pursuant to Human Rights Council resolution S-21/1*, A/HRC/29/CRP.4, 22 June 2015, para 497; Sayigh, *Armed Struggle and the Search for a State* (n 7) 636.

international humanitarian law, questions arise as to the extent to which this body of law fully applies to such acts of violence.

4.2 International Humanitarian Law's Blind Spot?

The principle of humane treatment is at the core of international humanitarian law.[96] That civilians and persons *hors de combat* must be treated humanely constitutes a rule of customary international law that applies in both international and non-international armed conflicts.[97] The ill-treatment of informers and other collaborators during conflict as described in the previous section constitutes a *prima facie* violation of this fundamental precept. The list of prohibited acts that inherently violate the principle of humane treatment in Common Article 3 of the 1949 Geneva Conventions was not specifically devised with the treatment to which wartime collaborators are subjected in mind, but it certainly reads like a catalogue of the cruelties of which they are so often victims: 'violence to life and person, in particular murder of all kinds, mutilation, cruel treatment and torture; [...] outrages upon personal dignity, in particular humiliating and degrading treatment; the passing of sentences and the carrying out of executions without previous judgment'.[98] Common Article 3's rules were reaffirmed and supplemented by the 'fundamental guarantees' set out in the 1977 Additional Protocols.[99] A hesitance to designate the measures taken against informers and other collaborators as clear breaches of these rules of international humanitarian law arises not from any failure to contravene the substance of the rules themselves[100]—although as Common Article 3 makes clear, and as discussed in the next section, capital punishment is not completely outlawed in times of armed conflict—but rather because of a prevailing uncertainty as to whether such rules are applicable to such conduct in every instance.

International humanitarian law in its early incarnations was devised on the basis of reciprocity and was concerned primarily with protecting the nationals of a state that fell into the hands of an opposing side as captured prisoners of war or as the inhabitants of occupied territory, as well as wounded, sick, or shipwrecked members of the armed forces irrespective of under whose control they fell.[101] While this body of law has considerably expanded the scope of its protections to encompass a greater range of persons, contemporary treaties continue to specify obligations which arise

[96] See generally Jean Pictet, 'The Principles of International Humanitarian Law' (1966) 6 No. 66 International Review of the Red Cross 455.

[97] Jean-Marie Henckaerts and Louise Doswald-Beck, *Customary International Humanitarian Law, Volume I: Rules* (CUP 2005) 306.

[98] Geneva Conventions 1949, art 3.

[99] Additional Protocol I, art 75; Additional Protocol II, art 6.

[100] See for example *From Madness to Hope: the 12-year war in El Salvador: Report of the Commission on the Truth for El Salvador*, UN Doc. S/25500, 1 April 1993, 162–163; *Report of the Sierra Leone Truth and Reconciliation Commission*, 2004, Volume 3A, 555–556; Colm Campbell and Ita Connolly, 'Making War on Terror? Global Lesson from Northern Ireland' (2006) 69(6) Modern Law Review 935, 952–3.

[101] Robert Cryer, Håkan Friman, Darryl Robinson, and Elizabeth Wilmshurst, *An Introduction to International Criminal Law and Procedure* (3rd edn, CUP 2014) 232.

towards the armed forces, civilian population, or property of the opposing side. The Third Geneva Convention encapsulates this approach almost in its entirety, while the Fourth Geneva Convention, for example, prohibits compelling protected persons 'of enemy nationality' to engage in work directly related to military operations.[102] The Rome Statute treats destroying or seizing 'the enemy's property' as a war crime.[103] Although the law of non-international armed conflict increasingly mirrors the rules applicable to international armed conflicts, there is not always a corresponding norm of humanitarian law which compels a state that is party to an armed conflict to treat its own nationals or their property on its territory as it would those of the enemy state in an international armed conflict.[104] Humanitarian law's development has been characterised by a discernible reluctance to have this body of law fully apply to how a party to an armed conflict might treats its own fighters or civilians.

With regard to informers and other collaborators, the previous chapter provided a number of examples of this approach, including the denial of prisoner of war status to captured defectors, the restrictions on protected person status under the Fourth Geneva Convention, and the potential to treat informers as spies. These illustrate the firm preference for such persons to be treated almost exclusively in accordance with national laws rather than through the framework of international humanitarian law. This body of law might be thus accused of having a blind spot when it comes to the treatment of those persons from its 'own side', including informers and other collaborators.

4.2.1 The Scope of War Crimes

Recent international jurisprudence serves to illustrate an occasional tendency to refrain from applying international humanitarian law to instances of a party to an armed conflict mistreating its own civilians or combatants. In the *Revolutionary United Front* case, for example, the Special Court for Sierra Leone was confronted with the killing of a fighter considered a security threat by members of the armed group alongside which he had fought. This accorded with the dictate of Revolutionary United Front (RUF) commander Issa Hassan Sesay that 'execution was the standard punishment for those RUF who connived with the enemy'.[105] The Special Court considered that this extrajudicial execution did not constitute a war crime, as 'the law of armed conflict does not protect members of armed groups from acts of violence directed against them by their own forces'.[106] Similarly, another killing was not viewed as a war crime, as the victim was not a member 'of the opposing armed group'.[107]

102 Fourth Geneva Convention, art 40.

103 Rome Statute of the International Criminal Court, arts 8(2)(b)(xiii), 8(2)(e)(xii).

104 See for example William A. Schabas, 'Al Mahdi Has Been Convicted of A Crime He Did Not Commit' (2017) 49 Case Western Reserve Journal of International Law 75, 88–9.

105 *Sesay, Kallon and Gbao*, Trial Chamber judgment (n 13) para 1399.

106 Ibid para 1451, 1455. See also paras 1454, 1457.

107 Ibid para 1457.

While these killings occurred in a non-international armed conflict, the Trial Chamber noted that:

The law of international armed conflict regulates the conduct of combatants vis-à-vis their adversaries and persons hors de combat who do not belong to any of the armed groups participating in the hostilities. In this respect, we recall that the field of application of the Third Geneva Convention is restricted to persons 'who have fallen into the power of the enemy.'[108]

The Chamber was firmly of the view that prisoner of war status could not apply to an armed group's own members:

It is trite law that an armed group cannot hold its own members as prisoners of war. The law of international armed conflict was never intended to criminalise acts of violence committed by one member of an armed group against another, such conduct remaining first and foremost the province of the criminal law of the State of the armed group concerned and human rights law. In our view, a different approach would constitute an inappropriate reconceptualisation of a fundamental principle of international humanitarian law. We are not prepared to embark on such an exercise.[109]

The prosecution did not challenge these findings, which went unaddressed in the appeal judgment.[110]

In the *Kononov* case before the European Court of Human Rights, the Chamber had to consider whether the killing of several Latvian villagers suspected of collaborating with the German occupying power amounted to a war crime.[111] Vasily Kononov, a Latvian national who was a member of a Soviet commando unit operating in Latvia during the Second World War, claimed that neither the 1907 Hague Regulations nor the Nuremberg Charter applied to 'acts of the members of an armed group perpetrated against fellow citizens'.[112] Moreover, he contended that as several of the villagers had been armed by the Germany occupation authorities, they were combatants rather than civilians and the partisans had a right 'to punish by death the armed accomplices of the Nazis'.[113]

The Chamber partly accepted the applicant's claims, holding that he had legitimate grounds for viewing several of the villagers, not as 'peaceable inhabitants' but as 'collaborators of the German army'.[114] The villagers were not entitled to be regarded as civilians, in the Chamber's view, and had been executed only after German-supplied rifles and grenades—'tangible evidence of their collaboration'—were found in their possession.[115] The attack on the villagers was not '*per se* contrary to the laws and customs of war' and thus international law provided no plausible legal basis for the applicant's conviction.[116] Judge Myjer, in his concurring opinion, considered that when the resistance 'silenced collaborators who had informed on

[108] Ibid para 1452. On the status of the armed conflict, see ibid paras 94–99.
[109] Ibid para 1451.
[110] *Prosecutor v Sesay, Kallon and Gbao*, Case No. SCSL-04-15-A, Appeals Chamber, Judgment, 26 October 2009.
[111] *Kononov v Latvia*, App No. 36376/04 (ECtHR 24 July 2008) paras 8–32.
[112] Ibid para 97. [113] Ibid para 100. [114] Ibid para 129.
[115] Ibid paras 131–132. [116] Ibid para 137.

Jews or persons in hiding, they had done the right thing',[117] but in hindsight, the killing of the Latvian villagers could be considered a criminal act.[118] Unlike the Special Court for Sierra Leone's holdings, the Chamber's finding in *Kononov* was overturned by the Grand Chamber of the European Court of Human Rights.[119] Nevertheless, it too stands as an example of how international humanitarian law seems to turn a blind eye to certain acts of otherwise unlawful violence occurring during situations of armed conflict.

The *Revolutionary United Front* and *Kononov* cases offer mere snapshots regarding the scope of the protections afforded by international humanitarian law, the reach of which has regularly been tested in the many other trials of persons accused of war crimes. With regard to informer and other collaborators, the recent jurisprudence from the International Criminal Court in the *Ntaganda* case is of particular relevance, given the finding that harms perpetrated against members of an armed group by fellow members of that group may constitute war crimes.[120] In addition to sexual violence against child soldiers specifically addressed in that case, the finding could also cover crimes perpetrated against members of an armed group that actively co-operate with another party during an armed conflict, such as by defecting, providing information, or offering other assistance. Before turning to the contemporary interpretation of international humanitarian law in this case law, it is worth touching on the position which prevailed prior to the adoption of the 1949 Geneva Conventions. The case law of the international and national military tribunals arising from the Second World War barely addressed the ill-treatment of collaborators, partly as there was more concern with calling to account those who had collaborated with the Axis powers, rather than those who may have attacked or mistreated them, but also because the laws of war as they then stood were not overly concerned with how a state treated its own nationals.

4.2.2 The Evolving Law of War Crimes and Crimes against Humanity

The principal treaties in force prior to the Second World War, the 1907 Hague Regulations and the 1929 Prisoners of War Convention, reflect the emphasis on protecting civilians and prisoners of war from being ill-treated by the enemy. While the International Committee of the Red Cross (ICRC) had been unsuccessful in its efforts to have states agree to a convention for the protection of civilians going beyond those in occupied territory, it would have only extended protection to enemy nationals on the territory of a belligerent had it been adopted.[121] The war crimes

[117] Ibid Concurring Opinion of Judge Myjer, para 9. [118] Ibid para 10.

[119] See *Kononov v Latvia*, App No. 36376/04 (ECtHR 17 May 2010).

[120] *Prosecutor v Ntaganda*, Appeals Chamber, Judgment on the appeal of Mr Ntaganda against the Second Decision on the Defence's challenge to the jurisdiction of the Court in respect of Counts 6 and 9, Case No. ICC-01/04-02/06 OA5, 15 June 2017.

[121] Projet de Convention Internationale Concernant la Condition et la Protection des Civils de Nationalité Ennemie qui se trouvent sur le Territoire d'un Belligérant ou sur un Territoire Occupé par Lui, Comité International de la Croix-Rouge, *Quinzième Conférence Internationale de la Croix-Rouge Tenue à Tokio Du 20 Au 29 Octobre 1934, Compte Rendu* (International Publishing and Printing Co. 1935).

provision of the Charter of the International Military Tribunal at Nuremberg reflected the state of the law by referring to war crimes against prisoners of war, as well as the civilian population 'of or in occupied territory'.[122] The ill-treatment of suspected collaborators by the authorities in Nazi Germany was not captured by the category of war crimes as prosecuted at Nuremberg. According to the United States Military Tribunal in the *Justice* case, both the Nuremberg Charter and the subsequently adopted Control Council Law No. 10 revealed 'the intent that the term "war crimes" shall be employed to cover acts in violation of the laws and customs of war directed against non-Germans, and shall not include atrocities committed by Germans against their own nationals'. [123]

In addition to this general limitation on the scope of war crimes, a number of other findings by national military court decisions of the Second World War are relevant in the context of collaborators. The case of *In re Pilz* concerned the prosecution of a German military doctor for the death of a Dutch national who had joined the German army during the occupation of the Netherlands and was subsequently shot by a German unit while attempting to escape and died after having been denied medical attention.[124] According to the Special Court of Cassation:

> The Hague Regulations of 1907 concerning the law and customs of war had not, however, been violated, since the object of the Regulations, and in particular Article 46, was to protect the inhabitants of an enemy-occupied country and not members of the occupying forces. The legal position of the latter was regulated not by international convention, but by the military law of the occupying Power.[125]

Even though he was a Dutch national who had been killed by German forces, the Special Court considered that this individual had 'belonged to the occupying army' and that by his voluntary enlistment he had 'forfeited the protection of the law of nations and had voluntarily submitted himself to the laws of the occupying Power'.[126] The Court failed to refer to the 1864 Geneva Convention which provided that '[w]ounded or sick combatants, to whatever nation they may belong, shall be collected and cared for'.[127] The Court's conclusion was that the acts in question did not amount to war crimes or crimes against humanity, and although they were crimes under German military law, they were outside the jurisdiction of the Dutch courts.[128]

[122] Agreement by the Government of the United States of America, the Provisional Government of the French Republic, the Government of the United Kingdom of Great Britain and Northern Ireland and the Government of the Union of Soviet Socialist Republics for the Prosecution and Punishment of the Major War Criminals of the European Axis, and Annex, Charter of the International Military Tribunal, London, 8 August 1945, art 6(b).

[123] *United States v Josef Alstoetter et al.*, 'The Justice Case', Military Tribunal III, Judgment, April 1949, III *Trials of War Criminals before the Nuernberg Military Tribunals* (1951) 972. A shortened version of the case is also available: *Trial of Josef Alstötter and Others (The Justice Trial)*, United States Military Tribunal, Nuremberg, 1947, VI *Law Reports of the Trials of War Criminals* (1948) 1.

[124] *In re Pilz*, Holland, District Court of the Hague (Special Criminal Chamber), 21 December 1949; Special Court of Cassation, 5 July 1950 (1950) 17 International Law Reports 391, 391.

[125] Ibid. [126] Ibid.

[127] Convention for the Amelioration of the Condition of Wounded in Armies in the Field, Geneva, 1864, art 6.

[128] *In re Pilz* (n 124).

In the *Motosuke* case, a Netherlands court-martial sitting in the Dutch East Indies was confronted with the summary execution of an Indonesian 'Dutch subject' who had joined a corps of volunteer combatants that served with the Japanese army during the occupation of the territory.[129] He was summarily executed by a firing squad on the orders of Lieutenant Motosuke after having shot a Japanese soldier. The defendant claimed that the execution was 'purely an internal matter of the Japanese army and did not come with the sphere of war crimes'.[130] The Court found that the killing was not contrary to the laws and customs of war, but treated it as a common law offence of 'intentional incitement to murder by abuse of authority'.[131] The Court drew on the terms of reference of the United Nations War Crimes Commission which limited war crimes to violations of the laws and customs of war perpetrated against Allied nationals.[132] The Commission had sought to avoid overly strict definitions of crimes, and while there was support amongst its members for 'the principle that the nationality of victims and the place of crime should not be regarded as decisive for the concept of war crimes', it could not achieve unanimity on a resolution which would have extended the category to include crimes committed by a belligerent against the nationals of a co-belligerent.[133]

As regards harms perpetrated against a state's own nationals, a new category of crimes was devised after the Second World War for the very purpose of dealing with these. Crimes against humanity constituted an innovation in the Nuremberg Charter, comprising certain offences committed against the civilian population and connected to the war, namely:

> murder, extermination, enslavement, deportation, and other inhumane acts committed against any civilian population, before or during the war, or persecutions on political, racial or religious grounds in execution of or in connection with any crime within the jurisdiction of the Tribunal, whether or not in violation of the domestic law of the country where perpetrated.[134]

This new category of crimes against humanity allowed leading Nazis to be prosecuted for the extermination of the Jews of Europe, as well as for the murder of political opponents in Germany itself; the Nuremberg Tribunal noted that '[t]he policy of persecution, repression, and murder of civilians in Germany before the war of 1939, who were likely to be hostile to the Government, was most ruthlessly carried out'.[135] It did not have jurisdiction over such crimes when committed before the outbreak of the war, however, 'revolting and horrible as many of these crimes were', owing to the nexus to other crimes laid down in the Charter.[136]

[129] *Trial of Susuki Motosuke*, Netherlands Temporary Court Martial at Amboina, Judgment, 28 January 1948, XIII *Law Reports of Trials of War Criminals* (1949)<?IBT> 126.

[130] Ibid 127. [131] Ibid. [132] Ibid 129.

[133] The United Nations War Crimes Commission, *History of the United Nations War Crimes Commission and the Development of the Laws of War* (H.M. Stationery Office 1948) 172–4. See *Trial of Albert Kesselring*, British Military Court at Venice, Italy, 17 February–6 May 1947, Case No. 44, VIII *Law Reports of Trials of War Criminals* 9.

[134] Nuremberg Charter, art 6(c).

[135] International Military Tribunal (Nuremberg), *Judgment and Sentences*, 1 October 1946 (1947) 41(1) American Journal of International Law 172, 172, 249.

[136] Ibid.

The Nuremberg judgment does not provide any clear examples of the ill-treatment or killing of collaborators being prosecuted as crimes against humanity, although references were made to the persecution of 'opponents' of Nazi Germany in occupied territories.[137] In the *Justice* case, the United States Military Tribunal considered the lawfulness of certain measures such as capital punishment taken against those considered as internal enemies of Nazi Germany. While the charges included with both war crimes and crimes against humanity, it was the latter category which gave the Tribunal jurisdiction to punish 'acts by Germans against German nationals', although it emphasised that this did not cover isolated acts but rather those meeting the definition of crimes against humanity and which were 'systematically organized and conducted by or with the approval of government'.[138]

The *Justice* case addressed the role of the judges, prosecutors, and officials of the Reich Ministry of Justice in implementing Nazi policies and punishing crimes against the state. German criminal law had defined such offences extremely broadly, and included various treasonable offences covering collaboration with an enemy, such as espionage.[139] Prescribed offences in occupied territory included '[f]avortism towards the enemy' and '[s]upport of members of an enemy army'.[140] These laws also served as a tool for extermination:

> The German criminal laws, through a series of expansions and perversions by the Ministry of Justice, finally embraced passive defeatism, petty misdemeanors and trivial private utterances as treasonable for the purpose of exterminating Jews or other nationals of the occupied countries. Indictments, trials and convictions were transparent devices for a system of murderous extermination, and death became the routine penalty.[141]

According to the Reich Ministry of Justice, lawyers had a duty to 'exterminate the traitors and saboteurs on the home front. The law offers enough expedients for this [...] any other culprit too who commits crimes by taking advantage of the circumstances of war sides with the enemy.'[142] Joseph Goebbels told German judges that they need no longer convince themselves of the guilt of an accused, as the Nazi state had to 'ward off its internal foes in the most efficient way and wipe them out entirely'.[143] The death penalty was imposed by German courts in thousands of cases.[144]

Despite the complete subjugation of law and legal process by the Nazi authorities—'[i]n place of the control of law there was substituted the control of National Socialist ideology as a guide to judicial action'—the Military Tribunal was hesitant to condemn all cases involving the imposition of the death penalty as amounting to crimes against humanity, including those against persons who could be considered collaborators.[145] For the Tribunal, this was partly because other countries also had resort to capital punishment, including in wartime; '[e]very nation recognizes the absolute necessity of more stringent enforcement of the criminal law in times of great emergency'.[146] With regard to restrictions on freedom of speech

[137] Ibid 287, 319–20.
[138] *United States v Josef Alstoetter et al.* (n 123) 973.
[139] Ibid 184–5, 193.
[140] Ibid 778–9, 1035.
[141] Ibid 20.
[142] Ibid 528–9.
[143] Ibid 453.
[144] Ibid 1025.
[145] Ibid 993, 1026.
[146] Ibid 1026.

and the severe punishments handed down for undermining military efficiency, the Tribunal considered that while these may have been 'revolting to our sense of justice [...] even under the protection of the Constitution of the United States a citizen is not wholly free to attack the Government or to interfere with its military aims in time of war'.[147]

As to whether the enforcement of these 'savage laws' constituted crimes against humanity, the Tribunal was not convinced that the invocation of the aggressive nature of Germany's actions against other countries was sufficient to render them so in every case, even though there were many instances of their enforcement in a discriminatory, arbitrary, and brutal manner.[148] The Tribunal accepted that an occupying power 'may, under the laws and customs of war, punish local residents who engage in fifth column activities hostile to the occupant', although some instances 'represented an unwarrantable extension of the concept of high treason'.[149] With regard to treason in Germany itself, the Tribunal did not condemn all prosecutions for this offence as crimes against humanity, and focused on instances where individual defendants had played a role in the application of the laws of treason retroactively, in annexed territories, and for purposes of racial extermination.[150]

Crimes against humanity could have served as a vehicle for addressing crimes perpetrated against civilians who collaborated with an opposing belligerent, but there are no prominent examples of such prosecutions after the Second World War. The *Justice* case suggests that Germany was entitled to prosecute and punish those presenting a genuine threat to its wartime security, although that authority was grossly abused. This jurisprudence also confirms that the laws of war at that time did not address crimes perpetrated against a state's own citizens, including members of its armed forces. The fate of collaborators during the Second World War went largely unaddressed in the Allied trials of Axis war criminals and many collaborators found themselves in the dock in its aftermath. While international humanitarian law was undergoing rapid development with the adoption of the post-war treaties, gaps have remained with regard to the treatment of collaborators during situations of armed conflict. Crimes against humanity, for example, which now apply in both peacetime and times of armed conflict, generally exclude crimes against members of armed forces.[151] Therefore, offences against members of the armed forces who may have defected or shared intelligence with the enemy would seem to fall outside of this category of crimes.[152] The continuing expansion of the law of war crimes since 1945, in contrast, may serve to accommodate crimes against such persons.

147 Ibid. 148 Ibid 1026–7. 149 Ibid 1028.

150 Ibid 1090, 1095, 1118–28.

151 Rome Statute of the International Criminal Court, art 7(1). See also *Prosecutor v Mrkšić et al.*, Case No. IT-95-13/1-T, Trial Chamber, Judgment, 27 September 2007, paras 448–464; *Prosecutor v Mrkšić and Šljivančanin*, Case No. IT-95-13/1-A, Appeals Chamber, Judgment, 5 May 2009, paras 23–44; Extraordinary Chambers in the Courts of Cambodia, Case File/Dossier No. 001/18-07-2007/ECCC/TC, Trial Chamber, Judgment, 26 July 2010, paras 302–312.

152 See however Cryer et al., *An Introduction to International Criminal Law* (n 101) 240–2.

4.2.3 Common Article 3 Expanded?

Protected person status, as discussed in Chapter 4, is generally not granted to a state's own nationals under the Third and Fourth Geneva Conventions. The fundamental guarantees in Common Article 3, however, are not subject to any such restriction and the article prohibits distinctions on the basis of 'race, colour, religion or faith, sex, birth or wealth, or any other similar criteria'. No reference is made to nationality, given that the provisions are intended to apply to conflicts 'not of an international character occurring in the territory of one of the High Contracting Parties'. In such conflicts, the protagonists and civilians, irrespective of whether they might be aligned with one side or the other, are thus likely to share the same nationality. Despite having been conceived for internal conflicts, Common Article 3 has become 'a minimum yardstick' for measuring acceptable conduct in both international and non-international armed conflicts.[153]

The rules in Common Article 3 are especially relevant for the treatment of informers or other collaborators and the scope of their application is broad; they apply to 'persons taking no active part in hostilities'. Article 75 of Additional Protocol I applies in an equally wide fashion to persons 'in the power of a Party to the conflict' and not benefitting from more favourable treatment elsewhere in the relevant instruments.[154] Neither Article 75 of Protocol I nor Article 4 of Additional Protocol II makes any reference to nationality, the latter insisting on humane treatment without adverse distinction of '[a]ll persons who do not take a direct part or who have ceased to take part in hostilities, whether or not their liberty has been restricted'.[155] Together these articles can be seen to comprise the minimum standard of treatment expected for all persons by all parties during all armed conflicts. For Jann Kleffner, 'it is hard to contemplate a situation in which a person who on a normative level should be entitled to the protections under Common Article 3 paragraph 1(1) would be deprived of such protections as a matter of law'.[156] Despite the lack of universal ratification of Additional Protocols I and II, the fundamental guarantees are considered as reflective of customary international law.[157]

Civilian informers and other collaborators would generally be entitled to the protection of the fundamental guarantees of Common Article 3 and the articles in the Additional Protocols addressing humane treatment and fair trial guarantees. As explored in Chapter 3, such persons could lose the protection from being the object of

[153] *Case Concerning Military and Paramilitary Activities in and Against Nicaragua, (Nicaragua v United States of America)*, Merits, 27 June 1986, General List No. 70, paras 218–219. See also *Prosecutor v Tadić*, Case No. IT-94-1-T, Trial Chamber, Judgment, 7 May 1997, para 607; *Prosecutor v Tadić*, Case No. IT-9-14-AR72, Appeals Chamber, Decision on the Defence Motion for Interlocutory Appeal on Jurisdiction, 2 October 1995, para 98.

[154] Additional Protocol I, art 75(1).

[155] Additional Protocol II, art 4(1).

[156] Jann K. Kleffner, 'The Beneficiaries of the Rights Stemming from Common Article 3' in Andrew Clapham, Paola Gaeta, and Marco Sassòli (eds), *The 1949 Geneva Conventions: A Commentary* (OUP 2015) 433, 446.

[157] See for example *Hamdan v Rumsfeld*, 548 U.S. 557 (2006); *Case Concerning Armed Activities on the Territory of the Congo (Democratic Republic of the Congo v Uganda)*, Judgment, 19 December 2005, General List No. 116, Separate Opinion of Judge Simma, para 28; *Report of the Secretary-General on the Establishment of a Special Court for Sierra Leone*, UN Doc. S/2000/915, 4 October 2000, para 14.

attack only for the limited time in which they might be considered as directly participated in hostilities. In *Kononov*, the Grand Chamber of the European Court of Human Rights emphasised that the victims could not be summarily executed when *hors de combat* even if they had committed 'war treason' (which it erroneously labeled as a violation of *jus in bello*).[158] Civilians could be arrested, tried, and punished but execution without trial was 'contrary to the laws and customs of war'.[159] While acknowledging the narrow exception created by direct participation in hostilities, international criminal tribunals have not demonstrated any hesitation in holding that the killing or ill-treatment of suspected civilian collaborators can amount to war crimes, although the cases have addressed crimes in non-international armed conflicts, where the nationality of the victim is not relevant.[160] Although one of the criteria used for assessing whether a nexus exists between an armed conflict and the conduct underlying an alleged war crime is 'the fact that the victim is a member of the opposing party',[161] this is not an essential requirement but rather a characteristic of most war crimes. The contemporary prosecution of war crimes committed against suspected civilian collaborators has not to date been impeded by the challenges concerning nationality or allegiance associated with grave breaches against protected persons in the context of international armed conflicts. Controversy has arisen, however, with regard to the judicial designation as war crimes offences committed by members of armed forces against other members on the same side.

Whether international humanitarian law addresses how a party to an armed conflict treats members of its own armed forces is of relevance for measures taken against members of a state's armed forces or armed opposition groups that might collaborate with the opposing side. The findings in *Pilz* and *Motosuke* that war crimes could not be committed against one's own armed forces reflected the prevailing view of the scope of the laws of war. The *Ntaganda* proceedings before the International Criminal Court have come to a different conclusion regarding the scope of war crimes. Defence counsel in *Ntaganda* asserted that humanitarian law 'does not protect persons taking part in hostilities from crimes committed by other persons taking part in hostilities on the same side of the armed conflict'.[162] The Pre-Trial Chamber did not dismiss this argument out of hand but rather determined that it needed to ask itself whether the child soldiers in question were taking a direct or active part in hostilities at the time they were victims of the crimes in question, namely rape and sexual slavery.[163] The Chamber accepted that certain protections under humanitarian law were foregone when persons took part in hostilities, but held that

[158] *Kononov v Latvia* (n 119) paras 194, 202. [159] Ibid para 204.

[160] See for example *Prosecutor v Limaj et al.*, Case No. IT-03-66-T, Trial Chamber, Judgment, 30 November 2005; *Prosecutor v Haradinaj et al.*, Case No. IT-04-84-T, Trial Chamber, Retrial Judgment, 29 November 2012; *Prosecutor v Fofana and Kondewa*, Case No. SCSL-04-14-A, Appeals Chamber, Judgment, 28 May 2008; *Sesay, Kallon and Gbao*, Trial Chamber Judgment (n 13).

[161] *Prosecutor v Kunarac, Kovac and Vukovic*, Case No. IT-96-23 & IT-96-23/1-A, Appeals Chamber, Judgment, 12 June 2002, para 59. See also *Prosecutor v Katanga and Chui*, Case No. ICC-01/04-01/07-PT, Pre-Trial Chamber I, Decision on the Confirmation of Charges, 30 September 2008, para 382.

[162] *Prosecutor v Ntaganda*, Case No. ICC-01/04-02/06, Pre-Trial Chamber II, Decision Pursuant to Article 61(7)(a) and (b), 9 June 2014, para 76.

[163] Ibid para 77.

the victims in this case 'cannot be considered to have taken active part in hostilities during the specific time when they were subject to acts of sexual nature, including rape', as these criminal acts 'logically preclude active participation in hostilities at the same time'.[164] But by asking the question in this manner, the Pre-Trial Chamber seemed to imply that participation in hostilities nullified humanitarian law's protections, even though many, such as the principle of unnecessary suffering, remain applicable.

The Pre-Trial Chamber's focus on the loss of civilian immunity from participation served to circumvent the question of whether such protections apply vis-à-vis members of the same armed group in the first place. In rejecting Ntaganda's jurisdictional challenge, the Trial Chamber focused on who is protected by the relevant rules of humanitarian law:

> While most of the express prohibitions of rape and sexual slavery under international humanitarian law appear in contexts protecting civilians and persons hors de combat in the power of a party to the conflict, the Chamber does not consider those explicit protections to exhaustively define, or indeed limit, the scope of the protection against such conduct.[165]

Citing the Martens Clause and the application of fundamental guarantees 'at any time and in any place whatsoever', the Trial Chamber held that the loss of immunity from being the object of attack for combatants does not provide a justification for sexual violence against such persons.[166] Recourse was also made to the revised commentary of the ICRC on the First Geneva Convention and the *jus cogens* nature of the prohibition of sexual slavery, before it was concluded that 'members of the same armed force are not *per se* excluded as potential victims of the war crimes of rape and sexual slavery'.[167] The Appeals Chamber essentially agreed with the Pre-Trial and Trial Chambers' ultimate findings, and offered a more refined if not unassailable analysis.

The Appeals Chamber unanimously concluded that members of armed forces or armed groups are not 'categorically excluded' from international law's protection from war crimes of rape and sexual slavery when committed by members of the same forces or group.[168] Demonstrating the existence of the armed conflict nexus would 'sufficiently and appropriately delineate war crimes from ordinary crimes'.[169] There is little doubt that this constitutes a departure from the traditional view that the laws of armed conflict do not generally address the treatment of members of armed forces by those on the same side; the Appeals Chamber acknowledged 'the seemingly unprecedented nature of this conclusion'.[170] But it noted that the First and Second Geneva Conventions include protections for members of a party's own armed forces, and that Common Article 3 offered 'unqualified protection'

164 Ibid para 79.

165 *Prosecutor v Ntaganda*, Case No. ICC-01/04-02/06, Trial Chamber VI, Second decision on the Defence's challenge to the jurisdiction of the Court in respect of Counts 6 and 9, 4 January 2017, para 47.

166 Ibid para 49.

167 Ibid paras 50–51, 54.

168 *Ntaganda*, Appeals Chamber Judgment (n 120) para 2.

169 Ibid.

170 Ibid para 67.

against certain acts irrespective of an individual's affiliation.[171] The ICRC's revised Commentary on the First Geneva Convention, which drew on an earlier decision from the *Ntaganda* proceedings, 'specifically observed that Common Article 3 protects members of armed forces against violations committed by the armed force to which they belong', it was claimed.[172] While the Appeals Chamber relied on the ICRC Commentary to support its own interpretation, it rejected as 'unpersuasive' the case law from the Second World War and the Special Court for Sierra Leone that had addressed aspects of this issue.[173] It found ultimately that 'in the absence of any general rule excluding members of armed forces from protection against violations by members of the same armed force, there is no ground for assuming the existence of such a rule specifically for the crimes of rape or sexual slavery'.[174] Cognisant of the risk presented by 'any undue expansion of the reach of the law of war crimes', the Appeals Chamber reiterated that the nexus requirement for war crimes must be rigorously applied.[175]

The *Ntaganda* findings represent a conscious effort to abandon the prevailing position concerning the extent to which international humanitarian law is concerned with how members of armed forces of a party to an armed conflict treat other members of the same forces. While the Appeals Chamber was correct regarding the First and Second Geneva Conventions, it stretched the scope of Common Article 3 beyond those members of armed forces that are *hors de combat*.[176] The ICRC's revised Commentary offers a more nuanced approach to the question of 'whether armed forces of a Party to the conflict benefit from the application of common Article 3 by their own Party', and seems more of a recommendation *de lege feranda*.[177] In considering the examples of trials of members of armed forces for alleged crimes or sexual abuse by members of the same Party, the Commentary states that '[t]he fact that the trial is undertaken or the abuse committed by their own Party should not be a ground to deny such persons the protection of common Article 3'.[178] The ICRC argues that the fundamental nature of Common Article 3 supports this interpretation, but adds importantly that:

> In many cases, of course, recourse to common Article 3 may not be necessary to make a Party to a conflict treat its own armed forces humanely, be it because a Party to a conflict will feel under a natural obligation to do so, because it will do so out of self-interest, or because, at least in the case of a State Party, domestic law and international human rights law require treatment at least equivalent to that of humane treatment in the sense of common Article 3.[179]

In the context of members of armed forces who assist the opposing belligerent, the practice of armed conflicts suggests a natural inclination of parties to resort to

[171] Ibid paras 61–62. [172] Ibid para 61. [173] Ibid paras 61–62.
[174] Ibid paras 65 (footnote omitted). [175] Ibid paras 68.
[176] Kevin Jon Heller, 'ICC Appeals Chamber says a war crime does not have to violate IHL', *Opinio Juris*, 15 June 2017 <http://opiniojuris.org/2017/06/15/icc-appeals-chamber-holds-a-war-crime-does-not-have-to-violate-ihl/> accessed 29 May 2019.
[177] ICRC, *Commentary on the First Geneva Convention: Convention (I) for the Amelioration of the Condition of the Wounded and Sick in Armed Forces in the Field*, (2nd edn, CUP 2016) 191.
[178] Ibid. [179] Ibid.

inhumane treatment or executions, often justified by the self-interest of deterring any future collaboration by their members. The application of international human rights law by non-state armed groups is of course contested, as the Commentary implicitly recognises here. As a matter of international humanitarian law, the ICRC advocates that all Parties 'should, as a minimum, grant humane treatment to their own armed forces based on common Article 3' where a conflict nexus exists.[180] Common Article 3 itself does not use the word 'should' but rather states that relevant persons 'shall in all circumstances be treated humanely'. This difference in wording is hardly an oversight.

Ntaganda is not the first time that an international criminal tribunal has offered radical interpretations of the law of war crimes on the basis of limited sources and reasoning that is open to challenge.[181] Such endeavours go against the general principle that ambiguous laws should be interpreted in the favour of the accused and may not accord with the views of states, the law's traditional architects.[182] Nevertheless, the findings have been welcomed and it remains unlikely that the International Criminal Court will depart subsequently from the views as expressed by the *Ntaganda* Pre-Trial, Trial and Appeals Chambers.[183] While the series of decisions has been sharply criticised,[184] its broadening of the scope of the law of war crimes may lead to light being cast on practices that have been insufficiently addressed previously, including prevalent sexual violence within armed forces.[185]

The International Criminal Tribunal for Yugoslavia has correctly observed that '[n]ot all unlawful acts occurring during an armed conflict are subject to international humanitarian law'.[186] The trial and treatment of informers and other collaborators frequently involves obvious illegality, although the relevant legal regime implicated may be less apparent at times. In the context of non-international armed conflicts, the ICRC revised Commentary stressed the conflict nexus requirement and that '[a]cts that have no such connection to the conflict generally remain regulated exclusively by domestic criminal and law enforcement regimes, within the boundaries set by applicable international and regional human rights law'.[187] The ill-treatment

180 Ibid 192.

181 See generally Shane Darcy, *Judges, Law and War: The Judicial Development of International Humanitarian Law* (CUP 2014).

182 See for example Rome Statute of the International Criminal Court, art 22(2); Darcy, *Judges, Law and War* (n 181) 261, 263, 279–85.

183 See for example Jann Kleffner, 'Friend or Foe? On the Protective Reach of the Law of Armed Conflict' in Mariëlle Matthee, Brigit Toebes, and Marcel Brus (eds), *Armed Conflict and International Law: In Search of the Human Face* (T.M.C. Asser Press 2013) 285; Tilman Rodenhäuser, 'Squaring the Circle: Prosecuting Sexual Violence Against Child Soldiers by their 'Own Forces' (2016) 14(1) Journal of International Criminal Justice 171.

184 See for example Michael A. Newton, 'Contorting Common Article 3: Reflections on the Revised ICRC Commentary' (2017) 45 Georgia Journal of International and Comparative Law 513; Heller, 'ICC Appeals Chamber says a war crime does not have to violate IHL' (n 176).

185 See for example Madeline Morris, 'By Force of Arms: Rape, War and Military Culture' (1996) 45(4) Duke Law Journal 641; T.S. Nelson, *For Love of Country: Confronting Rape and Sexual Harassment in the U.S Military* (Routledge 2002); Carol O'Brien, Jessica Keith, and Lisa Shoemaker, 'Don't Tell: Military Culture and Male Rape' (2015) 14(4) Psychological Services 357.

186 *Prosecutor v Aleksovski*, Case No. IT-95-14/1-T, Trial Chamber, Judgment, 25 June 1999, para 45.

187 ICRC, *Commentary on the First Geneva Convention* (n 177) 166.

of collaborators is connected to an armed conflict although humanitarian law has not always been applicable to such conduct. *Ntaganda* represents the latest attempt to expand the scope of humanitarian law via the law of war crimes in order to address unlawful acts occurring in armed conflict which previously fell solely within the domain of national law. The findings are nevertheless of considerable import for members of armed forces or groups that may have cooperated with the opposing side during an armed conflict. For armed opposition groups, significant challenges arise in terms of their capacity to meet certain demands of both international humanitarian law and human rights law, none more so than in ensuring that any trials are conducted in accordance with established fair trial guarantees.

4.3 Fair Trials and Capital Punishment

The lawfulness of the killing of informers and other collaborators during armed conflict outside of direct participation in hostilities usually hinges upon whether such individuals had previously been convicted of established criminal offences following a fair trial. The Prosecutor of the International Criminal Court has identified the ill-treatment and execution of Palestinians in Gaza accused of collaborating with Israel as potential war crimes.[188] As noted in Chapter 1, the United Nations Commission of Inquiry on the Gaza Conflict described these acts as war crimes, and noted that the executions were not carried out by the relevant authorities in accordance with the applicable rules of international law.[189] Amnesty International also condemned the summary killing of suspected Palestinian collaborators, advocating that any proceedings must 'fully respect international fair trial standards' and 'exclude the death penalty'.[190] Given the frequency with which suspected collaborators are killed during situations of armed conflict, this section examines the rules of international humanitarian law concerning fair trials and capital punishment, as well as relevant human rights law as applicable to both state and non-state parties to a conflict.

Violence to life and 'murder of all kinds' are prohibited absolutely under Common Article 3 of the 1949 Geneva Conventions and the Additional Protocols.[191] However, the language of Common Article 3 and the occasional silence in the corresponding articles of the Additional Protocols make it apparent that executions during times of armed conflict are not completely outlawed by humanitarian law. Common Article 3 prohibits 'the passing of sentences and the carrying out of executions without previous judgment pronounced by a regularly constituted court, affording all the judicial guarantees which are recognized as indispensable by civilized peoples'.[192]

188 Office of the Prosecutor, *Report on Preliminary Examination Activities 2016*, 14 November 2016, 28.

189 *Report of the detailed findings of the independent commission of inquiry* (n 95) para 502.

190 Amnesty International, *Strangling Necks* (n 94) 42.

191 Fourth Geneva Convention, art 3(1)(a); Additional Protocol I, art 75(2)(a); Additional Protocol II, art 4(2).

192 Fourth Geneva Convention, art 3(1)(d). See also Additional Protocol I, art 75(4); Additional Protocol II, art 6.

During times of armed conflict, the use of the death penalty is 'more frequent and the safeguards surrounding its use less stringent'.[193] International humanitarian law seeks to exclude the application of capital punishment to categories such as juveniles, pregnant women, or mothers of small children.[194] The 1949 Geneva Conventions countenance the use of the death penalty against both prisoners of war and protected persons in certain circumstances.[195] The death penalty might be imposed in occupied territory on protected persons that have engaged in espionage or serious acts of sabotage, if these were punishable by death under the law of the occupied territory.[196] The only prominent references to the death penalty in the ICRC Customary International Law Study are to the rules concerning children and women, and the prohibition of the '*summary* execution' of spies.[197] That the execution of spies is lawfully permitted in certain circumstances may contribute to a general perception of broader permissibility, particularly on the part of non-state armed groups.

International humanitarian law's permissive approach to capital punishment is not the last word on its lawfulness during conflict. As with fair trial rights, capital punishment falls into the third category of those identified by the International Court of Justice: 'some rights may be exclusively matters of international humanitarian law; others may be exclusively matters of human rights law; yet others may be matters of both these branches of international law'.[198] International human rights law insists on fair trial standards in any use of capital punishment, while also seeking the progressive restriction and indeed abolition of the death penalty.[199] The International Covenant on Civil and Political Rights encapsulates the standard approach of human rights law by restricting the death penalty to 'the most serious crimes' and requiring that any imposition of such a punishment 'only be carried out pursuant to a final judgement rendered by a competent court'.[200] Human rights law also shares the same approach of humanitarian law by excluding its application to certain categories of persons such as minors and pregnant women.[201]

Certain human rights instruments also aim at abolishing capital punishment 'in all circumstances' and have touched on its use during armed conflict.[202] The Second

193 William A. Schabas. *The Abolition of the Death Penalty in International Law* (3rd edn, CUP 2002) 211.

194 Additional Protocol I, arts 76(3) and 77(5); Additional Protocol II, art 6(4).

195 See Third Geneva Convention, arts 100–101; Fourth Geneva Convention, arts 68 and 75.

196 Fourth Geneva Convention, art 68.

197 Henckaerts and Doswald-Beck, *Customary International Humanitarian Law* (n 97) 391, 478–9, 482 (emphasis added).

198 *Legality of the Construction of a Wall in the Occupied Palestinian Territories*, Advisory Opinion, 9 July 2004, General List No. 131, para 106.

199 See generally Schabas. *The Abolition of the Death Penalty* (n 193); Jon Yorke (ed), *Against the Death Penalty: International Initiatives and Implications* (Ashgate 2008).

200 International Covenant on Civil and Political Rights (1966), entered into force 23 March 1976, 999 U.N.T.S. 171, art 6(2).

201 See for example International Covenant on Civil and Political Rights, art 6(4); Convention on the Rights of the Child (1989), entered into force 2 September 1990, 1577 U.N.T.S. 3, art 37(2); American Convention on Human Rights (1969), entered into force 18 July 1978, 1144 U.N.T.S. 123, art 4(5).

202 Protocol No. 13 to the Convention for the Protection of Human Rights and Fundamental Freedoms, concerning the abolition of the death penalty in all circumstances (2002), E.T.S. 187, art 1.

Optional Protocol to the International Covenant on Civil and Political Rights seeks an absolute prohibition but permits parties to enter a reservation allowing the death penalty 'in time of war pursuant to a conviction for a most serious crime of a military nature committed during wartime'.[203] This Protocol has eighty-five States parties, only a handful of which have entered a reservation of the type envisaged.[204] According to the United Nations Secretary General, 101 states are now abolitionist for all crimes, while 7 states are abolitionist for ordinary crimes only and retain the death penalty exceptionally, such as for 'military offences in time of war, or crimes against the State, such as treason, terrorism or armed insurrection'.[205] Fifty-one States are considered *de facto* abolitionist, but thirty-nine States remain retentionist, having imposed capital punishment in the period under review.[206] There has been a broadening of the range of offences to which the death penalty applies in several number of countries, including in Kenya where its Defence Forces Act 2012 sets out that an individual is liable 'to suffer death or any other punishment provided for by this Act if the offence is committed with intent to assist the enemy'.[207] In some countries, the death penalty remains mandatory for treason.[208] Overall, just under half the world's states retain the legal possibility of applying the death penalty during armed conflict.

Extrajudicial or summary executions of informers or other collaborators during armed conflict are obviously in violation of both treaty and customary international humanitarian law. Counterinsurgency operations in El Salvador provide an obvious example of such violations, given that the armed forces 'executed peasants, men, women and children, who had offered no resistance, merely because they were considered collaborators with the guerrillas'.[209] These killings were addressed by the Inter-American Court of Human Rights, which underscores how human rights obligations of a state may also apply alongside relevant obligations under humanitarian law. The codification of fair trial rights in international and regional human rights treaties often offers more detail and precision than the corresponding humanitarian law instruments and can serve as a means of interpreting Common Article 3's requirement of 'judicial guarantees which are recognized as indispensable by civilized peoples'.[210] The application of human rights standards concerning fair trials during

[203] Second Optional Protocol to the International Covenant on Civil and Political Rights (1989), entered into force 11 July 1991, 1642 U.N.T.S. 414, art 2(1). See also Protocol No. 6 to the Convention for the Protection of Human Rights and Fundamental Freedoms concerning the abolition of the death penalty (1983) E.T.S. 114, art 2.

[204] For ratification status and reservations see <https://treaties.un.org/Pages/Home.aspx?clang=_en> accessed 29 May 2019.

[205] *Capital punishment and implementation of the safeguards guaranteeing protection of the rights of those facing the death penalty: Report of the Secretary-General Report*, UN Doc. E/2015/49, 13 April 2015, 5, 8.

[206] Ibid 8–15.

[207] Ibid 14–15, Section 58(3)(a), Kenya Defence Forces Act, No. 25 of 2012.

[208] Ibid 34.

[209] Inter-American Court of Human Rights, *Case of the Massacres of El Mozote and Nearby Places v El Salvador*, Judgment, 25 October 2012, para 69.

[210] See for example International Covenant on Civil and Political Rights, arts 14–15; European Convention for the Protection of Human Rights and Fundamental Freedoms (1950), entered into force 3 September 1953, 213 U.N.T.S. 221, E.T.S. 5, arts 6–7; American Convention on Human Rights,

times of armed conflict may be constrained by the states of emergency regimes, the extraterritorial dimension of conflicts for some parties, and the unfortunate tendency to treat international humanitarian law in its entirety as *lex specialis*.[211]

States parties to human rights treaties are permitted to derogate from certain obligations in times of 'war or other public emergency threatening the life of the nation'.[212] As the United Nations Human Rights Committee has stated, this power cannot be invoked 'as justification for acting in violation of humanitarian law or peremptory norms of international law, for instance ... by deviating from fundamental principles of fair trial, including the presumption of innocence'.[213] Aside from the rule against retroactive application of criminal law, the articles addressed to fair trial rights are not designated as non-derogable during states of emergency. Nonetheless, the Human Rights Committee has drawn on the fundamental guarantees of international humanitarian law to assert that:

> Safeguards related to derogation, as embodied in article 4 of the Covenant, are based on the principles of legality and the rule of law inherent in the Covenant as a whole. As certain elements of the right to a fair trial are explicitly guaranteed under international humanitarian law during armed conflict, the Committee finds no justification for derogation from these guarantees during other emergency situations. [...] Only a court of law may try and convict a person for a criminal offence. The presumption of innocence must be respected.[214]

Even though certain aspects of fair trial rights might be derogated from during a state of emergency, fair trial guarantees may not be subjected to derogations that would 'circumvent the protection of nonderogable rights'.[215] The Human Rights Committee has specifically referred to the non-derogable nature of Article 6 of the Covenant in this context as meaning that 'any trial leading to the imposition of the death penalty during a state of emergency must conform to the provisions of the Covenant, including all the requirements of article 14'.[216]

arts 8–9; African Charter on Human and Peoples' Rights (1981), entered into force 21 October 1986, O.A.U. Doc. CAB/LEG/67/3 Rev. 5, art 7.

[211] See generally Orna Ben-Naftali (ed), *International Humanitarian Law and International Human Rights Law* (OUP 2011). On *lex specialis* see International Court of Justice, *Legality of the Threat or Use of Nuclear Weapons*, Advisory Opinion, 8 July 1996, General List No. 95, para 25; *Legality of the Construction of a Wall* (n 198) para 106; *Case Concerning Armed Activities on the Territory of the Congo* (n 157) paras 178–180. See also Chapter 5.

[212] European Convention on Human Rights, art 15(1). See also American Convention on Human Rights, art 27; International Covenant on Civil and Political Rights, art 4.

[213] Human Rights Committee, *General Comment No. 29—Article 4: Derogations during a state of emergency*, U.N. Doc. CCPR/C/21/Rev.1/Add.11, (2001), para 11.

[214] Ibid.

[215] Human Rights Committee, *General Comment No. 32—Article 14: Right to equality before courts and tribunals and to a fair trial*, U.N. Doc. CCPR/C/GC/32, 23 August 2007, para 6. See also Inter-American Court of Human Rights, *Judicial Guarantees in States of Emergency (Arts. 27(2), 25 and 8 of the American Convention on Human Rights)*, Advisory Opinion OC-9/87, October 6, 1987, Inter-Am. Ct. H.R. (Ser. A) No. 9 (1987).

[216] Human Rights Committee, *General Comment No. 32* (n 215) para 6. See also Human Rights Committee, *General Comment No. 36 (2018) on Article 6 on the International Covenant on Civil and Political Rights, on the right to life*, U.N. Doc. CCPR/C/GC/36, 30 October 2018, paras 31–51.

The advanced protection of fair trials under modern humanitarian law and human rights law renders extrajudicial executions of informers or other collaborators entirely indefensible as a matter of law. Furthermore, executions may only be imposed in accordance with the requirements of both bodies of law, including those concerning fair trials. The law as it stood before 1949 was less emphatic regarding wartime executions, with protective rules of a general nature at times giving way to contentious yet recognised exceptions. The 1907 Hague Regulations, for example, require respect for '[f]amily honour and rights' and 'the lives of persons', but it was accepted at the time that hostages might be taken from the civilian population and were liable to be executed, and that violations of the laws of war could be addressed by way of belligerent reprisals, including the reprisal killing of civilians as a last resort.[217] Spies, as previously discussed, were provided with only minimal protection under the laws of war. For Grotius, the severe punishment of captured spies was 'in accordance with that impunity which the law of war accords',[218] while Vattel supported the imposition of capital punishment on spies 'since we have scarcely any other means of guarding against the mischief they may do to us'.[219] And although the Lieber Code prescribed 'death by hanging' for spies, it emphasised the requirements of a trial in capital cases, stating the law of war does not allow for declaring persons as outlaws to be 'slain without trial by any captor'.[220] The 1874 Brussels Declaration introduced a 'guarantee of humanity' that spies would be tried in accordance with domestic law, while the Hague Regulations established as a rule of international law that '[a] spy taken in the act shall not be punished without previous trial'.[221] Case law relating to the Second World War conceded that enemy civilians might be killed in reprisal or as hostages under certain circumstances, as might spies or so-called *franc tireurs*, but not without a previous trial or some official process.[222]

The practice of the Second World War is replete with examples of the execution of prisoners of war, enemy civilians, and resistance fighters without trial or following only cursory proceedings. Although suspected informers and other collaborators were often simply murdered, some were subjected to a judicial process prior to execution, albeit not pursuant to a clear international legal obligation to do so. The 1943 trial in Krasnodar of eleven Soviet citizens for collaborating with the German armed forces during the occupation offers an example of Soviet practice concerning the trial and execution of those suspected of having aided the enemy,

[217] Hague Regulations 1907, art 46. On hostages and reprisals see Shane Darcy, *Collective Responsibility and Accountability Under International Law* (Transnational 2007) 83–92, 131–9; Frits Kalshoven, *Belligerent Reprisals* (Martinus Nijhoff 1971) 45–106.

[218] Hugo Grotius, *De Jure Belli ac Pacis Libri Tres*, Book III, Chapter IV, Section XVIII, 3 (first published 1646, tr Francis W. Kelsey, Vol. II, Carnegie Endowment for International Peace, Division of International Law 1925) 655–6.

[219] Emer de Vattel, *The Law of Nations*, Book III, *Of War*, Chapter X, §179 (first published 1758, Bela Kapossy and Richard Whatmore (eds), Liberty Fund, 2008) 582.

[220] Lieber Code 1863, arts 12–13, 88–91, 148.

[221] Hague Regulations 1907, art 30.

[222] See Darcy, *Collective Responsibility and Accountability* (n 217) 93–108, 139–45; Kalshoven, *Belligerent Reprisals* (n 217) 216–263; Kevin Jon Heller, *The Nuremberg Military Tribunals and the Origins of International Criminal Law* (OUP 2011) 380–381.

and contributed to the commission of atrocities.[223] Described as the first war crimes trial of the Second World War,[224] the eleven accused were charged with treason for having assisted a German SS unit with the killing of around 7,000 people, mostly Jewish, in poison gas vans, although it was their membership of an SS detachment that formed the basis for their convictions.[225] Those on trial had counsel appointed, but the legal procedure meant that they only met with the accused in court upon the commencement of the trial and cross-examination of witnesses was not permitted.[226] All eleven were found guilty. Eight were executed by hanging in front of a crowd of thousands which chanted 'Death to the traitors!' and the other three were sentenced to twenty-years' hard labour.[227] The harsh sentences and accompanying Soviet propaganda were aimed at 'deterring further collaboration'.[228] Others suspected of collaborating with the German occupier were not afforded due process when territories were liberated by the Red Army: 'In some villages even the whole population was murdered because of its positive attitude towards the Germans.'[229]

Thousands of Soviet trials of collaborators took place before military tribunals with limited due process guarantees for the accused. Indictments were usually handed down twenty-four hours before a trial started, the proceedings were not public, and there was no appeal allowed, although death sentences had to be 'reviewed by the responsible military councils and could be annulled by them'.[230] Tanja Penter has described how the Tribunal members were often inexperienced and uneducated, and that trials were compromised by 'falsification of evidence and witness testimonies, use of violence against defendants and witnesses, and corruption'.[231] Sentences were usually arbitrary and wrongful convictions occurred.[232] Despite the extremely broad Soviet understanding of collaboration, the Supreme Court sought to make some distinctions between 'collaborators' who actively assisted in German criminal activity and those 'accomplices' who assisted the German war effort.[233] Minor employees and those who engaged in resistance activities at the same time as collaboration were not punished so long as they did not contribute to German crimes.[234] In terms of offences, 'treason to the Motherland' was considered as more serious by the Soviets than crimes against humanity, and a number of individuals were punished for the former even when evidence pointed towards the latter.[235] It is not known, Penter concludes, 'how many of the tried collaborators committed real crimes and how many were tried mainly for political reasons'.[236]

[223] Ilya Bourtman, '"Blood for Blood, Death for Death": The Soviet Military Tribunal in Krasnodar, 1943' (2008) 22(2) Holocaust and Genocide Studies 246; I.F. Kladov, *The People's Verdict. A Full Report of the Proceedings of the Krasnodar and Kharkov German Atrocity Trials* (Hutchinson & Co. 1944).

[224] Penter, 'Local Collaborators on Trial' (n 54) 341; Durwood "Derry" Riedel, 'The U.S. War Crimes Tribunals at the Former Dachau Concentration Camp: Lessons for Today?' (2006) 24(2) Berkeley Journal of International Law 554, 562.

[225] Penter, 'Local Collaborators on Trial' (n 54) 351; Birstein, *SMERSH, Stalin's Secret Weapon* (n 28) 248.

[226] Birstein, *SMERSH, Stalin's Secret Weapon* (n 28) 248.

[227] Eric Lichtblau, *The Nazis Next Door: How America became a Safe Have for Hitler's Men*, (Mariner Books 2014) 49; Birstein, *SMERSH, Stalin's Secret Weapon* (n 28) 247–9.

[228] Penter, 'Local Collaborators on Trial' (n 54) 342. [229] Ibid 343.

[230] Ibid 345, 357. [231] Ibid 346–7. [232] Ibid 348–50. [233] Ibid 349–51.

[234] Ibid 350. [235] Ibid. [236] Ibid 359.

Considering the trials of Second World War collaborators through the lens of international law reveals a dearth of applicable rules as to how states could treat their own nationals at this time, as the drafters of the Nuremberg Charter had been aware.[237] Immediate post-war developments saw a tectonic shift in international law's approach to state sovereignty. The concept of human rights for all persons was embedded in the mandate of the United Nations, with two significant instruments adopted over two days in December 1948, the Universal Declaration of Human Rights and the Convention on the Prevention and Punishment of the Crime of Genocide.[238] With regard to fair trial rights, Article 10 of the Universal Declaration proclaims that '[e]veryone is entitled in full equality to a fair and public hearing by an independent and impartial tribunal, in the determination of his rights and obligations and of any criminal charge against him'. The Genocide Convention followed the example of crimes against humanity at Nuremberg in not limiting the victims of genocide to the nationals of an enemy state, as had been the case with war crimes. Common Article 3 of the 1949 Geneva Conventions marked international law's first foray into regulating situations of non-international armed conflict, and thus partly how a state could treat its own citizens during an armed conflict. However, the grave breaches articles of the 1949 Geneva Conventions almost exclusively cover serious offences committed against enemy persons or property. Common Article 3 established the legal requirement of fair trial prior to the imposition any sentences, including the death penalty.[239] The requirements of fair trial and regular trial were reiterated throughout the Geneva Conventions, including under the derogations regime of the Fourth Geneva Convention in relation to protected persons that may have engaged in hostile activity.[240] With the adoption of the 1977 Additional Protocols, the fair trial guarantees under international humanitarian law were not just reaffirmed, but also elaborated upon with some specification as regards the necessary due process requirements.[241]

Significantly, the relevant fair trial provisions under international humanitarian law apply to all parties to an armed conflict. In contrast to the treaties of human rights law which followed the Universal Declaration on Human Rights, and which create legal obligations for states to ensure the rights of a fair trial, the obligations under Common Article 3 and the Additional Protocols apply to both state and non-state armed opposition groups. What is considered conceptually challenging from a human rights perspective—the application of international law obligations to non-state actors—has long been accepted under international humanitarian law.[242] That is not to say that the unique nature of armed opposition groups and the contexts in

[237] See *Report of Robert H. Jackson United States Representative to the International Conference on Military Trials* (U.S. Government Printing Office 1949) 332–3.

[238] See for example Charter of the United Nations, 24 October 1945, 1 U.N.T.S. XVI, arts 1(3), 13(1)(b), 55, 56, 62(2), 68 and 76(c); Universal Declaration of Human Rights (1948), 10 December 1948, United Nations General Assembly Resolution 217 A(III); Convention on the Prevention and Punishment of the Crime of Genocide (1948), *entered into force* 12 January 1951, 78 U.N.T.S. 277.

[239] Geneva Conventions 1949, art 3(1)(d).

[240] Fourth Geneva Conventions, art 5.

[241] Additional Protocol I, art 75(4); Additional Protocol II, art 6.

[242] Clapham, *Human Rights Obligations of Non-State Actors* (n 1) 271–85.

which they operate do not present certain difficulties. The requirements of a fair trial before 'regularly constituted courts' that are independent, impartial, and offering 'all the judicial guarantees which are recognized as indispensable by civilized peoples' would not be within the capacity of many non-state armed groups.[243] The next section considers some relevant practice in light of these international legal obligations as arising in the trial and execution of informers and other collaborators by non-state parties to an armed conflict.

4.3.1 Non-State Armed Groups

Common Article 3 of the 1949 Geneva Conventions applies to 'each Party to the conflict' and expressly forbids 'the passing of sentences and the carrying out of executions without previous judgment pronounced by a regularly constituted court, affording all the judicial guarantees which are recognized as indispensable by civilized peoples'.[244] No further guidance is provided in the 1949 Geneva Conventions as to the precise meaning of the terms of this legal obligation. According to the United States Supreme Court:

> Common Article 3 obviously tolerates a great degree of flexibility in trying individuals captured during armed conflict; its requirements are general ones, crafted to accommodate a wide variety of legal systems. But *requirements* they are nonetheless.[245]

Pictet's Commentary explains the rationale behind the rule in Common Article 3—to avoid the killing of innocent persons due to the errors associated with summary justice—but does not elaborate on the safeguards which are essential 'even in time of war'.[246] Alongside the general codifications under international human rights law, more recent treaties of international humanitarian law have expanded on what is required for a trial to be considered fair and a sentence lawfully imposed during armed conflict.

Article 6 of Additional Protocol II, the direct descendant of the relevant Common Article 3 provision, addresses the required features of a court—it must offer 'the essential guarantees of independence and impartiality'—while also specifying certain fair trial rights procedural guarantees, including the presumption of innocence, *nullum crimen sine lege*, the right to be tried in one's presence, and to have 'all necessary rights and means of defence'.[247] Any reference to courts being 'regularly constituted' was deliberately omitted from the Protocol to avoid precluding compliance by non-state armed groups.[248] Additional Protocol I contains a similar but slightly

[243] Geneva Conventions 1949, art 3(1)(d); Additional Protocol II, art 6.

[244] Fourth Geneva Convention, art 3(1)(d).

[245] *Hamdan v Rumsfeld* (n 157) 635 [original emphasis].

[246] Jean S. Pictet (ed), *Commentary; IV Geneva Convention, Relative to the Protection of Civilian Person in Times of War* (ICRC 1958) 39.

[247] Additional Protocol II, art 6.

[248] Yves Sandoz, Christophe Swinarski, and Bruno Zimmermann (eds), *Commentary on the Additional Protocols of 8 June 1977 to the Geneva Conventions of 12 August 1949* (ICRC/Martinus Nijhoff Publishers 1987) 1376; Sandesh Sivakumaran, *The Law of Non-International Armed Conflict* (OUP 2012) 550.

longer list of procedural guarantees, and characterises the required judicial body as 'an impartial and regularly constituted court respecting the generally recognized principles of judicial procedure'.[249] A state's courts would be more likely to satisfy these requirements, compared with judicial mechanisms as may be employed by non-state groups. International human rights law emphasises the constitution of courts by law; the International Covenant on Civil and Political Rights, for example, establishes the right to 'a fair and public hearing by a competent, independent and impartial tribunal *established by law*'.[250] Yet the relevant articles of international humanitarian law do not specify that the rule can only be satisfied by state courts. It is accepted in principle that the courts of non-state entities providing for a fair trial can satisfy the requirements of Common Article 3 and the Protocols.[251] While the Rome Statute uses 'regularly constituted court' in its Common Article 3 war crimes, the Elements of Crimes emphasise independence, impartiality, and fair trial guarantees rather than the legal basis for the court's establishment.[252] Determining whether an armed group has met the necessary fair trial guarantees 'is a question of fact and needs to be determined on a case-by-case basis'.[253]

The practice of non-state armed groups establishing judicial bodies and trying individuals, including those suspected of being informers or collaborators with the enemy, pre-dates the adoption of the 1949 Geneva Conventions. During the Irish War of Independence, for example, the IRA conducted courts-martials of persons accused of informing, although many were also killed extrajudicially.[254] Courts-martials were conducted by IRA officers who had the power to impose fines, order the confiscation of property, or sentence those found guilty to exile or death.[255] The judges were usually the IRA officers holding the prisoner and despite counsel being allowed for the accused in some instances, the courts-martials were generally 'cursory affairs', with inconsistent sentences and enforcement, and thus frequent doubt about the guilt of the accused.[256] The proceedings allowed IRA members to draw 'moral comfort as well as a sense of legitimacy from using the language of due process to describe the steps by which civilian spies were killed'.[257]

[249] Additional Protocol I, art 75(4).

[250] International Covenant on Civil and Political Rights, art 14(1) (emphasis added).

[251] See generally Jonathan Somer, 'Jungle Justice: Passing Sentence on the Equality of Belligerents in Non-International Armed Conflict' (2007) 89 No. 867 International Review of the Red Cross 655; Sandesh Sivakumaran, 'Courts of Armed Opposition Groups; Fair Trials or Summary Justice?' (2009) 7 Journal of International Criminal Justice 489; Parth S. Gejji, 'Can Insurgent Courts be Legitimate within International Humanitarian Law?' (2013) 91 Texas Law Review 1525; Mark Klamberg. 'The Legality of Rebel Courts during Non-International Armed Conflicts, (2018) 16(2) Journal of International Criminal Justice 235; Murray, *The Human Rights Obligations of Non-State Armed Groups* (n 1) 208–20.

[252] Rome Statute of the International Criminal Court, art 8(2)(c)(iv); Knut Dörmann, *Elements of War Crimes under the Rome Statute of the International Criminal Court* (CUP 2002) 408–38.

[253] ICRC, *Commentary on the First Geneva Convention* (n 177) 236.

[254] See Eunan O'Halpin, 'Problematic Killing during the War of Independence and its Aftermath: Civilian Spies and Informers' in James Kelly and Mary Ann Lyons (eds), *Death and Dying in Ireland, Britain and Europe* (Irish Academic Press 2013) 317, 325; Paul McMahon, *British Spies and Irish Rebels: British Intelligence and Ireland 1916–1945* (Boydell Press 2008) 45.

[255] Ibid 323. [256] Ibid 324, 335–6. [257] Ibid 324.

More recent conflicts have replicated these practices, as non-state armed groups have had recourse to internal laws and legal processes in order to punish suspected collaborators, while also resorting to summary execution of suspected traitors at times. With regard to the latter, the Kurdish PKK has been accused of killing 'collaborators with Turkish forces, without any due process involved',[258] and of publicly displaying the corpses of those killed as traitors, often 'in the interests of organizational discipline'.[259] In relation to the former, Daragh Murray has observed that 'armed groups operating at all levels of sophistication typically provide some form of rule of law and administration of justice system. Indeed, establishing a police force or court system is often one of the first activities of an armed group'.[260] Codes of conduct of non-state armed groups have often identified spying or aiding the enemy as offences punishable by death.[261] The legal system established by Islamic State, for example, gave its courts jurisdiction over crimes such as espionage, treason, and collaborating with foreign interests.[262] The Taliban proclaimed that spies could be sentenced to death, with the authority to order an execution lying with 'the Imam, his Nayeb or the provincial judge or if no judge has been appointed, it lies with the authority of the provincial governor'.[263] Although referencing certain fair trial requirements, the Taliban's code of conduct effectively permitted executions without previous trial before a court, in contravention of Common Article 3.[264]

During the conflict in El Salvador, the FMLN established tribunals which 'passed sentence on, and executed, suspected government agents and collaborators'.[265] The organisation relied on both Common Article 3 and Additional Protocol II to claim that it was not necessary that such tribunals were 'set up according to government law in effect'.[266] While this interpretation would accord with the text of the relevant provisions, other fair trial shortcomings of these particular processes have been documented.[267] The Commission of Truth for El Salvador reiterated that

[258] Kerim Yildiz and Susan Breau, *The Kurdish Conflict: International Humanitarian Law and Post-Conflict Mechanisms* (Routledge 2010) 72.

[259] Amnesty International, *Turkey: No security without human rights*, AI Index: EUR/44/84/96, 1996, 26–28

[260] Murray, *The Human Rights Obligations of Non-State Armed Groups* (n 1) 205. See also Somer, 'Jungle justice' (n 251) 686.

[261] See for example Articles 58–59, General Order No. 1: An Order Promulgating a Code of Conduct Regulating the Affairs of the Bangsamoro Islamic Armed Forces, Prescribing its Powers, Duties and Functions, and Other Related Purposes, 2nd edn, June 2006 <http://theirwords.org/media/transfer/doc/sc_ph_milf_biaf_2006_09-9dbc781bd3fc677c268ce003582f4f58.pdf> accessed 29 May 2019. For the similar approach of the New People's Army in the Philippines see Olivier Bangerter and Nelleke van Amstel, 'A Collection of Codes of Conduct Issued by Armed Groups' (2011) 93 No. 882 International Review of the Red Cross 483, 489. See also Section 20(1)(c), (Provisional Order), Laws of the New Sudan, The SPLA Act, 2003 <http://theirwords.org/media/transfer/doc/1_sd_splm_a_2003_03-5fd4e4fabf407e670f236c8d3ecaf381.pdf> accessed 29 May 2019.

[262] Andrew F. March and Mara Revkin, 'Caliphate of Law', *Foreign Affairs*, 15 April 2015.

[263] Section 3, Articles 17–18, *The Islamic Emirate of Afghanistan Code of Conduct for the Mujahedin*, 2010, *reprinted in* Kate Clark, *The Layha: Calling the Taleban to Account*, Afghanistan Analysts Network, July 2011 <http://theirwords.org/media/transfer/doc/ut_af_taliban_2010_2009_2006_03-d8952e65095cf27bd9c8dbc5a328f8eb.pdf> accessed 29 May 2019.

[264] Ibid arts 18–19.

[265] Somer, 'Jungle justice' (n 251) 679.

[266] Ibid.

[267] See also Americas Watch, *Violation of Fair Trial Guarantees by the FMLN's Ad Hoc Courts*, 1990; *From Madness to Hope* (n 100) 44, 150.

'international humanitarian law does not permit the execution of civilians without a proper trial'.[268] As regards punishment, the legal code of the 'People's Courts' established by the Communist Part of Nepal-Maoist included a collaboration-type offence subject to a penalty of labour or imprisonment for anyone who 'commits or attempts to conspire or join the enemy'.[269] In Northern Ireland, an IRA training and induction manual specifically referred to 'punishing criminals, collaborators and informers', and urged its members to provide an explanation as to 'why we execute informers'.[270] Court-martials often involved torture and lead to sentences of death or grievous wounding.[271] These processes were said to allow suspected informers to 'defend themselves before a panel of three judges, retain counsel, and bring evidence and witnesses',[272] although they have been described as 'fairly arbitrary affairs so far as justice is concerned'.[273] In contrast to ordinary crimes which might come before such courts and which may not have harmed the armed group itself, offences of collaboration test most seriously the capacity of such bodies to deliver independent and impartial justice.

The public proclamation of such offences and applicable penalties prior to any prosecution or punishment by the courts of non-state armed groups can be considered as required by international humanitarian law, and may contribute to deterring collaboration with the enemy. Additional Protocol II gives specific expression to the rule against ex-post facto criminals laws or punishment as extensively codified in international human rights law:

> No one shall be held guilty of any criminal offence on account of any act or omission which did not constitute a criminal offence, under the law, at the time when it was committed; nor shall a heavier penalty be imposed than that which was applicable at the time when the criminal offence was committed.[274]

The phrase 'under the law' seems a deliberate acknowledgment of those laws promulgated by non-state armed groups, given that the equivalent provision in Additional Protocol I refers to 'a criminal offence under the national or international law to which he was subject at the time'.[275] The laws of non-state armed groups may duplicate or borrow from national laws, but would not constitute national law. As regards international law, armed opposition groups are arguably obliged to establish judicial bodies to punish violations of international humanitarian law, even though

268 *From Madness to Hope* (n 100) 162–3.

269 See Somer, 'Jungle justice' (n 251) 681.

270 See <http://cain.ulst.ac.uk/othelem/organ/ira/ira_green_book.htm> accessed 29 May 2019. See also Ron Dudai, 'Underground Penalty: The IRA's Punishment of Informers' (2018) 20(3) Punishment and Society 375.

271 Tim Pat Coogan, *The IRA: A History* (Roberts Rinehart Publishers 1994) 132.

272 Michael L. Gross, *The Ethics of Insurgency* (CUP 2015) 112.

273 Coogan, *The IRA* (n 271) 176.

274 Additional Protocol II, art 6(2)(c). See also Universal Declaration of Human Rights, art 11; International Covenant on Civil and Political Rights, art 15; European Convention on Human Rights, art 7. See also Rome Statute of the International Criminal Court, arts 22–24. On the principle of legality in relation to collaborator trials by states see Novick, *The Resistance versus Vichy* (n 31) 143–53; Paul M. Hayes, *Quisling: The Career and Political Ideals of Vidkun Quisling 1887–1945* (David and Charles 1971) 299–303.

275 Additional Protocol I, art 74(4)(c).

this body of law does not explicitly grant any legal authority to non-state actors to do so.[276]

Unlike the prosecution and punishment of possible war crimes by non-state actors, the legal basis for trying individuals for treason-type offences concerning collaboration with the enemy is not apparent, given that collaboration itself is not a violation of international humanitarian law per se. Furthermore, it places individuals in an invidious position of having to satisfy competing allegiance requirements from state and non-state authorities. Several non-state armed groups have provided for an offence of treason in their codes of conduct.[277] The National Resistance Army in Uganda provided for the death penalty for the offence of '[t]reason, that is to say, being an enemy agent, being an infiltrator, consciously giving information to the enemy [...] or subversion.[278] Where an armed opposition groups establishes offences of treason or collaboration, whether directed at members of the group itself or civilians, there might be no clear international or domestic legal basis for such offences.[279] A crime of treason promulgated by an armed opposition group that is party to a non-international armed conflict creates a 'a patently unworkable situation' for individuals, given that 'the law of the state would prohibit collaboration with the armed group, while the law of the armed group would prohibit collaboration with the state'.[280] An exception might arise where the authority of the state has been displaced by a non-state armed group exercising exclusive control over a territory and its population.[281] Crimes of treason would be less problematic where promulgated by an armed resistance group operating in occupied territory, given that no allegiance is owed to an occupying power.

A flexible approach to the meaning of 'the law' in Article 6 of Additional Protocol II might see the publicly promulgated codes of non-state armed groups as sufficient to satisfy the requirements of *nullum crimen sine lege*. Jonathan Somer has argued more generally for a looser interpretation of the requirement that courts of non-state armed groups have a legal basis and that greater emphasis instead be placed on the necessary judicial guarantees to accord with the reality of the practice of such actors: 'an IHL norm that all but prevents armed opposition groups from operating courts will remain merely a norm. These courts would continue to exist, but their "illegal" nature would obstruct efforts to improve compliance with judicial guarantees.'[282] An overly strict interpretation of these requirements could otherwise lead to a risk of indefinite detention by armed groups for the purposes of avoiding their international obligations.[283] Sandesh Sivakumaran, while being cognisant of the challenges and risks presented by non-state actor trials, considers that such trials offer a valuable alternative to summary execution, may contribute to law and order

[276] Murray, *The Human Rights Obligations of Non-State Armed Groups* (n 1) 220–1; ICRC, *Commentary on the First Geneva Convention* (n 177) 235.

[277] Olivier Bangerter, 'Internal Control: Codes of Conduct within Insurgent Armed Groups', *Small Arms Survey Occasional Paper no. 31* (2012) 15.

[278] Article 13(ii), National Resistance Army Code of Conduct <http://theirwords.org/media/transfer/doc/sc_ug_nra_02-56e734a47e81ad2ebace8f1ab67b1a73.pdf> accessed 29 May 2019.

[279] Murray, *The Human Rights Obligations of Non-State Armed Groups* (n 1) 224–5.

[280] Ibid 226. [281] Ibid. [282] Somer, 'Jungle justice' (n 251) 687. [283] Ibid.

where armed opposition groups control territory and a population, and can serve to reduce a climate of impunity.[284] While undoubtedly viewed as illegitimate by states, it cannot be ruled out that the courts of non-state armed groups may enjoy some support from the population as a forum for resolving disputes and delivering justice.[285]

The application of the death penalty by non-state actors against suspected informers or collaborators militates against any overly loose interpretation of the fair trial requirements under humanitarian law. The permissive approach of international humanitarian law to capital punishment, and its retention by certain states for offences of treason, might be interpreted by non-state actors as justification for their own resort to the execution of collaborators. The punishment of informers and other collaborators by non-state actors mirrors in many respects the past and at times continuing conduct of states. In light of the considerable difficulty in meeting fair trial standards, an absolute prohibition on issuing penalties of death has been suggested for armed groups, at the very least where the relevant state has abolished capital punishment.[286] Advocates against capital punishment have often found international humanitarian law lacking when seeking to pressure non-state actors to forgo penalties of death. In response to the execution by two collaborators by the Palestinian Authority, the Palestinian Centre for Human Rights criticised the resort to capital punishment, not as a violation of humanitarian law but as 'contrary to the fundamental principles of human rights and the rule of law'.[287] Hamas has claimed a legal basis for its treatment of collaborators, by relying on the Palestinian Liberation Organisation's 1979 revolutionary code, which included an offence of 'communicating with the enemy' or 'seeking and collaborating with [the] enemy'.[288] A spokesperson stated that '[t]he government will show no mercy to collaborators who stab our people in the back, and they will be held accountable according to the law'.[289]

Violation of the rules of humanitarian law requiring a fair trial prior to any imposition of capital punishment may amount to a war crime. The United Nations Independent Commission of Inquiry on the 2014 Gaza Conflict found that certain executions of collaborators violated common Article 3 and amounted to a war crime.[290] There has been no international case law to date on the war crime

[284] Sivakumaran, *The Law of Non-International Armed Conflict* (n 248) 550.

[285] Ibid 559. See also Frank Ledwidge, *Rebel Law: Insurgents, Courts and Justice in Modern Conflict* (Hurst & Company 2017) 65–83; Hyeran Jo, *Compliant Rebels: Rebel Groups and International Law in World Politics* (CUP 2015).

[286] Murray, *The Human Rights Obligations of Non-State Armed Groups* (n 1) 220. See also Klamberg, 'The Legality of Rebel Courts' (n 251) 253.

[287] Palestinian Centre for Human Rights, 'Searching for, and bringing to justice collaborators with the Israeli occupation is a legitimate right for the Palestinian people in the context of the rule of law', 26 October 2002, Ref: 125/2002. See also B'tselem, 'B'tselem strongly condemns executions of individuals suspected of collaborating with Israel', Press Release, 24 August 2014 <http://www.btselem.org/press_releases/20140824_btselem_condemns_executions> accessed 29 May 2019.

[288] Amnesty International, *Strangling Necks* (n 94) 15–16.

[289] Human Rights Watch, *Under Cover of War*, 20 April 2009, 14.

[290] *Report of the detailed findings of the independent commission of inquiry* (n 95) para 502.

of passing sentences and carrying out executions without a fair trial, although the execution of collaborators in Gaza may yet come before the International Criminal Court.[291] The formulation in the Rome Statute suggests that 'a determination that a specific fair trial guarantee has not been respected would not be equivalent to denial of a fair trial'.[292] The limited case law that does exist at the national level has found the denial of numerous fair trial guarantees: the Stockholm District Court in the *Sakhanh* case held that no fair trial had been provided prior to the execution of several Syrian government soldiers by rebels, including the accused:

> There have plainly not been any conditions, at the relevant time, to establish a court which fulfils the requirements of being independent and impartial, and which fulfils the fundamental requirements of a fair trial as established in international humanitarian law. And even if any judicial procedure that would resemble a trial had taken place, it can, considering what has been established regarding the point in time at which the procedure would have taken place, be ruled out that such a trial would have fulfilled fundamental requirements of a fair trial.[293]

The consequences for Sakhanh of participating in these executions was imprisonment for life, given their 'particularly severe criminality'.[294]

In his final report as Special Rapporteur on extrajudicial, summary, or arbitrary executions, Christof Heyns identified a potential dissonance between the comprehensive legal protection that the right to life enjoys and societal and cultural norms:

> it comes as no surprise that the right to life has spawned a coherent and sophisticated set of principles and rules that underlie its protection. At the same time, it should be recognized that this body of law is deeply affected by the prevailing mores, which to some degree change overtime, and in some cases differ between cultures.[295]

The law of armed conflict has historically been crafted to reflect the demands of states, often supported by the general population, that persons that collaborate with the enemy suffer death for their betrayal. Modern international humanitarian law has sought to restrict the resort to capital punishment by parties to an armed conflict and categorically forbids summary executions, yet the practice endures, most notably in the case of non-state armed groups. While it may be beyond their capacity to meet fair trial standards in certain instances, it is also clear that the resort to summary

[291] Office of the Prosecutor, *Report on Preliminary Examination Activities 2016* (n 188).

[292] William A. Schabas, *The International Criminal Court: A Commentary on the Rome Statute* (2nd edn, OUP 2016) 270–1.

[293] 'On the Establishment of Courts in Non-International Armed Conflicts by Non-State Actors'; Stockholm District Court Judgment of 16 February 2017, Case No. 3786-16 (tr Niklas Barke) reprinted in (2108) 16(2) Journal of International Criminal Justice 403, 422. See also Klamberg, 'The Legality of Rebel Courts' (n 251) 254–62.

[294] Ibid 424.

[295] *Report of the Special Rapporteur on extra-judicial, summary or arbitrary executions*, UN Doc. A/71/372, 2 September 2016, para 124.

killings of suspected informers or other collaborators is deliberate and purposefully undertaken in a brutal fashion in order to shock and deter. The ICRC has suggested that if a fair trial cannot be guaranteed, resort to detention by a non-state group might be considered, provided that the prohibition of arbitrary detention is observed,[296] yet this option has frequently been forgone. The killing of collaborators, extrajudicial or otherwise, is often a deliberate strategy that may reflect one of the 'prevailing mores' of many parties to an armed conflict, that those that serve the enemy are traitors deserving of such rough justice and that potential collaborators must be deterred. Such a motivation does not, however, render this conduct any less unlawful.

* * *

International humanitarian law tolerates members of armed forces or civilians providing assistance to an opposing belligerent during an armed conflict, but is largely unaccepting of much of the treatment that is meted out to such persons when their collaboration is discovered. Their trial and treatment must accord with the fundamental guarantees of international humanitarian law as enshrined in Common Article 3 of the 1949 Geneva Conventions and the Additional Protocols, yet parties to a conflict have often willingly disregarded such standards for the purpose of deterrence and in the taking of revenge against those considered to have betrayed them to their adversaries. Much of the ill-treatment meted out to those that in some way served the enemy constitutes a *prima facie* breach of international humanitarian law, yet as the chapter revealed, not all such acts of violence have fallen with the scope of the law governing situations of armed conflict.

The legal framework provided by international humanitarian law in this context has been incomplete given its past blind spot as to how a state might treat its own nationals. The law of war crimes has had a blinkered approach to the treatment of individuals considered as falling on the same side of party to the armed conflict. Nevertheless, in tracing the evolving scope of international humanitarian law, as well as the law of war crimes and crimes against humanity, this chapter has showed how judicial decision-making has sought to push the boundaries of international humanitarian law. In light of recent case law and the development of customary international law, parties to an armed conflict will find it increasingly difficult to argue that certain persons fall outside the protections of the Geneva Conventions and Additional Protocols. For non-state armed groups, their capacity for compliance with fair trial guarantees has often been the benchmark for assessing whether their punishment of suspected collaborators, particularly the imposition of capital punishment, is in keeping with their obligations under humanitarian law. More often than not, such groups have responded to collaboration with the enemy with violent and unlawful methods, mirroring how states themselves previously dealt with the phenomenon. While states may now be more likely to punish informers

[296] ICRC, *Commentary on the First Geneva Convention* (n 177) 236.

and other collaborators only as harshly as the law permits, it might also be asked if they are or should be restricted by international law from placing individuals in harm's way in the first place through encouraging collaboration for their benefit. With humanitarian law offering implied permission for the use of informers and other collaborators, the next chapter turns to consider how international human rights law might be addressed to the practice.

5

Human Rights, National Regulation, and Armed Conflict

The international legal framework applicable to situations of armed conflict no longer consists primarily of the treaties and customary rules of international humanitarian law, but also includes international human rights law.[1] Both bodies of law share core humanitarian concerns and can apply simultaneously during conflict, notwithstanding differences in origin, sources, enforcement, and outlook.[2] In analysing the role of international human rights law in relation to the subject of this book, this chapter begins by first considering how this body of law has been applied to the use of informers by state authorities in the context of policing, criminal justice, and national security. The focus of the chapter is on informers, so-called covert human intelligence sources, given that the other categories of collaborators examined in the book tend not be found outside the context of armed conflict, although many of the discussed human rights are relevant to all types of collaborators. While international human rights law and humanitarian law display a common if somewhat ambivalent approach to the use of informers, in that neither explicitly prohibits the practice itself but rather both outlaw abusive acts commonly associated with it, they diverge significantly when it comes to the regulation of the practice. In contrast to the law of armed conflict, which does not provide or require a detailed framework for regulating and overseeing the employing of informers, international human rights law expects that states have a legal basis which underpins the practice, and that they put in place measures to prevent and remedy abuse.

This chapter begins by analysing how international human rights law has been applied to the use, recruitment, and treatment of informers. Given the absence of any overt reference to the practice in human rights treaties, consideration is given to how human rights standards have been applied and interpreted by human rights courts

[1] See generally Gert Oberleitner, *Human Rights in Armed Conflict: Law, Practice, Policy* (CUP, 2015); Louise Doswald-Beck, *Human Rights in Times of Conflict and Terrorism* (OUP 2011); Orna Ben-Naftali (ed), *International Humanitarian Law and International Human Rights Law* (OUP 2011); Chandra Lekha Sriram, Olga Martin-Ortega, and Johanna Herman, *War, Conflict and Human Rights* (2nd edn, Routledge 2014); René Provost, *International Human Rights and Humanitarian Law* (CUP 2002).

[2] See for example Andrew Clapham, 'The Complex Relationship Between the Geneva Conventions and International Human Rights Law' in Andrew Clapham, Paola Gaeta, and Marco Sassòli (eds), *The 1949 Geneva Conventions: A Commentary* (OUP 2015) 701; Boyd van Dijk, '"Human Rights in War" On the Entangled Foundations of the 1949 Geneva Conventions' (2018) 112(4) American Journal of International Law 553.

To Serve the Enemy: Informers, Collaborators, and the Laws of Armed Conflict. Shane Darcy, Oxford University Press (2019). © Shane Darcy.
DOI: 10.1093/oso/ 9780198788898.001.0001

and monitoring bodies. Human rights law accommodates the use of informers but places certain restrictions on state authorities in their employment and offers some protective guarantees to individuals who might be recruited for such purposes or harmed by these activities. The right to life, freedom from torture and cruel, inhuman, or degrading treatment or punishment, the right to a fair trial, and the right to private and family life are often impacted upon by the practice of using informers. Although human rights bodies have engaged with certain elements of the practice, the influence of international human rights law on national law and policy concerning informers has been limited, with state authorities generally being resistant to regulation and oversight of such covert activities.

The use of informers by police and intelligence services is largely unseen and invariably secretive, but there is little doubt that national authorities place considerable stock in the role of informers in countering crime and threats to national security.[3] The second section of this chapter examines national approaches to regulating and overseeing the practice and shows that states have been reluctant to be overly prescriptive in this area to such an extent that the reliance on executive guidance and internal codes of conduct gives an impression that police and intelligence services act at times in a legal vacuum. The case study of Northern Ireland included in this section reinforces this perception. During the conflict in Northern Ireland, there was widespread use by state authorities of informers within paramilitary organisations, some of whom committed serious crimes, including murder.[4] While there was a demonstrable absence of legal regulation of the use of informers during the Troubles, national legislation has been adopted since the end of the conflict ostensibly to bring any use of covert human intelligence sources in line with the UK's human rights obligations.[5]

The final section of the chapter turns to consider the potential application of human rights law to the practice of using informers in times of armed conflict. Through the lens of the right to life, it explores the relevant protections provided by humanitarian law and international human rights law, the relationship between the two bodies of law, and the application of human rights law during armed conflicts, including those occurring outside of the territory of a party to the conflict. Consideration is then given to how obligations under human rights law, such as in relation to the right to life and the right to privacy, might be brought to bear on the practice of using informers during armed conflict. The chapter concludes by asking whether the requirement to comply with human rights law might be interpreted in such a way as to undermine the prevailing view as to the legality of using informers during armed conflict.

[3] See for example Roger Billingsley (ed), *Covert Human Intelligence Sources: The Unlovely Face of Police Work* (Waterside Press 2009); Roger Billingsley, Teresa Nemitz, and Philip Bean (eds), *Informers: Policing, Policy and Practice* (Routledge 2001).

[4] See for example *Statement by the Police Ombudsman for Northern Ireland on her Investigation into the circumstances surrounding the death of Raymond McCord Junior and related matters*, Belfast: Police Ombudsman for Northern Ireland, 22 January 2007, 7–8.

[5] See Regulation of Investigatory Powers Act 2000, s29.

5.1 International Human Rights Law

International human rights law and international humanitarian law as distinct yet overlapping branches of international are both ambivalent when it comes to the use of informers and other collaborators: while none of their principal treaties make any explicit reference to the lawfulness or otherwise of employing informers, the legality of the practice is accepted in principle, yet both bodies of law recognise and seek to mitigate the harm that frequently accompanies it. The prevailing interpretation of international humanitarian law as analysed in previous chapters has been that the use of informers and other collaborators by parties to an armed conflict is not prohibited, although it must accord with the established legal rules and principles applicable to the treatment of persons during situations of conflict. International human rights law adopts a largely similar approach, at least with regard to the use of informers in the context of policing, criminal justice and national security.[6] The United Nations Convention against Transnational Organised Crime is explicit in its endorsement of the use of informers, encouraging states parties to use persons 'who participate or who have participated in organized criminal groups' as a source of information.[7] In the context of policing, the European Court of Human Rights has acknowledged that the police 'are increasingly required to make use of undercover agents, informers and covert practices, particularly in tackling organised crime and corruption'.[8] In *Texeira de Castro v Portugal*, the Court held that the European Convention does not exclude the use of anonymous informants during investigations and 'where the nature of the offence so warrants'.[9]

International human rights law's permissive approach to the use of informers does not give states *carte blanche*. States remain bound by their human rights obligations towards individuals who are a source of information concerning actual or potential criminal or unlawful activity. As the United Nations Code of Conduct for Law Enforcement Officials sets out, '[i]n the performance of their duty, law enforcement officials shall respect and protect human dignity and maintain and uphold the human rights of all persons'.[10] The United Nations Global Counter-Terrorism Strategy has also emphasised the need for respecting human rights in the context of counter-terrorism: 'States must ensure that any measures taken to combat terrorism

[6] Richard Barrett and Tom Parker, 'Acting Ethically in the Shadows: Intelligence Gathering and Human Rights' in Manfred Nowak and Anne Charbord (eds), *Using Human Rights to Counter Terrorism* (Edward Elgar 2018) 236, 239–46, 262. On human rights law's tolerance of espionage more generally see John Kish, *International Law and Espionage* (Martinus Nijhoff 1995) 1–40; Ashley Deeks, 'Intelligence Communities and International Law: A Comparative Approach' in Anthea Roberts, Paul B. Stephan, Pierre-Hugues Verdier, and Mila Versteeg (eds), *Comparative International Law* (OUP 2018) 251.

[7] United Nations Convention against Transnational Organised Crime (2000) 2225 UNTS 209, art 26(1).

[8] *Ramanauskas v Lithuania* App no 74420/01 (ECtHR, 5 February 2008), para 49.

[9] *Texeiro de Castra v Portugal* App no 44/1997/828/1034 (ECtHR, 9 June 1998), paras 35–36.

[10] 'Code of Conduct for Law Enforcement Officials', adopted by United Nations General Assembly Resolution 34/169, 17 December 1979, art 2.

comply with their obligations under international law, in particular human rights law, refugee law and international humanitarian law.'[11]

The practice of using informers by police or intelligence services can evidently have an impact on a range of human rights, most prominently on the right to freedom from torture and inhuman or degrading treatment or punishment, which is relevant both to the recruitment of informers where coercion might be used, and to the protection of informers from retaliation by third parties for their activities. Recruitment might also engage the right to private and family life, while the right to life is invariably at issue for those who may face serious threats for having shared information with the authorities or provided evidence against members of criminal associations. In the context of criminal investigation and prosecutions, the use of information provided by informers may also give rise to fair trial concerns. This section analyses the law and admittedly limited body of decisions from a number of international and regional human rights bodies addressing the impact on human rights of the domestic practice of using informers. Human rights concerns arising in the context of post-conflict trials of collaborators or post-Soviet lustration measures are not addressed.[12]

International human rights law frequently contains the same or similar protections for individuals as those found in the law of armed conflict, some of which have been referred to in previous chapters. There is overlap between both bodies of law, as discussed in Chapter 4, with regard to the requirements of a fair trial in criminal proceedings and in the use of capital punishment. Of particular significance to the recruitment or treatment of informers is the absolute prohibition of torture as enshrined in both international humanitarian law and human rights law. The Convention Against Torture and Other Cruel, Inhuman or Degrading Treatment or Punishment acknowledges how torture has been used for purposes of information-gathering, defining torture as an act by which 'severe pain or suffering, whether physical or mental, is intentionally inflicted on a person for such purposes as obtaining from him or a third person information or a confession'.[13] General human rights treaties also prohibit torture in absolute terms irrespective of any claimed justification.[14] Any use of informers, therefore, must be in keeping with this non-derogable prohibition of torture.[15] The training of law enforcement,

[11] 'The United Nations Global Counter-Terrorism Strategy', General Assembly Resolution 60/288, 20 September 2006, U.N. Doc. A/Res/60/288, Annex IV.3.

[12] See for example *Kononov v Latvia*, App No. 36376/04 (ECtHR, 17 May 2010); *Vasiliauskas v Lithuania* App No. 35343/05 (ECtHR, 20 October 2015); *Zawisa v Poland*, App No. 37293/09 (ECtHR, 31 May 2011); *Žičkus v Lithuania*, App No. 26652/02 (ECtHR, 7 April 2009).

[13] Convention Against Torture and Other Cruel, Inhuman or Degrading Treatment or Punishment (1984) 1465 UNTS 85, art 1(1). See Michelle Farrell, *The Prohibition of Torture in Exceptional Circumstances* (CUP 2013) 241.

[14] See International Covenant on Civil and Political Rights (1966), entered into force 23 March 1976, 999 U.N.T.S. 171, art 7; European Convention of Human Rights (1950), entered into force 3 September 1953, 213 U.N.T.S. 221, E.T.S. 5, art 3; African Charter on Human and Peoples' Rights (1981), entered into force 21 October 1986, O.A.U. Doc. CAB/LEG/67/3 Rev. 5, art 5; American Convention on Human Rights (1969), entered into force 18 July 1978, 1144 U.N.T.S. 123, art 5(2).

[15] Convention Against Torture, art 2(2).

military, and other public officials who might use or recruit informers must address the prohibition of torture.[16]

While torture's categorical exclusion is present in both bodies of law, other related prohibitions under humanitarian law may have a less evident counterpart under human rights law. It will be recalled that it is forbidden to use coercion against individuals under the 1949 Geneva Conventions for purposes of gathering information.[17] An identical rule against physical and moral coercion is not found in the law of non-international armed conflict. The United States and others opposed the extension of the relevant rules of the 1949 Geneva Conventions, which do not 'of course apply to a Party's own nationals', for the stated reason that a state's nationals could use them 'to avoid having to give evidence during an inquiry or trial'.[18] The view also prevailed that such identical provisions were unnecessary, given the prohibitions on violence to life, health, and the physical or mental well-being of persons under Common Article 3 and Additional Protocol II.[19]

International human rights law clearly forbids coercion that would amount to torture or cruel, inhuman, or degrading treatment, but what of so-called moral coercion that might fall short of such practices? Does human rights law specifically exclude bribery, blackmail, or other forms of moral coercion that are so readily deployed by authorities in the recruitment of informers, or might it be concluded that such practices are implicitly forbidden? Human rights law has tended towards the enunciation of broadly enunciated standards, such as the right under the American Convention on Human Rights for every person 'to have his physical, mental, and moral integrity respected',[20] rather than highly prescriptive rules or listing specific practices that are forbidden. Nonetheless, a number of human rights treaties and declarations expressly prohibit coercion, including that which is aimed at restricting the exercise of certain rights or recruiting child soldiers.[21] Nonetheless, as will be recalled, the prohibition of coercion under humanitarian law as discussed in Chapter 2 is not absolute and human rights law similarly allows public authorities such as the police to act coercively and use reasonable force where necessary in the lawful performance of their duties.[22]

While not forbidding all recourse to coercive measures, international human rights law shares humanitarian law's awareness of the vulnerability of detained

[16] Ibid art 10(1).

[17] Third Geneva Convention, art 17; Fourth Geneva Convention, art 31.

[18] CDDH/III/SR.43, *Official Records of the Diplomatic Conference on the Reaffirmation and Development of International Humanitarian Law Applicable in Armed Conflicts, Geneva (1974–1977)*, Volume XV, 36.

[19] See CDDH/407/Rev.1 *Official Records* (n 18) 461.

[20] American Convention on Human Rights, art 5(1).

[21] See for example International Covenant on Civil and Political Rights, art 18(2); International Convention on the Protection of the Rights of All Migrant Workers and Members of their Families (1990) 429 U.N.T.S. 6193, art 12(2); Declaration on the Elimination of All Forms of Intolerance and of Discrimination based on Religion or Belief, UN Doc. A/36/684 (1981), art 1(2); Optional Protocol to the Convention on the Rights of the Child on the involvement of children in armed conflict, 25 May 2000, 2173 UNTS 222, art 3.

[22] See for example Helen Fenwick, *Civil Liberties and Human Rights* (4th edn, Routledge 2007) 1101–85.

persons to being recruited as informers against their will and seeks to protect such individuals from being coerced. The Body of Principles for the Protection of all Persons under any Form of Detention or Imprisonment, for example, states that '[i]t shall be prohibited to take undue advantage of the situation of a detained or imprisoned person for the purpose of compelling him to confess, to incriminate himself otherwise or to testify against any other person'.[23] The Rome Statute of the International Criminal Court states unequivocally that persons shall not be subjected to 'any form of coercion, duress or threat' during an investigation.[24] Access to a lawyer while in custody, the European Court of Human Rights has observed, 'constitutes an important counterweight to the vulnerability of suspects in police custody, provides a fundamental safeguard against coercion and ill-treatment of suspects by the police, and contributes to the prevention of miscarriages of justice'.[25]

Authorities are not prevented by human rights law from accepting voluntary or solicited offers of cooperation by detained persons, although it remains difficult, if not impossible at times, to draw a fine line between legitimate inducements and forms of moral coercion which international human rights law arguably condemns.[26] Detention might be considered as an inherently coercive situation that hinders or even negates an individual's exercise of free will, even if it would be naïve to consider that authorities would not seek to leverage the vulnerability of a detained individual in order to gain their cooperation. Human rights law has given state authorities a degree of latitude by only expressly forbidding the most serious forms of torture and ill-treatment, thus leaving some ambiguity that might be exploited in the absence of sufficient safeguards.[27] Recruitment of informers by police, for example, has relied upon 'legal blackmail'[28] where cooperation from those implicated in criminal activity is secured by offering concessions concerning bail, charges, or sentences, in informal circumstances with limited or no oversight, and thus significant potential for abuse.[29]

In addition to the restrictions on the methods that authorities might deploy in seeking to recruit informers, human rights law seeks to protect individuals from state interference in their private lives. The right to private and family life is of particular relevance to the recruitment of informers, as it seeks to prevent any arbitrary or unlawful interference by public authorities in the lives of individuals.[30] The American

[23] 'Body of Principles for the Protection of all Persons under any Form of Detention or Imprisonment', General Assembly Resolution 43/173, 9 December 1988, Principle 21.

[24] Rome Statute of the International Criminal Court, art 55(1)(b).

[25] *Ibrahim and Others v UK* App nos. 50541/08, 50571/08, 50573/08, and 40351/09 (ECtHR, 13 September 2016), para 255.

[26] Barrett and Parker, 'Acting Ethically in the Shadows' (n 6) 240.

[27] On the use of physical and verbal abuse in the recruitment of informers in the context of policing see Delores Jones-Brown and Jon M. Shane, *An Exploratory Study on the Use of Confidential Informants in New Jersey* (American Civil Liberties Union of New Jersey 2011) 9.

[28] Andrew Sanders, Richard Young, and Mandy Burton, *Criminal Justice* (OUP 2010) 329.

[29] Colin Dunningham and Clive Morris 'A Risky Business: The Recruitment and Running of Informers by English Police Officers' (1996) 19(2) Police Studies 1, 7; Sanders, Young and Burton, *Criminal Justice* (n 28) 328–9.

[30] See Sarah Joseph and Melissa Castan, *The International Covenant on Civil and Political Rights* (OUP 2013) 533–61; William A. Schabas, *The European Convention on Human Rights: A Commentary* (OUP 2016) 358–411.

Convention on Human Rights prohibits any 'arbitrary or abusive interference' in private life, while the right to privacy is notably absent from the African Charter.[31] Where public authorities seek to recruit or use an individual as an informer, this could constitute an interference in their private life, but would also interfere in the lives of those individuals about whom an informer provides information to public authorities. Such interference must be neither unlawful nor arbitrary in order to comply with human rights law.

The essential object of Article 8 of the European Convention is 'to protect the individual against arbitrary interference by public authorities'.[32] What constitutes arbitrary interference can be determined by reference to Article 8(2):

> There shall be no interference by a public authority with the exercise of this right except such as is in accordance with the law and is necessary in a democratic society in the interests of national security, public safety or the economic well-being of the country, for the prevention of disorder or crime, for the protection of health or morals, or for the protection of the rights and freedoms of others.[33]

To comply with the European Convention, the recruitment and use of informers by public authorities requires a legal basis, must satisfy the necessity requirement on one of the established grounds (which pointedly include national security and the prevention of crime), and must be proportionate, although parties to the treaty have enjoyed a 'margin of appreciation' in determining the appropriate measures to be taken.[34]

Human rights bodies and courts have elaborated upon these requirements, although not specifically in relation to the use and recruitment of informers by public authorities. With regard to a legal basis, the Human Rights Committee has explained that 'no interference can take place except in cases envisaged by the law', and such law must itself comply with the provisions, aims, and objectives of the International Covenant on Civil and Political Rights.[35] To avoid arbitrariness, the law in question must be sufficiently detailed:

> relevant legislation must specify in detail the precise circumstances in which such interferences may be permitted. A decision to make use of such authorized interference must be made only by the authority designated under the law, and on a case-by-case basis.[36]

For the European Court of Human Rights, measures entailing interference with an individual's rights under Article 8 must 'have some basis in domestic law [...] as

[31] American Convention on Human Rights, art 11(2).

[32] *P and S v Poland* App no 57375/08 (ECtHR, 30 October 2012), para 94.

[33] European Convention on Human Rights, art 8(2).

[34] See generally Schabas, *The European Convention on Human Rights* (n 30) 403; Andrew Legg, *The Margin of Appreciation in International Human Rights Law* (OUP 2012); Eyal Benvenisti, 'Margin of Appreciation, Consensus and Universal Standards' (1999) 31 New York University Journal of International Law and Politics 843.

[35] Human Rights Committee, *General Comment No. 16: Article 17 (Right to Privacy)*, Adopted at the Thirty Second Session, 8 April 1988, para 3.

[36] Ibid para 8.

opposed to a practice which does not have a specific legal basis',[37] as has often been the case with the use of informers, as discussed in the next section.

The European Court has emphasised that measures must be in accordance with the rule of law, meaning that the law itself must be accessible and foreseeable 'as to its effects', given that the exercise of executive power in secret entails evident 'risks of arbitrariness'.[38] The observations of the Court with regard to surveillance and monitoring of communications are apposite for the use of informers:

> because of the lack of public scrutiny and the risk of misuse of power, the domestic law must provide some protection to the individual against arbitrary interference with Article 8 rights. Thus, the domestic law must be sufficiently clear in its terms to give citizens an adequate indication as to the circumstances in and conditions on which public authorities are empowered to resort to any such secret measures. [39]

In the case of *Kruslin*, which had similarly concerned phone-tapping, the Court found against France as the system in place did not 'for the time being afford adequate safeguards against various possible abuses'.[40]

The existence of a legal basis authorising interference is not sufficient in and of itself for compliance with international human rights law. To avoid arbitrariness, according to the Human Rights Committee, any interference must comply with the provisions, aims, and objectives of the Covenant and be 'reasonable in the particular circumstances'.[41] Under the European Convention, the emphasis has been on necessity and proportionality in the application of Article 8.[42] While the European Court has held that 'national authorities enjoy a wide margin of appreciation in choosing how best to achieve the legitimate aim of protecting national security',[43] the legal discretion of a national executive or the judiciary must not be 'an unfettered power'.[44] Any interference with the right to private and family life must be 'necessary in a democratic society', based on one of the established grounds in Article 8, with the measures taken being proportionate to those legitimate aims. The relatively ambiguous and interrelated concepts of necessity and proportionality are applied by the European Court on a case-by-case basis in its determination of whether interference by States parties with the rights protected by Article 8 complies with the European Convention.[45] In the absence of a judicial determination, the covert

[37] *Big Brother Watch and Others v United Kingdom* App. No. 58170/13, 62322/14, 24960/15 (EctHR, 13 September 2018), para 305.

[38] Ibid 305–6.

[39] *Kopp v Switzerland* App No. 23224/94 (ECtHR, 25 March 1998), para 64.

[40] *Kruslin v France* App No. 11801/85 (ECtHR, 24 April 1990), para 35.

[41] Human Rights Committee, *General Comment No. 16* (n 35) para 4.

[42] Schabas, *The European Convention on Human Rights* (n 30) 404–6.

[43] *Big Brother Watch v United Kingdom* (n 37) para 314.

[44] *Weber and Saravia v Germany* App No. 54934/00 (ECtHR, 29 June 2006), para 94.

[45] See further Janneke Gerards, 'How to Improve the Necessity Test of the European Court of Human Rights' (2013) 11(2) International Journal of Constitutional Law 466; Alastair Mowbray, 'A Study of the Principle of Fair Balance in the Jurisprudence of the European Court of Human Rights' (2010) 10(2) Human Rights Law Review 289; Stavros Tsakyrakis, 'Proportionality: An Assault on Human Rights?' (2009) 7(3) International Journal of Constitutional Law 468.

nature of the practice of recruiting and using informers can presents serious challenges for assessing compliance with the principles of necessity and proportionality.

The use of informers in the context of criminal investigation and prosecutions may have implications for the fair trial rights of accused persons. Concerns regarding potential ulterior motives on the part of informers could undermine the reliability of their evidence.[46] Inducements offered to informers for their cooperation or any resort to coercion could taint the information or evidence they provide, while measures taken to protect their identities could undermine the right of an accused person to challenge witnesses against them.[47] The European Court of Human Rights has stated that 'the use of special investigative methods—in particular, undercover techniques—cannot in itself infringe the right to a fair trial', but must be 'kept within clear limits'.[48] Although it has accepted the use of anonymous informants during the investigation stage of certain crimes, 'the subsequent use of their statements by the court of trial to found a conviction is a different matter'.[49] In an earlier case, the European Court had found that the reliance on anonymous informants as witnesses at trial 'involved limitations on the rights of the defence which were irreconcilable with the guarantees contained in Article 6'.[50] In addition to providing evidence that may be questionable, informers may have been implicated in criminal activity themselves or acted as *agents provocateurs* and judges are often only able to provide a check on such activity in cases which come to trial and where the identity of an informer may become known.[51]

International human rights law is relevant not only to the methods of recruitment and to the use of informers in the context of criminal investigations or trials but also to the serious risks of harm faced by individuals who act as informers for national authorities. The right to life and freedom from torture and inhuman or degrading treatment or punishment are most relevant in this context, as informers, and their relatives, may require protection by the state from harm. Human rights law has played a more prominent role in addressing these consequences of informing, which have tended to be more overt, compared to the covert practices of state authorities in recruiting and deploying informers in the first place. The identity of an informer may become known in the course of criminal proceedings in which they give evidence, thus leaving them at risk of violent retaliation: a training manual on

[46] See for example Robert M. Bloom, *Ratting: The Use and Abuse of Informants in the American Justice System* (Praeger 2002); Alexandra Natapoff, *Snitching: Criminal Informants and the Erosion of American Justice* (New York University Press 2009); Matthew W. Gilliam, 'Whispering Sweet Nothings: How Jailhouse Snitches Subvert American Justice' in Sandra Guerra Thompson, Jennifer L. Hopgood, and Hillary K. Valderrama (eds), *American Justice in the Age of Innocence: Understanding the Causes of Wrongful Convictions and How to Prevent Them* (iUniverse Books 2011) 195.

[47] See for example International Covenant on Civil and Political Rights, art 14(3)(e); European Convention on Human Rights, art 6(3)(d); American Convention on Human Rights, art 8(2)(f).

[48] *Ramanauskas v Lithuania* (n 8) para 51.

[49] *Texeira de Castro v Portugal* App No. 44/1997/828/1034 (ECtHR, 9 June 1998), para 35. See also *Jasper v United Kingdom* App No. 27052/95 (EctHR, 16 February 2000); *Rowe and Davis v United Kingdom* App No. 28901/95 (EctHR, 16 February 2000); *Fitt v United Kingdom* App No. 29777/96 (ECtHR, 16 February 2000); *Donohue v Ireland* App No. 19165/08 (ECtHR 12 December 2013).

[50] *Kostovski v The Netherlands* App no 11454/85 (ECtHR, 20 November 1989), para 44.

[51] JUSTICE, 'Under Surveillance: Covert Policing and Human Rights Standards', 1998, 39.

human rights in the administration of justice prepared by the Office of the High Commissioner for Human Rights and the International Bar Association, specifically asks judges, prosecutors, and lawyers '[w]hat measures, if any, are taken in the country in which you work to help protect other witnesses, such as informers, whose lives may be in danger following their testimony?'[52]

The protection of informers in the context of criminal investigations is not specifically addressed by the European Convention itself, although the Committee of Ministers of the Council of Europe has adopted a recommendation on the protection of witnesses and 'collaborators of justice' who might face intimidation or violence. The recommendation defined a 'collaborator of justice' as:

> any person who faces criminal charges, or has been convicted of taking part in a criminal association or other criminal organisation of any kind, or in offences of organised crime, but who agrees to cooperate with criminal justice authorities, particularly by giving testimony about a criminal association or organisation, or about any offence connected with organised crime or other serious crimes.[53]

Member States were urged to take into consideration recommendations concerning protective measures when reviewing national criminal policy and practice, and developing relevant legislation. Protective measures or specific programme for informers, such as 'special penitentiary regimes', should be considered by States '[g]iven the essential role that collaborators of justice may play in the fight against serious offences'.[54] The Committee of Ministers also addressed the risks of further criminal activity by informers, recommending that:

> Adequate measures should be undertaken to protect against the risk of the collaborators of justice committing further crimes while under protection and therefore, even involuntarily, jeopardising the case in court. The intentional perpetration of an offence by a collaborator of justice under protection should, according to the relevant circumstances, imply the revocation of protection measures.[55]

Such a revocation could arguably leave a re-offending collaborator of justice exposed to reprisals for having previously cooperated with the authorities. The Committee of Ministers acknowledged generally the relevance of the European Convention and associated case law generally to this issue, but it was not until after the adoption of this recommendation that the European Court itself addressed cases concerning the requisite obligations of States parties in protecting those who have acted as informers.

The European Court of Human Rights has addressed the obligations of state authorities to protect informers from violence by third parties under Articles 2 and

[52] Office of the High Commissioner for Human Rights in cooperation with the International Bar Association, *Human Rights in the Administration of Justice: A Manual on Human Rights for Judges, Prosecutors and Lawyers* (United Nations 2003) 749.

[53] Recommendation Rec(2005)9 of the Committee of Ministers to Member States on the protection of witnesses and collaborators of justice (adopted by the Committee of Ministers on 20 April 2005 at the 924th meeting of the Ministers' Deputies).

[54] Ibid Principle 26.

[55] Ibid Principle 27.

3 of the Convention concerning the right to life and freedom from torture and inhuman or degrading treatment or punishment.[56] In the case of *DF v Latvia*, a police informant had been assaulted and threatened with murder on several occasions. While on trial he requested that he be detained in a prison section 'designated for holding detainees who have worked for law-enforcement institutions or collaborated with those institutions' because, he claimed, he had been subjected to 'repeated physical violence by other prisoners' for his previous collaboration with the police and owing to the charges against him of sexual crimes against minors.[57] The Court noted that the parties both agreed that 'prisoners who have previously collaborated with law-enforcement authorities are at a particular risk of inter-prisoner violence in Latvian prisons'.[58] The European Convention requires states to take measures to ensure that individuals, especially vulnerable persons in custody under state authorities' exclusive control, are not subject to torture or inhuman or degrading treatment or punishment, including at the hands of private persons:

> national authorities have an obligation to take all steps reasonably expected to prevent real and immediate risks to prisoners' physical integrity, of which the authorities had or ought to have had knowledge [...] This obligation is all the more true in cases when prisoners run a particularly heightened risk of ill-treatment by their fellow inmates, such as is the case with sexual offenders and police collaborators.[59]

Finding a violation of Article 3, the Court criticised the often lengthy and bureaucratic procedure for responding to requests to confirm an individual's collaboration with the police by law enforcement agencies and the lack of sufficient coordination among investigators, prosecutors, and prison authorities.[60]

Places of detention, such as prisons, often entail inherent limitations as to the measures that can be taken to protect those who have acted as informers, and such measures may themselves give rise to human rights concerns. Juan Mendez, the UN Special Rapporteur on torture, has observed the use of solitary confinement on a voluntary basis as a means to protect those 'at risk of injury, such as sex offenders, informants, and former correctional or law enforcement officers'.[61] For prisoners who have been committed to solitary confinement in the United States, it is somewhat ironic that they may be allowed to leave this cruel form of detention if they agree to become an informant, thus exposing themselves to potential harm in the future.[62]

The European Court of Human Rights has also considered the protection of police informers who face risks outside places of detention and has confirmed the

[56] See generally Alastair Mowbray, *The Development of Positive Obligations under the European Convention of Human Rights by the European Court of Human Rights* (Hart 2004) 1–66; Dimitris Xenos, *The Positive Obligation of the Statue under the European Convention on Human Rights* (2011).

[57] *DF v Latvia* App no 11160/07 (ECtHR, 29 October 2013), paras 10, 13.

[58] Ibid para 81.

[59] Ibid paras 83–84.

[60] Ibid para 92. See also *JL v Latvia*, App no 23893/06 (ECtHR, 17 April 2012).

[61] *Interim report of the Special Rapporteur on torture and other cruel, inhuman or degrading treatment or punishment*, A/66/268, 5 August 2011, para 43.

[62] *Report of the Special Rapporteur on torture and other cruel, inhuman or degrading treatment or punishment, Juan E. Mendez, Addendum, Observations on Communications transmitted to Governments and replies received*, A/HRC/25/60/Add.2, 11 March 2013, 128.

existence of a positive obligation in such contexts. The case of *R.R. and Others v. Hungary* concerned a former member of Serbian organised crime turned police informant and his family, who were denied admission to witness protection because of his alleged continued contact with a drugs gang. The applicants claimed a violation of Article 2 of the Convention as they were 'exposed to mortal danger' because of his cooperation with the authorities.[63] The Court referred to its established view that Article 2 may imply 'in certain well-defined circumstances a positive obligation on the authorities to take preventive operational measures to protect an individual whose life is at risk from the criminal acts of another individual'.[64] It explained that this obligation does not impose 'an impossible or disproportionate burden' on state authorities:

> not every claimed risk to life can entail for the authorities a Convention requirement to take operational measures to prevent that risk from materialising. [...] it must be established to its satisfaction that the authorities knew or ought to have known at the time of the existence of a real and immediate risk to the life of an identified individual or individuals from the criminal acts of a third party and that they failed to take measures within the scope of their powers which, judged reasonably, might have been expected to avoid that risk.[65]

The Court found inadmissible that part of the application relating to the informer himself, as the consequence of his exclusion from the witness protection scheme was a transfer to a stricter regime within the prison.[66] It accepted, however, that the other applicants, the informant's family members, faced a serious threat to their lives owing to 'the well-known nature of mafia conflicts and the applicants' unrefuted allegations about them being wanted by criminal circles—an assertion not implausible in the light of the first applicant's having become a collaborator of justice enabling the unravelling of internationally organised criminal activities'.[67] Hungary's authorities left them potentially exposed to such 'life-threatening vengeance' and this was contrary to the state's obligations under Article 2.[68]

European human rights case law thus confirms the obligation of states to protect from serious harm those who have collaborated with public authorities, particularly in the context of criminal justice. Other human rights bodies have also addressed the obligations associated with the right to life and freedom from torture or cruel and inhuman or degrading treatment or punishment, such as *non-refoulement*, but have only rarely touched upon such duties in relation to informers.[69] In one such instance, the United Nations Human Rights Committee found that Articles 6 and 7 of the International Covenant on Civil and Political Rights, concerning the right to life and freedom from torture, had not been violated by the forcible return to Russia

[63] *RR and Others v Hungary* App no 19400/11 (ECtHR, 4 December 2012), para 3.
[64] Ibid para 28. [65] Ibid para 29. [66] Ibid para 25. [67] Ibid para 30.
[68] Ibid para 32.
[69] On *non-refoulement* see for example David Weissbrodt and Isabel Hörtreiter, 'The Principle of Non-Refoulement: Article 3 of Convention Against Torture and Other Cruel, Inhuman or Degrading Treatment or Punishment in Comparison with the Non-Refoulement Provisions of Other International Human Rights Treaties' (1999) 5 Buffalo Human Rights Law Review (1999) 1; Aoife Duffy, 'Expulsion to face torture? *Non-refoulement* in International Law' (2008) 20 International Journal of Refugee Law 373.

of two asylum seekers who claimed to be at risk of torture or being killed as perceived collaborators of the Russian authorities and Wahhabi militants.[70] The Danish authorities had considered but not been persuaded of the veracity of the claims made by the applicants in seeking asylum. The Human Rights Committee emphasised 'the obligation of States parties not to extradite, deport, expel or otherwise remove a person from their territory where there are substantial grounds for believing that there is a real risk of irreparable harm such as that contemplated by articles 6 and 7 of the Covenant'.[71] The Committee showed deference to the national authorities by affirming that it was generally for the state in question to determine if such a risk exists. The Committee found that Denmark's asylum process was fair, and that based on the facts, it could not conclude that a real risk of treatment in violation of the Covenant was present.[72]

International human rights law has had a wide-ranging but somewhat ad hoc engagement with the practice of recruiting and using informers by state authorities, and with the attendant and often serious consequences that can arise both for individuals acting as covert human intelligence sources or for other persons impacted by their activity. The ultimately permissive approach of this body of law is accompanied by a recognition of the real risks to fundamental rights such as life, freedom from torture, fair trial, and privacy that the practice entails. Leaving aside this seeming ambivalence, key elements of a human rights-compliant approach to the use and recruitment of informers would include the requirements of an established legal basis, the designation of an appropriate authority, training for relevant public authorities, in particular to prevent torture, protective measures for those acting as informers, including witnesses in criminal proceedings, and accountability in the event of abuses occurring.

Further requirements that are considered necessary for a system governing the use of informers to comply with human rights have been identified by Arivander Sambei:

> It is essential that the use and deployment of CHIS is strictly regulated and employs a rigorous regime of source management. The system and oversight must be robust and able to withstand scrutiny. All dealings with CHIS and decisions as to their employment and tasking should be recorded. Any intelligence or potential evidential product discussed by a CHIS should be recorded and graded as to its potential use and disseminated. The interaction between intelligence agents and law enforcement officers should be undertaken by dedicated and specifically trained 'handlers', who in turn should be overseen by a 'controller' who is responsible for regulating the relationship between the handlers and the source.[73]

[70] *X and X v Denmark*, Communication No. 2186/2012, Views adopted by the Committee at its 112th session (22 October 2014), CCPR/C/112/D/2186/2012, 17 November 2014.

[71] Ibid para 7.3.

[72] Ibid para 7.5. See also *H and B v UK*, App nos 70073/10 and 44539/11 (ECtHR, 9 April 2013); *S.G. v Netherlands*, Decision, Communication No. 135/1999, CAT/C/32/D/135/1999 (Committee Against Torture, 14 May 2004).

[73] Arivinder Sambei, 'Intelligence Cooperation Versus Evidence Collection and Dissemination' in Larissa van den Herik and Nico Schrijver (eds), *Counter-Terrorism Strategies in a Fragmented International Legal Order: Meeting the Challenges* (CUP 2015) 212, 221 (footnote omitted).

In addition, as Dermot Walsh has noted, those tasked with handling informers must pay attention to matters such as informer credibility, anonymity, payment, motivation, usefulness, reliability, and the need for protective measures:

> The identity of the informer should be protected at all times, subject only to the requirements of justice in proving the innocence of the accused. Consideration should also be given to issues of informer safety, such as protection and relocation.[74]

Public authorities are required to be proactive when it comes to protection according to European case law. While a certain degree of secrecy is inevitable in the context of using covert human intelligence sources, transparency is required with regard to the legal basis underpinning the practice and to the basic principles and guidelines relied upon by relevant public authorities in the use and recruitment of informers.[75]

International human rights law does not itself explicitly lay out a comprehensive framework governing the recruitment and use of informers by states, nevertheless key components of such a framework can be determined from existing human rights treaties and case law, including those addressed to discrete human rights concerns associated with the practice that have come before international and regional human rights bodies. Not all aspects of the practice have been subject to the scrutiny of relevant bodies, however, most notably the fraught issue of state authorities permitting informers to engage in criminal activities in order to minimise the risk of their detection and to allow for their continued collaboration with the relevant authorities. A failure by a state to prevent serious crimes by an informer seems obviously contrary to its obligations under international human rights law where such crimes involve harm to the fundamental rights of others, notwithstanding a utilitarian claim that the informer's unlawful acts may be necessary for the prevention of a greater number of other crimes. The next section considers national approaches to the use of informers, including how state authorities address the potential commission of criminal activities by informers, with a particular focus on the situation in Northern Ireland.

5.2 National Approaches to the Regulation of Informers

Widespread agreement exists amongst public authorities on the necessity of employing informers, a practice that is considered as old as law enforcement itself.[76] Notwithstanding such acceptance and universal deployment, the concealed nature of this form of covert activity has meant that the precise modalities of the practice are often unknown and subjected to limited if any public scrutiny. While the use

[74] Dermot P.J. Walsh, *Human Rights and Policing in Ireland; Law, Policy and Practice* (Clarus Press 2009) 176–7.

[75] Ibid.

[76] Richard C. Donnelly, 'Judicial Control of Informants, Spies, Stool Pigeons, and Agent Provocateurs' (1951) 60(7) Yale Law Journal 1091, 1091. For an historical overview see Bloom, *Ratting* (n 46) 1–7.

of informers is evident in the policing and intelligence practices of many states,[77] the preponderance of literature has focused on the law, policy, and practice of a very limited number of jurisdictions.[78] Owing to limitations of space, this section continues somewhat in this vein by offering a case study of Northern Ireland which examines the numerous controversies surrounding the use of informers during the Troubles and the subsequent development of the UK's system for regulating the use of informers. This case study demonstrates the extent of the influence of human rights law on domestic practice regarding the use of informers during a situation of political violence approximating an armed conflict, and presages the discussion in this chapter's final section on the application of human rights standards during armed conflict. Before turning to Northern Ireland, some general observations can be made on national approaches to regulating the practice of employing informers by reference to some illustrative examples of domestic law, policy, and practice.

As is the case in situations of armed conflict, human rights abuses and corruption are often associated with the use of informers in the context of domestic criminal justice and intelligence gathering activities related to national security.[79] Nonetheless, and despite the requirement under international human rights law that any interference by public authorities in the private lives of individuals must be authorised by law, legal regulation of the recruitment and use of informers by public authorities is often absent. Peter Neyroud and Alan Beckley have found 'few international examples of a legislated framework for the use of informers' and concluded that governments have tended to address only those aspects of such covert policing that have given rise to public scandal.[80] While the use of covert human intelligence sources is regulated by national legislation in some countries,[81] in many states, reliance is instead placed upon internal codes of conduct or executive guidance for relevant authorities.

In the United States, there is a certain legal ambiguity surrounding the use of informers in policing and intelligence activities, despite the centrality of the practice to law enforcement. In lieu of federal legislation, mandatory guidelines have

[77] See Michael Fishwick, 'The European Perspective' in Billingsley, *Covert Human Intelligence Sources* (n 3) 123; Steven Greer, 'Where the Grass is Greener? Supergrasses in Comparative Perspective' in Billingsley, Nemitz, and Bean, *Informers* (n 3) 123; Anthony Minnaar, 'The Use of Informers: An Essential Tool in the Fight Against Crime?' (2011) 24(3) South African Journal of Criminology 83; Steve Hewitt, 'Forgotten Surveillance: Covert Human Intelligence Sources in Canada in a Post 9/11 World' in Michael Geist (ed), *Law, Privacy and Surveillance in the Post-Snowden Era* (University of Ottawa Press 2015) 45. See also N. Prabha Unnithan, *Crime and Justice in India* (Sage 2013); Børge Bakken, *Crime, Justice and Policing in China* (Rowman and Littlefield 2005).

[78] Specifically the United Kingdom and the United States, see for example Eugene Oscapella, 'A Study of Informers in England' (1980) Criminal Law Review 136; Billingsley, *Covert Human Intelligence Sources* (n 3); Billingsley, Nemitz, and Bean, *Informers* (n 3); Donnelly, 'Judicial Control of Informants' (n 76); Bloom, *Ratting* (n 46); Natapoff, *Snitching* (n 46); Gilliam, 'Whispering Sweet Nothings' (n 46).

[79] See generally Clifford S. Zimmerman, 'Toward a New Vision of Informants: A History of Abuses and Suggestions for Reform' (1994) 22 Hastings Constitutional Law Quarterly 81, 165; Sanders, Young, and Burton, *Criminal Justice* (n 28) 327–31; Calla Wahlquist, 'Gangsters, Cops and Lawyer X: The Police Informant Scandal that has Shocked Australia', *The Guardian*, 5 December 2018.

[80] Peter Neyroud and Alan Beckley, 'Regulating informers: The Regulation of Investigatory Powers Act, Covert Policing and Human Rights' in Billingsley, Nemitz, and Bean, *Informers* (n 3) 164, 173.

[81] Fishwick, 'The European Perspective' (n 77) 126.

been issued by the US Attorney General on the use of covert human intelligence sources by law enforcement agencies, including the Federal Bureau of Investigation (FBI).[82] Successive FBI Directors have emphasised the importance of covert human intelligence sources in US law enforcement,[83] notwithstanding the long-standing recognition of the 'problems inherent in the use of informants' and the need for accountability and control in order to minimise risk.[84] There are racial and class dimensions to the abuses associated with the use of informers in the United States,[85] as well as serious concerns surrounding the use of criminal informants and of informers acting as *agents provocateurs*.[86] The FBI has developed several internal guides and manuals for using informants in its investigations and operations, which have addressed instances where informants might engage in illegal activity.[87]

Ireland's police service, An Garda Síochána, similarly views the use of covert human intelligence sources as 'essential', such that a failure to maintain a capability to run informers effectively 'would fatally undermine the national and international law enforcement effort'.[88] There is no legislative framework in place covering the use of informers by An Garda Síochána, which is contrary to Ireland's obligations under international human rights law, with reliance placed instead on the unpublished 'Code of Practice for the Management and Use of Covert Human Intelligence Sources'.[89] Official and independent examinations of aspects of policing in Ireland have noted the absence of sufficient safeguards and the shortcomings of such self-regulation, and have recommended that consideration be given to the development of legislation governing the use of informers.[90] Given that informers have been

[82] Office of the Attorney General, 'The Attorney General's Guidelines Regarding the Use of FBI Confidential Human Sources', 2006; Office of the Attorney General, 'The Attorney General's Guidelines Regarding the Use of Confidential Informants', 2002.

[83] See for example William Webster, 'The Director: Why the FBI Needs Undercover Snoops', *Los Angeles Herald Examiner*, 2 June 1978, A-21; Dick Lehr, 'The Information Underworld: Police Reliance on Criminal Informants is a Dangerous Game for Both', *Boston Globe*, 16 October 1988, A27.

[84] James E. Hight, 'Avoiding the Informant Trap: A Blueprint for Control' (1998) 67 FBI Law Enforcement Bulletin 1, 5. See also Amanda J. Schreiber, 'Dealing with the Devil: An Examination of the FBI's Troubled Relationship with its Confidential Informants' (2001) 34 Colombia Journal of Law and Social Problems 301.

[85] Natapoff, *Snitching* (n 46) 101–19, 140–1. See also Peter Gill and Mark Phythian, *Intelligence in an Insecure World* (2nd edn, Polity Press 2012) 86–7.

[86] Ulrich Garms, 'The Preventive Criminal Justice Strategy Against Terrorism and its Human Rights Implications' in Nowak and Charbord, *Using Human Rights to Counter Terrorism* (n 6) 265, 289–92. Human Rights Watch and Columbia Law School Human Rights Institute, *Illusions of Justice: Human Rights Abuses in US Terrorism Prosecutions* (Human Rights Watch 2014); Wadie E. Said, 'The Terrorist Informant' (2010) 85 Washington Law Review 687.

[87] See for example Federal Bureau of Investigation, 'Confidential Human Source Policy Manual', 2007; Federal Bureau of Investigation, 'Confidential Human Source Validation Standards Manual', 2010; Federal Bureau of Investigation, 'Domestic Investigations and Operations Guide', 2011.

[88] *Public Statement by the Commissioner of An Garda Siochana on the Management and Use of Covert Human Intelligence Sources*, 2017, 4 <https://www.garda.ie/en/About-Us/Publications/Policy-Documents/Management-and-use-of-Covert-Human-Intelligence-Sources.pdf> accessed 30 May 2019.

[89] ibid. See also Walsh, *Human Rights and Policing in Ireland* (n 74) 195, 525.

[90] *Report of the Tribunal of Inquiry, Set up Pursuant to the Tribunal of Inquiry (Evidence) Acts 1921–2002 into Certain Gardaí in the Donegal Division, Report on Explosives 'Finds' in Donegal*, Dublin, Government Publications Office, 2004, 51–2, 460–1, 467–85; Garda Síochána Ombudsman Commission, *Special*

implicated in serious criminal activities,[91] recommendations have also been made to address shortcomings in training, supervision, informer registration, record-keeping, independent oversight, and transparency.[92] Where reforms and safeguards have been introduced, these have been criticised by some members of An Garda Síochána as onerous and inhibiting, in particular in relation to limitations concerning the use of intelligence from criminal informers.[93]

Significant risks attach to the use of informers who are close to or directly involved in criminal activity. Such persons are a valuable source of information given their proximity to ongoing or potential crimes, to the extent that police or other public authorities may be tempted to permit or turn a blind eye to criminal acts by those persons in order to keep them in place. The use of such participating informers or criminal informants is considered especially problematic in the United States, as it occurs in a context of 'tremendous official authority and discretion . . . with few legal limits'.[94] According to Alexandra Natapoff:

> The constraints that do exist tend to focus on the government's informational obligations rather than substantive limits on the way the government can use criminal informants, and even those informational obligations are tied to litigation and trials that occur infrequently. The end result of this laissez-faire, unregulated approach is that the American practice of using criminal informants is centrally shaped by individual decisions of police and prosecutors, with few external controls and little judicial oversight or legislative or public scrutiny.[95]

Similar concerns have been expressed by the Garda Siochána Ombudsman Commission in Ireland, given the lack of specific legislation, guidance, or procedures governing the use of criminal informers:

> The absence of such mechanisms for the use, in garda operations, of 'participating informants' creates significant risks, as in the Ombudsman Commission's view, it is not possible to effectively manage and place parameters on the extent to which such individuals are authorised to participate in criminality.[96]

The Commission expressed its view that where an informer may potentially participate in criminal activity with the knowledge of a state agency, such conduct should

Report by the Garda Ombudsman to the Minister for Justice, Equality and Defence, Issued pursuant to Section 80(5) of the Garda Síochána Act 2005, 9 May 2013, 1–8.

[91] Vincent Browne, 'Murderer served IRA and Garda but mostly himself', *Irish Times*, 8 January 1997; 'Cork man reveals he was Garda informer as he is jailed for gun attack on young woman', *Irish Examiner*, 14 February 2017.

[92] See for example *Report of the Tribunal of Inquiry* (n 90) 48, 461, 467, 485–8; Garda Síochána Ombudsman Commission, *Special Report* (n 90) 1–12.

[93] Jim Cusack, 'Garda punished for breaching informant rules', *Irish Independent*, 20 June 2013; Cormac O'Keefe, 'Informant system of limited use, say detectives', *Irish Examiner*, 14 November 2014. See also Garda Inspectorate, *Report of the Garda Síochána Inspectorate: Crime Investigation; Part 8: Intelligence-Led Policing*, 2014, 8.

[94] Natapoff, *Snitching* (n 46) 67. See also Michael L. Rich, 'Brass Rings and Red-Headed Stepchildren: Protecting Active Criminal Informants' (2012) 61(5) American University International Law Review 1433.

[95] Ibid. [96] Garda Síochána Ombudsman Commission, *Special Report* (n 90) 7–8.

'be subject to the utmost scrutiny and ethical considerations. Such scrutiny should be intrusive, robust and meticulously recorded.'[97]

In the United States, the Attorney General's Guidelines recognise that criminal activity by an informant can be permitted, but forbid the FBI from offering assurances of immunity to such persons:

> The FBI does not have any authority to make any promise or commitment that would prevent the government from prosecuting a Confidential Human Source for criminal activity that is not authorized [...]. An FBI Agent must exercise due diligence to avoid giving any person the erroneous impression that he or she has any such authority.[98]

With regard to 'otherwise illegal activity', the Attorney General's guidelines have established a system of authorisation, but emphasise that the FBI cannot authorise any acts of violence, except in self-defence, or acts that would be unlawful if carried out by law enforcement officials, such as trespass, breaking and entering, illegal wiretapping, or interception of post.[99] In addition to the detailed requirements of authorisation for illegal activity, the Attorney General has also established the need for written instructions, precautionary measures, monitoring, and record-keeping, as well as setting out a procedure for addressing instances of unauthorised illegal activity.[100] Despite the mandatory nature of the Attorney General's guidelines, an inspection by the Office of the Inspector General of the Department of Justice found 'significant problems in the FBI's compliance with Guidelines' provisions'.[101] A 2017 Bill before the House of Representatives proposed the Confidential Informant Accountability Act of 2017 which would require all Federal law enforcement agencies to report annually to Congress on serious crimes committed by confidential informants, whether authorised or not.[102] Previous attempts to have such a Bill enacted have been unsuccessful, although individual States have introduced legislation regulating aspects of the use of informers by police.[103]

The role of the judiciary in providing oversight of the use of informers in policing is generally limited, although judges can be more active where the integrity or fairness of specific criminal proceedings may be at issue. In Ireland, a retired High Court judge provides independent oversight of the system of informer handling by way of annual reports to the Minister of Justice,[104] although examination of whether there has been compliance with the Code of Practice does not involve a 'complete and

[97] Ibid 7–8.

[98] Office of the Attorney General, 'Guidelines Regarding the Use of FBI Confidential Human Sources' (n 82) 8.

[99] Ibid 30–1.

[100] Ibid 30–40. See also Federal Bureau of Investigation, 'Domestic Investigations and Operations Guide', 15 October 2011, §18.5.5 <https://www.documentcloud.org/documents/3416775-DIOG-Redactions-Marked-Redacted.html> accessed 30 May 2019.

[101] U.S. Department of Justice Office of the Inspector General, *The Federal Bureau of Investigation's Compliance with the Attorney General's Investigative Guidelines*, December 2005, 7.

[102] Confidential Informant Accountability Act of 2017, H.R. 1857—115th Congress (2017–2018).

[103] See for example HB 1221, Sixty-Fifth Legislative Assembly of North Dakota (2017); 'Rachel's Law', Florida Stat. Ann. 914.28 (2017).

[104] Minister for Justice and Equality Charlie Flanagan, Dáil Written Answers, 7 November 2017.

exhaustive investigation'.[105] The US Attorney General saw a limited judicial role in overseeing the use of covert human intelligence sources by the FBI, with court approval only required, for example, where authorities seek to use an individual on probation or parole as an informant.[106] Unlike in the case of warrants for intrusive surveillance,[107] judicial authorisation is generally not required for the deployment of informers and, as Raphael Bitton has noted, existing judicial scrutiny 'only cures harms ex post and lacks the ability to oversee an activity in an *ongoing* manner'.[108] The difficulty of ensuring oversight is even more pronounced in the context of the use of informers in intelligence gathering for national security, given that intelligence agencies are more impervious to public scrutiny.[109] While broad accountability and oversight of intelligence agencies may exist in the form of ministerial or parliamentary supervision,[110] the judicial role is often limited to inquiries, quasi-judicial commissions, or special courts sitting *in camera*.[111] Such oversight can be further hampered by the tendency of intelligence agencies to resort to blanket claims of secrecy on the basis of national security.[112]

International human rights law requires that the recruitment and use of informers be regulated by national law, and while this body of law has occasionally influenced the adoption by states of legislation for the use of informers by police and other public authorities,[113] the absence of an explicit requirement in the relevant international treaties, and the general ambivalence of this body of law towards the practice of using informers, has arguably contributed to the inertia of states in this context. In lieu of legislation, many states continue to rely on a system of self-regulation by police and intelligence agencies subject to broad political or judicial oversight which would seem unsuited to preventing corruption or harm to human rights. Existing limitations may also reflect the desire of public authorities such as the police and security services to retain an ambiguously regulated space that allows for relatively unencumbered resort to using informers as a valued if potential harmful means of information gathering. In Northern Ireland, informers were deployed by MI5, the British counter-intelligence and security agency, as well as by the army and

[105] See for example Letter from T.C. Smyth to Minister for Justice Francis Fitzgerald, *Re: Covert Human Intelligence Sources*, 5 October 2015. See also Walsh, *Human Rights and Policing in Ireland* (n 74) 714–15.

[106] Office of the Attorney General, 'Guidelines Regarding the Use of FBI Confidential Human Sources' (n 82) 23–5.

[107] Hewitt, 'Forgotten Surveillance' (n 77) 60.

[108] Raphael Bitton, 'In Law We Trust; The Israeli Case of Overseeing Intelligence' in Zachary K. Goldman and Samuel J. Rascoff (eds), *Global Intelligence Oversight: Governing Security in the Twenty-First Century* (OUP 2016) 141, 159 (original emphasis).

[109] See Kate Martin, 'Domestic Intelligence and Civil Liberties' in Christopher Andrew, Richard J. Aldrich, and Wesley K. Wark (eds), *Secret Intelligence: A Reader* (Routledge 2008) 358; Sambei, 'Intelligence cooperation versus evidence collection and dissemination' (n 73) 215, 222–3.

[110] Andrew, Aldrich, and Wark, *Secret Intelligence* (n 109) 311–13. See also Goldman and Rascoff, *Global Intelligence Oversight* (n 108); Steve Tsang (ed), *Intelligence and Human Rights in the Era of Global Terrorism* (Praeger Security International 2007); Thomas C. Bruneau and Steven C. Boraz (eds), *Reforming Intelligence: Obstacles to Democratic Control and Effectiveness* (University of Texas 2007).

[111] Andrew, Aldrich, and Wark, *Secret Intelligence* (n 109) 312.

[112] Gill and Phythian, *Intelligence in an Insecure World* (n 85) 170, 194.

[113] Ibid 164–5.

the police, the Royal Ulster Constabulary. As a case study, Northern Ireland aptly demonstrates the inherent risks associated with the deployment of informers in the absence of effective regulation, oversight and accountability.

5.2.1 The Case of Northern Ireland

The conflict in Northern Ireland from 1968 to 1998 was not accepted by the United Kingdom authorities as having qualified as an armed conflict within the meaning of international humanitarian law.[114] The level of organisation on the part of non-state armed groups, the large presence and engagement of British armed forces in Northern Ireland, the deaths of over 3,500 people during the thirty-year period of the Troubles, and the regular visits conducted by the International Committee of the Red Cross indicate, however, that the so-called Troubles were more than a mere situation of 'internal disturbances and tensions', although perhaps not of sufficient intensity throughout the period in question to qualify as an armed conflict.[115] While international humanitarian law was never formally applied, the United Kingdom's status as a party to the European Convention of Human Rights meant that human rights law was relevant for assessing state conduct.[116] Domestic law, including criminal law, was deployed against members of non-state paramilitary organisations in a context of enhanced emergency powers.[117]

In relation to the use of informers by state authorities, however, there were 'no rules', according to the Chief Constable of the Police Service of Northern Ireland: '[t]here was no regulatory framework for handling of informants' during the Troubles.[118] While informers were recruited and used on a considerable scale by the police, army, and security services, an official independent review found 'a wilful and abject failure by successive governments to provide the clear policy and legal framework necessary for agent-handling operations to take place effectively and within the law'.[119] This section examines the practice, policy, and law regarding informers both during and after the conflict in Northern Ireland, including how recent legal developments in the United Kingdom more explicitly link the deployment

[114] Steven Haines, 'Northern Ireland: 1968–1998' in Elizabeth Wilmshurst (ed), *International Law and the Classification of Conflicts* (OUP 2012) 117; Colm Campbell, '"Wars on Terror" and Vicarious Hegemons: The UK, International Law and the Northern Ireland Conflict' (2005) 54 International and Comparative Law Quarterly 321, 330–4.

[115] Additional Protocol II, art 1(2). See Fionnuala Ní Aoláin, *The Politics of Force: Conflict Management and State Violence in Northern Ireland* (Blackstaff 2000) 218–47

[116] See for example Brice Dickson, *The European Convention of Human Rights and the Conflict in Northern Ireland* (OUP 2010).

[117] See Dermot Walsh, *The Use and Abuse of Emergency Legislation in Northern Ireland* (Cobden Trust 1983); Jessie Blackburn, *Anti-Terrorism Law and Normalising Northern Ireland* (Routledge 1994).

[118] Eamon McCann, 'State role in killings by IRA changes everything', *Irish Times*, 28 January 2016. See generally Jon Moran, *From Northern Ireland to Afghanistan: British Military Intelligence Operations, Ethics and Human Rights* (Ashgate 2013) 23–66; Jon Moran and Clive Walker, 'Intelligence Powers and Accountability in the U.K.' in Goldman and Rascoff, *Global Intelligence Oversight* (n 108) 289.

[119] Rt Hon Sir Desmond de Silva, *The Report of the Patrick Finucane Review*, 12 December 2012, H.C. 802- I, 7.

of covert human intelligence sources by public authorities to the state's human rights obligations.

During the conflict in Northern Ireland, dozens of alleged informers were killed by paramilitary groups.[120] The IRA showed little sympathy for suspected informers, considering informing 'the ultimate crime', and often subjecting 'touts' to torture, ill-treatment, and execution after a cursory court martial.[121] The IRA Green Book specifically claimed that actions against domestic collaborators were 'morally justified'.[122] Counter-insurgency and policing operations in Northern Ireland relied heavily on informers, who were recruited by the police, army, and security services using a combination of coercive measures and inducements, such as promises of immunity from prosecution.[123] The use of such 'highly dubious methods' in Northern Ireland was nevertheless seen to have been effective in undermining the activities of the compromised armed groups.[124] The Provisional IRA adopted a cell structure to counter this threat from within,[125] yet informers continued to be active:

> Penetrating the group at a number of levels had several benefits, the most important being that if one agent was compromised, others (unknown to him or her) would remain in place. It also provided the security forces with the utilitarian option of sacrificing one agent in an attempt to protect the rest, should the PIRA suspect an informant at work. Yet such methods of operating began to venture into a grey area in terms of legality and moral acceptability.[126]

Although some high-profile examples of informers have become public,[127] the full extent to which informers have been used remains unknown, such disclosure not being in the interests of the parties to the conflict.[128] The use of 'supergrasses', informers who gave evidence in the trials of former colleagues in exchange for leniency

[120] Michael McKeown, 'Post-Mortem: An examination of the patterns of politically associated violence in Northern Ireland during the years 1969–2001 as reflected in the fatality figures for those years', 2009, 9, 18 <http://cain.ulst.ac.uk/victims/mckeown/mckeown01.pdf> accessed 30 May 2019; Rt Hon Sir Desmond de Silva, *The Report of the Patrick Finucane Review* (n 119) 91.

[121] Kevin Toolis, *Rebel Hearts: Journeys within the IRA's Soul* (Picador 1995) 194; Tim Pat Coogan, *The IRA: A History* (Roberts Rinehart Publishers 1994) 176.

[122] IRA, *The Green Book*, Vol. II, n.d., Section I(1) <http://cain.ulst.ac.uk/othelem/organ/ira/ira_green_book.htm> accessed 30 May 2019.

[123] Mark McGovern, 'Informers, Agents and the Liberal Ideology of Collusion in Northern Ireland' (2016) 9(2) Critical Studies on Terrorism 292, 295; J. Bowyer Bell, *The Secret Army: The IRA* (Poolbeg 1998) 485; B. Bamford, 'Intelligence in Northern Ireland' in Andrew, Aldrich, and Wark, *Secret Intelligence* (n 108), 259, 266.

[124] Bamford, 'Intelligence in Northern Ireland' (n 123) 259, 267. On infiltration by undercover agents see Kevin Fulton, *Unsung Hero: How I Saved Dozens of Lives as a Secret Agent Inside the IRA* (John Blake 2006). See also Jon Moran, 'Evaluating Special Branch and the Use of Informant Intelligence in Northern Ireland' (2010) 25(1) Intelligence and National Security 1; Thomas Leahy, 'The Influence of Informers and Agents on Provisional Irish Republican Army Military Strategy and British Counter-Insurgency Strategy, 1976–1994' (2014) 26(1) *Twentieth Century British History* 122.

[125] Colm Campbell and Ita Connolly, 'Making War on Terror? Global Lesson from Northern Ireland' (2006) 69(6) Modern Law Review 935, 953.

[126] Bamford, 'Intelligence in Northern Ireland' (n 123) 267.

[127] See for example Ian Cobain, 'How many murders can a police informer get away with?', *The Guardian*, 8 March 2018.

[128] Mark Urban, *Big Boys' Rules: The Secret Struggle against the IRA* (Faber and Faber 1992) 101.

and witness protection, also occurred in Northern Ireland.[129] While strongly advocated by the police, the reliance on such witnesses eventually proved unsuccessful in securing convictions, with evidence retracted at trial and doubts raised over the reliability of such individuals given the inducements involved.[130]

Official investigations of the activities of state-run informers since the end of the Troubles have confirmed that numerous agents were directly or indirectly involved in serious crimes, including the notorious murder of lawyer Patrick Finucane.[131] In a report on six murders in Loughinisland, a Police Ombudsman Commission found that informants were involved in the acquisition of weapons used 'in a wide range of murders', and concluded that 'some informants were protected by not asking them about certain crimes and hence not exploring their knowledge and potential culpability and also not proactively seeking intelligence on their potential involvement in those crimes. This meant that some informants were not investigated for serious matters. That is indefensible.'[132] In his independent review, Desmond de Silva, a former prosecutor of the Special Court for Sierra Leone, pointed to the absence of regulation of informers as a contributing factor to their involvement in criminality, concluding that '[m]any of the grave issues relating to the involvement of agents in the murder of Patrick Finucane must, therefore, be considered in the context of the wilful and abject failure by the UK Government to put in place adequate guidance and regulation for the running of agents'.[133]

One of the most high-profile alleged informers during the Troubles was Freddie Scappaticci, the head of internal security for the IRA and described by one British general as the army's 'golden egg' in Northern Ireland.[134] Known by the codename Stakeknife, Scappaticci's purported actions constitute one of the starkest examples of the propensity for high-level informants to be directly involved in criminal activities, including murder. Martin Ingram, a former agent handler of the British military intelligence's Force Research Unit in Northern Ireland, has explained the dilemma of Scappaticci providing information to the British authorities from within the IRA:

> Stakeknife produced high-grade intelligence, much of it read at the highest level of the political and security establishments. He was, without doubt, the jewel in the crown. The problem was, Stakeknife could only shine if he immersed himself in the activities of those he was reporting upon, including murder and other illegal acts.[135]

[129] Steven Greer, *Supergrasses: A Study in Anti-Terrorist Law Enforcement in Northern Ireland* (Clarendon Press 1995).

[130] Bamford, 'Intelligence in Northern Ireland' (n 123) 269; Ní Aoláin, *The Politics of Force* (n 115) 60–1.

[131] de Silva, *The Report of the Patrick Finucane Review* (n 119).

[132] Police Ombudsman for Northern Ireland, *Statutory Report: Public Statement by the Police Ombudsman in accordance with Section 62 of the Police (Northern Ireland) Act 1998. Relating to a complaint by the victims and survivors of the Murders at the Heights Bar, Loughinisland, 18 June 1994,* Belfast, 2016, 3, 37, 62, 82–3, 134, 137, 142–6.

[133] de Silva, *The Report of the Patrick Finucane Review* (n 119) 91.

[134] John Ware, 'Exposed: The murky world of spying during the Troubles', *Irish Times*, 11 April 2017.

[135] See Martin Ingram and Greg Harkin, *Stakeknife: Britain's Secret Agents in Ireland* (O'Brien Press 2004) 64. See also Bamford, 'Intelligence in Northern Ireland' (n 123) 272.

It has been claimed that Scappaticci was involved in the killing of a number of individuals in order to divert attention from himself as a possible informer.[136] These were not isolated incidents, as a 2007 report by the Police Ombudsman of Northern Ireland linked police informers to multiple murders, attempted murders, and various other serious crimes during the Troubles.[137] The Director of Public Prosecutions established *Operation Kenova*, an independent investigation into activities related to Stakeknife, in response to a classified Police Ombudsman report which linked Scappaticci to numerous killings carried out by the IRA's internal security.[138] In investigating whether evidence exists of criminal offences by State agents or alleged informants, *Operation Kenova* will have to consider whether 'lives were sacrificed' in order to protect Stakeknife as an informer.[139]

It is at least arguable that such ex post facto examinations of the conduct of informers and the state agencies employing them would not have been required had appropriate regulation, oversight, and accountability mechanisms been in place in Northern Ireland during the conflict. According to the independent review by de Silva, the implications of insufficient regulation of the use of informers within paramilitary organisations were that:

> agent-handlers and their superiors were expected to gather intelligence without clear guidance as to the extent to which their agents could become involved in criminal activity in order to achieve this objective. Intelligence officers were, in effect, being asked to perform a task that, in some cases, could not be achieved effectively in ways that were lawful. It is my view that those charged with upholding the law should never be put in the position of potentially having to break the law in order to discharge their official duties.[140]

Across the police, military, and security service the guidance in place was either unworkable or contradictory, or there was an absence of effective external oversight in relation to whether informers could engage in criminal activity in order to fulfil their roles as intelligence agents.[141]

The absence of a legal framework relating to the use of informers in Northern Ireland was not unintentional and has been interpreted by McGovern as giving rise to 'a space of legal obscurity and plausible deniability that facilitated counterinsurgency practice rather than hampering it'.[142] de Silva did not take issue with the use of informers during the conflict per se, finding that running such agents was 'one of the most effective methods by which the security forces could frustrate terrorist activity and save lives'.[143] The most valuable informers were those within paramilitary organisations, he accepted, who by necessity would be involved in criminal activity.[144] For de Silva, it was evident that navigating this terrain would require 'the

[136] Ingram and Harkin, *Stakeknife* (n 135) 80–1.

[137] *Statement by the Police Ombudsman for Northern Ireland on her Investigation into the circumstances surrounding the death of Raymond McCord Junior and related matters*, Belfast: Police Ombudsman for Northern Ireland, 22 January 2007, 7–8.

[138] Ware, 'Exposed: The murky world of spying during the Troubles' (n 134). [139] Ibid.

[140] de Silva, *The Report of the Patrick Finucane Review* (n 119) 7. [141] Ibid 6–7.

[142] McGovern, 'Informers, agents and the liberal ideology of collusion' (n 123) 302.

[143] de Silva, *The Report of the Patrick Finucane Review* (n 119) 68.

[144] Ibid 68–9. See also Moran, *From Northern Ireland to Afghanistan* (n 118) 57.

development of a detailed legal and policy framework, though I am fully conscious of how difficult drawing up such a framework would be'.[145] The broadly enunciated protections of the European Convention of Human Rights were applicable in Northern Ireland throughout the Troubles, but proved insufficient at prompting effective regulation and oversight by the United Kingdom authorities concerning the use of informers and at preventing the associated abuses of human rights.

Notwithstanding the absence of a clear and overarching legal or policy framework in Northern Ireland at the relevant time, internal guidelines were developed by various agencies, albeit in a piecemeal fashion and largely to ensure continued use of informers as a source of intelligence. For example, the recommendations implemented from the previously confidential 1980 Walker Report emphasised the importance of intelligence gathering and recruiting criminal suspects as potential agents, and led to greater coordination between the police, army, and intelligence services to avoid the arrest or prosecution of informers where possible.[146] Guidelines set out in a Home Office circular which predated the conflict were not applied by the Royal Ulster Constabulary as they were interpreted as only being suited to ordinary crimes and would hinder the gathering of intelligence.[147] A 1986 British Army directive laid down command, control, and handling arrangements for the military intelligence unit that was running informers. These instructions made it clear that it was 'unlawful for any person to authorise an illegal act', and required that preventive measures be taken where there was 'any possibility of a source becoming involved in criminality'.[148] This was interpreted, however, as not precluding the involvement of an agent in criminal activity if the purpose was to prevent an offence.[149] Internal instructions for the security services also contemplated that agents might be involved in criminal activity, subject to the advice of a legal adviser.[150]

Efforts by senior police and intelligence officers to have the British Government remedy the absence of a framework for handling agents proved unsuccessful during the conflict, as such requests effectively sought 'to make lawful active participation in serious terrorist criminality'.[151] Legislation was 'politically unobtainable', and any approval by Cabinet Ministers for draft guidelines devised by the Northern Ireland Office in 1990 was unlikely 'for fear that they may involve them in allegations of conspiratorial criminality'.[152] In the words of the Solicitor General, the draft guidelines were 'unpromising territory for ministerial approval', given their tolerance for informers engaging in criminal acts.[153] The Attorney General could not approve agent-handling guidelines which could be seen to condone in advance

[145] de Silva, *The Report of the Patrick Finucane Review* (n 119) 69.

[146] Royal Ulster Constabulary, 'Report on the Interchange of Intelligence between Special Branch and C.I.D., and on the R.U.C. Units Involved, including those in Crime Branch C1(1)', 1980 <https://s3-eu-west-1.amazonaws.com/caj.org.uk/2018/07/02111203/Walker-Report-1980.pdf> accessed 30 May 2019. See also Justin O'Brien, *Killing Finucane: Murder in Defence of the Realm* (Gill and Macmillan 2005) Appendix 1; McGovern, 'Informers, Agents and The Liberal Ideology of Collusion in Northern Ireland' (n 123) 296.

[147] See de Silva, *The Report of the Patrick Finucane Review* (n 119) 71.

[148] Ibid 72–3.

[149] Ibid 73.

[150] Ibid 75.

[151] Ware, 'Exposed: The murky world of spying during the Troubles' (n 134).

[152] de Silva, *The Report of the Patrick Finucane Review* (n 119) 83.

[153] Ibid 81.

the commission of criminal acts and raised doubts about whether informers could effectively claim a defence such as necessity against criminal charges.[154] Advocacy for a legislative framework ran up against political concerns about addressing such sensitive issues in Parliament, as well as claims regarding the frailty of the peace process.[155] The consequences for human rights of such inaction continue to reveal themselves.

5.2.1.1 Regulation of Investigatory Powers Act, 2000

Legislation providing the required regulation of the use of informers was adopted shortly after the end of the conflict in Northern Ireland in 1998. The Regulation of Investigatory Powers Act 2000 addresses concerns regarding the absence of statutory control over covert policing across the United Kingdom, including the use of informers, and was introduced in light of the Human Rights Act 1998 which gives domestic effect to the European Convention on Human Rights.[156] The Act sets out a scheme of authorisation and oversight of the conduct or use of covert human intelligence sources based on the principles of necessity and proportionality.[157] In keeping with the requirements of Article 8 of the European Convention on Human Rights, the Act lists the grounds on which the use of informers could be authorised include national security, preventing or detecting crime, preventing disorder, the economic well-being of the United Kingdom, public safety, public health, and revenue collection.[158] As it is addressed to informers, the Regulation of Investigatory Powers Act is significant in requiring relevant public authorities to have a structure and system in place which should ensure improved compliance with human rights standards.[159] While the Act puts the requirements of authorisation, oversight, and record-keeping on a statutory footing, concerns remain regarding the scheme of authorisation and the failure of the legislation to address the involvement of informers in criminal activities.

The Act requires that the use or conduct of informers must be authorised by a designated individual within the relevant public authority, such as the police, intelligence services, and armed forces, and that such authorisation must be on one of the established grounds and 'proportionate to what is sought to be achieved by the conduct or use'.[160] Judicial authorisation for the use or conduct of an informer is generally not required under the Act, although current or former members of the judiciary may play a role in general oversight by reviewing and reporting on

[154] Ibid 85–6. [155] Ibid 87–8.

[156] See Neyroud and Beckley, 'Regulating Informers' (n 80); JUSTICE, 'Under Surveillance' (n 51); Keir Starmer, Michelle Strange, and Quincy Whitaker, *Criminal Justice, Police Powers & Human Rights* (Blackstone 2001) 63–73; Simon McKay, *Covert Policing: Law and Practice* (OUP 2015) 214–87.

[157] RIPA 2000, s29(2). On the definition of a covert human intelligence source see s26(8).

[158] Ibid s29(3).

[159] For a critique in relation to other aspects of RIPA 2000 see Alan S. Reid and Nicholas Ryder, 'For Whose Eyes Only? A Critique of the United Kingdom's Regulation of Investigatory Powers Act 2000' (2001) 10(2) Information and Communications Technology Law 179.

[160] RIPA 2000, s29–30, Schedule I.

measures taken pursuant to the Act as Commissioners or by hearing complaints at the Investigatory Powers Tribunal.[161] The system of authorisation under the Act is one of 'self-authorisation', whereby a public authority itself authorises the conduct or use of informers, and has been criticised as such:

> It is arguable that that since in some circumstances the use of CHIS can be extremely intrusive that the voluntary and effectively internal self-authorisation of CHIS may be an inadequate protection in human rights terms and that similar strictures to those imposed for intrusive surveillance might have offered better protection.[162]

The Investigatory Powers Tribunal established under the Act can hear complaints regarding alleged breaches of the legislation, including claims relating to human rights, although there have been no judgments to date concerning the use of covert human intelligence sources. This may be because potential victims were unaware of the infringement of their privacy by the presence of authorised informer.[163]

Beyond the matter of authorisation, the Regulation of Investigatory Powers Acts addresses issues of oversight, record-keeping, and, to a limited degree, the security and welfare of informers. The Act requires that:

> there will at all times be a person holding an office, rank or position with the relevant investigating authority who will have day-to-day responsibility for dealing with the source on behalf of that authority, and for the source's security and welfare[164]

There must also be another person exercising 'general oversight of the use made of the source', as well as an individual responsible for maintaining a record of the use made of the covert source.[165] As regards security and welfare, the legislation does not clarify the scope of the relevant authorities obligations when using what is officially recognised as a 'high-risk covert technique'.[166] The Code of Practice published by the Home Office advocates for appropriate risk assessment before authorisation, including in instances where a source may need to be 'safely extracted' because of a refusal of authorisation.[167]

The Home Office Code of Practice problematically asserts that vulnerable individuals, those who may be 'unable to take care of themselves, or unable to protect themselves against significant harm or exploitation', can be used as covert sources in exceptional circumstances and subject to more stringent safeguards.[168] Minors have been used as informers in covert operations in the United Kingdom.[169] The

[161] Ibid ss61–63, but see however s32A. For an example of the reporting provided by the relevant Commissioners see Mark Waller, *Report of the Intelligence Services Commissioner for 2016*, HC/ 298, 23–6.

[162] Victoria Williams, *Surveillance and Intelligence Law Handbook* (OUP 2006) 152–3.

[163] RIPA 2000, ss65–70. See Sanders, Young, and Burton, *Criminal Justice* (n 28) 332.

[164] RIPA 2000, s29(5)(a). [165] Ibid s29(5)(b)–(e).

[166] Home Office, *Covert Human Intelligence Source Code of Practice*, 2014, 10.

[167] Ibid 42, 45–6. See also Roger Billingsley, 'Risk Management' in Billingsley, *Covert Human Intelligence Sources* (n 3) 155.

[168] Ibid 30.

[169] Damien Gayle and Ian Cobain, 'UK intelligence and police using child spies in covert operations', *The Guardian*, 19 July 2018; Damien Gayle and Ian Cobain, 'Home Office pressed for details over use of child spies', *The Guardian*, 17 August 2018.

use of children as covert intelligence sources can hardly be in keeping with the 'best interests of the child' under the Convention of the Rights of the Child.[170] While the Act and Code of Practice do not address the issues of protection and welfare in any detail, human rights law, as discussed in section 5.1, requires that informers facing a risk to their lives or safety must be protected by state authorities, such as by providing for relocation and a new identity.[171] Domestic case law has also shown that a duty of care towards informers might extend beyond 'physical welfare' to cover protection from financial loss.[172] Some informers for the British security services in Northern Ireland have claimed that the assurances made for securing their cooperation were not fulfilled.[173]

A duty of care has been found to apply to both potential and existing informants which precludes any threats to life or bodily integrity by police officers seeking to recruit or retain existing informers.[174] With regard to threats emanating from private actors, Freddie Scappaticci was unsuccessful in a legal challenge to the refusal of the Secretary of State for Northern Ireland to confirm his claim that he was not an informer for British military intelligence. The claim, as Lord Chief Justice Carswell explained:

> is founded on the proposition that since the making of the allegations has seriously endangered his life, the Government owes him a duty under Article 2 of the European Convention on Human Rights to reduce that danger by confirming that he is not Stakeknife. The minister's response is that it is Government policy to make no comment on intelligence matters and that she accordingly can neither confirm nor deny the allegations.[175]

To confirm or deny the identity of agents would put the person in question or another in 'immediate and obvious danger', according to the British government.[176] Despite finding 'a real and present danger' to Scappaticci's life, the Court accepted the State's argument that meeting the applicant's demands would have serious consequences for its intelligence-gathering capabilities.[177] Other measures of protection were offered by British security services, although Scappaticci is said to have rejected them: he was arrested but has not been charged in relation to a series of murders committed during his time as an alleged informer.[178]

[170] See Convention on the Rights of the Child (1989), *entered into force* 2 September 1990, 1577 UNTS 3, art 3(1). See also Sanders, Young, and Burton, *Criminal Justice* (n 28) 330; Hillel Cohen and Ron Dudai, 'Human Rights Dilemmas in Using Informers to Combat Terrorism: The Israeli–Palestinian Case' (2005) 17 Terrorism and Political Violence 229, 235–6.

[171] See further JUSTICE, 'Under Surveillance' (n 51) 51.

[172] *An Informer v A Chief Constable* [2012] EWCA Civ 197 (29 February 2012) 191.

[173] See for example 'IRA informer Raymond Gilmour found dead in Kent', *RTE*, 29 October 2016 <https://www.rte.ie/news/2016/1029/827858-ira-raymond-gilmour/> accessed 31 May 2019.

[174] *X v Ministry of Defence & Anor* [2017] NICA 66 (06 November 2017), para 44.

[175] *In the Matter of an Application by Freddie Scappaticci for Judicial Review*, High Court of Northern Ireland, Queen's Bench Division (Judicial Review), 18 August 2003, [2003] NIQB 56, 1. See also *In the Matter of an Application by Freddie Scappaticci for Judicial Review* High Court of Northern Ireland, Queen's Bench Division (Judicial Review), 17 June 2003, [2003] NIQB 40, 13.

[176] *Application by Freddie Scappaticci for Judicial Review*, 18 August 2003 (n 175) 6.

[177] Ibid 12.

[178] John Ware, 'How, and why, did Scappaticci survive the IRA's wrath' *Irish Times*, 15 April 2017; Henry McDonald and Iain Cobain, 'IRA informers "Stakeknife" arrested in murder investigation', *The Guardian*, 30 January 2018.

The Regulation of Investigatory Powers Act leaves unresolved the key concern at the heart of the Scappaticci affair: the involvement of informers in serious criminal activity. The Act avoids the issue entirely, while the Home Office's Code of Practice simply states that neither the Act nor the Code 'is intended to affect the existing practices and procedures surrounding criminal participation of CHIS'.[179] John Stevens, a former police Commissioner who was tasked with investigating collusion in Northern Ireland between state and paramilitary forces, advocated the urgent adoption of guidelines 'on the use of CHIS in countering terrorism'.[180] With the thorniest of all issues concerning the use of informers effectively unaddressed by the Act and accompanying Code of Practice, it is effectively left to the discretion of relevant public authorities. It is doubtful therefore, as Desmond de Silva has concluded, that the legislation and Code of Practice 'provides a real resolution to these difficult issues given that it provides little guidance as to the limits of the activities of covert human intelligence sources'.[181]

British police and intelligence services have produced internal guidance addressed to the involvement of informers in criminal activity, both prior and subsequent to the adoption of the Regulation of Investigatory Powers Act. Such documents, however, have not always been publicly available. For example, the unpublished Guidelines of the Association of Chief Police Officers in the United Kingdom, which incorporate Home Office guidance from 1969, provide that:

> Participating informants are persons whose involvement, without authority, in an activity could or has led to their arrest and prosecution. Police officers must not counsel, incite or procure the commission of a crime by a participating informant. A participating informant's role must be considered essential; he or she should only play a minor role and not actively engage in planning or committing a crime. A participating informant must be instructed not to act as an agent provocateur. The court must never be knowingly misled over the role played by a participant informant.[182]

Guidelines addressed to the use of covert human intelligence sources who participate in criminality have also been produced by MI5. The Official Guidance, a public version of which has been heavily redacted, offers an explanation as to 'the circumstances in which agent-running sections may use agents who participate in criminality'.[183]

MI5's guidance begins by noting that the Regulation of Investigatory Powers Act neither provides immunity from prosecution for a participating informer nor for informers to be authorised take part in criminal acts, and that MI5 'has established its own procedure for authorising the use of agents participating in crime'.[184]

[179] Home Office, *Covert Human Intelligence Source Code of Practice* (n 166) 7. See however Alistair Gillespies (2000) 'The Legal Use of Participating Informers', 5 Web Journal of Current Legal Issues.

[180] John Stevens, 'Stevens Enquiry: Overview and Recommendations' 17 April 2003, Recommendation 10.

[181] de Silva, *The Report of the Patrick Finucane Review* (n 119) 91.

[182] Cited in JUSTICE, 'Under Surveillance' (n 51) 48.

[183] 'Guidelines on the use of Agents who participate in Criminality (Official Guidance)', March 2011 <https://reprieve.org.uk/press/tribunal-to-consider-whether-mi5-covert-agents-can-commit-serious-criminal-offences/> accessed 31 May 2019.

[184] Ibid para 4.

This may be necessary and proportionate 'in order to secure or maintain access to intelligence that can be used to save life or disrupt more serious criminality, or to ensure that agent's continued safety, security and ability to pass such intelligence'.[185] Authorisation for the use of an agent participating in crime may be made if:

1. there is a real prospect that the agent will be able to provide information concerning serious crime [. . .]
2. the required information cannot readily be obtained by any other means; and
3. the need for the information that may be obtained by the use of the agent justifies his use notwithstanding the criminal activity.[186]

The only allusion of the Official Guidance to potential limits on the criminal acts in which an informer can be involved is in the proportionality requirement which seemingly requires an authorising officer to decide if the potential harm to the public interest from the agent's criminal activity is outweighed by the benefit that may be provided and 'the benefit is proportionate to the criminal activity in question'.[187] The terms employed suggest a considerable discretion given the subjective assessment of state agents on whether to authorise criminal activity, in effect in deciding if such law-breaking is for the greater good. There is no operational oversight provided by the Intelligence Services Commissioner, who engages in a retrospective examination of a sample of authorisations. Such reviews commenced only in 2012 following a request from Prime Minister David Cameron, who stressed to the Commissioner that such oversight 'would not provide endorsement of the legality of the policy'.[188]

MI5 accepts that authorisation to engage in criminal activity does not grant immunity from prosecution. It warns agent handers not to 'encourage, counsel or procure' the commission of a criminal offence except that which is covered by the relevant authorisation.[189] There is an admission in the document that the organisation may seek to avoid prosecution of those involved in criminality:

> An authorisation of the use of a participating agent has no legal effect and does not confer on either the agent or those involved in the authorisation process any immunity from prosecution. Rather, the authorisation will be the Service's explanation and justification of its decisions should the criminal activity of the agent come under scrutiny by an external body, e.g. the police or prosecuting authorities. In particular, the authorisation process and associated records may form the basis of representations by the Service to the prosecuting authorities that prosecution is not in the public interest. Accordingly, any such authorisation should, on its face, clearly establish that the criteria for authorisation are met, in terms which will be readily understood by a prosecutor.[190]

The emphasis on accurate record-keeping in the guidance, therefore, could serve the purpose of bolstering calls by MI5 that particular participating informers should

[185] Ibid para 4. [186] Ibid paras 6–8. [187] Ibid para 8.

[188] 'Letter from David Cameron to Sir Mark Waller', 27 November 2012 <https://reprieve.org.uk/wp-content/uploads/2018/10/1-Letter-PM-to-Sir-Mark-Waller-27-Nov-12.pdf> accessed 31 May 2019.

[189] 'Guidelines on the use of Agents who participate in Criminality' (n 183) para 13.

[190] Ibid para 9.

not be prosecuted.[191] Although the document provides only a partial picture of the policy guiding the practice of using criminal informers, it confirms the institutional acceptance of the practice, its tenuous legality, and the absence of unambiguous limits on the criminal conduct in which informers might engage.

The Regulation of Investigatory Powers Act 2000 goes some way towards meeting the demands of international human rights law, specifically the requirements of Article 8 of the European Convention of Human Rights of a legal basis for the interference inherent in the use of informers, and adherence to the principles of necessity and proportionality. Concerns remain that a minimalist approach to compliance with human rights has been taken by the United Kingdom given the presence of certain ambiguities and blind spots in the legislation, the continued reliance on self-authorisation, and the failure to address the use of criminal informers.[192] The Act's effectiveness relies in large part on the honesty of the relevant public authorities and their willingness to comply.[193] It is argued that the legislation has led to the hiding of police informers and given rise to a 'more secret and thus less controllable, system of informers over which RIPA merely draws a presentational veil'.[194] With regard to criminal informers, the legislation facilitated a hands-off approach by avoiding the issue, arguably one which a legislature could not be seen to condone. The matter was left to be regulated internally by relevant public authorities who have placed considerable stock in their use.[195] The reliance on unpublished internal guidance presents serious difficulties for ensuring compliance with domestic and international human rights law standards, and allows the practice to occur in a legally ambiguous sphere. A judicial role in authorisation going beyond reviewing and reporting after the fact might ensure more robust oversight and reduce the risks of abuse and corruption, although it may be impractical to require the involvement of judges at an operational level.[196] Judges, moreover, might be viewed by some relevant authorities as potential obstacles to the authorisation of criminal activity. When it comes to the involvement of informers in crimes, the Regulation of Investigatory Powers Act represents a potentially dangerous continuation of the status quo.[197]

191 Ibid para 11.

192 Sanders, Young, and Burton, *Criminal Justice* (n 28) 333; Cara Hirsch, 'Policing Undercover Agents in the United Kingdom: Whether the Regulation of Investigatory Powers Acts Complies with Regional Human Rights Obligations' (2001) 25(5) Fordham International Law Journal 1282.

193 Sanders, Young, and Burton, *Criminal Justice* (n 28) 331–2.

194 Ibid 332–4.

195 Bradley W.C. Bamford, 'Intelligence in Northern Ireland' (n 123) 274–5; David Omand, 'Ethical Guidelines in Using Secret Intelligence for Public Security' (2006) 19(4) Cambridge Review of International Affairs 613, 622.

196 On the judicial role see JUSTICE, 'Under Surveillance' (n 51) 49–50; Clive Harfield, 'The Regulation of CHIS' in Billingsley, *Covert Human Intelligence Sources* (n 3) 43, 53–4; Gillespies, 'The Legal Use of Participating Informers' (n 179).

197 See Daniel Holder, 'Covert Policing, and Collusion, Running Informants and the Human Rights Framework' in *Covert Policing and Ensuring Accountability: Ten Years on from the Cory Collusion Inquiry Reports, Where Now?* (Committee on the Administration of Justice and University of Ulster Transitional Justice Institute 2015) 21.

5.3 Rights in Conflict

This final section considers in brief the application of human rights law to the recruitment, use and treatment of informers in times of armed conflict. A growing consensus has emerged that human rights law applies in situations of armed conflict, including extraterritorially in certain operations, notwithstanding the existence of unexplored aspects of the evolving relationship between international humanitarian law and human rights law.[198] While the use of informers during armed conflict raises similar concerns to those identified by human rights bodies outside the context of conflict, including for example the potential for tainting criminal trials or detention proceedings,[199] the application of human rights law to the practice during armed conflict remains underexplored. This section considers the application of human rights law in times of conflict and its relationship with international humanitarian law through an analysis of the right to life, particularly those aspects of the right of relevance in the context of informing. As will be discussed, the application of human rights law during armed conflict opens the door for the potential application of regulatory frameworks developed at the national level for the use of covert human intelligence sources, such as the Regulation of Investigatory Powers Act 2000.

The activities of informers during situations of armed conflict almost invariably give rise to concerns for human life. The lives of those who collaborate with an opposing side, those about whom they share information, and even those who employ informers may be gravely endangered in this context.[200] Not all such killings necessarily involve violations of international humanitarian law, and there may be occasions in which information from an informer can contribute to the prevention of unlawful deaths in war, such as by verifying the nature of certain targets or by facilitating the disruption of a planned attack, possibly by using lethal force.[201] The protection of life is at the core of both international humanitarian law and international human rights law, which take distinguishable but at times overlapping approaches. International humanitarian law does not outlaw all killing, but prohibits attacks on civilians and others *hors de combat* and insists on adherence to principles of necessity, distinction, proportionality, and unnecessary suffering during the conduct of hostilities.[202] International human rights law seeks to ensure the right of life of all persons

[198] See generally Doswald-Beck, *Human Rights in Times of Conflict and Terrorism* (n 1); Ben-Naftali, *International Humanitarian Law and International Human Rights Law* (n 1); Marko Milanovic, *Extraterritorial Application of Human Rights Treaties: Law, Principles and Policy* (OUP 2011).

[199] See for example Lisa Hajjar, *Courting Conflict: The Israeli Military Court System in the West Bank and Gaza* (University of California Press 2005) 111, 114, 198, 211; B'Tselem and HaMoked, *Asbolute Prohibition: The Torture and Ill-Treatment of Palestinian Detainees*, May 2007, 60–2.

[200] For an example of an informer killing his handlers see Joby Warrick, 'Humam Al-Balawi: The Triple Agent', *Newsweek* 19 June 2011.

[201] On the lawfulness of lethal attacks based on information supplied by informers see generally Nils Melzer, *Targeted Killings in International Law* (OUP 2008); Noam Lubell, *Extraterritorial Use of Force against Non-State Actors* (OUP 2010); Michael L. Gross, 'Fighting by Other Means in the Mideast: A Critical Analysis of Israel's Assassination Policy' (2003) 51 Political Studies 1, 5–7.

[202] See generally Ian Park, *The Right to Life in Armed Conflict* (OUP 2018); Doswald-Beck, *Human Rights in Times of Conflict and Terrorism* (n 1) 161–93.

by forbidding any arbitrary deprivation of life, establishes positive obligations for states in this regard, and requires adequate remediation in the event of violation.[203] While humanitarian law and human rights law may have differing outlooks, emphases, and approaches to the protection of life, during an armed conflict, both are relevant, as they are 'complementary, not mutually exclusive'.[204]

Before turning to human rights law, some reference can be made to relevant rules of international humanitarian law concerning the protection of life during armed conflict and practice as it relates to informers. As the 1907 Hague Regulations made clear, this body of law has long required respect for 'the lives of persons', especially outside the context of hostilities.[205] During hostilities, members of armed forces and persons directly participating in hostilities, including informers in some limited instances, might be lawfully targeted with lethal force,[206] although obligations exist for parties to an armed conflict to avoid unnecessary harm, even allowing for the forcible transfer of civilians for their protection.[207] With regard to informers, handlers have taken precautions to protect these 'assets', by warning them of the risks faced, as British army recruiters did in Iraq,[208] or by the extended detention of a newly recruited Palestinian informer to avoid arousing suspicion.[209] In Afghanistan, the CIA base at Khost had a building specifically designed for meetings with informants, 'separated by high walls and guarded by private security contractors armed with assault rifles ... lined on one side by a large awning to further shield operatives from view as they came and left... [and] surrounded by CIA officers and free from any possibility of detection by al-Qaeda spies'.[210] Informers only knew the names and saw the faces of their handlers, so as to minimise the information that might be divulged if they were exposed.[211] While some states whose armed forces relied on local informers in Afghanistan provided relocation to those individuals, others failed to do so, with the result that some exposed informers were killed.[212]

International humanitarian law itself does not specify precautions to be taken in the use of informers to ensure their protection, although an obligation to do so could be read into the treaty requirements that parties must ensure 'the lives of persons', 'public order and safety', and 'respect for and protection of the civilian

[203] ibid. See also International Covenant on Civil and Political Rights, arts 2(3) and 6.

[204] Human Rights Committee, *General Comment No. 31—Article 2: The Nature of the General Legal Obligation Imposed on States Parties to the Covenant*, U.N. Doc. CCPR/C/21/Rev.1/Add.3, 26 May 2004, para 11.

[205] Hague Regulations 1907, art 46.

[206] Additional Protocol I, arts 48–60 and discussion in Chapter 3.

[207] Jean-Marie Henckaerts and Louise Doswald-Beck, *Customary International Humanitarian Law, Volume I: Rules* (CUP 2005) Rule 129, 457–62.

[208] Mark Urban, *Task Force Black: the Explosive True Story of the SAS and the Secret War in Iraq* (Little, Brown 2010) 198.

[209] Mossab Hassan Yousef, *Son of Hamas* (Authentic Media 2014) 84.

[210] Joby Warrick, *The Triple Agent: The Al-Qaeda Mole who Infiltrated the CIA* (Vintage Books 2012) 3.

[211] Ibid 145. See also Nicky Hager and Jon Stephenson, *Hit & Run; The New Zealand SAS in Afghanistan and the Meaning of Honour* (Potton & Burton 2017) 19.

[212] Hager and Stephenson, *Hit & Run* (n 211) 94–5.

population'.[213] An example of measures taken to protect informers and other collaborators at risk of attack is the relocation in 2005 by Israeli authorities of the residents of Dahaniya, 'an Israeli-guarded village in the Gaza Strip that was tainted by its reputation as a haven for Palestinians who collaborated with Israel'.[214] While the Fourth Geneva Convention generally prohibits individual or mass forcible transfers of protected persons, an occupying power 'may undertake total or partial evacuation of a given area if the security of the population or imperative military reasons so demand'.[215] Voluntary internment is also conceived as a potential protective measure for protected persons at risk of harm from the general population, although such a measure can only be applied to 'aliens' in the territory of a party to a conflict and would not be permissible in occupied territory, even 'in the case of civilians who have collaborated with the occupying power in a way that provokes the hostility of the general population'.[216] That an occupying power which accedes to a request for voluntary internment by civilian collaborators could be in breach of the Convention is indicative of how international humanitarian law has generally overlooked the phenomenon and consequences of collaboration and neglected to provide a legal regime requiring regulation of their use, including measures to protect the lives of informers or other collaborators that go beyond the rules and principles of general application to all persons in situations of armed conflict.

The existence of gaps in international humanitarian law was traditionally addressed by recourse to the Martens Clause as first appeared in the 1899 Hague Regulations:

> Until a more complete code of the laws of war is issued, the High Contracting Parties think it right to declare that in cases not included in the Regulations adopted by them, populations and belligerents remain under the protection and empire of the principles of international law, as they result from the usages established between civilized nations, from the laws of humanity, and the requirements of the public conscience.[217]

Recourse to the public conscience is fraught in the context of informers and other collaborators, given the public hostility frequently directed at those perceived as traitors, although 'the laws of humanity' at the very least serve to remind parties to an armed conflict of the requirement of humane treatment.[218] In the context of the

[213] See for example Hague Regulations 1907, arts 43 and 46; Geneva Conventions 1949, art 3; Additional Protocol I, arts 10(2), 48, and 75(1); Additional Protocol II, art 4(1).

[214] 'Israel Relocates "Collaborators"', *LA Times*, 30 August 2005; Chris McGreal, 'Collaborators fear for their lives as Palestinians prepare to reclaim Gaza', *The Guardian*, 11 August 2005.

[215] Fourth Geneva Convention, art 49.

[216] Nils Melzer, *International Humanitarian Law: A Comprehensive Introduction* (ICRC 2016), 192. See Fourth Geneva Convention, arts 42(2), 68, and 78.

[217] Hague Regulations 1899, preamble. See also Additional Protocol II, preamble. See also Hague Convention IV 1907, preamble; Fourth Geneva Convention, art 158; Additional Protocol I, art 1(2).

[218] For varying interpretations of the Clause see Antonio Cassese, 'The Martens Clause: Half a Loaf or Simply Pie in the Sky?' (2000) 11(1) European Journal of International Law 187; Emily Crawford, 'The Modern Relevance of the Martens Clause' (2006) VI ISIL Yearbook of International Humanitarian Law 1; Theodor Meron, 'The Martens Clause, Principles of Humanity, and Dictates of Public Conscience' (2000) 94 American Journal of International Law 78; Rupert Ticehurst, 'The Martens Clause and the Laws of Armed Conflict' (1997) 37 No. 317 International Review of the Red Cross 125.

use of informers during armed conflict, the omissions of international humanitarian law can be remedied to an extent by recourse to international human rights law. Although similarly demonstrating some ambivalence towards the practice as humanitarian law, this body of law has developed a rich jurisprudence addressing the obligations of states with regard to the right to life in general, as well as requirements for any interference in the lives of individuals by public authorities, as discussed in the first section of this chapter. The application of human rights law in times of armed conflict is increasingly accepted in principle, but is not without its challenges in practice.

Decisions of international courts and human rights bodies have confirmed the application of international human rights law during times of armed conflict, including extraterritorially such as in occupied territories, and clarified the relationship between human rights law and international humanitarian law.[219] The International Court of Justice held that the right to life applies during armed conflict, that the protection of the International Covenant on Civil and Political Rights 'does not cease in times of war' with the exception of human rights that may lawfully be derogated from under states of emergency regimes.[220] A state's human rights obligations can apply extraterritorially where its officials or forces exercise effective control over persons or territory.[221] According the United Nations Human Rights Committee:

> This includes persons located outside any territory effectively controlled by the State, whose right to life is nonetheless impacted by its military or other activities in a direct and reasonably foreseeable manner. [...] States parties must respect and protect the lives of individuals located in places, which are under their effective control, such as occupied territories, and in territories over which they have assumed an international obligation to apply the Covenant. [...] Given that the deprivation of liberty brings a person within a State's effective control, States parties must respect and protect the right to life of all individuals arrested or detained by them, even if held outside their territory.[222]

With international humanitarian law also applying in such instances, the interaction between both bodies of law has thus required consideration in the case law.

The International Court of Justice has held that the determination of whether an arbitrary deprivation of the right life has occurred during armed hostilities requires recourse to 'the applicable *lex specialis*, namely, the law applicable in armed conflict which is designed to regulate the conduct of hostilities'.[223] For the UN Human

[219] See for example Gentian Zyberi, *The Humanitarian Face of the International Court of Justice* (Intersentia 2008); Christine Byron, 'A Blurring of the Boundaries: The Application of International Humanitarian Law by Human Rights Bodies' (2007) 47 *Virginia Journal of International Law* 839.

[220] International Court of Justice, *Legality of the Threat or Use of Nuclear Weapons*, Advisory Opinion, 8 July 1996, General List No. 95, para 25.

[221] See for example *Legality of the Construction of a Wall in the Occupied Palestinian Territories*, Advisory Opinion, 9 July 2004, General List No. 131; *Case Concerning Armed Activities on the Territory of the Congo (Democratic Republic of the Congo v Uganda)*, Judgment, 19 December 2005, General List No. 116; *Al-Skeini and others v United Kingdom* App no 55721/07 (ECtHR, 7 July 2011); *Al-Jedda v United Kingdom*, App No. 27021/08 (ECtHR, 7 July 2011).

[222] Human Rights Committee, *General Comment No. 36 (2018) on Article 6 on the International Covenant on Civil and Political Rights, on the right to life*, UN Doc. CCPR/C/GC/36, 30 October 2018, para 63.

[223] *Legality of the Threat or Use of Nuclear Weapons*, (n 220) para 25.

Rights Committee, lethal force that is inconsistent with the rules and principles of international humanitarian law could entail an arbitrary deprivation of life under Article 6 of the Covenant.[224] The description of humanitarian law as *lex specialis*, as used by the International Court of Justice, can give the mistaken impression of the subordination of human rights law to humanitarian law, even though the Court's holdings do not support such a restrictive interpretation:

As regards the relationship between international humanitarian law and human rights law, there are thus three possible situations: some rights may be exclusively matters of international humanitarian law; others may be exclusively matters of human rights law; yet others may be matters of both these branches of international law. In order to answer the question put to it, the Court will have to take into consideration both these branches of international law, namely human rights law and, as *lex specialis*, international humanitarian law.[225]

The application of the *lex specialis* rule does not imply that one body of law displaces the other in its entirety, but rather that a general rule gives way to a more specific rule.[226]

On the use, recruitment, and treatment of informers, both international humanitarian law and international human rights law share common prescriptions which apply to the practice, such as the prohibition of coercion and the requirements of fair trial as discussed in previous chapters. However, as demonstrated, international human rights law establishes more extensive obligations in relation to the right to life and the right to privacy that are of significant relevance to the practice of using informers. Such obligations can apply during situations of armed conflict. With regard to the positive obligations under the right to life, for example, the Human Rights Committee has elaborated on the content of the duty to protect:

States parties are thus under a due diligence obligation to undertake reasonable positive measures, which do not impose on them disproportionate burdens, in response to reasonably foreseeable threats to life originating from private persons and entities, whose conduct is not attributable to the State. Hence, States parties are obliged to take adequate preventive measures in order to protect individuals against reasonably foreseen threats of being murdered or killed by criminals and organized crime or militia groups, including armed or terrorist groups.[227]

Of particular relevance to the use of informers during armed conflict, the Committee spoke of the requirement to take 'special measures of protection towards persons in situation of vulnerability whose lives have been placed at particular risk because of specific threats or pre-existing patterns of violence'.[228] Such measures could include the provision of police protection or consensual protective custody.[229] States parties

[224] Human Rights Committee, *General Comment No. 36* (n 222) para 64.

[225] *Legality of the Construction of a Wall* (n 221) para 106. See also *Democratic Republic of the Congo v Uganda* (n 221) paras 175–178. See for example Michael J. Dennis, 'Application of Human Rights Treaties Extraterritorially in Times of Armed Conflict and Military Occupation' (2005) 99(1) American Journal of International Law 119.

[226] Clapham, 'The Complex Relationship' (n 2) 730–1, 735.

[227] Human Rights Committee, *General Comment No. 36* (n 222) para 21.

[228] Ibid. para 23. [229] Ibid.

to the Covenant are also required to investigate 'alleged or suspected violations of article 6 in situations of armed conflict in accordance with the relevant international standards'.[230] The European Court of Human has affirmed the application of positive obligations concerning the right to life in times of armed conflict occurring outside the territory of a state party to the Convention.[231]

Privacy has never been a prominent issue for international humanitarian law, although it is evident that infringements of the right to privacy can occur during situations of armed conflict.[232] In the *Wall* Advisory Opinion, the International Court of Justice specifically mentioned that the article on privacy in the International Covenant on Civil and Political Rights, Article 17, is applicable in the Palestinian territories occupied by Israel, although it did not elaborate on the implications.[233] As discussed earlier in this chapter, the use of informers constitutes an interference in the lives of individuals which must have a legal basis and accord with principles of necessity and proportionality in order to comply with human rights law. That a state's obligations with regard to the right to private life continue to apply during armed conflict in respect of those persons over whom effective control is exercised means that a state must fulfil these established requirements when using and recruiting informers. Although the right itself may be derogable,[234] it is at least arguable that the safeguards concerning the right to privacy also go some way towards fulfilling the requirements of those non-derogable rights of relevance to the use of informers, in particular the right to life and freedom from torture or cruel, inhuman, or degrading treatment.

While human rights law is becoming more firmly embedded in legal practice concerning armed conflict, there has been limited application in the context of wartime intelligence activities. The military manuals of several major powers addressed to the operational aspects of in armed conflict, including the use of informers, recognise that a range of laws apply to such intrinsically risky activities. For example, the US *Commanders Guide to Human Intelligence* attributes the 'numerous regulatory and legal requirements' to the 'political and operational sensitivity and inherently dangerous nature of source operations'.[235] The US Army field manual on intelligence states that:

> Commanders should be aware that intelligence collection is enabled by, and subject to, laws, regulations, and policies to ensure proper conduct of intelligence operations. While there

[230] Ibid.

[231] See for example *Jaloud v The Netherlands* Appl No. 47708/08 (ECtHR 20 November 2014); *Al-Skeini and others v United Kingdom* (n 221). See also *Varnava and others v Turkey* App no 16064/90 (ECtHR 18 September 2009).

[232] See Doswald-Beck, *Human Rights in Times of Conflict and Terrorism* (n 1), 444–64; Daragh Murray, *Practitioner's Guide to Human Rights Law in Armed Conflict* (OUP 2016) 120–1, 152–4, 309–15; Peter Rowe, *The Impact of Human Rights Law on Armed Forces* (CUP 2006) 41–50; Henckaerts and Doswald-Beck, *Customary International Humanitarian Law* (n 207) 382–3.

[233] *Legality of the Construction of a Wall* (n 221) para 128.

[234] See generally Marko Milanovic, 'Extraterritorial Derogations from Human Rights in Times of Armed Conflict' in Nehal Bhuta (ed), *The Frontiers of Human Rights: Extraterritoriality and its Challenges* (OUP 2016) 55.

[235] United States, *Commander's Guide to Human Intelligence (HUMINT)*, 20 August 2012, A-5.

are too many to list here specifically, categories of these legal considerations include United States Codes (USCs), Executive Orders, National Security Council Intelligence Directives (NCSIDs), Army Regulations, United States Signal Intelligence Directives (USSIDs), SOFAs, ROE, and other international laws and directives.[236]

With regard to relevant international law, key field manuals concerning human intelligence tend to make explicit reference only to the law of armed conflict, primarily the 1949 Geneva Conventions.[237] Notwithstanding some continued recalcitrance towards the application of human rights law in armed conflict, the absence of direct reference to human rights in this context may also reflect how the required element of effective control is not always present in the context of an international armed conflict. Most informers, however, could be considered as falling under the effective control of the party to an armed conflict that recruits them. For a State party to the International Covenant on Civil and Political Rights, the circumstances of the use of such individuals as a source of information during conflict, including the potentially serious harms they face, would in many instances render them 'persons over whose enjoyment of the right to life it exercises power or effective control'.[238]

For a non-international armed conflict occurring on the territory of a state, the application of its human rights obligations is relatively more straightforward. A distinction between categories of conflict for the purposes of intelligence gathering is recognised in Canada's counter-insurgency operations manual, which suggests less restraints in traditional armed conflict or 'conventional operations', than in counter-insurgency (COIN) operations:

> Intelligence gathering in a COIN campaign will, in all probability, lack the freedom that may be enjoyed in conventional operations. The primacy of civilian political control, the balance between efforts to defeat the insurgency and those expended on crime prevention and resolution, the need to share with other agencies, legal limitations and the need for admissible evidence for prosecution will all constrain the gathering of intelligence. Military intelligence staffs may find themselves in unfamiliar circumstances, subordinated to civilian control and methods of operating (particularly when supporting police).[239]

This recognition of the constraining effect of national laws and structures, envisaged here as applying to a potential non-international armed conflict on Canadian territory, reinforces the view that such 'legal limitations' as inhere in a state's human rights obligations have not been embedded in the framework applicable to all armed conflicts, particularly those that are international in nature. Canada's *Law of Armed Conflict* manual, for example, makes only fleeting reference to human rights.[240]

[236] United States Army, *Intelligence*, Field Manual (Headquarters, Department of the Army May 2004) 4–7. See also 6–44.

[237] See for example United States Army, *Human Intelligence Collector Operations*, Headquarters, Department of the Army, September 2006, FM 2–22.3 (FM34-52), A-1; British Army Field Manual, Volume I, Part 10, *Countering Insurgency*, Army Code 71876, October 2009, 3–36, 12–20; Canada Land Force, *Counter-Insurgency Operations*, National Defence Headquarters, 13 December 2008, B-GL-323-004/FP-003, 4A-2.

[238] Human Rights Committee, *General Comment No. 36* (n 222) para 21.

[239] Canada Land Force, *Counter-Insurgency Operations* (n 237) 7–2.

[240] Canada, *Joint Doctrine Manual: Law of Armed Conflict at the Operational and Tactical Levels*, (Office of the Judge Advocate General, 2001) 1–1, 2–2.

Other military manuals replicate in some respects the approach of national police and intelligence authorities to the use of covert human intelligence sources, such as by requiring appropriate training for agent handlers and adherence to applicable guidelines concerning targets for recruitment, without explicitly referring to human rights in this context.[241]

The United Kingdom has been more forthright in its acceptance that human rights law can apply in the context of armed conflict outside its territory in certain circumstances.[242] This is also confirmed by findings of the European Court on Human Rights in relation to the actions of British forces in Iraq.[243] While the general *Joint Service Manual* does not specifically refer to human rights law in the context of the use of informers, other sources have addressed the relevance and applicability of this body of law. The Home Office, for example, has advised that the Regulation of Investigatory Powers Act 2000 can apply extraterritorially in light of its role in giving effect to European Convention obligations:

> The Human Rights Act 1998 applies to all activity taking place within the UK. This should be taken to include overseas territories and facilities which are within the jurisdiction of the UK. Authorisations under the 2000 Act may therefore be appropriate for overseas covert operations occurring in UK Embassies, military bases, detention facilities, etc., in order to comply with rights to privacy under Article 8 of the ECHR.[244]

The jurisdictional scope referred to here seems narrower than the prevailing international case-law, including that emanating from the European Court of Human Rights which has applied the Convention to certain security operations undertaken by British forces in Iraq.[245]

A seemingly different understanding of the scope of application of the Regulation of Investigatory Powers Act can be found in a 2009 British Army field manual on counter-insurgency, which claims that the legislation 'does not, as a matter of law, apply outside Britain [but], it is applied overseas by reason of [Ministry of Defence] policy'.[246] This manual endorses the application of the Act given the human rights risks associated with intelligence gathering from a civilian population, including this risk of reprisals against those providing information: 'While it may, at first sight, appear to be cumbersome on operations it provides a well established regulatory framework for such operations and reduces the chances of improper conduct and abuse'. To this end, a legal adviser needs to be involved in 'the planning and conduct of all HUMINT and surveillance operations'.[247]

[241] United States, *Commander's Guide to Human Intelligence* (n 235) A-5.

[242] United Kingdom Ministry of Defence, *The Joint Service Manual of the Law of Armed Conflict* (OUP 2004) 215.

[243] See for example *Al-Skeini and others v United Kingdom* (n 221); *Al-Jedda v United Kingdom* (n 221).

[244] Home Office, *Covert Human Intelligence Source Code of Practice* (n 166) 32.

[245] *Al-Skeini and others v United Kingdom* (n 221) paras. 141–140. See further Noam Lubell, 'Human Rights Obligations in Military Occupation' (2012) 96 No. 885 International Review of the Red Cross 317.

[246] British Army Field Manual, *Countering Insurgency* (n 237) 3–36, 12–20.

[247] Ibid 12–20.

Such developments constitute an important recognition of the role of human rights law in the recruitment and use of informers during armed conflict. Certain matters remain to be addressed, such as the extent to which it might be considered that informers can participate in criminal activities, given that separate UK legislation specifically allows for authorisation of Secret Service Intelligence agents to engage in acts outside of the United Kingdom for which they would be liable if carried out domestically.[248] Notwithstanding, this nascent application of relevant human rights standards and domestic law to the use of informers during armed conflict can serve to complement and indeed supplement the existing rules of international humanitarian law.

* * *

International human rights law shares humanitarian law's seeming ambivalence towards the recruitment and use of informers, in that it accepts the permissibility of the practice in general, but seeks to place restrictions on aspects of the practice in light of the inherent risks to specific human rights. This body of law does not explicitly provide a comprehensive and detailed set of rules governing the use of informers but rather offers a framework applicable to the practice based on existing human rights obligations. The holdings of various international and regional human rights bodies have elaborated on the implications for the right to life, freedom from torture, inhuman, or degrading treatment, the right to a fair trial and the right to privacy in relation to the use informers in the context of policing, criminal justice, and national security. Of particular importance is the obligation of states to regulate the use of informers and ensure that it takes place in accordance with the law. While states invariably accept the legitimacy and necessity of the practice, they have usually failed to ensure that it occurs within a legislative framework which might serve to prevent abuse and provide accountability.

The case study of Northern Ireland demonstrated the lethal threat to human rights arising from an unregulated system of running informers by police, military, and intelligence services, the implications of which are still being assessed. Despite having failed to develop sufficient rules and oversight of the use of informers during the Northern Ireland conflict, which was not treated as an armed conflict under international humanitarian law, the United Kingdom now recommends the application of its domestic legislation governing the use of covert human intelligence sources and which gives effect to its human rights obligations, during situations of armed conflict, including those occurring outside of its territory. This approach reflects the increasing acceptance of the role of human rights law during armed conflict, and constitutes a significant development in the law and practice of wartime intelligence gathering.[249]

As demonstrated in this chapter, human rights and humanitarian law overlap considerably in their approach to the use of informers. However, human rights law

[248] Intelligence Services Act 1994, s7.

[249] See Peter Gill, 'Security Intelligence and Human Rights: Illuminating the "Heart of Darkness"?' (2009) 24(1) Intelligence and National Security 78.

distinguishes itself from humanitarian law in a number of important respects in this context, two of which merit being repeated. First is that this body of law requires that the interference in the lives of individuals that the use of informers entails be subject to legal regulation and a system of authorisation which ensures adherence to the principles of necessity and proportionality. It is not the use of informers per se that raises human rights concerns, it has been argued, but rather reliance by states on 'unregulated systems of informers'.[250] Second is that international human rights law has established positive obligations in relation to the right to life and freedom from torture, cruel, and inhuman treatment which require states to be proactive in addressing threats from private parties of which they knew or ought to have known.

Informers are almost invariably at risk from the activities they engage in and which have been fostered and exploited by state authorities. As the risks of harm and the scope for ensuring protective measures will vary on a case-by-case basis, it would perhaps be reading too much into human rights law and its positive obligations to claim that the prevailing view as to the essential legality of using informers, including during armed conflict, is fatally undermined at this stage by this evolving body of law. As to the risks to other persons presented by the participation of informers in criminal activity, it has been claimed that preventing such involvement would be tantamount to banning the practice of using informers itself.[251] State authorisation of criminal activity by informers, however, sits most uneasily with human rights, particularly where serious criminality is involved. That the toleration or granting of permission for such activity arises in opaque and legally ambiguous contexts strongly shows the need for human rights law needs to provide a more assertive and overt censure of this fraught aspect of the practice of using informers.

The extraterritorial application of human rights in armed conflict may have been initially motivated by the absence of individual remedies under international humanitarian law, although it now serves a broader purpose in complementing the law of armed conflict in a range of areas. The view of Judge Bonello of the European Court of Human Rights that 'those who export war ought to see to the parallel export of guarantees against the atrocities of war' indicates that humanitarian law has required the bolstering that is offered by human rights law.[252] This is certainly evident in the context of using informers. Meeting the requirements for a human rights compliant system of running informers, such as an established legal basis, prior authorisation, adequate training, reporting, and record-keeping, appropriate oversight, and sufficient protective measures, may prove more onerous in the context of armed conflict, but equally, the grave risks for human rights, including the right to life, that are often associated with the use of informers in national contexts are magnified and more acute during situations of armed conflict.

[250] Cohen and Dudai, 'Human Rights Dilemmas' (n 170) 229–30.
[251] Moran, *From Northern Ireland to Afghanistan* (n 118) 57.
[252] *Al-Skeini and others v United Kingdom* (n 221) Concurring Opinion of Judge Bonello, para. 38.

Conclusion

The ubiquity of the practice of informing and other forms of collaboration involving assistance to an opposing side during a situation of armed conflict is not openly reflected in the detailed legal framework that has been specifically designed and adopted to address the conduct of parties to an armed conflict. International humanitarian law has had an ambivalent approach to wartime collaboration in that it adopts a largely a permissive stance towards voluntary cooperation with an enemy and implicitly recognises the unlawfulness of the practice under domestic law, yet seeks to prohibit parties to an armed conflict from forcing individuals to provide assistance against their will or from punishing alleged collaborators in cruel or inhumane ways in light of the coercion and abuse that frequently accompany the practice. How the law of armed conflict addresses the phenomenon of collaboration is analogous to its stance on armed conflict itself in that it does not prohibit states or non-state armed groups from engaging in hostilities but rather seeks to mitigate the harm caused by conflict through regulating their conduct to the extent possible.

International humanitarian law does not outlaw the waging of armed conflict—the *jus ad bellum* does, to some degree—and can even be seen to facilitate it, as its main concern is the alleviation of some of the suffering that war usually entails, rather than preventing conflict itself.[1] National law may restrain the use of force by states, and prohibit it on the part of non-state entities, but international humanitarian law is not concerned with the question of whether force has been used lawfully but rather how it is used. Despite the undoubted illegality under national legal systems of most forms of collaboration examined in this book, states have decided not to prohibit such conduct under the international law of armed conflict. Motivated primarily by self-interest, states have taken the somewhat hypocritical approach of allowing international law to shield the betrayal of an opposing belligerent by its soldiers or citizens, while at the same time subjecting such to stern sanctions under domestic law when carried out by their own nationals. The book has shown that states actively encourage and welcome cooperation from an enemy's nationals when

[1] See for example Samuel Moyn, 'A War without Civilian Deaths? What Arguments for a More Humane War Conceal', The New Republic, 23 October 2018; Samuel Moyn, 'Civil Liberties and Endless War' (2015) 62(4) Dissent 57; Chris af Jochnick and Roger Normand, 'The Legitimation of Violence: A Critical History of the Laws of War' (1994) 35 Harvard International Law Journal 49.

To Serve the Enemy: Informers, Collaborators, and the Laws of Armed Conflict. Shane Darcy, Oxford University Press (2019). © Shane Darcy.
DOI: 10.1093/oso/ 9780198788898.001.0001

it is in their favour, but condemn in the strongest terms any such betrayal that is to their detriment.[2]

In a similar vein to how international humanitarian law largely eschews concern for the lawfulness of any use of force or the justness of a cause that a party to an armed conflict may be fighting for,[3] this body of law is not concerned with passing any judgment on the legality of individuals choosing to provide assistance to an opposing party. And just as it seeks to ensure that all parties to an armed conflict respect its rules and fundamental guarantees, it also demands humane treatment of all those who are not taking an active part in hostilities, including captured enemy personnel and members of the civilian population, irrespective of which side they fought on, supported, or belonged to. While this general statement may be a true reflection of the current *jus in bello*, humanitarian law's concern with preventing ill-treatment has not encompassed all acts of violence associated with an armed conflict, including those directed against alleged informers and other collaborators. During the early development of the law of war, several states even stuck firmly to the view that civilians could be coerced into providing information to an opposing belligerent that had occupied the territory of their country. While this feared 'incubus' was not formalized by the drafters of the 1907 Hague Regulations,[4] international humanitarian law has allowed some latitude for parties to an armed conflict to make use of an enemy's personnel and population against it. A proposal during the drafting of Additional Protocol I that medics treating injured fighters should report potential criminal activity was opposed because '[d]octors should not be turned into informers or intelligence agents'.[5] Civilians or captured members of armed forces, on the other hand, could, subject to the broad though not absolute prohibition of coercion.

The practice of wartime collaboration has habitually involved coercion, violence, and recrimination. Whether it be in the recruitment and use of informers to meet the perpetual demands for intelligence, or in the compelling of captured members of armed forces or civilians to engage in military operations as occurred during the Second World War, parties to an armed conflict have frequently placed perceived military needs over the safety and well-being of individuals. Other forms of assistance to the enemy, such as bureaucratic collaboration, propaganda, interpreting, or labour, as detailed in Chapter 1, may have more likely been offered on a voluntary basis, notwithstanding the inherently coercive context of armed conflict. Such willing support to an opposing side has rendered its proponents open to violent retaliation both during and after conflict. States

[2] As has been the case with espionage more generally, see Simon Chesterman, *One Nation under Surveillance* (OUP 2011) 27.

[3] See however Article 1(4) of Additional Protocol I which refers to 'armed conflicts in which peoples are fighting against colonial domination and alien occupation and against racial régimes in the exercise of their right of self-determination'.

[4] See discussion in Chapter 2, section 2.1.

[5] *Official Records of the Diplomatic Conference on the Reaffirmation and Development of International Humanitarian Law Applicable in Armed Conflicts, Geneva (1974–1977)*, Volume XI, 182. See also ibid 443.

and non-state armed groups alike have sought to make use of informers and other collaborators in times of armed conflict, and both have been implicated to varying degrees in the coercion and retribution that have so often characterised the practice. It is in relation to these latter aspects that international humanitarian law has been most relevant.

The lengthy gestation of the overarching rule of international humanitarian law that civilians or members of armed forces cannot be compelled to serve in the forces of the enemy, engage in military activities, or divulge information is as much a reflection of the reluctance of states to forego such a claimed power as it is of the slow pace of humanitarian law's general evolution. During the preparation of the 1874 Brussels Declaration and the Hague Regulations of 1899 and 1907, states debated and disagreed over the extent to which civilians in particular might be made to serve the enemy in some way. The 1949 Geneva Conventions brought greater certainty regarding the prohibition of coercion against prisoners of war or civilians in occupied territory, yet allowed some exceptions, such as in relation to judges or other officials in occupied territory, as discussed in Chapter 2. An identical replication of the prohibition of coercion is not found in the law of non-international armed conflict, thus implying lesser restrictions on states that are engaged in fighting against non-state armed groups. Moreover, the relative ambiguity of the prohibition of physical and moral coercion, and the absence of any international mechanism tasked with overseeing its observance, grants considerable freedom of action to states in their use and recruitment of informers and other collaborators during armed conflict. The risk of abuse is increased by the frequently covert nature of recruitment activities, although where practices have come to light, national judicial authorities have on occasion imposed restrictions on military forces going beyond the strictures of international humanitarian law.[6] This is exceptional though, as judicial interventions have tended to be addressed only to the brutal consequences faced by those alleged to have assisted the enemy.

It is apparent that the activities of informers and other collaborators may render them lawful targets under the law of armed conflict or impact on their status under this legal framework, even though no specific category has been created for them. Participation in military operations and intelligence gathering in certain limited circumstances may amount to direct participation in hostilities, and international humanitarian law offers little protection to those who may have been coerced into engaging in such actions. The firm desire of states to limit the protections afforded to those who have assisted an opposing belligerent in an international armed conflict is evident in the general exclusion of a state's own nationals from the categories of prisoners of war and protected persons under the Third and Fourth Geneva Convention as discussed in Chapter 3. Subject to the basic fundamental guarantees of Common Article 3 and the Additional Protocols where applicable, states have retained the right to deal with such individuals under national law. Those most likely to suffer recrimination for treasonous activities associated with an armed conflict

[6] See discussion in section 2.2.

have fallen at times into a blind spot of international humanitarian law. Recent jurisprudence seeking to expand the scope of the law of war crimes, as outlined in Chapter 4, may serve to bring the ill-treatment directed against those alleged to have assisted the other side more squarely within the purview of international humanitarian law, albeit at the expense of the principle of legality. Regardless of this, it remains evident that international humanitarian law has only partially and at times inadvertently been addressed to the common wartime practice of collaboration and its consequences.

The overall ambivalence of international humanitarian law towards collaboration with an opposing belligerent during armed conflict is deliberate as it allows parties to an armed conflict to make use of an enemy's personnel or population who are willing to provide assistance whether for financial, ideological, or other reasons. Subjecting the practice to the rules against coercion and ill-treatment should prevent the abuse and cruelties that have regularly featured in the recruitment, use, and treatment of informers and other collaborators throughout the history of armed conflict. Yet, it is at least arguable that the permissive stance of the law of armed conflict towards voluntary assistance to an opposing side during an armed conflict partly contributes to this cruel treatment and violence. The law's accommodation of the practice grants it legitimacy and does little to dissuade parties to an armed conflict from seeking such cooperation from those ostensibly on the other side. The relatively ambiguous aspects of the prohibition of coercion have been exploited, as have the oppressive circumstances of armed conflict, to ensure that the services of even reluctant collaborators can be employed. For parties to an armed conflict that may recruit informers and other collaborators without purposefully resorting to physical or moral coercion, such individuals may find themselves caught in an inherently coercive situation characterised by serious and enduring risks to their lives and well-being. The violent and often unlawful reprisals taken by non-state armed groups arise from a lack of capacity to respond to the threat of collaboration by judicial means, as well as demands for revenge, the need to deter others from assisting the opposition, or other grievances. In a number of conflicts examined in this book, including the Second World War, East Timor, and South Africa, non-state parties have at times directed more of their attacks against suspected informers and collaborators than against enemy forces.

In this light, it is appropriate to ask how the law of armed conflict might evolve to improve the prevention of the seemingly inevitable abuse that accompanies collaboration as a perennial feature of armed conflict? Might such an evolution encompass a prohibition of involuntary as well as voluntary assistance to an opposing belligerent during armed conflict, such as exists under domestic law, or would it be more feasible to insist on meaningful regulation of the practice of wartime collaboration as addressed in Chapter 5? The prospects of an outright prohibition are negligible, as this would run contrary to the conventional view of the necessity of using collaborators in wartime despite concerns associated with the practice. With regard to informers, for example, the UK *Joint Service Manual* views them as a lawful means of gathering information about the enemy, which is 'essential if commanders are to be able to verify potential targets as military objectives and take precautions for the protection of the civilian population'.[7] Despite the negative view of collaborators, they are considered an indispensable component of many operations, including the control of territory: long-term military occupations, for example, 'are unthinkable without them'.[8] While informers may provide intelligence of value to a party to an armed conflict, it is not the sole reason for their employment, as their presence or suspected presence alone within a party to an armed conflict can itself seriously undermine operational efficiency by promoting distrust and paranoia amongst its members.[9] Informers, however, are not drawn solely from the membership of armed groups, and reliance on civilian informers can also have similar harmful effects on the civilian population itself.

The use of informers during an armed conflict, as in the case of domestic policing, criminal justice, and national security, may serve the military, security, or intelligence needs of state authorities, but it brings with it serious risks of harm to the human rights of individuals and to society through instilling fear and division within communities.[10] The latter may at times be a desired rather than unfortunate by-product:

> People tend to think that information gathering lies at the heart of any collaboration strategy, but occupation regimes benefit just as much, if not more, from the culture of deception that it engenders and the way this culture corrodes the occupied society. Neighbors learn to distrust one another precisely because they know that anyone could be an informant. Activist and militant networks break down once the poison of collaboration has been injected into their bodies. [...] The resulting social disintegration is the kind favored by occupation forces—a divided society is one that has trouble resisting.[11]

The activities of informers and other collaborators, the divisions they may engender, and the harm to human rights that the practice frequently involves can have lasting effects that extend beyond the end of armed conflict. According to the Truth and Reconciliation Commission of South Africa:

> one the most destructive legacies of the past is the labelling of sometimes innocent people as 'informers' or collaborators. Individuals and their families were killed, assaulted, harassed and ostracised as a result of this stigmatisation. Many people still live with the daily experience of rejection because they were identified as informers during the period of the Commission's mandate.[12]

[7] United Kingdom Ministry of Defence, *The Joint Service Manual of the Law of Armed Conflict*, (OUP 2004), 63 (footnotes omitted).

[8] Neve Gordon, 'Talking about collaborators', *L.A. Review of Books*, 25 February 2014.

[9] United States Army, *Field Manual 3-24, Counterinsurgency*, (Headquarters, Department of the Army December 2006) 1–19.

[10] Michael L. Gross, *The Ethics of Insurgency* (CUP 2015) 109; Steve Hewitt, *Snitch! A History of the Modern Intelligence Informer* (Continuum, 2010) 3–5; Ron Dudai, 'Informers and the Transition in Northern Ireland' (2012) 52 British Journal of Criminology 32, 33; Kiran Sarma, 'Informers and the Battle Against Republican Terrorism: A Review of 30 Years of Conflict' (2005) 6(2) Police Practice and Research 165, 178; Dermot P.J. Walsh, *Human Rights and Policing in Ireland: Law, Policy and Practice* (Clarus Press 2009) 715.

[11] Gordon, 'Talking about collaborators' (n8). See also Hillel Cohen and Ron Dudai, 'Human Rights Dilemmas in Using Informers to Combat Terrorism: The Israeli–Palestinian Case' (2005) 17 Terrorism and Political Violence 229, 239–40.

[12] *Truth and Reconciliation Commission of South Africa Report*, 1998, Volume 5, 307.

Reckoning with the phenomenon of collaboration in the aftermath of armed conflict has involved trials, lustration, amnesties, and truth commissions, as well acts of retaliatory violence and public humiliation.[13]

Notwithstanding these harmful aspects of the practice, authorities seem unlikely to forego relying upon informers and other collaborators as a means of pursuing various wartime aims. Yet previously accepted practices have fallen out of favour over time and eventually been proscribed under international humanitarian law.[14] The early treaties saw the successful inclusion of a rule against coercing civilians to divulge information to an invading or occupying force, despite the prior widespread practice. In the words of the Dutch representative at the Second Hague Peace Conference: 'Should the inhabitants who must remain apart from the struggle be forced to supply the lack of instruction and foresight of the invader? If a State has not sufficient means to make war let it keep the peace or make peace. It is not for us to make war easy.'[15] An outright prohibition that would restrain further the waging of conflict may be unthinkable for states at present. Closer regulation of the practice may therefore be more feasible, yet above all should be viewed as necessary, if the employment of informers and other collaborators is to retain any legitimacy and to operate in compliance with human rights.

International human rights law shares a similar approach to international humanitarian law with regard to the subject matter of this book, in that none of its treaties are explicitly addressed to the practice of using informers or other collaborators during situations of armed conflict, yet a number of its general rules and standards can be brought to bear on the practice. In contrast to humanitarian law, and as explored in Chapter 5, international human rights law offers an emerging body of decisions from various courts and UN bodies that has examined human rights concerns related to various aspects of the use of informers in domestic contexts. While accepting in principle the permissibility of the practice, such jurisprudence demonstrates that state authorities must abide by relevant human rights standards which give rise to an expectation of the legal regulation of the practice. National regulation of the use of informers in a domestic context has been notably lacking, with a few states having begun to legislate in this area. The consequences of an absence of regulation of the use of so-called covert human intelligence sources was evident in the case study of Northern Ireland, where alleged informers were implicated in serious criminal activity. The Police Ombudsman for Northern Ireland stated in 2018 that although 'the widespread use of informants saved lives [...] an absolute position

[13] See generally Jon Elster, *Retribution and Reparation in the Transition to Democracy* (CUP 2006); István Deák, Jan T. Gross, and Tony Judt (eds), *The Politics of Retribution in Europe: World War II and its Aftermath* (Princeton University Press 2000); Benajmin Frommer, *National Cleansing: Retribution Against Nazi Collaborators in Postwar Czechoslovakia* (CUP 2005); István Deák, *Europe on Trial: The Story of Collaboration, Resistance, and Retribution During World War II* (Westview Press 2015); Dudai, 'Informers and the Transition in Northern Ireland' (n 10).

[14] Hostage taking, for example, was not prohibited by treaty until the adoption of the 1949 Geneva Conventions. See Shane Darcy, *Collective Responsibility and Accountability under International Law* (Transnational 2007) 81–115.

[15] Second Meeting of the Second Commission, 14 August 1907, *The Proceedings of the Hague Peace Conferences; The Conference of 1907*, Volume III (OUP 1921) 10.

that failures were few and far between and that the end justified the means is not borne out by the evidence'.[16] If states are unprepared to abandon such a means of intelligence gathering, before, during, and after armed conflict, then the matter of regulation needs to be adequately addressed.

Earlier in the book it was asked whether the inherent harms and risks associated with the use of informer and other collaborators during situations of armed conflict required an alternative reading of international law as to the permissibility of the practice. While neither international humanitarian law nor international human rights law either expressly or impliedly object to state authorities using informers or other collaborators, it is submitted that the practice is permissible under international only if it is sufficiently regulated so as to minimize harm to human rights or violations of the principles and applicable rules of international humanitarian law. The unregulated use of informers and other collaborators carries serious risks of abuse, corruption, and the violation of human rights.[17] As to the form of such regulation, a human-rights based approach would require a clear legislative basis, transparency where appropriate, accountability of relevant actors, independent oversight, reporting, training of officials, and the maintenance of adequate records. The absence of a properly regulated system leaves states exposed to liability for the acts of their officials and those from the opposing side's armed forces or civilian population from whom they have received assistance.[18] For non-state armed groups, incentives for treating informers and other collaborators in conformity with humanitarian law and human rights may include greater legitimacy with the public or international actors. The challenges of adequately regulating the practices examined in this book cannot be overstated, nor should regulation be considered a panacea for preventing all abusive conduct by state and non-state armed groups alike in this context. Nevertheless, it is past time that such a pervasive and risk-laden practice continues to take place for the most part in the shadow of the law.

[16] 'Victimhood and dealing with the Past in Northern Ireland'—by Police Ombudsman Dr Michael Maguire, Queens University Belfast, 14 May 2018 <http://eamonnmallie.com/2018/05/the-chief-constable-and-the-police-ombudsman-in-drive-to-tackle-legacy-of-the-past/> accessed 30 May 2019.

[17] Cohen and Dudai, 'Human Rights Dilemmas in Using Informers' (n 11) 229.

[18] Sigrid Redse Johansen, 'The Occupied and The Occupier: The Case of Norway' in Kjetil Mujenović Larsen, Camilla Guldahl Cooper, and Gro Nystuen, *Searching for a 'Principle of Humanity' in International Humanitarian Law* (CUP 2013) 206, 216–220. See also Raphael Bitton, 'In Law We Trust: The Israeli Case of Overseeing Intelligence' in Zachary K. Goldman and Samuel J. Rascoff (eds), *Global Intelligence Oversight: Governing Security in the Twenty-First Century* (OUP 2016) 141, 158.

Select Bibliography

BOOKS

Andrew C., Aldrich R.J., and Wark W.K. (eds), *Secret Intelligence: A Reader* (Routledge 2009).

Arai-Takahashi Y., *The Law of Occupation: Continuity and Change of International Humanitarian Law, and its Interaction with International Human Rights Law* (Martinus Nijhoff 2009).

Bassiouni M.C., *Crimes against Humanity: Historical Evolution and Contemporary Application* (CUP 2011).

Ben-Naftali O. (ed.), *International Humanitarian Law and International Human Rights Law* (OUP 2011).

Bennett R., *Behind the Battle: Intelligence in the War with Germany 1939–1945* (Pimlico 1999).

Bhuta N. (ed.), *The Frontiers of Human Rights: Extraterritoriality and its Challenges* (OUP 2016).

Billingsley R. (ed.), *Covert Human Intelligence Sources: The Unlovely Face of Police Work* (Waterside Press 2009).

Billingsley R., Nemitz T., and Bean P. (eds), *Informers: Policing, Policy and Practice* (Routledge 2001).

Birstein V.J., *SMERSH, Stalin's Secret Weapon: Soviet Military Intelligence in World War II* (Biteback Publishing 2011).

Black E., *IBM and the Holocaust: The Strategic Alliance between Nazi Germany and America's Most Powerful Corporation* (2nd edn, Crown Books 2012).

Bloom R.M., *Ratting: The Use and Abuse of Informants in the American Justice System* (Praeger 2002).

Boothy W.H., *The Law of Targeting* (OUP 2012).

Bordoff M. and Okazaki T. (eds), *Economies under Occupation: The Hegemony of Nazi Germany and Imperial Japan in World War II* (Routledge 2015).

Bowyer Bell J., *The Secret Army: The IRA* (Poolbeg 1998).

Brody J.K., *The Trial of Pierre Laval: Defining Treason, Collaboration and Patriotism in World War II France* (Routledge 2010).

Brook T., *Collaboration: Japanese Agents and Local Elites in Wartime China* (Harvard University Press 2005).

Broun K.S., *Saving Nelson Mandela: The Rivonia Trial and the Fate of South Africa* (OUP 2012).

Bruneau T.C. and Boraz S.C. (eds), *Reforming Intelligence: Obstacles to Democratic Control and Effectiveness* (University of Texas 2007).

Bunting M., *The Model Occupation: The Channel Islands Under German Rule 1940–1945* (Harper Collins 1995).

Cassese A. (ed.), *The Oxford Companion to International Criminal Justice* (OUP 2009).

Cassese A., *Realizing Utopia: The Future of International Law* (OUP 2012).

Cassese A., Gaeta P., Baig L., Fan M., Gosnell C., and Whiting A., *Cassese's International Criminal Law* (OUP 2013).

Chesterman S., *One Nation under Surveillance* (OUP 2011).

Clapham A., Gaeta P., and Sassòli M. (eds), *The 1949 Geneva Conventions: A Commentary* (OUP 2015).

Cohen H., *Army of Shadows: Palestinian Collaboration with Zionism, 1917–1948* (Haim Watzman tr, University of California Press 2008).
Crawford E., *The Treatment of Combatants and Insurgents Under the Law of Armed Conflict* (OUP 2010).
Crawford E., *Identifying the Enemy: Civilian Participation in Armed Conflict* (OUP 2015).
Cryer R., Friman H., Robinson D., and Wilmshurst E., *An Introduction to International Criminal Law and Procedure* (3rd edn, CUP 2014).
Dahl H.F., *Quisling: A Study in Treachery* (Anne-Marie Stanton-Ife tr, CUP 1999).
Davies P., *Dangerous Liaisons: Collaboration and World War Two* (Pearson Longman 2004).
de Guttry A., Capone F., and Paulussson C., *Foreign Fighters under International Law and Beyond* (TMC Asser Press 2016).
Deák I., *Europe on Trial: The Story of Collaboration, Resistance, and Retribution During World War II* (Westview Press 2015).
Deák I., Gross J.T., and Judt T. (eds), *The Politics of Retribution in Europe: World War II and its Aftermath* (Princeton University Press 2000).
Dickson B., *The European Convention of Human Rights and the Conflict in Northern Ireland* (OUP 2010).
Domke M., *Trading with the Enemy in World War II* (Central Book Company 1944).
Dörmann K., *Elements of War Crimes under the Rome Statute of the International Criminal Court* (CUP 2002).
Doswald-Beck L., *Human Rights in Times of Conflict and Terrorism* (OUP 2011).
Douglas L., *The Right Wrong Man: John Demjanjuk and the Last Great Nazi War Crimes Trial* (Princeton University Press 2016).
Elster J., *Retribution and Reparation in the Transition to Democracy* (CUP 2006).
Fenwick H., *Civil Liberties and Human Rights* (4th edn, Routledge 2007).
Fleck D. (ed.), *The Handbook of International Humanitarian Law* (3rd edn, OUP 2013).
Fortin K., *The Accountability of Armed Groups under Human Rights Law* (OUP 2017).
French D., *The British Way in Counter-Insurgency 1945–1967* (OUP 2011).
French D., *Fighting EOKA: The British Counter-Insurgency on Cyprus 1955–1959* (OUP 2015).
Gieseke J., *The History of the Stasi: East Germany's Secret Police 1945–1990* (D Burnett tr, Berghahn 2014).
Gill P. and Phythian M., *Intelligence in an Insecure World* (2nd edn, Polity Press 2012).
Goldman Z.K. and Rascoff S.J. (eds), *Global Intelligence Oversight: Governing Security in the Twenty-First Century* (OUP 2016).
Gordon B.M., *Collaborationism in France during the Second World War* (Cornell University Press 1980).
Greenberg K.J. and Dratel J.L. (eds), *The Torture Papers: The Road to Abu Ghraib* (CUP 2005).
Greer S., *Supergrasses: A Study in Anti-Terrorist Law Enforcement in Northern Ireland* (Clarendon Press 1995).
Gross M.L., *The Ethics of Insurgency* (CUP 2015).
Hager N. and Stephenson J., *Hit & Run: The New Zealand SAS in Afghanistan and the Meaning of Honour* (Potton & Burton 2017).
Hajjar L., *Courting Conflict: The Israeli Military Court System* (University of California Press, 2005).
Hansen R., *Disobeying Hitler: German Resistance in the Last Year of WWII* (Faber and Faber 2014).
Hastings M., *The Secret War: Spies, Codes and Guerillas 1939–1945* (William Collins 2015).

Hayes P.M., *Quisling: The Career and Political Ideals of Vidkun Quisling 1887–1945* (David and Charles 1971).

Heller K.J., *The Nuremberg Military Tribunals and the Origins of International Criminal Law* (OUP 2011).

Henckaerts J.-M. and Doswald-Beck L., *Customary International Humanitarian Law, Volume I: Rules* (CUP 2005).

Henckaerts J.-M. and Doswald-Beck L., *Customary International Humanitarian Law, Volume II: Practice* (CUP 2005).

Herman M., *Intelligence Power in Peace and War* (CUP 1996).

Hilberg R., *The Destruction of the European Jews: Volume III* (Holmes & Meier 1985).

Hirshfeld G., *Nazi Rule and Dutch Collaboration: The Netherlands Under German Occupation 1940–1945* (OUP 1988).

Holmes C., *Searching for Lord Haw-Haw: The Political Lives of William Joyce* (Routledge 2016).

Imlay T. and Horn M., *The Politics of Industrial Collaboration during World War II: Ford France, Vichy and Nazi Germany* (CUP 2014).

Ingram M. and Harkin G., *Stakeknife: Britain's Secret Agents in Ireland* (O'Brien Press 2004).

Jo H., *Compliant Rebels: Rebel Groups and International Law in World Politics* (CUP 2015).

Kalshoven F. and Zegveld L., *Constraints on the Waging of War* (4th ed, CUP 2011).

Kalyvas S.N., *The Logic of Violence in Civil War* (CUP 2006).

Kaplan A., *The Collaborator: The Trial & Execution of Robert Brassilach* (University of Chicago Press 2000).

Keegan J., *Intelligence in War: Knowledge of the Enemy from Napoleon to Al-Qaeda* (Alfred A. Knopf 2003).

Kershaw I., *To Hell and Back; Europe 1914–1949* (Penguin Books 2016).

Kish J., *International Law and Espionage* (Martinus Nijhoff 1995).

Kitson F., *Low Intensity Operations: Subversion, Insurgency, Peace-Keeping* (Faber and Faber 1971).

Larsen K.M., Cooper C.G., and Nystuen G. (eds), *Searching for a 'Principle of Humanity' in International Humanitarian Law* (CUP 2013).

Lech R., *Broken Soldiers* (University of Illinois Press 2000).

Ledwidge F., *Rebel Law: Insurgents, Courts and Justice in Modern Conflict* (Hurst & Company 2017).

Legg A., *The Margin of Appreciation in International Human Rights Law* (OUP 2012).

Lekha Sriram C., Martin-Ortega O., and Herman J., *War, Conflict and Human Rights* (2nd edn, Routledge 2014).

Lichtblau E., *The Nazis Next Door: How America became a Safe Have for Hitler's Men*, (Mariner Books 2014).

Littlejohn D., *Patriotic Traitors: A History of Collaboration in German-Occupied Europe 1940–1945* (Heineman 1972).

Lubell N., *Extraterritorial Use of Force against Non-State Actors* (OUP 2010).

Marrus M.R. and Paxman R.O., *Vichy France and the Jews* (Stanford University Press 1981).

Mason H.L., *The Purge of Dutch Quislings; Emergency Justice in the Netherlands* (Springer 1952).

Matthee M., Toebes B., and Brus M. (eds), *Armed Conflict and International Law: In Search of the Human Face* (TMC Asser Press 2013).

McKay S., *Covert Policing: Law and Practice* (OUP 2015).

McMahon P., *British Spies and Irish Rebels: British Intelligence and Ireland 1916–1945* (Boydell Press 2008).

McNeilly M., *Sun Tzu and the Art of Modern Warfare* (OUP 2001).

Melzer N., *Targeted Killings in International Law* (OUP 2008).
Melzer N., *International Humanitarian Law: A Comprehensive Introduction* (ICRC 2016).
Milanovic M., *Extraterritorial Application of Human Rights Treaties: Law, Principles and Policy* (OUP 2011).
Moran J., *From Northern Ireland to Afghanistan: British Military Intelligence Operations, Ethics and Human Rights* (Ashgate 2013).
Mueller M., *Canaris: The Life and Death of Hitler's Spymaster* (Naval Institute Press 2007).
Müller I., *Hitler's Justice: The Courts of the Third Reich* (D. Lucas Schneider tr, Harvard University Press 1991).
Murray D., *The Human Rights Obligations of Non-State Armed Groups* (Hart 2016).
Natapoff A., *Snitching: Criminal Informants and the Erosion of American Justice* (New York University Press 2009).
Ní Aoláin F., *The Politics of Force: Conflict Management and State Violence in Northern Ireland* (Blackstaff 2000).
Niebergall-Lackner H., *Status and Treatment of Deserters in International Armed Conflicts*, (Brill/Nijhoff 2016).
Novick P., *The Resistance versus Vichy: The Purge of Collaborators in Liberated France* (Columbia University Press 1968).
Nowak M. and Charbord A. (eds), *Using Human Rights to Counter Terrorism* (Edward Elgar 2018).
O'Brien J., *Killing Finucane: Murder in Defence of the Realm* (Gill and Macmillan 2005).
Oberleitner G., *Human Rights in Armed Conflict: Law, Practice, Policy* (CUP 2015).
Park I., *The Right to Life in Armed Conflict* (OUP 2018).
Paxton R.O., *Vichy France: Old Guard and New Order 1940–1944* (Columbia University Press 2001).
Perrin B. (ed.), *Modern Warfare: Armed Groups, Private Militaries, Humanitarian Organizations, and the Law* (UBC Press 2012).
Pictet J.S. (ed.), *Commentary; IV Geneva Convention, Relative to the Protection of Civilian Person in Times of War* (ICRC 1958).
Plavnieks R., *Nazi Collaborators on Trial during the Cold War: Victor Arājs and the Latvian Auxiliary Security Police* (Palgrave MacMillan 2018).
Rings W., *Life with the Enemy: Collaboration and Resistance in Hitler's Europe 1939–1945* (J. Maxwell Brownjohn tr, Doubleday & Co. 1982).
Roberts A., Stephan P.B., Verdier P.H. and Versteeg M. (eds), *Comparative International Law* (OUP 2018).
Rogers A.P.V., Law *on the Battlefield* (3rd edn, Manchester University Press 2012).
Rowe P., *The Impact of Human Rights Law on Armed Forces* (CUP 2006).
Sanders A., Young R., and Burton M., *Criminal Justice* (OUP 2010).
Schabas W.A., *The Abolition of the Death Penalty in International Law* (3rd edn, CUP 2002).
Schabas W.A., *The European Convention on Human Rights: A Commentary* (OUP 2015).
Schabas W.A., *The International Criminal Court: A Commentary on the Rome Statute* (2nd ed, OUP 2016).
Schmitt M. and Pejic J. (eds), *International Law and Armed Conflict: Exploring the Faultlines; Essays in Honour of Yoram Dinstein* (Martinus Nijhoff 2007).
Shehadeh R., *Occupier's Law: Israel and the West Bank* (Institute for Palestine Studies Washington DC 1985).
Sivakumaran S., *The Law of Non-International Armed Conflict* (OUP 2012).
Solis G., *The Law of Armed Conflict: International Humanitarian Law in War* (CUP 2010).
Steinberg D.J., *Philippine Collaboration in World War II* (University of Michigan Press 1967).

Stern J. and Berger J.M., *ISIS: The State of Terror* (Harper Collins 2015).
Sweeney J.A., *The European Court of Human Rights in the Post-Cold War Era: Universality in Transition* (Routledge 2013).
Szanajda A., *Indirect Perpetrators: The Prosecution of Informers in Germany, 1945–1965* (Rowman and Littlefield 2010).
Tessler M.A., *A History of the Israeli–Palestinian Conflict* (Indiana University Press 1994).
Thuo Gathii J., *War, Commerce, and International Law* (OUP 2010)
Toolis K., *Rebel Hearts: Journeys within the IRA's soul* (Picador 1995).
Trunk I., *Judenrät: The Jewish Councils in Eastern Europe under Nazi Occupation* (University of Nebraska Press 1972).
Tsang S. (ed.), *Intelligence and Human Rights in the Era of Global Terrorism* (Praeger Security International 2007).
Urban M., *Big Boys' Rules: The Secret Struggle against the IRA* (Faber and Faber 1992).
Urban M., *Task Force Black: The Explosive True Story of the SAS and the Secret War in Iraq* (Brown 2010).
Van den Herik L. and Schrijver N. (eds), *Counter-Terrorism Strategies in a Fragmented International Legal Order: Meeting the Challenges* (CUP 2015).
van Engeland A., *Civilian or Combatant? A Challenge for the 21st Century* (OUP 2011).
Vaughan H., *Sleeping with the Enemy: Coco Chanel's Secret War* (Alfred A. Knopf 2011).
von Lingen K. (ed.), *Debating Collaboration and Complicity in War Crimes Trials in Asia, 1945–1956* (Palgrave MacMillan 2017).
Walsh D., *The Use and Abuse of Emergency Legislation in Northern Ireland* (Cobden Trust 1983).
Walsh D., *Human Rights and Policing in Ireland: Law, Policy and Practice* (Clarus Press 2009).
Warrick J., *The Triple Agent: The Al-Qaeda Mole Who Infiltrated the CIA* (Vintage Books 2012).
Weale A., *Patriot Traitors: Roger Casement, John Amery and the Real Meaning of Treason* (Viking 2001).
Weill S., *The Role of National Courts in Applying International Humanitarian Law* (OUP 2014).
West R., *The New Meaning of Treason* (The Viking Press 1964).
Williams C., *Pétain: How the Hero of France Became a Convicted Traitor and Changed the Course of History* (Palgrave McMillan 2005).
Williams V., *Surveillance and Intelligence Law Handbook* (OUP 2006).
Wilmshurst E. (ed.), *International Law and the Classification of Conflicts* (OUP 2012).
Xenos D., *The Positive Obligation of the Statue under the European Convention on Human Rights* (2011).
Yildiz K. and Breau S., *The Kurdish Conflict; International Humanitarian Law and Post-Conflict Mechanisms* (Routledge 2010).
Yorke J. (ed.), *Against the Death Penalty: International Initiatives and Implications* (Ashgate 2008).
Young C.S., *Name, Rank, and Serial Number: Exploiting Korean War POWs at Home and Abroad* (OUP 2014).
Zyberi G., *The Humanitarian Face of the International Court of Justice* (Intersentia 2008).

JOURNAL ARTICLES

'Coercion: A Defense to Misconduct while a Prisoner of War' (1954) 29(4) Indiana Law Journal 603.
'Misconduct in the Prison Camp: A Survey of the Law and Analysis of the Korean Cases' (1956) 56(5) Columbia Law Review 709.

'Wartime Collaborators: A Comparative Study of the Effect of their Trials on the Treason Law of Great Britain, Switzerland and France' (1946–1947) 56(7) Yale Law Journal 1210.
af Jochnick C. and Normand R., 'The Legitimation of Violence: A Critical History of the Laws of War' (1994) 35 Harvard International Law Journal 49.
Akande D., 'Clearing the Fog of War? The ICRC's Interpretive Guidance on Direct Participation in Hostilities' (2010) 59 International and Comparative Law Quarterly 181.
Akande D. and Hill-Cawthorne L., 'The Lieber Code and the Regulation of Civil War in International Law' (2015) 53(3) Columbia Journal of Transnational Law 638.
Baker M., 'Interpreters and Translators in the War Zone: Narrated and Narrators' (2010) 16(2) The Translator 197.
Baxter R., 'The Duty of Obedience to the Belligerent Occupant' (1950) 27 British Yearbook of International Law 235.
Baxter R., 'So-called "Unprivileged Belligerency": Spies, Guerillas, and Saboteurs' (1951) 28 British Yearbook of International Law 323.
Ben-Naftali B. and Tuval Y., 'Punishing International Crimes Committed by the Persecuted: The Kapo Trials in Israel' (1950s–1960s)' (2006) 4 Journal of International Criminal Justice 128.
Bitton R., 'Intelligence Agents, Autonomous Slaves and the U.S. Supreme Court's Wrong (and Right) Concept of Personal Autonomy' (2014) 7(1) European Journal of Legal Studies 4.
Black P., 'Foot soldiers of the Final Solution: The Trawniki Training Camp and Operation Reinhard' (2011) 25(1) Holocaust and Genocide Studies 1.
Bourtman I., '"Blood for Blood, Death for Death": The Soviet Military Tribunal in Krasnodar 1943' (2008) 22(2) Holocaust and Genocide Studies 246.
Byron C., 'A Blurring of the Boundaries: The Application of International Humanitarian Law by Human Rights Bodies' (2007) 47 Virginia Journal of International Law 839.
Campbell C., '"Wars on Terror" and Vicarious Hegemons: The UK, International Law and the Northern Ireland Conflict' (2005) 54 International and Comparative Law Quarterly 321.
Cheah W.L., 'Dealing with Desertion and Gaps in International Humanitarian Law: Changes of Allegiance in the Singapore War Crimes Trials' (2018) 8(2) Asian Journal of International Law 350.
Chesterman S., 'The Spy Who Came in from the Cold War: Intelligence and International Law' (2006) 27 Michigan Journal of International Law 1071.
Civiletti B.R., 'Intelligence Gathering and the Law: Conflict or Compatibility' (1980) 48(6) Fordham Law Review 883.
Clause J.D., 'The Status of Deserters under the 1949 Geneva Prisoner of War Convention' (1961) 11 Military Law Review 15.
Clayton G. and Thomson A., 'The Enemy of My Enemy is My Friend ... The Dynamics of Self-Defence Forces in Irregular War: The Case of the Sons of Iraq' (2014) 37(11) Studies in Conflict and Terrorism 920.
Cohen H. and Dudai R., 'Human Rights Dilemmas in Using Informers to Combat Terrorism: The Israeli–Palestinian Case' (2005) 17 Terrorism and Political Violence 229.
Deeks A., 'Confronting and Adapting: Intelligence Agencies and International Law' (2016) 102(3) Virginia Law Review 599.
Demarest G.B., 'Espionage in International Law' (1996) 24(2) Denver Journal of International Law and Policy 321.
Dennis M.J., 'Application of Human Rights Treaties Extraterritorially in Times of Armed Conflict and Military Occupation' (2005) 99(1) American Journal of International Law 119.

Dethlefsen H., 'Denmark and the German Occupation: Cooperation, Negotiation or Collaboration?' (1990) 15(1-2) Scandinavian Journal of History 193.

Donnelly R.C., 'Judicial Control of Informants, Spies, Stool Pigeons, and Agent Provocateurs' (1951) 60 (7) Yale Law Journal 1091.

Doswald-Beck L., 'The Right to Life in Armed Conflict: Does International Humanitarian Law Provide All the Answers' (2006) 88 (864) International Review of the Red Cross 881.

Drumbl M., 'Victims who Victimise' (2016) 4(2) London Review of International Law 217.

Dudai R. and Cohen H., 'Triangle of Betrayal: Collaborators and Transitional Justice in the Israeli–Palestinian Conflict' (2007) 6 International Journal of Human Rights 37.

Dudai R., 'Informers and the Transition in Northern Ireland' (2012) 52 British Journal of Criminology 32.

Dudai R. 'Underground Penalty: The IRA's Punishment of Informers' (2018) 20(3) Punishment and Society 375.

Dunningham C. and Morris C. 'A Risky Business: The Recruitment and Running of Informers by English Police Officers' (1961) 19(2) Police Studies 1.

Elliot E., 'Andrei Vlasov: Red Army General in Hitler's Service' (1982) 46(2) Military Affairs 84.

Elster J., 'Redemption for Wrongdoing: The Fate of Collaborators after 1945' (2006) 50 Journal of Conflict Resolution 324.

Finnegan J.P., 'The Evolution of US Army HUMINT: Intelligence Operations in the Korean War' (2011) 55(2) Studies in Intelligence 57.

Fletcher G.P., 'Ambivalence about Treason' (2004) 82 North Carolina Law Review 1611.

Gejji P.S., 'Can Insurgent Courts be Legitimate within International Humanitarian Law?' (2013) 91 Texas Law Review 1525.

Gerards J., 'How to improve the necessity test of the European Court of Human Rights' (2013) 11(2) International Journal of Constitutional Law 466.

Gill P., 'Security Intelligence and Human Rights: Illuminating the 'Heart of Darkness'?' (2009) 24(1) Intelligence and National Security 78.

Grevers H., 'Re-education in Times of Transitional Justice: The Case of the Dutch and Belgian Collaborators after the Second World War' (2015) 22(5) European Review of History 711.

Gross M.L., 'Fighting by Other Means in the Mideast: A Critical Analysis of Israel's Assassination Policy' (2003) 51 Political Studies 1.

Gurcan M., 'Arming Civilians as a Counterterror Strategy: The Case of the Village Guard System in Turkey' (2015) 8(1) Dynamics of Asymmetric Conflict 1.

Henderson I., 'Civilian Intelligence Agencies and the Use of Armed Drones' (2010) 13 Yearbook of International Humanitarian Law 133.

Hirsch C., 'Policing Undercover Agents in the United Kingdom: Whether the Regulation of Investigatory Powers Acts Complies with Regional Human Rights Obligations' (2001) 25(5) Fordham International Law Journal 1282.

Hoffmann S., 'Collaborationism in France during World War II' (1968) 40(3) The Journal of Modern History 375.

Hwang D., 'Wartime Collaboration in Question: An Examination of the Postwar Trials of the Chinese Collaborators' (2005) 6(1) Inter-Asia Cultural Studies 75.

Jones K., 'From the Horse's Mouth: Luftwaffe POWs as Sources for Air Ministry Intelligence during the Battle of Britain' (2000) 15(4) Intelligence and National Security 60.

Juvinall B., 'Heaven or Hell? The Plight of Wartime Interpreters of the Iraq and Afghanistan Conflicts living in the U.S.' (2013) 21(1) Michigan State International Law Review 205.

Kalyvas S.N., 'Collaboration in Comparative Perspective' (2008) 15(2) European Review of History 109.

Kalyvas S.N., 'Ethnic Defection in Civil War' (2008) 41 Comparative Political Studies 1043.

Klamberg M., 'The Legality of Rebel Courts during Non-International Armed Conflicts (2018) 16(2) Journal of International Criminal Justice 235.

Koreman M., 'The Red Tape Option: Bureaucratic Collaboration and Resistance in Vichy France' (2000) 9(2) Contemporary European History 261.

Lauterpacht H., 'The Problem of the Revision of the Law of War' (1952) 29 British Yearbook of International Law 360.

Leahy T., 'The Influence of Informers and Agents on Provisional Irish Republican Army Military Strategy and British Counter-Insurgency Strategy, 1976–1994' (2014) 26(1) Twentieth Century British History 122.

Levy J.S. and Barbieri C., 'Trading with the Enemy during Wartime' (2004) 13(3) Security Studies 1.

Loeffel R., 'Treasonous Conduct: Assessing the Wartime Activities, Post-War Trials and Tribulations of Australian Collaborators in the Second World War' (2009) 55(1) Australian Journal of Politics and History 17.

Lutes Hillman E., 'Disloyalty among Men in Arms: Korean War POWs at Court-Martial' (2004) 82 (5) North Carolina Law Review 1629.

Marrus M.R., 'Coming to Terms with Vichy' (1995) 9(1) Holocaust and Genocide Studies 23.

McDermott J., 'Trading with the Enemy: British Business and the Law during the First World War' (1997) 32(2) Canadian Journal of History 201.

McGovern M., 'Informers, Agents and the Liberal Ideology of Collusion in Northern Ireland' (2016) 9(2) Critical Studies on Terrorism 292.

Minnaar A., 'The Use of Informers: An Essential Tool in the Fight Against Crime?' (2011) 24(3) South African Journal of Criminology 83.

Moran J., 'Evaluating Special Branch and the Use of Informant Intelligence in Northern Ireland' (2010) 25(1) Intelligence and National Security 1.

Morgenstern F., 'Asylum for War Criminals, Quislings and Traitors' (1948) 25 British Yearbook of International Law 382.

Omand D., 'Ethical Guidelines in Using Secret Intelligence for Public Security' (2006) 19(4) Cambridge Review of International Affairs 613.

Oppenheim B., Steele A., Vargas J.F., and Weintraub M., 'True Believers, Deserters, and Traitors: Who Leaves Insurgent Groups and Why' (2015) 59(5) Journal of Conflict Resolution 794.

Oscapella E., 'A Study of Informers in England' (1980) Criminal Law Review 136.

Otto R., 'Neighbours as Human Shields? The Israel Defence Forces' "Early Warning Procedure" and International Humanitarian Law' (2004) 86 (856) International Review of the Red Cross 771.

Penter T., 'Local Collaborators on Trial: Soviet War Crimes Trials under Stalin 1943–1953' (2008) 49(2/3) Cahiers du Monde Russe 341.

Reid A.S. and Ryder N., 'For Whose Eyes Only? A Critique of the United Kingdom's Regulation of Investigatory Powers Act 2000' (2001) 10(2) Information and Communications Technology Law 179.

Rich M.L., 'Brass Rings and Red-Headed Stepchildren: Protecting Active Criminal Informants' (2012) 61(5) American University International Law Review 1433.

Rodenhäuser T., 'Squaring the Circle; Prosecuting Sexual Violence Against Child Soldiers by their "Own Forces"' (2016) 14(1) Journal of International Criminal Justice 171.

Sadat Wexler L., 'Reflections on the Trial of Vichy Collaborator Paul Touvier for Crimes Against Humanity in France' (1995) 20(1) Law and Social Inquiry 191.

Said W.E., 'The Terrorist Informant' (2010) 85 Washington Law Review 687.

Sarma K., 'Informers and the Battle Against Republican Terrorism: A Review of 30 Years of Conflict' (2005) 6(2) Police Practice and Research 165.

Sassoli M., 'The Status, Treatment and Repatriation of Deserters Under International Humanitarian Law' (1985) Yearbook / International Institute of Humanitarian Law 9.

Schmitt M.N., 'The Interpretive Guidance on the Notion of Direct Participation in Hostilities: A Critical Analysis' (2010) 1 Harvard National Security Law Journal.

Sivakumaran S., 'Courts of Armed Opposition Groups: Fair Trials or Summary Justice?' (2009) 7 Journal of International Criminal Justice 489.

Somer J., 'Jungle Justice: Passing Sentence on the Equality of Belligerents in Non-International Armed Conflict' (2007) 89 International Review of the Red Cross 867.

Sperber M.H., 'John Walker Lindh and Yaser Esam Hamdi: Closing the Loophole in International Humanitarian Law for American Nationals Captured Abroad while Fighting with Enemy Forces' (2004) 40 American Criminal Law Review 159.

Tamari S., 'In League with Zion: Israel's Search for a Native Pillar' (1983) 12(4) Journal of Palestine Studies 41.

van Dijk B., 'Human Rights in War" On the Entangled Foundations of the 1949 Geneva Conventions' (2018) 112(4) American Journal of International Law 553.

Waller J.H., 'The Double Life of Admiral Canaris' (1996) 9 (3) International Journal of Intelligence and Counter Intelligence 271.

Wilkbanks M. and Karsh E., 'How the "Sons of Iraq" Stablized Iraq' (2010) 17(4) Middle East Quarterly 57.

Wilson P., 'The Myth of International Humanitarian Law' (2017) 93 (3) International Affairs 563.

Wood N., 'Memory on Trial in Contemporary France: The Case of Maurice Papon' (199) 11(1) History and Memory 41.

Zanasi M., 'Globalizing Hanjian: The Suzhou Trials and the Post-World War II Discourse on Collaboration' (2008) 113(3) American Historical Review 731.

Zimmerman C.S., 'Toward a New Vision of Informants: A History of Abuses and Suggestions for Reform' (1994) 22(81) Hastings Constitutional Law Quarterly 165.

Index

Note: *For the benefit of digital users, indexed terms that span two pages (e.g., 52–53) may, on occasion, appear on only one of those pages*